MW00619893

The
HR Handbook:
Workplace Solutions
from A to Z

Easy-to-use format covering such topics as:

- Hiring Practices
- Termination
- Dress Codes
- Recordkeeping

- Discipline
- Employee Handbooks
- Discrimination
- Compensation and Benefits

**Progressive Business
—— Publications ——**

Progressive Business Publications
370 Technology Dr.
Malvern, Pennsylvania 19355

Copyright © 2011 by Progressive Business Publications.
All rights reserved. No part of this publication may be reproduced by any means, electronic
or mechanical, including photocopying, without prior written permission from the publisher.
Printed in the United States of America.

> "This publication is designed to provide accurate and authoritative information in regard to
> the subject matter covered. It is sold with the understanding that the publisher is not engaged
> in rendering legal, accounting or other professional service. If legal advice or other expert
> assistance is required, the services of a competent professional person should be sought."—
> *from a Declaration of Principles jointly adopted by a Committee of the American Bar
> Association and a Committee of Publishers and Associations.*

ISBN 978-1-933043-60-9

Published 2011   by: Progressive Business Publications

Application for Preassigned Control Number pending.

Cover design by Jennifer Erb

TABLE OF CONTENTS

CHAPTER ONE
Successful Hiring Practices

CHAPTER FOUR
Personnel Development and Retention

TABLE OF CONTENTS

CHAPTER FIVE
Discipline and Termination

CHAPTER SIX
Discrimination

CHAPTER SEVEN
Posting and Recordkeeping Requirements

TABLE OF CONTENTS

CHAPTER EIGHT
Forms

INTRODUCTION

We are excited to introduce this edition of *The HR Handbook: Workplace Solutions from A to Z.* Designed for the busy human resources professional, this easy-to-use book presents a unique combination of materials designed to help you effectively and efficiently manage a broad spectrum of personnel-related issues. Case summaries, source materials, forms, checklists and practical guidance are organized into chapters by subject area for easy reference. A comprehensive index and case tables make it easy to quickly find the information you need.

Rely on *The HR Handbook: Workplace Solutions from A to Z* with confidence to navigate the difficult challenges human resources professionals face on a regular basis.

ABOUT THE EDITORS

Curt J. Brown is the group publisher of the Center for Education & Employment Law. Prior to assuming his present position, he gained extensive experience in business-to-business publishing, including management of well-known publications such as *What's Working in Human Resources, What's New in Benefits & Compensation, Keep Up to Date with Payroll, Supervisors Legal Update,* and *Facility Manager's Alert.* Mr. Brown graduated from Villanova School of Law and graduated magna cum laude from Bloomsburg University with a B.S. in Business Administration. He is admitted to the Pennsylvania bar.

Thomas D'Agostino is a managing editor at the Center for Education & Employment Law and is the editor of *Higher Education Legal Alert.* He graduated from the Duquesne University School of Law and received his undergraduate degree from Ramapo College of New Jersey. He is a past member of the American Bar Association's Section of Individual Rights and Responsibilities as well as the Pennsylvania Bar Association's Legal Services to Persons with Disabilities Committee. Mr. D'Agostino is admitted to the Pennsylvania bar.

Tim Gould is senior editor/group publisher for the Human Resources publications of Progressive Business Publications. He is currently managing editor of the semi-monthly newsletter *What's Working in Human Resources,* and serves as editor of the website *HRMorning.com.*

Dan Wisniewski is the editor of *What's Working in Human Resources* and *WhatsWorkinginHR.com.* In the past, he has also worked extensively on providing content for *HR Legal Training Online.* Dan is a graduate of St. Joseph's University and holds a Bachelor of Arts in English. He is currently pursuing his graduate degree in journalism at Temple University.

HOW TO USE YOUR HANDBOOK

We have designed *The HR Handbook: Workplace Solutions from A to Z* in an accessible format for you to use as a research and reference tool toward prevention of legal problems.

Research Tool

As a research tool, our guide book allows you to conduct your research on two different levels – by topics or cases.

Topic Research

♦ If you have a general interest in a particular **topic** area, our **table of contents** provides descriptive chapter headings containing detailed subheadings from each chapter.

➤ For your convenience, we also include the chapter table of contents at the beginning of each chapter.

Example:
For information on interviewing, the table of contents indicates that a discussion of this topic begins in Chapter One on page 10:

CHAPTER ONE
Successful Hiring Practices

♦ If you have a specific interest in a particular **issue**, our comprehensive **index** collects all of the relevant page references to particular issues.

Example:
 For information on open enrollment, the index provides references to all of the text dealing with benefits instead of only the text dealing with open enrollment:

Benefits, 51-120
    Dental benefits, 55
    Employee assistance programs, 57-58
    Health insurance, 51-53
    Judicial decisions, 62-70
➤   Open enrollment, 61
    Prescription drug benefits, 53-54
    Real-life success stories, 71-75
    Reform law and, 54-55
    Retirement benefits, 58-60
        401(k) plans, 58-59
        403(b) plans, 59
        Defined benefit plans, 58

Case Research

♦ If you know the **name** of a particular case, our **table of cases** will allow you to quickly reference the location of the case.

Example:
 If someone mentioned a case named *Nationwide Mutual Insurance Co. v. Darden,* looking in the table of cases, which has been arranged alphabetically, the case would be located under the "N" section.

N

National League of Cities v. Usery, 307
➤ Nationwide Mutual Insurance Co. v. Darden, 64
NCAA v. Tarkanian, 389
New England Stone, LLC v. Conte, 39
Newport News Shipbuilding and Dry Dock Co. v. EEOC, 352

✓ Each of the cases summarized in the guide book also contains the case citation, which will allow you to access the full text of the case if you would like to learn more about it. *See How to Read a Case Citation, p. 395.*

◆ If your interest lies in cases from a **particular state**, our **table of cases by state** will identify the cases from your state and direct you to their page numbers.

Example:
    If cases from California are of interest, the table of cases by state, arranged alphabetically, lists all of the case summaries contained in the handbook from California.

➡️ **CALIFORNIA**

AT&T Corp. v. Hulteen, 234, 350
Bay Area Laundry and Dry Cleaning Pension Trust Fund v. Ferbar
    Corp. of California, Inc., 69
Beck v. PACE Int'l Union, 68
Black & Decker Disability Plan v. Nord, 66
California Brewers Ass'n v. Bryant, 336
California Federal Savings and Loan Ass'n v. Guerra, 353
Chevron U.S.A. v. Echazabal, 222, 371

✓ Remember, the judicial system has two court systems – state and federal court – which generally function independently from each other. *See The Judicial System, p. 391.* We have included the federal court cases in the table of cases by state according to the state in which the court resides. However, federal court decisions often impact other federal courts within that particular circuit. Therefore, it may be helpful to review cases from all of the states contained in a particular circuit.

We hope you benefit from the use of *The HR Handbook: Workplace Solutions from A to Z.* If you have any questions about how to use the guide book, please contact Thomas D'Agostino at tdagostino@pbp.com.

TABLE OF CASES

TABLE OF CASES

TABLE OF CASES

TABLE OF CASES BY STATE

TABLE OF CASES BY STATE

CHAPTER ONE

Successful Hiring Practices

I. TOPIC OVERVIEW

Employees are the lifeblood that determine whether companies thrive or flounder, and new hires represent a significant investment that should be made only after careful forethought and planning. Employers who fail to identify and avoid the pitfalls associated with the task of hiring qualified and suitable candidates run the risk of exposing themselves to legal liability.

Employers use a variety of measures to determine whether applicants are a good fit for open positions. Among the tools most frequently utilized are physical and mental tests, psychological examinations, and of course the traditional interview process, during which the applicant's intelligence, aptitude level and personality are gauged.

Though "discrimination" is a word that justifiably strikes fear in the hearts of human resources professionals, not all discrimination in employment is prohibited. In fact, the gist of what employers do during the hiring process is discriminate against applicants who are perceived to be less qualified. It is only when discrimination is based on a protected characteristic, such as race or disability, that it becomes taboo.

Employers also have to be careful not to let information about prior union activity, National Guard duty, lawsuits against former employers, marital status and (in some states) sexual orientation affect their decision-making process.

II. EFFECTIVE RECRUITING: FINDING THE BEST CANDIDATES

A. Overview

It may sound overly elementary, but it's not: A critical key to finding the right candidate for a job is to begin by carefully defining the need you are trying to fill and the skillset that will be required to fill it.

Too often, employers launch headlong into the search process before taking sufficient time to stop and think precisely about what they are seeking. The search for the right candidate should begin in earnest only after this need and the attributes of a desirable candidate have been clearly defined. Before the search process begins, make sure these questions have been clearly answered: What exactly is the job, and what skills are necessary to do it?

Once the need has been defined, the question becomes: What is the best way to find the right person to fill it?

Among the most common methods are the following:

- **Print advertising** in local newspapers, trade magazines, etc.
- **Evaluation of internal candidates.** Many experts believe this is often the best way to fill open positions.
- **Use of job-related websites**, such as *careerbuilder.com* and *monster.com.*
- **Incentive programs.** Offering current employees a cash reward for referring a qualified candidate can be an effective tool.
- **Employment agencies and executive search firms.**
- For some positions, a visit to local **trade schools' job placement offices** can produce suitable applicants.
- **Networking** with other industry professionals.

B. Q&As

1. We're looking to bolster our recruiting efforts. Is Twitter a viable recruiting resource?

It can be, says Briana Marrah *(Brianam@parkerlepla.com)* of Parker LePla Consultants. Twitter is best for publicizing info like job openings. But if you want to interact with applicants or give them more info about your company, a social media hub like Facebook is best.

2. Could we run into any legal trouble by placing a job posting only on Facebook?

It's probably safe, says San Diego employment law attorney Rich Paul. It's illegal to use a recruiting channel that excludes certain demographics, but these days you could probably show that social media's universally used.

As to whether it's permissible to check social media for other personal info (for example, religion), it likely comes down to timing. If you do it before deciding to call someone in for an interview, you could run into trouble. But if you do it afterward, when you've already met the person, it's probably safe since you've already gone ahead with a serious interview.

3. We're having a tough time getting solid info from applicants' references besides dates of employment, job titles, and starting/ending salaries. Any ideas to help us get more insightful information?

Instead of asking references to tell you something, ask them to confirm something for you, says Mel Kleiman *(mkleiman@humetrics.com)*.

Most managers are instructed to keep tight-lipped about former employees, so enlist the help of applicants. Ask them how their former manager would rank them on a part of their job performance. When you get the dreaded, "I can't comment on that" from references, try this:

"I understand. So I asked (applicant's name) how he thought you'd rank him on dependability, and he said 'above average' because he did Jobs X, Y and Z for you last year. Can you confirm that?"

C. Real-Life Success Stories

1. Successfully tried new recruiting approach

We weren't finding the type of new hires that we wanted.

In the past, our recruiting approach was less strategic: When new positions opened up, we'd post to every major online job board.

We thought that'd help us reach the greatest number of potential hires and, subsequently, enable us to find the best quality employees.

But that wasn't always turning out to be the case. We found that some of the candidates we attracted via job boards didn't meet the requirements we were looking for. Plus, we'd get tons of resumes – all of which we had to sort through.

Taking a step back

So we decided to scale back the posts we make on job boards. Instead, we adopted a tiered effort, splitting the recruiting duties between members of the recruiting staff.

Some sift through resumes and pass along the most-qualified candidates for a second look. Others proactively pursue applicants for higher-level jobs.

We still use job boards, but our approach has become more strategic. We now use the boards selectively, particularly when we know we're trying to attract a broader range of candidates.

Now we get fewer resumes and better applicants. The payoff's clear. As an example, 80% of managers hired in 2010 were highly skilled, better quality candidates.

(A VP of talent acquisition for a bank in Pittsburgh)

2. New recruiting approach worked wonders

We're a small firm, and it's easy for our managers to get busy and forget things. Where we saw the biggest issues: the hiring process.

Example: Sometimes managers forgot to include specific qualifications for candidates when they posted a new position online. The result? Almost 200 resumes for HR and managers to comb through.

We wanted supervisors to buy in to the fact that even though we're all busy, a little effort up front can save a ton of time later – especially in hiring.

We'd done group manager training before, but we wanted something else.

'We're here to help'

So we drew up a presentation and scheduled time to speak with each department head and the managers below him or her in small groups.

We gave them concrete examples of how their mistakes had cost us time and money, and how much time they could save by doing one or two small things.

Afterward, we opened the floor to questions – not just issues limited to the presentation, but any issues on supervisors' minds.

The response was unanimous – managers got a lot out of the session.

Now we schedule time to meet and present different topics to each department several times a year.

The best part: Managers very rarely make mistakes during the hiring process anymore.

(An HR manager of a bank in Oklahoma City)

3. Input from employees bolstered hiring

Something was off with our hiring process.

We were looking for applicants with a certain personality who'd be a good cultural fit for our company.

But for some reason we kept striking out.

The problem reached a climax when we lost a couple of new workers.

We needed to come up with a new system to keep from having to try out multiple candidates for each open position.

Getting to know you

The solution: Get out on the floor. We spoke with supervisors and asked if we could spend a day among employees while they were working.

After we got the OK, we took a day to interact with workers and observe how they worked as a team. We even came in at night to observe workers on the third shift.

Once we knew the kind of personality that thrives in our workplace – for example, people who work the third shift need to be self-motivated and quick thinkers – we had a solid template for the kind of applicants we were looking for.

And after we started matching candidates against that template, we were able to pinpoint the exact people we wanted to hire.

Now that we've done that, we've been able to get the right person for the job – the first time.

(An HR manager of a Midwestern dairy distributor)

4.   Online program gave applicants needed info

We were looking for a surefire way to lock up solid applicants.

We weren't having trouble finding good candidates, but we wanted to be aggressive and sell applicants on what we had to offer them right away.

The answer turned out to be right under our nose.

Gave them info upfront

After we determined we wanted to bring applicants in for an interview, we decided to let them access the online orientation program we'd designed for new hires.

Once interviews had been scheduled, we sent applicants an email with a link to the program's website, and a user name and password to log in.

The orientation program has info on our salary ranges, benefits and 401(k) program – in other words, everything candidates usually shy away from asking about.

Now, when candidates come in for an interview, they have a better idea about areas that'll factor into their decision – and a better sense if it's what they're looking for in a new position.

Applicants say the program's been invaluable.

In fact, current staff members have told us that the orientation website was what made the difference in deciding our company was the right fit for them.

(A director of HR for a college in Michigan)

5.   Our own people got us new hires we wanted

We'd been following the same old pattern when we were recruiting: posting jobs on career sites and talking to staffing firms.

The problem was, these methods were super costly for the company. The staffing firms alone were charging monstrous fees.

And if money wasn't a big enough issue, I was spending too much time sorting through resumes and doing phone interviews.

There had to be a simpler way to find good hires. We knew in-house referrals worked for other companies. Maybe we could make them work for us.

Asked for help

As we suspected, our skilled employees knew others in their field.

We asked for a few names and they were happy to comply. They gave us the goods on folks they thought were qualified, hard-working and team players.

We were amazed at the quality of the candidates. We finally found the people we wanted.

Since this referral plan was put in place, we've not only cut hiring costs, I have more time to focus on other tasks.

The best part: Our employees are so psyched about referring their friends, we don't have to offer financial incentives.

(An HR manager for a contractor in Texas)

6. Narrowed our focus, found the right people

Like a lot of companies, we were worried – employees were retiring, and we didn't have qualified people to replace them.

The local paper didn't push many applicants our way anymore. The pool of applicants seemed to be getting smaller.

That's when we realized we were shopping in the wrong department.

We'd been using a shotgun approach. What we really needed was a laser beam – on a much smaller target.

Since we were looking for specialized labor, we had to get our name to the specialists – the qualified employees out in the field.

Found a better source

We flipped through our industry's trade journals for ideas. And we realized – the answer was right in our hands. Experienced workers read the journals for the latest industry news.

They were our best potential applicants. So we advertised our company's career opportunities in the next issue. By using an industry publication, we were able to zero in on the audience we needed.

And the resumes started pouring in when we made a direct connection with qualified people in our field.

Best of all: We found and hired quality employees we needed to replace our retiring workers.

(An HR director for a school district in Oregon)

7. Found new hires in unexpected spot

We had a major recruiting problem when the local technical college closed down.

Since most of our new hires had to have specialized training, we couldn't rely on classified ads or job posting boards.

Those methods just wouldn't attract the kind of talent we were looking for. We had to come up with a new way to find qualified applicants – and quickly.

We didn't have time to search for new contacts, but what if we could make something happen with our existing resources?

Right under our nose

So we looked at our current memberships in industry organizations. And we noticed that we hadn't been active in a group that held meetings in our area on a regular basis.

We got actively involved in the group. We used the opportunity to network, and announce open positions. We left fliers for members to pass along to qualified friends.

An added bonus: The group set up an internal email exchange where members could post job openings and share industry news.

Our "problem" turned into a golden opportunity. Now, we have a new source for recruiting – and a new pipeline of industry news.

(An office manager for a medical clinic in Alabama)

8. Try before you buy managerial solution

Some of our supervisors were nearing retirement, which meant it was time to start hiring new managers.

And we were not looking forward to that.

Recruiting and training supervisors took a long time and a lot of money.

And when a potential manager didn't work out, that was company time and money wasted.

There had to be a more efficient way to bring on supervisors.

So we took some inspiration from an unlikely place – our temp workers.

We used temps to get us through busy patches. If they put in great work, we hired them full time.

Could that work for managers too?

Managers waiting in the wings

Next time we needed temps, we asked the temp agency only to send us workers with supervisory experience.

If they were dependable enough workers, we brought them on full time – and we started giving them full managerial training.

When the training didn't work out, it was no problem – the workers just went back to their normal jobs.

But most of the workers flourished – and that's helped us put our future managerial plans in place.

Now, we've got employees waiting in the wings to replace our managers when they do retire – and we've saved time and money in the process.

(An HR supervisor for a recycling plant in Rhode Island)

9. *Expanded referrals helped our recruiting*

Our main recruiting program involved attending local trade shows and job fairs, just to put our face out in the community.

But we didn't have much success at those.

After some brainstorming, we considered a referral program, similar to ones we'd seen other companies have success with.

However, for the program to succeed, we knew we'd need to tailor it to our specific needs.

We're in a niche market, and finding the right people can be difficult.

More money, less time

So we set up our program a little differently from other companies:

- **Doubled the money.** Like most employers, we paid employees a flat fee when we hired a worker they referred to us. But when we were having a hard time finding applicants for a specific position, we doubled the monetary reward.
- **Shortened the time span.** Most companies wait until referrals have been with the company for six months before rewarding the workers who referred them. But we wanted staff members to refer people to us now – so we shortened that time period to 30 days.

Now we fill 30 to 40 positions a year from referrals – because we know our program strikes a chord with our employees.

(A VP of HR for a welding company in Illinois)

10. *Reduced recruiting and hiring headaches by shifting our focus*

We were beginning to wonder whether our recruiting and training budgets were being used efficiently.

When we were looking for employees, we'd write out classified ads and pay a boatload of money to run them in the newspaper or online.

But more times than not, an employee would stop us in the hallway or come to our office and say, "I heard we have an open position. I know someone who'd be a great fit here!"

Or: "I'd personally like to apply for the job that just opened up."

When we followed up with the worker or the person they suggested, we typically found those were the employees who worked out the best in the end.

After this happened a couple times, we got to thinking: Maybe starting our recruiting process outside company walls wasn't the best idea.

An inside job

So we focused our recruiting process on two areas: referrals and internal recruiting.

- **Referrals.** We instituted a referral program, with a cash incentive for employees who refer successful job candidates.
- **Internal recruitment.** We posted open positions internally first to give our current employees a chance to make a change or advance.

We assumed no employee would recommend someone who'd make them look bad, and we were right – the referral system has been a great success, and brought us some of our best workers.

And not posting open positions externally has saved us time and money – and we'd much rather promote from within anyway.

Our new recruiting ideas have really worked out well.

Solving our training problems came next.

Training subsidy

When we did have to hire from outside the company, we hit the same roadblock many companies hit: Some workers just didn't make it through training.

Was there some way to protect ourselves if that happened?

We networked, and called some of our peers – and we found exactly what we were looking for.

And we found if we hired people directly off unemployment, those new workers were eligible to have half of their wages reimbursed to the company during their training period.

Of course, we only hire people off unemployment if they are the best candidate for the position.

But even if they're great applicants, they still require training – and we've got some financial protection if they don't work out in the end.

More time for pressing matters

Our new recruiting and training strategies are working out nicely for us.

And best of all? We have more time and money to devote to other HR matters now.

(A benefits coordinator for an engineering company in Michigan)

11. Revamped hiring process helped unearth hard-to-find candidates

We were having a heck of a time finding the skilled talent we needed to fill our open positions.

We initially thought we just weren't reaching the right applicant pool. The right candidates had to be out there somewhere, right?

So we partnered with some contingency search firms to try and find those perfect employees.

No dice.

Could that mean the problem was on our end?

Maybe it was time for us to take a look at our hiring process.

'First date'

Our application process was put together by a recruiter, and, like all recruiters, he wanted to gather as much info as possible on each potential candidate.

So we got tons of info from applicants before we ever spoke to them. Problem was, applying for a job with us was a painfully time-consuming process. We finally figured out we were likely losing candidates before they even submitted their resume.

So we decided to revamp the initial application process. Now, all we ask from candidates is some demographic info and their resume – what we refer to as a "first date." The whole deal takes about five minutes.

Even with that little bit of info, we know which employees we want to pursue for a phone interview.

After we initiated the new process, we immediately saw an increase in applicants.

24 hours, 5 references

We'd managed to make the initial application process easier, but we wanted to go further. Our next problem point? References.

Like most companies, we called the references that applicants provided to us. But sometimes it took days for us to get in touch with them. We always assumed that was part of the process – but did it have to be?

We found the answer on the Internet. Basically, here's how it worked: Applicants asked their references to email their feedback to a web-based "clearinghouse." The clearinghouse then sent the comments to us – anonymously.

It was a godsend. Where it used to take three to five days to get candidates' references on the phone, we heard from nearly all the references within 24 hours.

And because it was anonymous, we got a lot more useful insight into the candidates than we ever got over the phone.

Proof positive

Was revamping our hiring process worth it? Well, before we revamped hiring, we had positions that had been open for a year. Now we've filled them.

That's proof enough for us.

(An HR business partner for an energy company in California)

III. INTERVIEWING

A. Overview

For most employers, the job interview plays a critical role in the search process – and for good reason. The interview provides advantages that are lacking with respect to other methods of evaluation. The face-to-face interaction of the interview enables employers to gauge the skills, experiences, personality and cultural fit of an applicant like no other assessment tool.

Interview questions should focus on how the applicant's skill set and previous experience match up with the job's requirements. Though the interview is a uniquely flexible tool, it is nonetheless wise to approach it with a defined sense of structure. Straying too far from a script increases the odds of committing a costly mistake, such as making a legally forbidden inquiry or a statement that is wrongfully perceived by the applicant as an assurance that a job offer is forthcoming.

It is a good idea to begin by offering a detailed description of the job before proceeding to a scripted but adjustable set of questions. Consistent, objective questions that relate entirely to the applicant's ability to meet legitimate job requirements are the hallmark of effective, legal interviews.

Many pitfalls endanger the unwary employer with respect to the interview process, and several areas of inquiry are strictly off limits. Some prohibited questions, such as those explicitly addressing disability, national origin or religion, are clearly to be avoided. But others may seem relatively innocuous and yet pose a distinct legal risk. For example, even questions relating to credit history may subject an employer to a claim of unlawful discrimination on the theory that the practice has an unlawfully disparate impact on a protected class of individuals.

B. Real-Life Success Stories

1. *One question got applicants to open up*

We were having a difficult time getting candidates to open up during interviews.

Interviews can be scary, we know. But some candidates with great potential were so nervous that it was hard for them to calm down and talk to us.

Answers revealed 3 things

So we sat down and brainstormed ways to get applicants talking.

It helps that we're interviewing constantly, so we had many opportunities to try new ideas.

After some trial and error, we found one question that worked: "What do you think are the three most important traits one should have to be successful in this position?"

We usually ask this in the beginning of the interview because it's not a hard question – but it gets people talking.

Candidates' answers reveal a lot. We're able to tell:

- how well the candidate understands what the job involves
- how well the candidate is able to see things from the employer's perspective, and
- how much thought they've put into assessing their own fit for the job.

Since we've introduced that one question, we've really gotten applicants to open up – and that's helped us find some great hires.

(An HR consultant for a broadcasting company in Toronto)

2. *Stopped managers' interview mistakes*

Our managers, as great as they were, sometimes made mistakes while interviewing candidates.

Every once in a while, we'd hear that a manager had made an interview faux pas – for example, asked an applicant how old he was. We couldn't have that happen.

The problem: We didn't have the budget for a high-profile training program.
Whatever we came up with would need to be in-house, and not break the bank to boot.

Informal but effective

So we came up with a two-tiered solution.

First, someone in HR spoke informally with each offending manager.

This wasn't a formal dressing down so much as a reminder – albeit an important one – about what is and isn't acceptable to ask in interviews.

That got managers' attention, but we wanted to make sure the info stuck.

So every once in a while we email a short but relevant article about interviewing do's and dont's to managers – something they can read quickly but also get a lot out of.

The managers have responded well, and we always get a couple of positive comments about the emails.

And it seems to have worked – we haven't heard about any inappropriate questions in interviews since.

(An HR director for a church in Houston)

3.   Centralized hiring saved time, money

We were missing opportunities to hire good candidates because we didn't have a centralized approach.

Candidates applied to specific departments, each with its own hiring team – but there wasn't a system for sharing information between teams.

Often, we'd realize that candidates rejected for one position would have fit well in another department.

Even if we recommended that someone apply to another department, they'd have to start over with paperwork and interviews – a waste of time and money.

We needed to start working together to get the most qualified applicants in the best positions.

Everybody get together

We got all our hiring personnel in one location to improve communication and adopted a standard system for applications.

When an applicant interviewed for a position, the interviewer would evaluate whether they might be a better fit elsewhere.

If applicants were referred to another department, we could pass along information seamlessly.

Thanks to increased cooperation, we've eliminated redundant hiring procedures, saving time and money.

And we've been able to keep good applicants within the company, matching workers' skills to positions.

(An HR manager of a food company in Kansas)

C. Checklists

☑ CHECKLIST

Avoiding Dangerous Questions

Federal laws against discrimination ban interviewers from asking applicants questions in several key areas. Here's a checklist:

❑ Race
❑ Color
❑ Sex
❑ Religion
❑ National origin
❑ Birthplace
❑ Age
❑ Disability
❑ Marital/family status.

Although those categories seem fairly straightforward, interviewers sometimes unwittingly run into problems with what seem like perfectly innocent questions. A list of specific things interviewers can't ask:

❑ An applicant's birth date.
❑ How long an applicant has lived at his or her current address.
❑ The surname of the applicant's father.
❑ The name of the church or synagogue the applicant attends.
❑ The ages of the applicant's children (if the applicant has volunteered the information about having children).
❑ An applicant's childcare arrangements.
❑ How an applicant would travel to work.
❑ Whether an applicant rents or owns his/her home.
❑ Whether the applicant has outstanding debts.
❑ If the applicant's ever been arrested.
❑ Whether an applicant suffers from a disability.
❑ Whether an applicant has ever filed a workers' compensation claim.

IV. BACKGROUND CHECKS

A. Overview

"Background check" is the term used to describe a number of varying informational reports that are sought by employers to learn more about job applicants and confirm the accuracy of reported information. The category includes criminal record checks, credit history checks and checks of driving records. Other areas that can be addressed by background checks include past employment, education and workers' compensation history.

A federal law called the Fair Credit Reporting Act strictly regulates the ability of employers to obtain such reports if they are prepared by a consumer reporting agency. Even a check of a reference provided by an applicant is covered by the act's requirements if the reference is verified by an outside reference-checking agency. Employers who check references on their own are not subject to the act.

Among the Fair Credit Reporting Act's most important requirements is the requirement that employers notify applicants in writing – and obtain their written permission – before seeking to obtain a report from a consumer reporting agency. The law also requires employers to take certain steps if they intend to use the results of the reports to take an adverse action against an applicant, such as denying him employment.

Various state laws further regulate the background check process.

For some occupations, such as those involving contact with children, a background check may be mandatory. In many cases, these mandatory checks are limited to a criminal records check.

Background checks serve another important purpose: They can shield employers from claims of negligent hiring and related claims in the event that an applicant is hired and subsequently causes harm to others while on the job.

B. Q&As

1. *We're going to start searching applicants' social media profiles. Should we do it ourselves or hire a third party to conduct it?*

Do it in-house, says Nicholas Walker *(clientservices@ogletreedeakins.com)* of the labor and employment law firm Ogletree Deakins.

The Fair Credit Reporting Act comes into play here. The bill governs "employment background checks for the purposes of hiring" and applies if "an employer uses a third-party screening company to prepare the check."

Under the law, if you hire a third party, you'll need to tell applicants of the investigation, get the candidates' OK to conduct the search, and notify them if the report is used to make an adverse decision.

2. *Can we request that candidates give us their social media passwords as part of the application process?*

You probably shouldn't, says Molly DiBianca *(mdibianca@ycst.com)* of the Delaware Employment Law Blog. You could instead gain that info by:

*   requiring candidates to grant your online "friend" request for 24 to 48 hours, or
*   asking candidates to log in to their social media pages during the interview in the presence of an HR staffer.

3. *We've heard that doing Facebook or Google searches on applicants and employees may violate federal discrimination laws. Is that true?*

Possibly, says Adria B. Martinelli *(amartinelli@ycst.com)* from the Delaware Employment Law Blog.

It's illegal for employers to acquire genetic info, such as family history of disease, on applicants or staff under the Genetic Information Nondiscrimination Act (GINA).

Even a cursory Internet search that reveals a worker ran in a cancer research fundraiser in support of her mother with cancer could be a violation.

Employers aren't in violation if the info they get is from "publicly available" sources, but the Equal Employment Opportunity Commission hasn't decided yet if info from Internet searches is "publicly available."

For now, be wary – a stray remark after genetic info is found could link causation between membership in a protected class and a firing.

4. *We want candidates to be up front with us about anything that may show up when we do a background check. What's the best way to go about that?*

Tell candidates that you'll give them a chance to explain themselves, no matter what's on their records, says hiring expert Mel Kleiman *(mkleiman@humetrics.com).*

Frame it like this: The worst-case scenario is when an interviewer asks a candidate if anything will show up on a background check and the applicant says no – and then the check turns up some prior conviction. At that point, it's too late for candidates to speak up and explain.

Tell applicants they should explain anything that may show up before you start the checking process. And stress that not all black marks on a person's record are deal-killers. For example, if an otherwise qualified 43-year-old candidate was arrested when he was 17, that's not something likely to affect your hiring decision.

5. *We recently interviewed a candidate who previously worked at a company that we have a close business relationship with. Are we allowed to talk with people we know at the company about the worker even if she hasn't provided them as references?*

Definitely, says Mel Kleiman *(mkleiman@humetrics.com).* You are permitted to ask for additional information on applicants from previous employers, even if the candidate has not officially given them to you as references.

Even if you're not familiar with the supervisor or manager you're calling, you can always ask, "Is there anyone else you recommend I talk to who could give me good information about this applicant?"

C. Checklists

☑ CHECKLIST

Background Checks

Evey company that does a background check on an applicant must get a permission to do so. But it's in firms' best interests to let a candidate know just what he or she is agreeing to. Here are three pieces of information companies will want to be transparent about on their background check forms.

❏ The firm can contact a lot of organizations. By signing a background check permission form, candidates are giving permission for a company to check with a number of organizations and institutions with which the applicant has been associated. These include but aren't limited to present or past employers, schools, financial institutions, credit agencies, law enforcement agencies, and city, state, county and federal courts.

❏ A photocopy is as good as an original. Companies should also let applicants know that any photocopy of their signed background check permission form can count as a substitute for the original.

❏ Written notice is waived. Finally, firms should include a note that by signing the form, they've waived present or past employers from having to give the candidate written authorization that they're releasing information about him or her.

D.   Statutes and Regulations

Fair Credit Reporting Act (Relevant Provisions)
§ 604. Permissible purposes of consumer reports [15 U.S.C. § 1681b]

(b) Conditions for Furnishing and Using Consumer Reports for Employment Purposes.

(1) *Certification from user.* A consumer reporting agency may furnish a consumer report for employment purposes only if

(A) the person who obtains such report from the agency certifies to the agency that:

(i) the person has complied with paragraph (2) with respect to the consumer report, and the person will comply with paragraph (3) with respect to the consumer report if paragraph (3) becomes applicable; and

(ii) information from the consumer report will not be used in violation of any applicable Federal or State equal employment opportunity law or regulation; and

(B) the consumer reporting agency provides with the report, or has previously provided, a summary of the consumer's rights under this title, as prescribed by the Federal Trade Commission under section 609(c)(3) [§ 1681g].

(2) Disclosure to Consumer.

(A) *In general.* Except as provided in subparagraph (B), a person may not procure a consumer report, or cause a consumer report to be procured, for employment purposes with respect to any consumer, unless –

(i) a clear and conspicuous disclosure has been made in writing to the consumer at any time before the report is procured or caused to be procured, in a document that consists solely of the disclosure, that a consumer report may be obtained for employment purposes; and

(ii) the consumer has authorized in writing (which authorization may be made on the document referred to in clause (i)) the procurement of the report by that person.

(B) *Application by mail, telephone, computer, or other similar means.* If a consumer described in subparagraph (C) applies for employment by mail, telephone, computer, or other similar means, at any time before a consumer report is procured or caused to be procured in connection with that application –

(i) the person who procures the consumer report on the consumer for employment purposes shall provide to the consumer, by oral, written, or electronic means, notice that a consumer report may be obtained for employment purposes, and a summary of the consumer's rights under section 615(a)(3); and

(ii) the consumer shall have consented, orally, in writing, or electronically to the procurement of the report by that person.

(C) *Scope.* Subparagraph (B) shall apply to a person procuring a consumer report on a consumer in connection with the consumer's application for employment only if –

(i) the consumer is applying for a position over which the Secretary of Transportation has the power to establish qualifications and maximum hours of service pursuant to the provisions of section 31502 of title 49, or a position subject to safety regulation by a State transportation agency; and

(ii) as of the time at which the person procures the report or causes the report to be procured the only interaction between the consumer and the person in connection with that employment application has been by mail, telephone, computer, or other similar means.

(3) Conditions on use for adverse actions.

(A) *In general.* Except as provided in subparagraph (B), in using a consumer report for employment purposes, before taking any adverse action based in whole or in part on the report, the person intending to take such adverse action shall provide to the consumer to whom the report relates –

(i) a copy of the report; and

(ii) a description in writing of the rights of the consumer under this title, as prescribed by the Federal Trade Commission under section 609(c)(3).

(B) *Application by mail, telephone, computer, or other similar means.*

(i) If a consumer described in subparagraph (C) applies for employment by mail, telephone, computer, or other similar means, and if a person who has procured a consumer report on the consumer for employment purposes takes adverse action on the employment application based in whole or in part on the report, then the person must provide to the consumer to whom the report relates, in lieu of the notices required under subparagraph (A) of this section and under section 615(a), within 3 business days of taking such action, an oral, written or electronic notification –

(I) that adverse action has been taken based in whole or in part on a consumer report received from a consumer reporting agency;

(II) of the name, address and telephone number of the consumer reporting agency that furnished the consumer report (including a toll-free telephone number established by the agency if the agency compiles and maintains files on consumers on a nationwide basis);

(III) that the consumer reporting agency did not make the decision to take the adverse action and is unable to provide to the consumer the specific reasons why the adverse action was taken; and

(IV) that the consumer may, upon providing proper identification, request a free copy of a report and may dispute with the consumer reporting agency the accuracy or completeness of any information in a report. July 30, 2004.

(ii) If, under clause (B)(i)(IV), the consumer requests a copy of a consumer report from the person who procured the report, then, within 3 business days of receiving the consumer's request, together with proper identification, the person must send or provide to the consumer a copy of a report and a copy of the consumer's rights as prescribed by the Federal Trade Commission under section 609(c)(3).

(C) *Scope.* Subparagraph (B) shall apply to a person procuring a consumer report on a consumer in connection with the consumer's application for employment only if –

(i) the consumer is applying for a position over which the Secretary of Transportation has the power to establish qualifications and maximum hours of service pursuant to the provisions of section 31502 of title 49, or a position subject to safety regulation by a State transportation agency; and

(ii) as of the time at which the person procures the report or causes the report to be procured the only interaction between the consumer and the person in connection with that employment application has been by mail, telephone, computer, or other similar means.

(4) Exception for national security investigations.

(A) *In general.* In the case of an agency or department of the United States Government which seeks to obtain and use a consumer report for employment purposes, paragraph (3) shall not apply to any adverse action by such agency or department which is based in part on such consumer report, if the head of such agency or department makes a written finding that–

(i) the consumer report is relevant to a national security investigation of such agency or department;

(ii) the investigation is within the jurisdiction of such agency or department;

(iii) there is reason to believe that compliance with paragraph (3) will–

(I) endanger the life or physical safety of any person;

(II) result in flight from prosecution;

(III) result in the destruction of, or tampering with, evidence relevant to the investigation;

(IV) result in the intimidation of a potential witness relevant to the investigation;

(V) result in the compromise of classified information; or

(VI) otherwise seriously jeopardize or unduly delay the investigation or another official proceeding.

(B) *Notification of consumer upon conclusion of investigation.* Upon the conclusion of a national security investigation described in subparagraph (A), or upon the determination that the exception under subparagraph (A) is no longer required for the reasons set forth in such subparagraph, the official exercising the authority in such subparagraph shall provide to the consumer who is the subject of the consumer report with regard to which such finding was made –

(i) a copy of such consumer report with any classified information redacted as necessary;

(ii) notice of any adverse action which is based, in part, on the consumer report; and

(iii) the identification with reasonable specificity of the nature of the investigation for which the consumer report was sought.

(C) *Delegation by head of agency or department.* For purposes of subparagraphs (A) and (B), the head of any agency or department of the United States Government may delegate his or her authorities under this paragraph to an official of such agency or department who has personnel security responsibilities and is a member of the Senior Executive Service or equivalent civilian or military rank.

(D) *Report to the Congress.* Not later than January 31 of each year, the head of each agency and department of the United States Government that exercised authority under this paragraph during the preceding year shall submit a report to the Congress on the number of times the department or agency exercised such authority during the year.

(E) *Definitions.* For purposes of this paragraph, the following definitions shall apply:

(i) The term "classified information" means information that is protected from unauthorized disclosure under Executive Order No. 12958 or successor orders.

(ii) The term "national security investigation" means any official inquiry by an agency or department of the United States Government to determine the eligibility of a consumer to receive access or continued access to classified information or to determine whether classified information has been lost or compromised.

V. DRUG TESTING

A. Overview

Employers have good reason to do all they can to keep illegal drug use out of the workplace. Drug abuse among employees can lead to a variety of problems, such as increased tardiness, absenteeism, lack of productivity and violent and/or criminal behavior.

Although private employers are afforded a degree of latitude when it comes to testing job applicants, privacy concerns and a patchwork of varying state laws play into the mix. Some states ban pre-employment drug testing until after an offer of employment has been extended. In addition, employers may need to provide written notice that testing is required. For a list of state laws regulating pre-hiring drug testing by employers, go to *http://www.dol.gov/asp/programs/ drugs/said/StateLaws.asp.*

Challenges to drug testing in the private sector are less likely to succeed than their counterparts in the public sector. This is largely because the federal Constitution's Fourth Amendment only prohibits unreasonable searches and seizures by the government and does not regulate searches by employers.

Any drug testing program must be uniformly applied to all similarly situated applicants. It is best to advise applicants early on in the process that testing may be required. In addition, the confidentiality of test results must be maintained.

B. Judicial Decisions

♦ A Massachusetts job applicant was given a conditional job offer and required to pass a drug screen, which included a test for nicotine. As part of its wellness plan, the company had a policy of not hiring smokers. The applicant submitted a urine sample and began working for the company pending the test results. When his urine tested positive for nicotine, he was told he would not be permanently hired. He sued, asserting that he had been "fired" in violation of his ERISA rights. A federal court ruled against him, noting that he was not an employee who "may become eligible to receive a benefit from an employee benefit plan." **His "regular" employment was clearly contingent on passing the background check and urinalysis screening.** He also could not claim a violation of his privacy rights because he smoked in public and received a warning after his supervisor noticed his cigarettes on his dashboard. *Rodrigues v. EG Systems d/b/a Scotts Lawnservice,* 639 F.Supp.2d 131 (D. Mass. 2009).

◆ A North Carolina applicant with depression, bipolar disorder and ADHD received a conditional offer of employment, contingent on passing a drug test. He did not mention that he was taking medication for his condition and tested positive for amphetamines. When the job offer was withdrawn, he did not contact the company's medical review officer to provide proof that he was taking legal medication. Instead, he sued under the ADA. A federal court ruled for the company, noting that **its drug-free workplace policy did not improperly prohibit employees' use of prescription drugs**. In fact, several other applicants had contacted the medical review officer after testing positive for amphetamines, and provided documentation that they were taking prescription medication. They were subsequently hired. Thus, the company did not discriminate against the applicant. *Meyer v. Qualex, Inc.,* 388 F.Supp.2d 630 (E.D.N.C. 2005).

◆ After Wal-Mart offered a West Virginia applicant a job, it required her to give a urine sample. The test came back negative for drugs and the employee began working. She later quit and sued the company for invasion of privacy. The case reached the Supreme Court of Appeals of West Virginia, which noted that an employer may not require an employee to submit to drug testing unless it has a reasonable good-faith suspicion of drug use, or the employee's job responsibilities involve public safety or the safety of others. However, **in the pre-employment context, the individual has a lower expectation of privacy**. Background checks, references and medical examinations all contribute to that lower expectation. The urine sample requirement did not violate the employee's privacy rights. *Baughman v. Wal-Mart Stores,* 592 S.E.2d 824 (W.Va. 2003).

◆ A manager accepted a conditional offer of employment that required him to pass a drug test prior to beginning the job. He succeeded in delaying the test until four days after his eventual date of hire and then submitted a test indicating marijuana use. The employer withdrew its offer of employment, and the manager sued, claiming that he could not be tested for drugs without individualized suspicion of drug use. The Court of Appeal of California noted that the state **approved of drug testing without individualized suspicion for job applicants**. Suspicionless testing is appropriate in such cases, because prospective employers have not had the opportunity to observe them and may have a need to evaluate their drug usage. In contrast, an employer generally should not have to resort to suspicionless testing of current employees. In this case, the manager had not performed any work for the new employer and was properly viewed as a job applicant. An applicant could not avoid drug testing by delaying a test beyond the date of hire. *Pilkington Barnes Hind v. Superior Court (Visbal)*, 77 Cal.Rptr.2d 596 (Cal. Ct. App. 1998).

♦   An electrical contractor hired employees for construction projects in North and South Carolina. A labor organization charged that the contractor violated federal labor law at the North Carolina site by refusing to hire, threatening and interrogating union-affiliated applicants, and for devising and enforcing a drug testing policy to discourage union activities. The union also claimed that the contractor failed to offer work to 16 union-affiliated employees at the South Carolina site based on their union activities or sympathies. The National Labor Relations Board (NLRB) affirmed the findings of an administrative law judge (ALJ) in favor of the union and ordered the contractor to reinstate two union-affiliated employees who had been fired for refusing to take a drug test. The contractor appealed. The Fourth Circuit rejected the contractor's claim that the ALJ was biased and held that the contractor had committed unfair labor practices. However, the drug testing policy had been **legitimately enacted in response to information that employees of other contractors at the two work sites were using drugs**. The drug testing policy had been uniformly applied to all new employees. The court reversed the NLRB's decision concerning the drug testing policy. *Eldeco, Inc. v. NLRB,* 132 F.3d 1007 (4th Cir. 1997).

VI. VERIFYING ELIGIBILITY (I-9)

A. Overview

A federal law called the Immigration Reform and Control Act of 1986 aims to curb illegal immigration by making it more difficult for illegal immigrants to find employment in the United States. Under the law, all United States employers must complete and maintain Employment Eligibility Verification Forms, also known as I-9s, for all employees who are newly hired to work in the United States. Employers who fail to meet the law's requirements relating to I-9s are subject to civil and criminal penalties.

The I-9 form has three sections. The first section, which must be completed between the time a job offer is accepted and the employee's first day of work, includes basic identifying information such as the employee's name, address and Social Security number.

Within three business days from the date that employment begins, the new employee must provide the employer an original document indicating his identity and employment authorization. Examples of documents that may be offered include a U.S. Passport and a Permanent Resident Card.

Also within three business days of the start of employment, the employer must complete the second section of the I-9 form by recording information relating to the provided documentation and certifying that it has examined the documentation and that it appears to be genuine.

The third section of the I-9 form is used to update information relating to the employee or to reverify his eligibility for employment. This section is completed, for example, when an employment authorization document expires and a new one is substituted in its place.

Employers must retain completed I-9 forms until either three years from the date of hire or one year of the date of termination – whichever is later.

I-9s may not be used as a way to screen job applicants.

B. Q&As

1. *We've been scanning I-9 certifications into our electronic database for some time now. Can we throw away the paper versions once we've done so?*

Generally, yes, provided that your electronic system satisfies the requirements set by U.S. Citizenship and Immigration Services, says Molly DiBianca *(mdibianca@ycst.com)* of the Delaware Employment Law Blog *(tinyurl.com/dbnzse).*

Once you fill out a paper I-9 form and scan the original signed document, you're free to get rid of the paper copy.

Careful, though: Make sure you back up the electronic files in more than one place. You never know when a mishap could wipe out all your I-9 info.

2. *There's been some confusion on how long we have to complete a worker's I-9 form for E-Verify. Please set the record straight – do we have three or four days?*

It can get tricky, says Bernhard Mueller *(bernhard.mueller@ ogletreedeakins.com)* of the law firm Ogletree Deakins.

You must fill out Section 1 at the time a new worker is hired. Section 2 must be completed "within three business days of hire." But the jury's still out on if the day of hire counts into those three days or not.

Best bet: Play it safe. If you hire a worker on Monday, complete Section 1 that day and Section 2 no later than Wednesday.

The following are select questions from the *Handbook for Employers: Instructions for Completing Form I-9* from the U.S. Citizenship and Immigration Services. The full form can be found here: *http://www. uscis.gov/files/form/m-274.pdf.*

3. *Do citizens and noncitizen nationals of the United States need to complete Form I-9?*

Yes. While citizens and noncitizen nationals of the United States are automatically eligible for employment, they too must present the required documents and complete a Form I-9. U.S. citizens include persons born in the United States, Puerto Rico, Guam, the U.S. Virgin Islands, and the Commonwealth of the Northern Mariana Islands U.S. noncitizen nationals are persons who owe permanent allegiance to the United States, which include those born in American Samoa, including Swains Island.

4. *If someone accepts a job with my company but will not start work for a month, can I complete Form I-9 when the employee accepts the job?*

Yes. The law requires that you complete Form I-9 only when the person actually begins working for pay. However, you may complete the form earlier, as long as the person has been offered and has accepted the job. You may not use the Form I-9 process to screen job applicants.

5. *Do I need to fill out Forms I-9 for independent contractors or their employees?*

No. For example, if you contract with a construction company to perform renovations on your building, you do not have to complete Forms I-9 for that company's employees.

The construction company is responsible for completing Forms I-9 for its own employees. However, you may not use a contract, subcontract or exchange to obtain the labor or services of an employee knowing that the employee is unauthorized to work.

6. *May I fire an employee who fails to produce the required documents within three business days of his or her start date?*

Yes. You may terminate an employee who fails to produce the required document or documents, or an acceptable receipt for a document, within three business days of the date employment begins.

7. *What happens if I properly complete and retain a Form I-9 and DHS discovers that my employee is not actually authorized to work?*

You cannot be charged with a verification violation. You will also have a good faith defense against the imposition of employer sanctions penalties for knowingly hiring an unauthorized individual, unless the government can show you had knowledge of the unauthorized status of the employee.

8. *May I specify which documents I will accept for verification?*

No. The employee may choose which document(s) he or she wants to present from the Lists of Acceptable Documents. You must accept any document (from List A) or combination of documents (one from List B and one from List C) listed on Form I-9 and found in Part Eight of this Handbook that reasonably appear on their face to be genuine and to relate to the person presenting them. To do otherwise could be an unfair immigration-related employment practice in violation of the anti-discrimination provision in the INA. Individuals who look and/or sound foreign must not be treated differently in the recruiting, hiring, or verification process.

9. *What is my responsibility concerning the authenticity of document(s) presented to me?*

You must examine the document(s), and if they reasonably appear on their face to be genuine and to relate to the person presenting them, you must accept them. To do otherwise could be an unfair immigration-related employment practice. If the document(s) do not reasonably appear on their face to be genuine or to relate to the person presenting them, you must not accept them.

10. May I accept an expired document?

No. Expired documents are no longer acceptable for Form I-9. However, you may accept Employment Authorization Documents (Forms I-766) and Permanent Resident Cards (Forms I-551) that appear to be expired. For example, Temporary Protected Status (TPS) beneficiaries whose Employment Authorization Documents (Forms I-766) appear to be expired may be automatically extended in a *Federal Register* notice. These individuals may continue to work based on their expired Employment Authorization Documents (Forms I-766) during the automatic extension period specified in the *Federal Register* notice. When the automatic extension of the Employment Authorization Document (Form I-766) expires, you must reverify the employee's employment authorization.

11. May I accept a photocopy of a document presented by an employee?

No. Employees must present original documents. The only exception is that an employee may present a certified copy of a birth certificate.

12. When I review an employee's identity and employment authorization documents, should I make copies of them?

If you participate in E-Verify and the employee presents a document used as part of Photo Matching, currently the U.S. passport and passport card, Permanent Resident Card (Form I-551) and the Employment Authorization Document (Form I-766), you must retain a photocopy of the document he or she presents.

Other documents may be added to Photo Matching in the future. If you do not participate in E-Verify, you are not required to make photocopies of documents. However, if you wish to make photocopies of documents other than those used in E-Verify, you must do so for all employees. Photocopies must not be used for any other purpose. Photocopying documents does not relieve you of your obligation to fully complete Section 2 of Form I-9, nor is it an acceptable substitute for proper completion of Form I-9 in general.

13. My new employee presented two documents to complete Form I-9, each containing a different last name. One document matches the name she entered in Section 1. The employee explained that she had just gotten married and changed her last name, but had not yet changed the name on the other document. Can I accept the document with the different name?

You may accept a document with a different name than the name entered in Section 1 provided that you resolve the question of whether the document reasonably relates to the employee. You also may wish to attach a brief memo to Form I-9 stating the reason for the name discrepancy, along with any supporting documentation the employee provides. An employee may provide documentation to support his or her name change, but is not required to do so. If, however, you determine that the document with a different name does not reasonably appear to be genuine and to relate to her, you may ask her to provide other documents from the Lists of Acceptable Documents on Form I-9.

14. The name on the document my employee presented to me is spelled slightly differently than the name she entered in Section 1 of Form I-9. Can I accept this document?

If the document contains a slight spelling variation, and the employee has a reasonable explanation for the variation, the document is acceptable as long as you are satisfied that the document otherwise reasonably appears to be genuine and to relate to him or her.

15. How do I correct a mistake on an employee's Form I-9?

The best way to correct Form I-9 is to line through the portions of the form that contain incorrect information, then enter the correct information. Initial and date your correction. If you have previously made changes on Forms I-9 in White-Out instead, USCIS recommends that you attach a note to the corrected Forms I-9 explaining what happened. Be sure to sign and date the note.

16. Can I contract with someone to complete Forms I-9 for my business?

Yes. You can contract with another person or business to verify employees' identities and employment authorization and to complete Forms I-9 for you. However, you are still responsible for the contractor's actions and are liable for any violations of the employer sanctions laws.

17. How can I protect private information on Forms I-9?

Since Form I-9 contains an employee's private information, and you are required to retain forms for specific periods of time, you should ensure that you protect that private information, and that it is used only for Form I-9 purposes. To protect employees' private information, ensure that completed Forms I-9 and all supporting documents, including photocopies of documents, as well as information regarding employment authorization if you participate in E-Verify, are stored in a safe, secure location that only authorized individuals can access. For more information on protecting electronically stored Forms I-9, see Part 3.

C. Checklists

☑ CHECKLIST

Acceptable Documentation

These documents establish both identity and eligibility to work in the United States.

Documents that Establish Both Identity and Employment Eligibility
1. U.S. Passport (unexpired or expired).
2. Certificate of U.S. Citizenship (Form N-560 or N-561).
3. Certificate of Naturalization (Form N-550 or N-570).
4. Unexpired foreign passport, with an attached Form I-94 indicating unexpired employment authorization.
5. Permanent Resident Card or Alien Registration Receipt Card with photograph (Form I-551).
6. Unexpired Temporary Resident Card (Form I-688).
7. Unexpired Employment Authorization Card (Form I-688A).
8. Unexpired Reentry Permit (Form I-327).
9. Unexpired Refugee Travel Document (Form 1-571).
10. Unexpired Employment Authorization Document issued by the Department of Homeland Security (DHS) that contains a photograph (Form I-688B).

Documents that Establish Identity
An employee needs to present both proof of identity and proof of employment eligibility. These documents establish an employee's identity.
1. Driver's license or ID card issued by a state or outlying possession of the United States provided it contains a photograph or information such as name, date of birth, gender, height, eye color, and address.
2. ID card issued by federal, state or local government agencies or entities, provided it contains a photograph or information such as name, date of birth, gender, height, eye color, and address.
3. School ID card with a photograph.
4. Voter's registration card.
5. U.S. Military card or draft record.
6. Military dependent's ID card.
7. U.S. Coast Guard Merchant Mariner Card.
8. Native American tribal document.
9. Driver's license issued by a Canadian government authority.

For persons under age 18 who are unable to present a document listed above, collect:

10. School record or report card.
11. Clinic, doctor or hospital record.
12. Daycare or nursery school record.

Documents that Establish Employment Eligibility

One of these documents must be presented in addition to the document establishing proof of identity.

1. U.S. social security card issued by the Social Security Administration (other than a card stating it is not valid for employment).
2. Certification of Birth Abroad issued by the Department of State (Form FS-545 or Form DS-1350).
3. Original or certified copy of a birth certificate issued by a state, county, municipal authority or outlying possession of the United States bearing an official seal.
4. Native American tribal document.
5. U.S. Citizen ID Card (Form I-197).
6. ID Card for use of a Resident Citizen in the United States (Form I-179).
7. Unexpired employment authorization document issued by DHS (other than those listed under List A).

Additional Form I-9 Employer Responsibilities

- Make sure your I-9 Forms are filled out correctly. Follow the directions exactly.
- Employers must keep each employee I-9 Form on file for at least three years, or for one year after employment ends, whichever is longer.
- Keep and make copies of the original documents supplied by your employees – not required, but advised. Keep only the minimum number of documents required and store the I-9 forms and document photocopies separate from your employee files.
- If changes are made to the I-9 document, change them on the original form and initial and date the changes. Don't fill out a new form.
- Re-verify expiring work authorizations and do not allow the employee to work if their documentation has expired.
- Be sure to respond according to timing instructions and guidelines if you receive a Social Security Administration no-match letter that indicates a certain number of your employees have unverifiable Social Security numbers.

D. Statutes and Regulations

Immigration Reform and Control Act of 1986 (Relevant Provisions)
TITLE I – CONTROL OF ILLEGAL IMMIGRATION

PART A – EMPLOYMENT
SEC. 101. CONTROL OF UNLAWFUL EMPLOYMENT OF ALIENS.

(a) IN GENERAL –

(1) NEW PROVISION. – Chapter 8 of title II is amended by inserting after section 274 (8 U.S.C. 1324) the following new section:

UNLAWFUL EMPLOYMENT OF ALIENS
SEC. 274A. (a) "8 USC 1324a" MAKING EMPLOYMENT OF UNAUTHORIZED ALIENS UNLAWFUL. –

(1) IN GENERAL. – It is unlawful for a person or other entity to hire, or to recruit or refer for a fee, for employment in the United States –

(A) an alien knowing the alien is an unauthorized alien (as defined in subsection (h)(3)) with respect to such employment, or

(B) an individual without complying with the requirements of subsection (b).

(2) CONTINUING EMPLOYMENT. – It is unlawful for a person or other entity, after hiring an alien for employment in accordance with paragraph (1), to continue to employ the alien in the United States knowing the alien is (or has become) an unauthorized alien with respect to such employment.

(3) DEFENSE. – A person or entity that establishes that it has complied in good faith with the requirements of subsection (b) with respect to the hiring, recruiting, or referral for employment of an alien in the United States has established an affirmative defense that the person or entity has not violated paragraph (1)(A) with respect to such hiring, recruiting, or referral.

(4) USE OF LABOR THROUGH CONTRACT. – For purposes of this section, a person or other entity who uses a contract, subcontract, or exchange, entered into, renegotiated, or extended after the date of the enactment of this section, to obtain the labor of an alien in the United States knowing that the alien is an unauthorized alien (as defined in subsection (h)(3)) with respect to performing such labor, shall be considered to have hired the alien for employment in the United States in violation of paragraph (1)(A).

(5) USE OF STATE EMPLOYMENT AGENCY DOCUMENTATION. – For purposes of paragraphs (1)(B) and (3), a person or entity shall be deemed to have complied with the requirements of subsection (b) with respect to the hiring of an individual who was referred for such employment by a State employment agency (as defined by the Attorney General), if the person or entity has and retains (for the period and in the

manner described in subsection (b)(3)) appropriate documentation of such referral by that agency, which documentation certifies that the agency has complied with the procedures specified in subsection (b) with respect to the individual's referral.

(b) EMPLOYMENT VERIFICATION SYSTEM. – The requirements referred to in paragraphs (1)(B) and (3) of subsection (a) are, in the case of a person or other entity hiring, recruiting, or referring an individual for employment in the United States, the requirements specified in the following three paragraphs:

(1) ATTESTATION AFTER EXAMINATION OF DOCUMENTATION. –

(A) IN GENERAL. – The person or entity must attest, under penalty of perjury and on a form designated or established by the Attorney General by regulation, that it has verified that the individual is not an unauthorized alien by examining –

(i) a document described in subparagraph (B), or

(ii) a document described in subparagraph (C) and a document described in subparagraph (D).

A person or entity has complied with the requirement of this paragraph with respect to examination of a document if the document reasonably appears on its face to be genuine. If an individual provides a document or combination of documents that reasonably appears on its face to be genuine and that is sufficient to meet the requirements of such sentence, nothing in this paragraph shall be construed as requiring the person or entity to solicit the production of any other document or as requiring the individual to produce such a document.

(B) DOCUMENTS ESTABLISHING BOTH EMPLOYMENT AUTHORIZATION AND IDENTITY. – A document described in this subparagraph is an individual's –

(i) United States passport;

(ii) certificate of United States citizenship;

(iii) certificate of naturalization;

(iv) unexpired foreign passport, if the passport has an appropriate, unexpired endorsement of the Attorney General authorizing the individual's employment in the United States; or

(v) resident alien card or other alien registration card, if the card –

(I) contains a photograph of the individual or such other personal identifying information relating to the individual as the Attorney General finds, by regulation, sufficient for purposes of this subsection, and

(II) is evidence of authorization of employment in the United States.

(C) DOCUMENTS EVIDENCING EMPLOYMENT AUTHORIZATION. – A document described in this subparagraph is an individual's –

(i) social security account number card (other than such a card which specifies on the fact that the issuance of the card does not authorize employment in the United States);

(ii) certificate of birth in the United States or establishing United States nationality at birth, which certificate the Attorney General finds, by regulation, to be acceptable for purposes of this section; or

(iii) other documentation evidencing authorization of employment in the United States which the Attorney General finds, by regulation, to be acceptable for purposes of this section.

(D) DOCUMENTS ESTABLISHING IDENTITY OF INDIVIDUAL. – A document described in this subparagraph is an individual's –

(i) driver's license or similar document issued for the purpose of identification by a State, if it contains a photograph of the individual or such other personal identifying information relating to the individual as the Attorney General finds, by regulation, sufficient for purposes of this section; or

(ii) in the case of individuals under 16 years of age or in a State which does not provide for issuance of an identification document (other than a driver's license) referred to in clause (ii), documentation of personal identity of such other type as the Attorney General finds, by regulation, provides a reliable means of identification.

(2) INDIVIDUAL ATTESTATION OF EMPLOYMENT AUTHORIZATION. – The individual must attest, under penalty of perjury on the form designated or established for purposes of paragraph (1), that the individual is a citizen or national of the United States, an alien lawfully admitted for permanent residence, or an alien who is authorized under this Act or by the Attorney General to be hired, recruited, or referred for such employment.

(3) RETENTION OF VERIFICATION FORM. – After completion of such form in accordance with paragraphs (1) and (2), the person or entity must retain the form and make it available for inspection by officers of the Service or the Department of Labor during a period beginning on the date of the hiring, recruiting, or referral of the individual and ending –

(A) in the case of the recruiting or referral for a fee (without hiring) of an individual, three years after the date of the recruiting or referral, and

(B) in the case of the hiring of an individual –

(i) three years after the date of such hiring, or

(ii) one year after the date the individual's employment is terminated, whichever is later.

(4) COPYING OF DOCUMENTATION PERMITTED. – Notwithstanding any other provision of law, the person or entity may copy a document presented by an individual pursuant to this subsection and may retain the copy, but only (except as otherwise permitted under law) for the purpose of complying with the requirements of this subsection.

(5) LIMITATION ON USE OF ATTESTATION FORM. – A form designated or established by the Attorney General under this subsection and any information contained in or appended to such form, may not be

used for purposes other than for enforcement of this Act and sections 1001, 1028, 1546, and 1621 of title 18, United States Code.

(c) NO AUTHORIZATION OF NATIONAL IDENTIFICATION CARDS. – Nothing in this section shall be construed to authorize, directly or indirectly, the issuance or use of national identification cards or the establishment of a national identification card.

*****

SEC. 102. UNFAIR IMMIGRATION-RELATED EMPLOYMENT PRACTICES.

(a) IN GENERAL. – Chapter 8 of title II is further amended by inserting after section 274A, as inserted by section 101(a), the following new section:

UNFAIR IMMIGRATION-RELATED EMPLOYMENT PRACTICES

SEC. 274B. "8 USC 1324b" (a) PROHIBITION OF DISCRIMINATION BASED ON NATIONAL ORIGIN OR CITIZENSHIP STATUS. –

(1) GENERAL RULE. – It is an unfair immigration-related employment practice for a person or other entity to discriminate against any individual (other than an unauthorized alien) with respect to the hiring, or recruitment or referral for a fee, of the individual for employment or the discharging of the individual from employment –

(A) because of such individual's national origin, or

(B) in the case of a citizen or intending citizen (as defined in paragraph (3), because of such individual's citizenship status.

(2) EXCEPTIONS. – Paragraph (1) shall not apply to –

(A) a person or other entity that employs three or fewer employees,

(B) a person's or entity's discrimination because of an individual's national origin in the discrimination with respect to that person or entity and that individual is covered under section 703 "42 USC 2000e-2" of the Civil Rights Act of 1964, or

(C) discrimination because of citizenship status which is otherwise required in order to comply with law, regulation, or executive order, or required by Federal, State, or local government contract, or which the Attorney General determines to be essential for an employer to do business with an agency or department of the Federal, State, or local government.

(3) DEFINITION OF CITIZEN OR INTENDING CITIZEN. – As used in paragraph (1), the term "citizen or intending citizen' means an individual who –

(A) is a citizen or national of the United States, or

(B) is an alien who –

(i) is lawfully admitted for permanent residence, is granted the status of an alien lawfully admitted for temporary residence under section 245A(a)(1), "8 USC 1255" is admitted as a refugee under section 207, "8 USC 1157" or is granted asylum under section 208, "8 USC 1158" and

(ii) evidences an intention to become a citizen of the United States through completing a declaration of intention to become a citizen; but does not include (I) an alien who fails to apply for naturalization within six months of the date the alien first becomes eligible (by virtue of period of lawful permanent residence) to apply for naturalization or, if later, within six months after the date of the enactment of this section and (II) and alien who has applied on a timely basis, but has not been naturalized as a citizen within 2 years after the date of the application, unless the alien can establish that the alien is actively pursuing naturalization, except that time consumed in the Service's processing the application shall not be counted toward the 2-year period.

(4) ADDITIONAL EXCEPTION PROVIDING RIGHT TO PREFER EQUALLY QUALIFIED CITIZENS. – Notwithstanding any other provision of this section, it is not an unfair immigration-related employment practice for a person or other entity to prefer to hire, recruit, or refer an individual who is a citizen or national of the United States over another individual who is an alien if the two individuals are equally qualified.

(b) CHARGES OF VIOLATIONS. –

(1) IN GENERAL. – Except as provided in paragraph (2), any person alleging that the person is adversely affected directly by an unfair immigration- related employment practice (or a person on that person's behalf) or an officer of the Service alleging that an unfair immigration-related employment practice has occurred or is occurring may file a charge respecting such practice or violation with the Special Counsel (appointed under subsection (c)). Charges shall be in writing under oath or affirmation and shall contain such information as the Attorney General requires. The Special Counsel by certified mail shall serve a notice of the charge (including the date, place, and circumstances of the alleged unfair immigration-related employment practice) on the person or entity involved within 10 days.

(2) NO OVERLAP WITH EEOC COMPLAINTS. – No charge may be filed respecting an unfair immigration-related employment practice described in subsection (a)(1)(A) if a charge with respect to that practice based on the same set of facts has been filed with the Equal Employment Opportunity Commission under title VII of the Civil Rights Act of 1964 "42 USC 2000e" unless the charge is dismissed as being outside the scope of such title. No charge respecting an employment practice may be filed with the Equal Employment Opportunity Commission under such title if a charge with respect to such practice based on the same set of facts has been filed under this subsection, unless the charge is dismissed under this section as being outside the scope of this section.

(c) SPECIAL COUNSEL. –

"(1) APPOINTMENT. – The President shall appoint, by and with the advice and consent of the Senate, a Special Counsel for Immigration-Related Unfair Employment Practices (hereinafter in this section referred to as the 'Special Counsel') within the Department of Justice to serve for a term of four years. In the case of a vacancy in the office of the Special Counsel the President may designate the officer or employee who shall act as Special Counsel during such vacancy.

(2) DUTIES. – The Special Counsel shall be responsible for investigation of charges and issuance of complaints under this section and in respect of the prosecution of all such complaints before administrative law judges and the exercise of certain functions under subsection (j)(1).

(3) COMPENSATION. – The Special Counsel is entitled to receive compensation at a rate not to exceed the rate now or hereafter provided for grade GS-17 of the General Schedule, under section 5332 of title 5, United States Code.

(4) REGIONAL OFFICES. – The Special Counsel, in accordance with regulations of the Attorney General, shall establish such regional offices as may be necessary to carry out his duties.

(d) INVESTIGATION OF CHARGES. –

(1) BY SPECIAL COUNSEL. – The Special Counsel shall investigate each charge received and, within 120 days of the date of the receipt of the charge, determine whether or not there is reasonable cause to believe that the charge is true and whether or not to bring a complaint with respect to the charge before an administrative law judge. The Special Counsel may, on his own initiative, conduct investigations respecting unfair immigration-related employment practices and, based on such an investigation and subject to paragraph (3), file a complaint before such a judge.

(2) PRIVATE ACTIONS. – If the Special Counsel, after receiving such a charge respecting an unfair immigration-related employment practice which alleges knowing and intentional discriminatory activity or a pattern or practice of discriminatory activity, has not filed a complaint before an administrative law judge with respect to such charge within such 120-day period, the person making the charge may (subject to paragraph (3)) file a complaint directly before such a judge.

(3) TIME LIMITATIONS ON COMPLAINTS. – No complaint may be filed respecting any unfair immigration-related employment practice occurring more than 180 days prior to the date of the filing of the charge with the Special Counsel. This subparagraph shall not prevent the subsequent amending of a charge or complaint under subsection (e)(1).

(e) HEARINGS. –

(1) NOTICE. – Whenever a complaint is made that a person or entity has engaged in or is engaging in any such unfair immigration-related employment practice, an administrative law judge shall have power to issue and cause to be served upon such person or entity a copy of the

complaint and a notice of hearing before the judge at a place therein fixed, not less than five days after the serving of the complaint. Any such complaint may be amended by the judge conducting the hearing, upon the motion of the party filing the complaint, in the judge's discretion at any time prior to the issuance of an order based thereon. The person or entity so complained of shall have the right to file an answer to the original or amended complaint and to appear in person or otherwise and give testimony at the place and time fixed in the complaint.

(2) JUDGES HEARING CASES. – Hearings on complaints under this subsection shall be considered before administrative law judges who are specially designated by the Attorney General as having special training respecting employment discrimination and, to the extent practicable, before such judges who only consider cases under this section.

(3) COMPLAINANT AS PARTY. – Any person filing a charge with the Special Counsel respecting an unfair immigration-related employment practice shall be considered a party to any complaint before an administrative law judge respecting such practice and any subsequent appeal respecting that complaint. In the discretion of the judge conducting the hearing, any other person may be allowed to intervene in the said proceeding and to present testimony.

(f) TESTIMONY AND AUTHORITY OF HEARING OFFICERS. –

(1) TESTIMONY. – The testimony taken by the administrative law judge shall be reduced to writing. Thereafter, the judge, in his discretion, upon notice may provide for the taking of further testimony or hear argument.

(2) AUTHORITY OF ADMINISTRATIVE LAW JUDGES. – In conducting investigations and hearings under this subsection and in accordance with regulations of the Attorney General, the Special Counsel and administrative law judges shall have reasonable access to examine evidence of any person or entity being investigated. The administrative law judges by subpoena may compel the attendance of witnesses and the production of evidence at any designated place or hearing. In case of contumacy or refusal to obey a subpoena lawfully issued under this paragraph and upon application of the administrative law judge, an appropriate district court of the United States may issue an order requiring compliance with such subpoena and any failure to obey such order may be punished by such court as a contempt thereof.

(g) DETERMINATIONS. –

(1) ORDER. – The administrative law judge shall issue and cause to be served on the parties to the proceeding an order, which shall be final unless appealed as provided under subsection (i).

(2) ORDERS FINDING VIOLATIONS. –

(A) IN GENERAL. – If, upon the preponderance of the evidence, an administrative law judge determines that any person or entity named in the complaint has engaged in or is engaging in any such unfair immigration- related employment practice, then the judge shall state his findings of fact and shall issue and cause to be served on such person or entity to cease and desist from such unfair immigration-related employment practice.

(B) CONTENTS OF ORDER. – Such an order also may require the person or entity –

(i) to comply with the requirements of section 274A(b) with respect to individuals hired (or recruited or referred for employment for a fee) during a period of up to three years;

(ii) to retain for the period referred to in clause (i) and only for purposes consistent with section 274(b)(5), "8 USC 1324" the name and address of each individual who applies, in person or in writing, for hiring for an existing position, or for recruiting or referring for a fee, for employment in the United States;

(iii) to hire individuals directly and adversely affected, with or without back pay; and

(iv)(I) except as provided in subclause (II), to pay a civil penalty of not more than $1,000 for each individual discriminated against, and

(II) in the case of a person or entity previously subject to such an order, to pay a civil penalty of not more than $2,000 for each individual discriminated against.

(C) LIMITATION ON BACK PAY REMEDY. – In providing a remedy under subparagraph (B)(iii), back pay liability shall not accrue from a date more than two years prior to the date of the filing of a charge with an administrative law judge. Interim earnings or amounts earnable with reasonable diligence by the individual or individuals discriminated against shall operate to reduce the back pay otherwise allowable under such subparagraph. No order shall require the hiring of an individual as an employee or the payment to an individual of any back pay, if the individual was refused employment for any reason other than discrimination on account of national origin or citizenship status.

(D) TREATMENT OF DISTINCT ENTITIES. – In applying this subsection in the case of a person or entity composed of distinct, physically separate subdivisions of each of which provides separately for the hiring, recruiting, or referring for employment, without reference to the practices of, and not under the control of or common control with, another subdivision shall be considered a separate person or entity.

(3) ORDERS NOT FINDING VIOLATIONS. – If upon the preponderance of the evidence an administrative law judge determines that the person or entity named in the complaint has not engaged or is not engaging in any such unfair immigration-related employment practice, then the judge shall state his findings of fact and shall issue an order dismissing the complaint.

(h) AWARDING OF ATTORNEYS' FEES. – In any complaint respecting an unfair immigration-related employment practice, an administrative law judge, in the judge's discretion, may allow a prevailing party, other than the United States, a reasonable attorney's fee, if the losing party's argument is without reasonable foundation in law and fact.

(i) REVIEW OF FINAL ORDERS. –

(1) IN GENERAL. – Not later than 60 days after the entry of such final order, any person aggrieved by such final order may seek a review of such order in the United States court of appeals for the circuit in which the violation is alleged to have occurred or in which the employer resides or transacts business.

(2) FURTHER REVIEW. – Upon the filing of the record with the court, the jurisdiction of the court shall be exclusive and its judgment shall be final, except that the same shall be subject to review by the Supreme Court of the United States upon writ of certiorari or certification as provided in section 1254 of title 28, United States Code.

(j) COURT ENFORCEMENT OF ADMINISTRATIVE ORDERS. –

(1) IN GENERAL. – If an order of the agency is not appealed under subsection (i)(1), the Special Counsel (or, if the Special Counsel fails to act, the person filing the charge) may petition the United States district court for the district in which a violation of the order is alleged to have occurred, or in which the respondent resides or transacts business, for the enforcement of the order of the administrative law judge, by filing in such court a written petition praying that such order be enforced.

(2) COURT ENFORCEMENT ORDER. – Upon the filing of such petition, the court shall have jurisdiction to make and enter a decree enforcing the order of the administrative law judge. In such a proceeding, the order of the administrative law judge shall not be subject to review.

(3) ENFORCEMENT DECREE IN ORIGINAL REVIEW. – If, upon appeal of an order under subsection (i)(1), the United States court of appeals does not reverse such order, such court shall have the jurisdiction to make and enter a decree enforcing the order of the administrative law judge.

(4) AWARDING OF ATTORNEY'S FEES. – In any judicial proceeding under subsection (i) or this subsection, the court, in its discretion, may allow a prevailing party, other than the United States, a reasonable attorney's fee as part of costs but only if the losing party's argument is without reasonable foundation in law and fact.

(k) TERMINATION DATES. –

(1) This section shall not apply to discrimination in hiring, recruiting, referring, or discharging of individuals occurring after the date of any termination of the provisions of section 274A, under subsection (1) of that section.

(2) The provisions of this section shall terminate 30 calendar days after receipt of the last report required to be transmitted under section 274A(j) if –

(A) the Comptroller General determines, and so reports in such report that –

(i) no significant discrimination has resulted, against citizens or nationals of the United States or against any eligible workers seeking employment, from the implementation of section 274A, or

(ii) such section has created an unreasonable burden on employers hiring such workers; and

(B) there has been enacted, within such period of 30 calendar days, a joint resolution stating in substance that the Congress approves the findings of the Comptroller General contained in such report.

The provisions of subsections (m) and (n) of section 274A shall apply to any joint resolution under subsection (l) of such section.".

(b) NO EFFECT ON EEOC AUTHORITY. – Except as may be specifically provided in this section, "8 USC 1324b note" nothing in this section shall be construed to restrict the authority of the Equal Employment Opportunity Commission to investigate allegations, in writing and under oath or affirmation, of unlawful employment practices, as provided in section 706 of the Civil Rights Act of 1964 (42 U.S.C. 2000e-5), or any other authority provided therein.

(c) CLERICAL AMENDMENT. – The table of contents is amended by inserting after the item relating to section 274A (as added by section 101(c)) the following new item: "Sec. 274B. Unfair immigration-related employment practices."

VII. NON-COMPETE AGREEMENTS

A. Overview

Particularly in specialized areas, employers often require employees to enter into non-compete agreements that prohibit employees from leaving their employment and competing with the former employer. Generally, a non-compete agreement is not valid unless it is supported by consideration. In other words, the employee who agrees not to compete must get something in return. Several relevant court rulings have discussed what this "something" can be. For employers, a safe route to take is to have an applicant sign a non-compete as a condition of employment. In such cases, the promise to employ is valid consideration for the employee's assent to the non-compete agreement.

To be valid, non-compete agreements must be reasonable with respect to key three aspects:
- scope (What activity does the agreement ban?)
- geographic area (Where is the employee banned from competing?), and
- time (For how long must the employee refrain from competing?).

Each agreement will be examined based on the individual circumstances. If its terms are deemed to be more restrictive than necessary to preserve the employer's legitimate interests, it will likely be deemed invalid in court.

B. Judicial Decisions

◆   The COO of a company in Rhode Island signed a contract that **barred him from competing with the company in the New England area for two years if he was fired for "cause."** When he violated a direct order not to deliver granite to a customer until the customer paid for the order, the president of the company fired him on the spot. He acquired a competing business, and his former employer sued to enjoin him from competing. In his defense, he asserted that the company should have given him due process (notice and a hearing) before firing him for cause. The Rhode Island Supreme Court disagreed. The COO admittedly defied the president's directive, giving the president a good-faith basis to fire him for cause. As a result, by the terms of the non-compete clause, he was barred from opening the competing business. *New England Stone, LLC v. Conte,* 962 A.2d 30 (R.I. 2009).

◆   The manager of a trucking company in St. Louis made plans to leave the company and join a competitor. She let the renewal deadline for the company's lease of its premises pass without informing company officials, then **gave confidential information about the company to the competitor**. When the company sued her for breach of the duty of loyalty (and sued the competitor for conspiracy), she claimed that as an at-will employee who had never signed a non-compete agreement, she could not be held liable. A jury and the Missouri Supreme Court disagreed. However, the verdict ($54,000 against the manager and $254,000 against the competitor) could not stand because it included preparations the manager made. Instead, the jury could only consider actions taken beyond the preparation stage. The case had to be re-tried. *Scanwell Freight Express STL, Inc. v. Chan,* 162 S.W.3d 477 (Mo. 2005).

◆   A North Carolina publisher of internal company magazines hired a general manager to oversee the production of several magazines, including one for a furniture company's employees. The general manager hired an assistant to help him. Neither employee signed a non-compete agreement. Later, when the publisher, general manager and assistant entered into discussions with the furniture company about renewing the contract, the assistant quit. She formed a competing business with the general manager and contracted with the furniture company to publish the magazine. The general manager then resigned. The publisher sued the general manager and the assistant for breach of the duty of loyalty as well as deceptive trade practices. A trial court dismissed the case, but the court of appeals reversed in part, finding that the general manager may have breached a duty of loyalty to the employer. On further appeal, the Supreme Court of North Carolina ruled that **the general manager was not in a fiduciary relationship with the employer such that he could be held liable for breach of duty**, and the employer failed to show that he engaged in unfair or deceptive trade practices. *Dalton v. Camp,* 548 S.E.2d 704 (N.C. 2001).

C. Q&As

1. *We recently discovered that a potential new hire of ours is under a nationwide non-compete agreement.*

    We've never heard of anything that far-reaching before. Is it legal?

    It's legal, says Michael Greco *(mgreco@laborlawyers.com)*. But the former employer's obligated to answer yes to this question: "Can this employee hurt you anywhere in the country?" If the former worker has access to confidential info, for example, then the non-compete is likely enforceable.

2. *Normally, when staff members leave our company, we go over their non-compete with them, stressing what they can and can't do under the agreement.*

    But we recently had a worker bolt and didn't get to go over the necessary info. We'd still like to emphasize how serious we are about the non-compete. How can we do that?

    Mail a copy of the applicable non-compete agreement to the worker at his or her home address, says Heather Zalar Steele *(hsteele@laborlawyers.com)* on the Non-Compete and Trade Secrets Blog.

    In the future, if you can't put together the specific documentation in time, simply advise the worker of the firm's general non-compete and confidential info policy.

    Remind the employee that you demand compliance with all post-employment non-competes and that you'll take action to enforce the contract if necessary.

3. *As part of our severance agreement with departing employees, we've been considering including a non-compete agreement. Are there any problems we could run into in doing this?*

    Very possibly, says attorney Christopher Stief *(cstief@laborlawyers.com)*.

    Unlike during the hiring and employment process, where your company has a legitimate business interest in its workers, the termination process changes your relationship with your employees. When you fire workers for cause, you're essentially saying they're no longer of use to you. Therefore, you don't have a legitimate business interest to protect.

    If you include this in your severance agreement and sue a worker who goes to a competitor, it's entirely possible a judge would rule in the employee's favor.

4. *A former employee is now self-employed, in direct competition with us. We're thinking about using non-compete agreements, but we've heard some doubts about their effectiveness. Any advice?*

    Laws vary in different states, says attorney Marshall Tanick, but the basic thing to remember is that the contract must be reasonable if it is to be upheld.

    The contract has to be designed to protect the business – not just penalize the employee for leaving the company.

Another key point: Non-competes need to be specific about such things as time periods and geographic boundaries.

An agreement that bars a former employee from working in a industry forever, anywhere in the world, obviously doesn't have much chance of standing up in court.

5. *We're considering tying our non-compete agreement to our annual bonus. If workers don't violate their non-compete, they'd receive and keep the final merit and performance bonus they receive when they leave us. However, if they do violate the non-compete, we'd be permitted to take the bonus money back. Would this be an enforceable policy?*

In most states that should be enforceable, says employment attorney Christopher Stief *(cstief@laborlawyers.com).*

One problem: Some states say you have to give employees something more than what they'd normally receive to make the non-compete enforceable – so tying it to their final bonus might not work. Linking the non-compete to an additional bonus could be an acceptable alternative in those states.

6. *Is there a difference in enforcing a non-compete for an employee who resigns versus a worker who's terminated?*

Most of the time, you can't enforce a non-compete if you terminate an employee, says Michael Greco *(mgreco@laborlawyers.com).*

Why? Judges have held if you terminate an employee for non-performance, you deem them worthless, and therefore can't consider them a legitimate threat to your company.

When can you terminate an employee and still enforce a non-compete?

When the worker's fired for a reason other than performance – such as sexually harassing a co-worker.

D. Checklists

☑ CHECKLIST

Non-competes

Non-competes are a solid way to protect a company's trade secrets and confidential information, but they can also result in massive headaches – especially when firms create ones that are unenforceable or overly broad. Firms should follow these five tips for compiling a reasonable yet enforceable non-compete agreement:

❑ **Pick the restriction that fits your company's needs.** Not every worker plans on establishing a competing business down the road, so companies should choose the restrictions they plan to enforce carefully. The most common types of restrictions include non-compete, client non-solicit, employee non-solicit and non-disclosure.

❑ **Keep the scope reasonable.** An overly broad agreement is often the death knell for a non-compete. To keep a court from striking down your agreement, lay out a time frame and geographic region that make the most sense for protecting your company.

❑ **Specificity is your friend.** The more you tailor your agreement to a specific position and job a worker will be doing, the more likely a court will be to uphold your agreement.

❑ **Communicate often.** Employers should make it clear to workers what info is confidential, and have a clear policy in place about returning devices such as cell phones or laptops that may contain sensitive subject matter.

❑ **Get it signed.** Once all the hard work's done, this should be the easy part, but it often slips through the cracks. Firms should always get the employee to sign and date a non-compete.

CHAPTER TWO

Compensation and Benefits

I. COMPENSATION

A. Overview

Issues relating to the payment of compensation to employees are governed in large part by a federal law called the Fair Labor Standards Act (FLSA). This law sets requirements relating to the payment of wages (including overtime), establishes rules relating to recordkeeping and sets restrictions on the employment of children.

While the FLSA sets a federal minimum hourly wage, many states have their own minimum wage laws. If a particular state's law requires a higher minimum hourly wage than the minimum hourly wage set by the federal law, employees must be paid the higher hourly rate.

There are some exemptions to the FLSA's general rules. These exemptions apply to specified businesses and types of work.

One notable FLSA exemption is the one that excuses employers from complying with otherwise applicable minimum wage and overtime pay requirements with respect to employees who qualify as executive, administrative, professional, computer or outside sales employees.

Over the years, various state and federal laws have helped to shape United States labor practices, particularly:

- **Fair Labor Standards Act (FLSA) of 1938** established minimum wage, overtime pay and recordkeeping standards for employees in the private sector, as well as in federal, state and local governments. FLSA requires employees be paid:

  1. at least minimum wage. Therefore, except for required payroll taxes, employers can't make deductions in employees' pay, such as for loans, uniforms, etc., that would result in them making below minimum wage for that pay period.

  2. overtime pay at a rate not less than one and one-half times the regular rate of pay after 40 hours of work in a workweek.

- An amendment to the FLSA, the **Fair Minimum Wage Act of 2007**, gradually raised federal minimum wage from $5.15 per hour to $7.25 effective July 24, 2009.

- **Equal Pay Act of 1963** makes it illegal to pay women lower rates for the same job strictly on the basis of their sex. The wage gap between men and women narrowed, but remained significant, leading to the Lilly Ledbetter Fair Pay Act of 2009.

- **The Lilly Ledbetter Fair Pay Act of 2009** reaffirms that discriminatory compensation decisions based on sex, as well as race, age, disability, etc., are illegal. More significant, it establishes a rolling time frame for filing wage discrimination claims. Previously, victims of pay discrimination only had 180 days from the date of the first unfair paycheck to file a claim. But the Ledbetter act restarts the clock each time the employee receives a paycheck reflecting the discriminatory practice.

- **The Davis Bacon and Related Acts (DBRA)** was established in 1931. It requires all contractors and subcontractors working on federal construction contracts or federally assisted contracts in excess of $2,000, to pay laborers and mechanics no less than the prevailing wage rates and fringe benefits determined by the Secretary of Labor for similar types of laborers and mechanics employed on similar projects in the area. The wage rates and fringe benefits must be included in the contract.

1. Employment Status

Proper employee classification is essential to ensure compliance with wage and hourly laws. Employee classifications include:

- **Exempt employees** are not eligible for overtime pay.
- **Non-exempt employees** are eligible for overtime pay.
- **Non-exempt salaried employees** are covered by FLSA minimum wage and overtime pay provisions. These employees must be paid overtime even though they're paid on a salary basis and must be making at least minimum wage when their weekly salary is broken down into hours.

(Note: When an employee is subject to both state and federal minimum wage laws, the employee is entitled to the higher minimum wage.)

2. Recordkeeping for Overtime Purposes

According to the DOL, employers are required to keep the following employee info on file:

1. Name and social security number
2. Address and ZIP code
3. Birth date if younger than 19
4. Sex and occupation
5. Time and day of week workweek begins
6. Hours worked each day, and total hours worked each workweek
7. Basis on which wages are paid (hourly rate and what it is, weekly salary or piecework)
8. Total daily or weekly straight-time earnings
9. Total overtime earnings for the workweek
10. All additions to/deductions from employees' wages
11. Total wages paid each pay period, and
12. Date of payment and the pay period covered by the payment.

3. Tracking Time

Employers can use any timekeeping method they choose to track hours and ensure overtime is paid, including a time clock, swipe card or manual process, as long as it's complete, accurate and consistent.

Independent contractors typically determine what type of services need to be performed and how they'll be done, while the clients paying for the services usually determine the desired end result. Independent contractors aren't entitled to overtime pay, and their earnings are subject to self-employment tax.

There are three tests to determine if an individual meets the requirements of independent contractor status.

1. **The General Test** has three criteria:
   - *Economic independence.* The service provider is in a position to either profit or lose money as a result of performing the job, and is significantly invested in the assets of his/her business or incurs unreimbursed expenses consistent with industry practice. The

unreimbursed expenses must equal at least 2% of gross income during the taxable year.

- *Workplace independence.* The service provider either operates out of his/her own principal place of business, works at various sites for the service recipient or uses his/her own equipment to perform the service.
- *Written Contract.* The service recipient and service provider have a written contract stating the worker won't be treated as an employee and is responsible for his/her own taxes and benefits. (*Note:* The service recipient must file a Form 1099 for an independent contractor.)

2. **The Incorporation Test** applies if the worker conducts business as a corporation or limited liability company, and has a written contract stating he/she isn't an employee and will be responsible for his/her own taxes and benefits. (Note: Under the incorporation option, the limit on the number of independent contractors a service recipient can hire in a year equates to the greater of 3% of employees in the preceding year or 10 employees.)

3. **The Twenty Factor Test** was developed by the Internal Revenue Service (IRS). The criteria concerns three key areas: The worker's control over the work performed, integration into the business and ability to directly benefits from his/her labor.

Here's an abridged version of the IRS' 20-Factor Test.

A worker is usually an employee if the following conditions or situations exist:

1. The worker is required to comply with *instructions* about when, where and how he/she must work.
2. The employer *trains* the worker by requiring an experienced employee to work with the worker, educating the worker through correspondence, requiring the worker to attend meetings, or through other methods.
3. The worker's services are *integrated* into business operations, and the worker is subject to direction and control of the employer.
4. The worker's services are *rendered personally,* and the employer is presumably interested in the methods used to complete the services, as well as in the result.
5. The employer *hires, supervises, and pays assistants* for the worker, indicating control over the worker on the job.
6. There's a *continuing relationship* between the worker and the employer, even if it's at irregular intervals.
7. The employer sets *specific hours of work* for the worker.
8. The worker is working *essentially full time* for the employer, and presumably not free to do work for other employers.
9. The work is performed on the *employer's premises,* especially when the work could be done elsewhere. (*Note:* The fact that work is done off the employer's premises doesn't necessarily make the worker an independent contractor.)

10. The worker is required to perform services in an *order or sequence* set by an employer, indication control over the worker.

11. The worker is required to submit regular *oral or written reports* to an employer.

12. The worker is paid by the *hour, week or month,* rather than by the job or on a straight commission basis.

13. The employer pays for the worker's *business or travel expenses.*

14. The employer furnishes the worker with significant *tools, materials or other equipment.*

15. The employer has a *right to discharge* the worker, and the worker must obey the employer's instructions in order to stay employed. (*Note:* An independent contractor can only be fired if the work being performed doesn't meet the agreed-upon specifications.)

16. The worker has the *right to terminate* his /her relationship with the employer at any time without being held liable, say for breach of contract.

The worker is usually an **independent contractor** if the following conditions or situations exist:

17. The worker *significantly invests* in facilities used to perform services.

18. The worker can *experience profit or loss* as a result of his/her services.

19. The worker performs *for more than one firm at a time.*

20. The worker makes his/her *services available to the general public* on a regular and consistent basis.

Tipped workers can be paid as little as $2.13 per hour, as long as their estimated tips bring their earnings up to the current federal minimum wage. It's important for employers to check their states' laws regarding this class of employees. For example, some states:

- allow employers to take a "tip credit" and pay a lower hourly rate, if employees' tips average at least $30 a month in gratuities.
- require higher hourly wages for tipped employees.
- don't allow tip polling that includes workers like busboys, bartenders and dishwashers who don't actually serve customers.

Interns in the for-profit private sector are typically considered employees. Unlike trainees, they must be paid at least the minimum wage and overtime compensation for working over 40 hours in a workweek.

Applying the following six criteria helps determine if someone is an intern:

1. The internship is similar to training which would be given in an educational environment, even though it includes actual operation of the employer's facilities and resources.

2. The internship experience is for the benefit of the intern.

3. The intern doesn't displace regular employees, but works under close supervision of existing staff.

4. The employer providing the opportunity doesn't derive any immediate advantages or benefits from the activities of the intern;

and could possible experience delays in operations resulting from the internship.
5. The intern isn't entitled to a job at the conclusion of the internship.
6. The employer and intern both understand the intern isn't entitled to wages for the time spent in the internship.

4. Hours

Full-time employment; part-time employment: FLSA doesn't define full-time or part-time employment. This is typically determined by the employer.

Flexible work schedule: An alternative to the traditional 9-to-5, 40-hour workweek that lets employees vary their arrival and/or departure times. Employees typically work a set number of hours per pay period and are present during a specific "core time." FLSA doesn't address flexible work schedules. This is typically determined by the employer.

Break periods: Federal law doesn't require lunch or coffee breaks. However, most states have a mandatory 30-minute lunch period for each eight hours of work, which isn't compensable. And if an employer permits a short break, it is considered compensable work hours included in the total hours worked. (*Note:* These hours must be taken into account when determining overtime.)

5. Extra Compensation

Sign-on bonus: This is usually offered to new employees with unique, critical skills or for essential occupations when there's a bona fide, and documented, labor shortage and recruitment or retention is difficult. The sign-on bonus agreement must detail the nature and amount of the payment(s) and the dates of payout. (*Note:* It's a good idea to consider paying the bonus at the end of the first pay period.)

Retention bonus: This is a strategy used to retain an employee through a critical business cycle. The retention period can last up to three years or simply cover the duration of a particular project with a specific start and end date. The bonuses range from position to position, and:
• are paid in one lump sum, or
• are paid in installments throughout the course of the critical business cycle.

Spot bonus award: An employer may decide to reward an employee on the spot for achievements that deserve special recognition. Spot bonus awards are usually determined by the immediate supervisor and any higher-level staff member.

Pay-for-performance plans: These bonus plans often involve a substantial percentage of an employee's annual income and can be tied to a number of factors – individual achievement, team performance, departmental performance or overall company performance. These bonuses are often paid on a yearly basis, but in recent years, as many firms' performance has begun to show some short-term volatility, they've been computed quarterly or even monthly.

Severance plans: These are programs that pay an employee following termination, either as an individual or part of a larger reduction-in-force.

Amounts vary – some companies figure them based on years of service (Example: One week's current salary for every year worked for the company), while others pay a predetermined flat amount. Normally, the departing employee signs a waiver agreeing not to bring future legal action against the employer as a condition of receiving the severance payment.

6. Workers' Compensation

The **Federal Employees' Compensation Act (FECA)** provides comp benefits to employees disabled as the result of an injury or occupational disease sustained while performing their job duties. It would cover destruction of medical braces, artificial limbs and other prosthetic devices. The FECA also provides benefits to dependents if job-related injury or disease causes the employee's death.

The FECA is administered by the Office of Workers' Compensation Programs (OWCP), U.S. Department of Labor, and administers the four major disability compensation programs summarized here:

1. **The Energy Employees Occupational Illness Compensation Program** covers eligible employees and former employees of the U.S. Department of Energy, its contractors and subcontractors and certain survivors of these individuals.

2. **The Federal Employees' Compensation Program** provides wage replacement benefits, medical treatment, and other benefits to federal workers, or their dependents, who are injured at work or acquire an occupational disease.

3. **The Longshore and Harbor Workers' Compensation Program** provides compensation benefits to workers for disability resulting from an injury or an employment-related occupational disease occurring on navigable United States waters or in adjoining shoreside areas.

4. **The Black Lung Benefits Program** provides monthly payments and medical benefits to coal miners totally disabled from pneumoconiosis (black lung), as well as monthly payments to eligible surviving dependents.

Under the Federal Employees' Compensation Act, workers must provide medical and factual evidence to establish five basic elements:

1. The claim was filed within the time limits set by the FECA.
2. The injured or deceased person was an employee within the meaning of the FECA.
3. The employee actually developed a medical condition in a particular way.
4. The employee was performing duties of the job when the event(s) leading to the claim occurred.
5. The medical condition found resulted from the event(s) leading to the claim.

B. Real-Life Success Stories

1. Eased staffers into pay process change

We decided to look into making direct deposit mandatory.

For one thing, our paycheck distribution process had become too time-consuming for our supervisors to go around handing out checks to their staffers.

And then there were the occasional mishaps – such as checks getting lost or misplaced.

First, we double-checked that there were no rules stopping us from requiring staff members to sign up for direct deposit.

Then we worked with our primary banker and credit union provider to make sure everyone had access to some type of bank account.

Plenty of notice

In the month leading up to the change, we covered everything involved with the change extensively in our monthly employee newsletter.

We also held staff member meetings and distributed payroll stuffers in the weeks leading up to the switch to mandatory direct deposit.

The change was a tremendous success for everyone involved.

Supervisors no longer have to hand out checks, there are no issues with pay being lost and employees love the convenience of not having to go to the bank to get paid.

(A VP of HR for a grocery store in Louisiana)

2. Change in payroll processing paid off

Our pay period structure was causing managers a lot of problems.

It left only one day for the managers to approve their employees' time cards before payroll had to be processed.

And whenever that day fell on a holiday, it really screwed things up.

It caused a lot of stress for everyone and often led to inaccuracies.

So for the new year, we decided to move our pay day back one day in the week.

This extra day would give us more time to process payroll.

Small change, big benefit

But, of course, we first had to make sure switching our pay day wouldn't be an issue for employees – especially those who had automatic withdrawals set up from their bank accounts.

We sent out an email to employees explaining why we were switching the pay day.

It ended up working out great. Employees had sufficient notice to plan for the change, and it went off without a hitch.

Now, managers always have time to review time cards for accuracy.

Plus, my department doesn't have the headache of trying to rush through payroll to meet the direct deposit deadline.

(A payroll and benefits manager for a credit union in California)

II. BENEFITS

A. Overview

ERISA, the Employee Retirement Income Security Act of 1974, 29 U.S.C. § 1001 *et seq.,* is a comprehensive federal statute that imposes uniform rules and standards upon private pension and welfare benefit plans. It describes the fiduciary responsibilities of plan administrators and specifies rules for pension participation, funding, vesting and financial reporting.

ERISA preempts all state laws "as they may now or hereafter relate to any employee benefit plan described in section 1003(a) of this title...." Because the question of ERISA applicability frequently determines the outcome of pension litigation, a substantial body of law has developed concerning whether a particular state law "relates to" a plan described by ERISA.

Defined benefit plans consist of a general pool of assets rather than individual dedicated accounts. Under these plans, employees are entitled to a fixed periodic payment upon retirement, and employers generally bear the risk of investment. If there is under-funding of plan assets, the employer must make up the difference. On the other hand, if there is a surplus of plan assets, the employer may reduce or suspend its contributions.

Defined contribution plans are more common. Under these plans, the employer's contribution is fixed, and the employee receives whatever level of benefits the amount contributed on his or her behalf will provide. Each beneficiary is entitled to whatever assets are dedicated to his or her individual account. Employees bear the risk of loss and reap the rewards of high returns.

1. Employer-Sponsored Health Insurance

Health insurance is arguably the most important benefit a company can offer its employees. Employer-sponsored healthcare plans fall into two basic categories: fully insured and self-insured.

Fully insured health plan: When an employer-sponsored health plan is fully insured, it means the employer's insurance company is ultimately responsible for the company's healthcare costs, and the employer is required to pay the premiums.

Self-insured health plan: With these plans, the employer provides its workers with medical coverage out of its own assets. A self-insured health plan passes all the risks directly onto the employer. Employers, however, can then purchase stop loss insurance to lower their risk.

Stop-loss provision of a self-funded plan: A stop-loss provision in a self-funded plan limits an employer's losses to a set dollar amount. So, if the claim costs are higher than a certain predetermined amount, an insurance carrier will then cover the excess amount.

While employer-sponsored health insurance is divided into two major categories, companies have a number of options when it comes to finer points of their group health plan. To clarify, here's how a group health plan is defined under the *Employee Retirement Income Security Act (ERISA)*:

"*A group health plan* is an employee benefit plan established or maintained by an employer or an employee organization – such as a union – or both, that provides medical care to employees or their dependents directly or through insurance, reimbursement or otherwise."

Here are the most prevalent employer-sponsored group health plan options:

Preferred provider organization (PPO): A PPO is an organization or network of physicians, hospitals or other healthcare providers that offers volume discounts to companies that sponsor group health plans. Employers then normally offer financial incentives for the employees for using the "preferred providers" within the plan's network.

Health maintenance organization (HMO): An HMO is a prepaid group medical service organization that stresses preventive care. The Public Health Service Act (Health Maintenance Organization Act) of 1973 defines an HMO plan as "an organized system for the delivery of comprehensive health maintenance and treatment services to voluntarily enrolled members for a prenegotiated, fixed, periodic payment." Unlike PPO plans, HMOs require plan members to select a primary care physician who is responsible for managing and coordinating all of the participants' healthcare services. If an HMO plan member needs to see a specialist or have a diagnostic service done, the member's primary doctor must provide him or her with a referral. If the member doesn't have a referral and chooses to see a doctor outside of the HMO network, the care received likely won't be covered under the terms of the insurance plan.

Point of service (POS): A health plan where the level of benefits received depends on how an employee elects to receive care at the "point of service" of that care. Example: If an employee's care begins with the gatekeeper physician in the network, the plan will pay more than if the care was received outside of the network.

Consumer-driven health plan (CDHP): In general, any health plan that attempts to control medical costs by helping plan participants to make more informed choices about the quality and efficiency of their health care is a CDHP. The most popular CDHPs today include a high deductible (an amount that must be satisfied by the plan member in the event of a catastrophic event) combined with a tax savings account like a health savings account, health reimbursement arrangement or a flexible spending account.

High-deductible health plan (HDHP): An HDHP is a plan option that includes lower premium costs and higher deductibles than traditional plans such as PPOs or HMOs. In addition, HDHPs must also include a health savings account (HSA) or some other pre-tax option such as a flexible spending account or health reimbursement account. Here are the definitions for the major tax-advantaged options added to an HDHP:

Health savings account: A tax-advantaged account created for the benefit of a participant covered under an HDHP. Contributions can be made by the employer or the employees, and unused funds roll over from year to year. HSAs are owned by the account beneficiary, so the account belongs to the employee or plan participant.

Health reimbursement arrangement (HRA): These arrangements are established and exclusively funded by employers. HRAs are also tax-free accounts where employees can use the funds in HRAs for general healthcare expenses before using traditional coverage. However, unlike HSAs or FSAs, these arrangements are called "theoretical accounts." This means money isn't actually in an individual account where an employee can invest money. HRA balances that are there at year-end can roll over and be used to cover future medical costs.

Flexible spending account (FSA): With FSAs, employees can set aside money on a pretax basis to pay for eligible unreimbursed medical and dependent care expenses. Unlike HRAs and HSAs, FSA funds not used by the end of the year are lost to the employer. In addition, FSAs are subject to annual maximum limits and forfeiture rules set by the IRS.

Indemnity plan: An indemnity plan gives participants complete freedom when it comes to selecting doctors, hospitals and other providers of healthcare benefits. Indemnity plans are usually the most expensive plan option available.

2. Prescription Drug Benefits

In addition to offering a group health plan, the vast majority of companies cover employees' prescription drug expenses in some way. According to the Society for Human Resource Management (SHRM), 96% of employers offer some type of prescription drug benefits.

Prescription drug benefits can either be included as part of an employer-sponsored group health plan or as a separate – or "carved out" – plan. Normally, when prescription drugs are administered during an employee's hospital stay, the health plan will absorb the entire cost as part of the covered inpatient hospital charges. However, when prescriptions are prescribed outside of a hospital stay, payment is often subject to a deductible and co-pay by the employee.

Some of the more common employer prescription drug plan features include:

Formulary plans: A formulary is a list of covered drugs in the employer's pharmacy plan. A health plan normally only covers the prescription drugs that are listed on its formulary. Formulary plans are meant to limit employee coverage only to drugs that have been on the market for a certain amount of time – and that have proved effective in treating certain medical conditions. These plans focus on the most cost-effective, clinically proven prescription drug available for treating specific conditions.

Mail-order pharmacy services: Mail-order services usually give workers a 90-day supply of their prescription each time they place an order for a specified co-payment. These plans help to save money because the prescription drugs are obtained at volume discount prices from the manufacturer.

Tiered prescription drug pricing: With a tiered structure, employees are charged co-payments according to what tier the drugs are classified under; the higher the tier, the more expensive the drug. Example: In a three-tier model, the lowest (or first tier) co-payment is assigned to the generics on the plan's formulary; the second tier charge is for preferred drugs on the formulary or drugs without any generic equivalents; and the third tier – and most expensive co-payment – is assigned to nonformulary, nonpreferred brand-name drugs. While a three-tier model is still the most popular among employers, some companies are rolling out four- and five-tier co-payment structures.

Many employers also utilize the services of a **Pharmacy Benefits**

Manager (PBM). A PBM is an individual or a company that manages an employer's pharmacy benefits. PBMs generally handle tasks like, establishing and maintaining a formulary, negotiating prices with drug manufacturers and wholesalers, approving and processing claims, and providing the health plans with occasional financial and utilization reports.

3. The Effects of the Reform Law on Healthcare Benefits

The healthcare reform law – officially titled the **Patient Protection and Affordable Care Act (PPACA)** – went into effect on March 23, 2010. The reform law was designed to overhaul the entire healthcare system in the United States over the next several years and, in some ways, has already begun to do so.

Bottom line: Health reform has the potential to alter the way employers' offer health insurance to their employees, as well as the plan options available.

Major changes are in place now

Here are some of the major healthcare reform law changes that are in place right now:

- Dependents can remain on their parent's health insurance plan even if they're employed elsewhere or are not enrolled in school
- Insurance companies cannot discriminate against children with pre-existing conditions
- Insurance plans are barred from imposing lifetime caps on insurance coverage (there are also rules in place regulating annual limits on health coverage – until annual limits are prohibited altogether on Jan. 1, 2014)
- Insurers are prohibited from dropping covered employees who become ill
- Small employers – with fewer than 25 employees with an average annual wage of less than $50,000 – are eligible for tax credits for purchasing group health insurance
- New health plans must cover certain preventive services – like mammograms and colonoscopies – without charging a deductible, co-pay or coinsurance, and
- Employees can no longer use tax-advantaged accounts like flexible spending or health savings accounts for the reimbursement of over-the-counter drugs – unless the drugs are insulin or prescribed by a doctor.

What changes are coming?

There are a number of reform law changes slated to take effect between 2012 and 2018, including:

- Use of electronic health records to reduce paperwork and administrative burdens, cut costs, reduce medical errors and improve care quality (2012)
- Healthcare claims and appeals rules (2012)
- Reporting of health costs on employees' W-2s (2013 W-2s for large

employers; 2014 W-2s for small employers)
- The creation of multi-state health exchanges to compete with the health insurance marketplace and the mandate that all individuals carry health insurance (2014)
- Employers are prohibited from imposing waiting periods of more than 90 days for employees to be eligible for health coverage (2014), and
- A 40% excise tax on health plans with premiums higher than $10,200 for single coverage and more than $27,500 for family plans (2018).

Delayed and repealed provisions

A number of health reform changes have been either delayed or thrown out completely, such as:
- Nondiscrimination rules which prohibit group health plan from offering health coverage to highly compensated employees that isn't available to all company employees (delayed until the feds release further guidance)
- 1099 reporting rules that would've required employers to track and report any payments to every vendor they paid more than $600 to during the course of the year (repealed)
- Free Choice Vouchers which would've allowed workers who make less than 400% of the federal poverty level to get a healthcare voucher if their company-sponsored healthcare coverage cost them between 8% and 9.8% of their total income (repealed).

A much more detailed description of all of the health reform changes – in a year by year format – can be found here: *http://healthreform.kff.org/Timeline.aspx.*

4. Miscellaneous Health Benefits

Dental benefits

Today, most companies provide some type of dental health benefits for their employees. Like standard health benefits, there are a number of plan options to choose from. However, two of the most common options are:

Dental Health Maintenance Organization (DHMO): This option provides workers with a range of dental services for a set fee. Participants in a DHMO are required to receive care from a participating provider. Also, regardless of the care received by the participant, dentists will still receive a set fee each month from each participant.

Dental Preferred Provider Organization (DPPO): A DPPO is a fee-for-service program that lets participants choose to go to any dentist they'd like, but offers financial incentives if participants opt to go with dentists who are part of the preferred provider organization network.

Wellness Programs

The idea of "wellness" has grown tremendously in popularity over the past decade, and most employers offer at least one type of wellness program to employees. A basic working definition of a wellness program is any program offered to employees that is designed to help them maintain a high level of health and well-being through using strategies like proper diet, exercise, stress management and injury prevention.

Wellness programs can be individualized or group based – and can include rewards for participation, or results or penalties for failure to participate. These programs come in all different shapes and sizes; however, all wellness programs have one thing in common: All wellness programs must comply with the Health Insurance Portability and Accountability Act (HIPAA).

Under HIPAA, there are two basic wellness programs from which companies have to choose:

- A program that does not depend on health status factors, and
- A program that does depend on health status factors.

Wellness programs that do not depend on health status factors (also known as "participatory wellness programs"): With this program, either no reward is offered or the reward isn't related to an individual's health. Example: A healthcare premium discount that's given to employees' who participate in a smoking-cessation program, but don't have to actually quit smoking to receive the discount.

Wellness programs that do depend on health status factors (also known as 'health-contingent wellness programs'): The conditions for obtaining a reward are based on whether or not an individual satisfies a standard related to a health factor.

Wellness programs that depend on health status factors are required to meet HIPAA's five nondiscrimination requirements:

The 20% rule. The size of the reward – or penalty – set by your wellness program can't exceed 20% of the total cost of health coverage for employees.

The promotion of good health and disease prevention. According to the feds, a wellness program must exist to promote employees' good health and prevent disease. Bottom line: Your wellness program must treat everyone equally. As long as the wellness program helps employees improve their health and imposes "reasonable standards" for the rewards, it passes this non-discrimination requirement.

The 'clean slate' rule. Every eligible participant in a wellness program must be given the chance – a.k.a. a clean slate – to earn health plan-related rewards and incentives – at least once per year for as long as the program is in place.

The "good-faith effort" rule. The most important of the HIPAA requirements, the good-faith effort rules states that employers can't "discriminate based on a health risk factor." Basically, companies must reward employees enrolled in a wellness program if they make a good-effort to lose weight, quit smoking, etc., even if the end result was a failure.

The "reasonable alternative" rule. If a company has an employee who's not capable of achieving the goals required to earn the rewards the wellness program offers, HIPAA requires the company to offer that employee a reasonable alternative way to earn the wellness program's rewards.

Common wellness initiatives

Employers can roll out a single-phrase wellness program or combine several initiatives together.

Here are some of the most common wellness components employers are using today:

Biometric screenings: These are short health examinations that determine an employee's risk level for specific diseases and medical conditions. The screenings normally check a number of biometric measures, like: cholesterol levels, blood pressure and blood glucose levels, as well as measurement of an employee's height, weight and body mass index (BMI). All test results are confidential.

Health Risk Assessments (HRA): An HRA is a questionnaire used to determine an employee's current health status and potential future health risks the employee may be vulnerable to. These questionnaires usually refer to a number of different lifestyles and behavioral activities.

Wellness newsletters: This is one of the most common features of an employer-sponsored wellness program. Wellness newsletters are written exclusively to provide employees with info about various health and wellness topics.

Wellness consultant/coach: Many companies bring in professionally trained consultants to help employees hit – and maintain – their health and wellness goals.

Weight-loss programs: A cornerstone of many employer-sponsored wellness initiatives is some type of a weight-loss program.

Smoking-cessation programs: While these programs can vary greatly from company to company, the end goal is always the same: to help employees quit smoking.

Chronic-condition management programs: These programs focus exclusively on workers with chronic conditions – like diabetes, asthma, heart disease – to help improve the employees' overall health and minimize the chances of major problems down the road.

Generally, an employer will contract with its insurance provider or a third-party vendor to implement a chronic condition management program. The most basic programs may include nothing more than a nurse reminding workers with diabetes to check their blood sugar or take insulin regularly.

However, detailed programs will gather and analyze an array of data – prescription utilization, lab results, inpatient/outpatient visits, etc., to come up with a long-term plan to help employees make the lifestyle changes needed to avoid major medical incidents in the future.

Employee Assistance Programs (EAPs)

In addition to physical wellness, employers normally have programs in place to help employees with their mental and emotional health. The most common: Employee assistance programs (EAPs).

These are employer-sponsored programs to help workers deal with problems at work and personal difficulties that may be hurting overall job performance. EAPs have proven to be effective at helping companies to reduce absenteeism, improve morale, boost productivity and even lower healthcare costs.

Generally, EAPs offer employees assessments, counseling and referrals to professional services for a number of different career and personal issues. Some (but not all) of the more common issues EAPs help employees with include:

drug and alcohol abuse, mental health disorders, marriage or family difficulties, domestic violence, and legal and/or financial concerns.

5. Retirement Benefits

The Employee Retirement Income Security Act of 1974 (ERISA) sets minimum standards for most voluntarily established pension and health plans in private industry, as a way to protect individuals participating in these plans. In addition, ERISA:

- requires plans to provide participants with plan info, including details regarding plan features and funding
- provides fiduciary responsibilities for those who manage and control plan assets
- requires plans to establish a grievance and appeals process for participants to get benefits from their plans, and
- gives participants the right to sue for benefits and breaches of fiduciary duty.

ERISA doesn't cover group health plans established or maintained by the government or churches for their employees, or plans maintained solely to comply with applicable workers' compensation, unemployment or disability laws.

Retirement Plans

There are two basic types of employer-sponsored retirement plans: **defined-contribution plans and defined-benefit plans**. The key difference between the two is which party bears the responsibility for the performance of the plan's invested contributions.

- *Defined Contribution plans* are those where the employee contributes a given amount per pay period to his or her own retirement account. Once the employer has made the agreed-upon contribution to the employee's account, the investment risk lies entirely with the account holder (the employee).
- *Defined Benefit plans* are the traditional pension arrangements, where employers set aside money in a company-controlled fund for distribution to employees after they retire. The payments can be based on various factors, like time spent with the company and salary received over a given period. Since the employer is responsible for delivering a set pension amount to its employees during their retirement, the investment risk falls on the company.

Defined contribution plans include: 401(k) plans, which allow employees to set aside part of their salaries – tax free – to put in a retirement fund they control. Plan contributions are invested in mutual funds, stocks, bonds and other investment vehicles. The amount deferred isn't taxable until it's withdrawn or distributed from the plan. Some 401(k) plans let employees make contributions on an after-tax basis, and these amounts are tax-free when withdrawn.

For 2011, the maximum amount of compensation an employee can defer to a 401(k) plan is $16,500. Employees age 50 or older by the end of the year can make additional catch-up contributions of up to $5,500.

The money in the plan grows tax-deferred like individual retirement accounts (IRAs). But while IRA distributions can be made at any time, a "triggering event" is required for distributions to occur from a 401(k) plan, including:

- The employee's retirement, death, disability or separation from service with the employer
- The employee reaches age 59 1/2
- The employee experiences a hardship as defined under the plan, if the plan permits hardship withdrawals, and
- Upon the termination of the plan.

Required minimum distributions (RMDs) must begin at age 70 1/2, unless the participant is still employed and the plan allows RMDs to be deferred until retirement. Distributions will be counted as ordinary income and assessed a 10% early distribution penalty if the distribution occurs before age 59 1/2 unless an exceptions applies, such as:

- The distributions occur after the death or disability of the employee.
- The distributions occur after the employee separates from service, providing the separation occurs during or after the calendar year that the employee attains age 55.
- The distribution is made to an alternate payee under a qualified domestic relations order (QDRO).
- The employee has deductible medical expenses exceeding 7.5% of adjusted gross income.
- The distributions are taken as a series of substantially equal periodic payments over the participant's life or the joint lives of the participant and beneficiary.
- The distribution represents a timely correction of excess contributions or deferrals.
- The distribution is as a result of an IRS levy on the employee's account.
- The distribution is not taxable.

Employees can access their plan balances through loans, but there are restrictions. For example, the option is available at the employer's discretion. If allowed, then up to 50% of the employee's vested balance can be accessed, providing the amount doesn't exceed $50,000. It usually has to be repaid within five years. However, loans used for primary home purchases can be repaid over longer periods. But any unpaid balance left at the end of the term could be considered a distribution and taxed and penalized accordingly.

403(b) plans are similar to 401(k) plans, but they're specifically for employees of non-profit organizations, such as hospitals, museums, public foundations, churches, research organizations, and public educational systems. Participants typically invest in either annuities or mutual funds. Employees may make salary deferral contributions that are usually limited by regulatory caps.

Traditional individual retirement accounts (IRAs) can be opened by anyone with earned income, and is a tax-deferred retirement savings account. Taxes are paid only when an individual makes withdrawals in retirement. Deferring taxes means all of the dividends, interest payments and capital gains can compound each year without being hindered by taxes, so the IRA grows much faster than a taxable account.

Roth individual retirement accounts (IRAs) are similar to traditional IRAs, but contributions are not tax deductible and qualified distributions are tax free. Similar to other retirement plan accounts, non-qualified distributions from a Roth IRA may be subject to a penalty upon withdrawal. A qualified distribution is one that is taken at least five years after the taxpayer establishes his or her first Roth IRA and when he or she is age 59.5, disabled, using the withdrawal to purchase a first home (limit $10,000), or deceased (in which case the beneficiary collects).

Current contribution levels:

- **Under 50 years of age at the end of 2011:** The maximum contribution that can be made to a traditional or Roth IRA is the smaller of $5,000 or the amount of taxable compensation for 2011. This limit can be split between a traditional IRA and a Roth IRA but the combined limit is $5,000.

- **50 years of age or older before the end of 2011:** The maximum contribution that can be made to a traditional or Roth IRA is the smaller of $6,000 or the amount of taxable compensation for 2011. This limit can be split between a traditional IRA and a Roth IRA but the combined limit is $6,000.

Companies offering defined-benefit plans have three different pension obligations:

1. **Projected Benefit Obligation (PBO)** is the present value of the future retirement/pension benefits earned by an employee to date, based on expected future increases in earnings.

2. **Accumulated Benefit Obligation (ABO)** is the present value of the future retirement/pension benefits earned by an employee to date, ignoring any expected future increases in earnings.

3. **Vested Benefit Obligation (VBO)** is the present value of the future retirement/pension benefits earned by an employee to date, granted they have been fully vested. (*Note:* VBO doesn't consider any future service by the employee.)

6. Additional Considerations

Automatic Enrollment

Under most 401(k) plans, when an eligible employee doesn't make an affirmative election to defer salary under the plan, ERISA permits employers to **automatically enroll** the employee at the default contribution amount. However, the law also gives employees the right to a minimum 30-day decision period to opt-out of automatic contributions before they begin. Plus, there is usually a 90-day "second-chance" opt-out opportunity that allows an employee to cancel participation and get an immediate refund of any automatic contributions made through the effective date of the cancellation.

The default contribution rate must be a uniform percentage of pay for all employees automatically enrolled in the plan. But plans are permitted to have different default rates for union vs. non-union employees, for different unions, and for different "qualified separate lines of business." Employers can have graduated default rates, such as 1% in the first year, 2% in the second year, etc., maxing out at 10% in the tenth year.

Before opting for automatic enrollment, employers need to decide:

1. Which employees will be subject to automatic enrollment, whether only employees who don't have an affirmative election on file, or only new employees hired after the arrangement was first adopted
2. Appropriate default contribution rate(s)
3. Where default contributions should be invested until the employee exercises investment control, and
4. Initial set-up and ongoing administrative costs.

Voluntary (or Supplemental) Benefits

In addition to healthcare and retirement benefits, many employers also offer employees certain voluntary benefits. Voluntary – or employee-paid – benefits are supplemental benefit plans that companies provide on a voluntary basis. Some of the more typical voluntary benefits include:

- Life insurance (term or premium)
- Disability income supplements (long and short term)
- Vision
- Transportation and parking benefits
- Long-term care benefits, and
- Homeowners' insurance.

Open Enrollment

Open enrollment is one of the most important components of employer-sponsored benefits. The **open enrollment period** – also known as the annual enrollment period – is the time period when employees can sign up for or change elections for their employer-sponsored benefits. Most employers use this time period to focus on educating workers about their benefits options, as well as any changes that have taken place since the previous open enrollment – plan changes, new plan options, different insurance provider, etc. The majority of open enrollment periods rely on a meeting – or a series of meetings – where the employer, the healthcare provider/broker or both communicate directly with employees about their benefits options. For calendar year plans (plans beginning on Jan. 1), the open enrollment period is usually anywhere from a several weeks to a few months prior to the plan's effective date.

Summary Plan Descriptions (SPDs)

Under ERISA, employers are required to provide employees with an explanation about certain benefits programs (healthcare options, retirement benefits, etc.) in a language that can be easily understood by an average employee. SPDs need to be updated when plan changes are made.

B. Judicial Decisions

♦   A former employee sued his ex-employer, alleging that he had asked the company to make certain changes to his 401(k) investments and that it had never made the changes. He asserted that this failure "depleted" his interest in the plan by approximately $150,000 and amounted to a breach of fiduciary duty under ERISA. A South Carolina federal court granted pretrial judgment to the company, and the Fourth Circuit affirmed. The U.S. Supreme Court vacated and remanded the case, holding that although Section 502(a)(2) of ERISA does not provide a remedy for individual injuries distinct from plan injuries, **ERISA does authorize recovery for fiduciary breaches that impair the value of plan assets in a participant's individual account**. Here, the misconduct alleged by the employee fell squarely within the statutory duties imposed by ERISA. This was a different situation than a defined benefit plan, where participants are entitled to a fixed payment (like from a pension). Here, fiduciary misconduct could reduce a participant's benefits below the amount he would otherwise receive. Further proceedings were necessary. *LaRue v. DeWolff, Boberg & Associates, Inc.,* 552 U.S. 248, 128 S.Ct. 1020, 169 L.Ed.2d 847 (2008).

♦   Participants in a multiemployer pension plan in Illinois retired after accruing enough pension credits to qualify for early retirement payments under a "service only" pension scheme that paid them the same monthly benefit they would have received had they retired at the usual age. They were only 39 at the time. The plan prohibited them from taking jobs as construction workers (but not as supervisors) if they wanted to continue receiving pension payments. They took supervisory construction jobs so as to be able to receive pension benefits in addition to their salaries. The plan then expanded its definition of barred employment to include any construction industry job, and stopped payments when the participants did not leave their supervisory jobs. They sued to recover the suspended benefits, claiming that the suspension violated the "anti-cutback" rule of ERISA, which prohibits any pension plan amendment that would reduce a participant's "accrued benefit."

    A federal court ruled for the plan, but the Seventh Circuit reversed, holding that imposing new conditions on rights to benefits already accrued violated the anti-cutback rule. The U.S. Supreme Court affirmed, holding that ERISA Section 204(g) prohibits an amendment expanding the categories of barred post-retirement employment so as to suspend payment of early retirement benefits already accrued. Here, the suspension of benefits allowed by **the plan amendment had the effect of reducing an early retirement benefit that had been promised**. *Cent. Laborers' Pension Fund v. Heinz,* 541 U.S. 739, 124 S.Ct. 2230, 159 L.Ed.2d 46 (2004).

♦   A Washington state law automatically revoked, upon divorce, the designation of a spouse as beneficiary to a life insurance policy or employee benefit plan. When a divorced employee died in a car accident, his children sought the proceeds of his life insurance policy and his pension plan, even though his ex-wife was still named on both documents. Also, both documents were governed by ERISA. A question arose as to whether ERISA preempted the state law, making the children the recipients of the proceeds. The U.S. Supreme Court ruled that **ERISA preempted the state law**. To rule otherwise would require plan administrators to familiarize themselves with the statutes of all 50 states. ERISA allowed them to pay out proceeds per the plan documents. Thus, the ex-wife was entitled to the proceeds. *Egelhoff v. Egelhoff*, 532 U.S. 141, 121 S.Ct. 1322, 149 L.Ed.2d 264 (2001).

♦   The Retirement Equity Act of 1984 allows participants in survivor's annuity plans to designate a beneficiary other than their spouse only with the spouse's consent. A Louisiana telecommunications employee with a wife and three sons participated in several ERISA-qualified retirement plans. Following the death of his wife, the employee remarried. When he died several years later, his sons submitted claims against his estate based upon the first wife's will for his undistributed retirement benefits, including a savings plan, an employee stock ownership plan, and a survivor's annuity. A federal court held that the sons were entitled to a share of the retirement benefits under Louisiana community property law. The Fifth Circuit affirmed. The U.S. Supreme Court held that ERISA preempted the state law that allowed the first wife to transfer (upon her death) an interest in undistributed pension plan benefits. **The surviving spouse was entitled to receive the survivor's annuity since she had not waived her rights or consented to the designation of the sons as beneficiaries.** She was also entitled to the stock shares and the savings plan proceeds, since the claims of the sons were based on community property law and were inconsistent with ERISA's anti-alienation provision. *Boggs v. Boggs*, 520 U.S. 833, 117 S.Ct. 1754, 138 L.Ed.2d 45 (1997).

♦   A class of former employees of the Kaiser Steel Corporation, who participated in the company's ERISA-qualified retirement plan, brought suit for the plan's losses against an actuary employed by the company. They alleged that the actuary had knowingly participated in misfeasance by plan fiduciaries. Kaiser had hired the actuary when it began to phase out its steel-making operations, prompting early retirement by a large number of plan participants. The actuary failed to change the plan's actuarial assumptions to reflect the additional costs imposed by the retirements. As a result, Kaiser did not adequately fund the plan, and its assets became insufficient to satisfy its obligations. When the plan was terminated, the former employees began receiving only the benefits guaranteed by ERISA, which were substantially lower than the fully vested pensions due them under the plan. After a California federal court and the Ninth Circuit dismissed the complaint, the U.S. Supreme Court affirmed. ERISA Section 502(a)(3) permits plan participants to bring civil actions to obtain "appropriate equitable relief" to redress violations of the plan. The Court determined that **requiring the actuary to make the plan whole for the losses it sustained would not constitute "appropriate equitable relief."** What the employees were seeking here was compensatory damages, not "equitable relief." *Mertens v. Hewitt Associates*, 508 U.S. 248, 113 S.Ct. 2063, 124 L.Ed.2d 161 (1993).

♦   One of the trustees of a sheet metal workers' pension fund embezzled over $375,000 from the union. Two pension plans contended that the trustee had forfeited his right to receive benefits as a result. They also asserted that even if he had not forfeited his benefits, those benefits should be paid to the union and not to him. A Colorado federal court held that because there was a judgment against the trustee for $275,000, a constructive trust should be imposed on the trustee's benefits until the judgment was paid off. The Tenth Circuit affirmed. The U.S. Supreme Court held that the constructive trust violated the prohibition on assignment or alienation of pension benefits called for by ERISA. Here, although the trustee had stolen money from the union, he had not stolen money from the pension funds. Even if the Labor-Management Reporting and Disclosure Act authorized the imposition of a constructive trust when a union officer breached his fiduciary duties, that did not override ERISA's anti-alienation provision. ERISA reflected a congressional policy choice to **safeguard a stream of income for pensioners even if that prevented others from obtaining relief for the wrongs done to them**. The Court reversed and remanded the case. *Guidry v. Sheet Metal Workers National Pension Fund*, 493 U.S. 365, 110 S.Ct. 680, 107 L.Ed.2d 782 (1990).

On remand, the union and the trustee agreed that the trustee's monthly pension payments would be made to a bank account opened specifically to receive the pension funds, and that the funds would then be subject to garnishment by the union. The Tenth Circuit noted that Section 206(d)(1) protection did not extend to the funds once the plan participant asserted dominion over them. Since the garnishment action was not "against the plan," it was not prohibited by ERISA. *Guidry v. Sheet Metal Workers Local No. 9*, 10 F.3d 700 (10th Cir. 1993).

♦   A North Carolina insurance agent sold insurance for competitors after his relationship with an insurer was terminated. When the insurer sought to avoid paying his retirement benefits on the grounds that he violated a non-compete clause, he sued. The U.S. Supreme Court noted that the agent's ERISA claim could succeed only if he was an employee. Because ERISA's definition of "employee" as "any individual employed by an employer" was not helpful, the Court suggested **assessing and weighing all the elements of an employment relationship**, including: the location of the work, the duration of the relationship between the parties, the method of payment, and the provision of employee benefits, among others. The Court reversed and remanded the case for a determination of whether the agent qualified as an employee under traditional agency law. *Nationwide Mutual Insurance Co. v. Darden*, 503 U.S. 318, 112 S.Ct. 1344, 117 L.Ed.2d 581 (1992).

♦   An employee in Texas went through a divorce, during which his wife agreed to divest herself of all rights to his employee benefit, retirement and pension plans. However, the divorce decree did not spell out a number of specific things necessary for it to be considered a "qualified domestic relations order." Nor did the employee change the beneficiary designation on his savings and investment plan (SIP). He did appoint his daughter as a new beneficiary for his pension and retirement plan. When he died, the SIP administrator paid

$400,000 to the ex-wife. His estate sued under ERISA. The case reached the U.S. Supreme Court, which held that the administrator properly paid the benefits to the ex-wife. **The employee never changed the beneficiary designation on the SIP even though the plan provided an easy way for him to do so.** *Kennedy v. Plan Administrator for DuPont Savings and Investment Plan,* 129 S.Ct. 865, 172 L.Ed.2d 662 (U.S. 2009).

♦   A Sears employee was diagnosed with a heart condition that prevented her from performing her job. She received disability benefits under the company's plan for 24 months, and applied for Social Security benefits as well. An administrative law judge found her eligible for benefits, which Sears' insurer took by right of offset. Sears' insurer then found her ineligible for long-term disability benefits on the ground that she could do sedentary work. She sued under ERISA. An Ohio federal court ruled for the insurer, the Sixth Circuit reversed, and the U.S. Supreme Court affirmed the ruling for the employee. The Court noted **the conflict of interest where an insurer decides if an employee is eligible for benefits and is also responsible for paying the claim.** *Metropolitan Life Insurance Co. v. Glenn,* 554 U.S. 105, 128 S.Ct. 2343, 171 L.Ed.2d 299 (2008).

♦   After a Maryland employee and her husband were injured in an automobile accident, the employee's ERISA-covered health insurance plan paid the couple's medical expenses. They then sued several third parties for injuries they suffered as a result of the accident. The health plan administrator sent them a letter asserting a lien on any proceeds from the lawsuit. After the lawsuit settled for $750,000, the plan administrator sued to recover the medical expenses it had paid. A federal court ordered the couple to reimburse the plan administrator for the medical expenses, and the Fourth Circuit affirmed in part. The U.S. Supreme Court also affirmed, noting that **the plan properly provided for beneficiaries to reimburse the plan from any recovery from outside sources.** This was a claim for equitable relief that could be brought under ERISA. The couple had to reimburse the plan. *Sereboff v. Mid Atlantic Medical Services, Inc.,* 547 U.S. 356, 126 S.Ct. 1869, 164 L.Ed.2d 612 (2006).

♦   Two Texas employees sued their health plan administrators when their respective HMOs refused to cover their physicians' recommended medical treatment and they suffered medical setbacks as a result. Federal courts dismissed the cases as preempted by ERISA, but the Fifth Circuit reversed. On further appeal, the U.S. Supreme Court reversed the Fifth Circuit, noting that **ERISA preempted their state law claims for medical negligence.** The employees' claims fell squarely within the parameters of Section 502(a), which has extraordinary preemptive power and which allows plan participants to sue to enforce rights or recover benefits under their plans. Here, contrary to the employees' argument, the plan administrators were making eligibility decisions, not treatment decisions. Also, the failure of the plans to cover the requested treatment was the proximate cause of the employees' injuries, not the denial of coverage. *Aetna Health Care v. Davila,* 542 U.S. 200, 124 S.Ct. 2488, 159 L.Ed.2d 312 (2004).

◆ A Black & Decker employee alleged that a mild degenerative disc condition made him eligible for long-term disability benefits under ERISA. Although his personal physician backed up his claim, a separate neurologist recommended by Black & Decker concluded that he could perform "sedentary work" if aided by pain medication. Based on this opinion and the recommendation of its insurer, Black & Decker denied the employee's claim. He sued in a California federal court to overturn this determination. The judge ruled in favor of Black & Decker, but the U.S. Court of Appeals for the Ninth Circuit reversed, holding that the company had not come up with adequate reasons for rejecting the opinion of the employee's treating physician. The Supreme Court, however, disagreed. It held that **plan administrators are not obliged to accord special deference to the opinions of treating physicians** when making benefit determinations under ERISA. The statute and its regulations "require 'full and fair' assessment of claims and clear communication to the claimant of the 'specific reasons' for benefit denials," the Court explained. "But these measures do not command plan administrators to credit the opinions of treating physicians over other evidence relevant to the claimant's medical condition." *Black & Decker Disability Plan v. Nord,* 538 U.S. 822, 123 S.Ct. 1965, 155 L.Ed.2d 1034 (2003).

◆ Employees of a railway subsidiary were entitled to railroad retirement benefits and pension, health and welfare benefits under collective bargaining agreements covered by ERISA. When the contract between the railway and the subsidiary was terminated, the railway hired another service to do the work. The new contractor retained some of the subsidiary's employees; however, it was not required to make railroad retirement contributions and its welfare plan was inferior to the subsidiary's plan. Employees who continued to work for the new contractor sued the railroad, the subsidiary and the new contractor in a California federal court, asserting that the manner of the discharge interfered with their pension and welfare benefits. The court dismissed the ERISA claims. The Ninth Circuit reinstated the claim for interference with pension benefits, but agreed that ERISA did not protect employees from elimination of welfare benefits that did not vest.

The U.S. Supreme Court found that Section 510 of ERISA prevents an employer from discharging a plan participant or beneficiary for the purpose of interfering with the attainment of any right to which the participant might be entitled. Section 510 draws no distinction between those rights that vest under ERISA and those that do not. Further, **although an employer has the right to unilaterally amend or eliminate a welfare benefit plan, Section 510 requires the employer to follow the plan's formal amendment process.** The Court vacated the judgment and remanded the case for further proceedings. *Inter-Modal Rail Employees Ass'n v. Atchison, Topeka and Santa Fe Railway Co.,* 520 U.S. 510, 117 S.Ct. 1513, 137 L.Ed.2d 763 (1997).

◆ A manufacturer transferred its money-losing divisions to a new subsidiary and told employees in these divisions that their benefits and salaries would remain the same if they transferred. Many employees transferred to the subsidiary, which went into receivership within two years. Employees and retirees who participated in the subsidiary's welfare benefit plan asserted that the manufacturer fraudulently induced them to accept the transfers. They sued in an Iowa federal court, which held that the manufacturer violated its obligation under ERISA to administer the plan in the employees' interest. The court awarded damages to the participants and ruled that they had a right to appropriate equitable relief including reinstatement into the manufacturer's plan. The U.S. Court of Appeals, Eighth Circuit, affirmed much of the district court decision but disallowed a $46 million damage award.

The manufacturer appealed to the U.S. Supreme Court, which found that the manufacturer had been **acting as both a plan fiduciary and an employer when it promised to preserve employee benefits and salaries after the transfer**. Accordingly, its actions were held to the standard of fiduciary care that subjected it to potential ERISA liability. The Court rejected the argument that ERISA did not allow individual equitable relief, and affirmed the lower court decisions. *Varity Corp. v. Howe,* 516 U.S. 489, 116 S.Ct. 1065, 134 L.Ed.2d 130 (1996).

◆   A corporation maintained and administered a single-employer health plan for its employees. After closing a New Jersey facility, the corporation's executive vice president notified retirees of the facility by letter that their post-retirement health benefits were being terminated. The retirees sued the corporation, alleging that the company's summary plan description lacked a valid amendment procedure and that the action constituted a plan amendment. The court agreed with the retirees and ordered the corporation to pay them over $2.6 million in benefits. The Third Circuit affirmed.

The U.S. Supreme Court agreed with the corporation that the minimal language in its summary plan description satisfied the amendment procedure requirement of ERISA Section 402(b)(3). Under the plan description, the corporation "reserve[d] the right at any time to amend the plan. ..." ERISA creates no substantive entitlement to employer-provided welfare benefits and employers are allowed to freely modify, amend or terminate welfare plans under most circumstances. **A plan that simply identified the person or persons having authority to amend a plan necessarily indicated the amendment procedure.** The Court reversed and remanded the case. *Curtiss-Wright Corp. v. Schoonejongen,* 514 U.S. 73, 115 S.Ct. 1223, 131 L.Ed.2d 94 (1995).

◆   A corporation operated a self-funded healthcare plan under which plan members agreed to reimburse it for benefits paid if the member recovered on a claim in a liability action against a third party. The daughter of a plan member was seriously injured in an automobile accident, and the plan paid part of her medical expenses. A negligence action against the driver of the vehicle settled, and the plan member refused to reimburse the plan, asserting that Pennsylvania law precluded subrogation by the plan. A federal court held that the state statute prohibited the plan from enforcing the subrogation provision. The case reached the U.S. Supreme Court, which stated that ERISA preempted the application of the Pennsylvania law, and that the plan could seek subrogation. State laws that directly regulate insurance are "saved" from preemption, but this does not apply to **self-funded employee benefit plans** because they are not insurance for purposes of such laws. *FMC Corp. v. Holliday,* 498 U.S. 52, 111 S.Ct. 403, 112 L.Ed.2d 356 (1990).

◆   A District of Columbia workers' compensation statute required employers who provided health insurance for their employees to furnish equivalent health insurance coverage for injured employees eligible for workers' compensation benefits. An employer sued the district and its mayor, claiming that the act was preempted by ERISA. The U.S. Supreme Court held that **employer-sponsored health insurance programs are subject to ERISA regulation,** and any state law imposing requirements by reference to such covered programs is preempted by ERISA. ERISA superseded the workers' compensation act because the act related to a covered plan. The district could not require employers to provide equivalent health insurance coverage for injured employees eligible for workers' compensation. *District of Columbia v. Greater Washington Board of Trade,* 506 U.S. 125, 113 S.Ct. 580, 121 L.Ed.2d 513 (1992).

◆   A paper company and its parent entity employed 2,600 people in seven paper mills. A union represented employees covered by 17 of the companies' defined benefit pension plans. When the companies filed for bankruptcy, they considered, as ERISA allows, terminating the plans through the purchase of annuities. The union proposed that the companies merge the plans with its multi-employer pension plan, conveying the plans' assets to the union's plan, which would then assume the liabilities of the companies' plans. However, the companies discovered that by purchasing annuities, they could satisfy their obligations to plan participants and retain a $5 million surplus. They rejected the union's proposal and purchased the annuities. A California bankruptcy court ruled that the companies breached a fiduciary duty to fully consider the union's proposal, and the Ninth Circuit agreed. The U.S. Supreme Court reversed. It noted that the Pension Benefit Guaranty Corporation (PBGC) – the entity administering the federal insurance program that protects plan benefits – took the position that **ERISA did not permit merger as a method of terminating a defined benefits plan because the statute provides for merger as an alternative to plan termination**. The PBGC's interpretation was reasonable. *Beck v. PACE Int'l Union,* 551 U.S. 96, 127 S.Ct. 2310, 168 L.Ed.2d 1 (2007).

◆   The Multi-employer Pension Plan Amendments Act of 1980 (MPPAA), 29 U.S.C. §§ 1381-1461, requires employers who withdraw from under-funded multi-employer pension plans to pay a withdrawal liability. Employers may contest an assessed liability but are required to make payments pending appeal. An employer made contributions to a multi-employer pension fund for laundry workers in the San Francisco Bay area for several years and then ceased making contributions. The fund's trustees demanded payment of a withdrawal liability and notified the employer of its payment options. The employer refused to make payments. However, the fund did not sue the employer until eight years after it withdrew from the fund and over six years after missing its first scheduled payment. A federal court dismissed the case as barred by the MPPAA's six-year statute of limitations, and the Ninth Circuit affirmed.

The fund appealed to the U.S. Supreme Court, which rejected the employer's claim that its withdrawal commenced the statute of limitations, because the MPPAA does not require a withdrawing employer to pay anything until the plan demands payment. **The cause of action did not accrue until the employer was assessed a liability, notified of the amount and means of payment, and failed to make a required payment.** Although over six years had passed from the employer's failure to pay the first installment, the fund was entitled to recover all but the first of the installment payments. The Court reversed and remanded the lower court decisions. *Bay Area Laundry and Dry Cleaning Pension Trust Fund v. Ferbar Corp. of California, Inc.,* 522 U.S. 192, 118 S.Ct. 542, 139 L.Ed.2d 553 (1997).

♦   The MPPAA requires employers who withdraw from under-funded multi-employer pension plans to pay a fair share of the plan's unfunded liabilities. It gives withdrawing employers the option to pay their withdrawal liability in a lump sum, or to amortize the amount in level annual payments "calculated as if the first payment was made on the first day of the plan year following the plan year in which the withdrawal occurs and as if each subsequent payment was made on the first day of each subsequent plan year." A Wisconsin brewing company withdrew from an under-funded plan with a withdrawal charge of $23.3 million. Although the plan and the brewery agreed on the amount of withdrawal liability, the parties disagreed on the amount of interest that had accrued during the withdrawal year. The case reached the U.S. Supreme Court, which stated that **nothing in the MPPAA required withdrawing employers to pay an actuarially perfect fair share of withdrawal liability**. The MPPAA provision describing withdrawing employer liability did not cause interest to start accruing during the withdrawal year itself. Rather, it called for calculation as if the first payment was made on the first day of the plan year following the plan year in which withdrawal occurs. Because a withdrawing employer owed nothing to a plan until the plan demanded payment as set forth by the MPPAA, the employer was unable to determine its liability until sometime after the beginning of the withdrawal year. The Court affirmed the decision for the brewery. *Milwaukee Brewery Workers' Pension Plan v. Jos. Schlitz Brewing Co.,* 513 U.S. 414, 115 S.Ct. 981, 130 L.Ed.2d 932 (1995).

♦   A former employee of a closely held corporation claimed that the corporation and a corporate officer/shareholder violated ERISA by failing to properly administer the corporation's employee pension plan. The former employee sued the corporation and the officer/shareholder, obtaining a judgment of $187,000 against the corporation. The former employee was unable to collect on his judgment, even though the shareholder/officer continued to take cash out of the corporation as a favored creditor. The former employee then sued the corporate officer for engaging in a civil conspiracy to siphon assets from the corporation to prevent satisfaction of the ERISA judgment. The court allowed the employee to collect his judgment from the officer. The Fourth Circuit, affirmed, but the Supreme Court reversed. **ERISA contains no authority for imposing liability for an existing ERISA judgment against a third party.** There were no independent grounds for a federal court to exercise jurisdiction in this case under a corporate veil-piercing argument. There was also no merit to the former employee's argument that a federal court could exercise jurisdiction over the matter as factually interdependent with and related to the prior lawsuit. Because the case was based on theories of relief that did not exist, the district court lacked jurisdiction to hear it. *Peacock v. Thomas*, 516 U.S. 349, 116 S.Ct. 862, 133 L.Ed.2d 817 (1996).

◆ The U.S. Supreme Court held that the **Coal Industry Retiree Health Benefit Act of 1992 unconstitutionally deprived a Massachusetts employer of property** by requiring it to fund healthcare benefits for retired coal miners and their dependents, which created a severe, disproportionate and retroactive burden on the employer. The Act imposed severe retroactive liability on a class of employers that could not have anticipated it, and the liability was substantially disproportionate to the parties' experience. The employer's liability under the act was estimated at $50 to $100 million, even though it had employed no miners since before 1965, when the retirement and healthcare benefits offered were far less extensive. The act retroactively divested the employer of property long after it believed its liabilities were settled. *Eastern Enterprises v. Apfel*, 524 U.S. 498, 118 S.Ct. 2131, 141 L.Ed.2d 451 (1998).

◆ A corporation sold a subsidiary and terminated the ERISA retirement plan it funded. As a single-employer plan, all accrued benefits automatically vested. The corporation paid out the benefits that had vested, including non-reduced early retirement benefits to those employees who met both the age (62) and years of service (30) requirements. A group of employees who did not meet both requirements sued the corporation because it recouped nearly $11 million. They maintained that it was first required to distribute contingent early retirement benefits, even if unaccrued, before recouping plan assets. A Virginia federal court ruled for the corporation, and the Fourth Circuit reversed. The case reached the U.S. Supreme Court, which held that **the section of ERISA, under which this lawsuit was brought, did not create benefit entitlements** but merely provided for the orderly distribution of plan assets. However, since there were two alternative sections of ERISA, which could potentially lead to a recovery by the employees, the Court remanded the case. *Mead Corp. v. Tilley*, 490 U.S. 714, 109 S.Ct. 2156, 104 L.Ed.2d 796 (1989).

◆ A New York corporation filed for Chapter 11 bankruptcy (reorganization). At that time, it was the sponsor of three defined benefit pension plans covered by Title IV of ERISA that were chronically under-funded. At the corporation's request, the Pension Benefit Guaranty Corporation (PBGC) terminated the plans. The corporation and its employees then **negotiated new pension arrangements that provided substantially the same benefits as before**. The PBGC then issued a notice of restoration to undo the termination because the new "follow-on" plans were abusive of the insurance program. When the corporation refused to comply with the restoration, a lawsuit followed. The U.S. Supreme Court found that the PBGC's restoration decision was not arbitrary or capricious. As such, the corporation had to restore the plans that had been terminated. *Pension Benefit Guaranty Corp. v. LTV Corp.*, 496 U.S. 633, 110 S.Ct. 2668, 110 L.Ed.2d 579 (1990).

C. Real-Life Success Stories

1. *We personally brought benefits info to staff*

We were worried our staffers didn't have a clear understanding of their benefits options.

Sure, we did the usual things: email reminders with useful links and info, comprehensive open enrollment education, etc. But how many times do people see something in their inbox and say, "I'll get to it later"?

We wanted to be 100% sure our staff knew all of the benefits we offered, what had changed since last year and what options would work best. So we decided to go old-school with our benefits communications.

Old-fashioned walk-around

We began going cubicle to cubicle to talk up our open enrollment and any changes that had taken place with our benefits.

Employees felt much more comfortable talking one on one, and we were able to answer questions and convince staffers to use their benefits more wisely.

Example: After our first year of cube-to-cube chats, we had a 20% increase in employees' flexible spending accounts.

Thanks to our personalized benefits education, we're absolutely certain employees understand their options – and use them correctly.

Plus, the face-to-face contact helps build trust in our HR staff.

As a result, employees are much more apt to come to us for advice or coaching.

(An HR manager from a publications firm in Illinois)

2. *Benefits FAQ: A real time-saving tool*

Employees' benefits-related questions were taking up a lot of our time.

We were glad to provide the info, but it seemed like we were answering the same questions over and over.

Plus, we were juggling a lot of other responsibilities.

If we could cut down on the calls, emails and visits to the department to get these questions answered, we'd have more time to do other work.

That's when we decided to create a frequently-asked-questions (FAQ) page on our company intranet.

Top 10 list

We focused on the top 10 issues that came up, which included:
- change of address or marital status
- dependent eligibility, and
- enrollment dates.

With the help of IT, we added a search field. If the info they need isn't on the FAQ page, they contact us.

The FAQ makes a great handout to distribute at open enrollment, especially for those who don't visit the site. And we include it as a handout in our employee orientations.

Now that the FAQ is our employees' first stop for info, we're being contacted less frequently – and we have more time for other responsibilities.

(An office manager for a clinic in Arizona)

3.   Wellness partnership: Key we needed for results we wanted

If we were going to get anything out of our wellness program, we had to commit for the long haul.

Our early attempts at wellness consisted of directing staff to phone lines and online resources for chronic disease management and lifestyle tips.

But staffers weren't following up on the suggestions, and our healthcare costs continued to rise each year.

Our efforts to promote these resources just weren't enough to keep the services front-of-mind.

Wellness connection

If we really wanted our employees to get involved in wellness, we'd have to jump in with both feet. Our solution: Create an on-site program.

And there'd have to be flexibility in what we offered to accommodate around-the-clock shifts.

After researching our options, we decided to partner with an organization providing face-to-face wellness coaching and related services to employees in the workplace.

We had two wellness coaches available during a set number of hours each month to cover all three shifts.

Employees could schedule private meetings with the coaches to work on things like:

- setting and meeting healthy goals
- behavior and lifestyle changes
- tobacco cessation and nutrition
- stress and weight management, and
- on-the-job injury prevention.

The coaches were available via email or phone when not on-site.

Plus, they regularly coordinated companywide programs, like lunch 'n learn presentations, yoga classes, weight-management competitions, and blood pressure screenings.

The wellness coaches also performed risk assessments and biometric testing, tracked progress in a confidential database and regularly followed up with employees.

The combined data was recorded and reported biannually to show us the progress and improvements among our employees.

Seeing is believing

The best part: We didn't even need to use incentives to get employees to participate. Our wellness coaches helped them realize the true incentive was their improved quality of life.

And the employees making healthy changes then became our best advocates to help us get the word out.

Our rates haven't gone down due to health reform, but the rate increases we've experienced have been below the national average for two years in a row.

We're confident there's a direct correlation to the wellness coaching programs. These serve as visual reminders and help keep employees motivated and focused on health.

Going forward, we're sure the service will pay for itself as the employees' healthy behaviors kick in.

(A corporate communications officer for a pharmaceutical development firm in Pennsylvania)

4. Session boosted our 401(k) participation

Our employees wanted more help with financial planning advice, and they were looking to us for some guidance.

So we contacted our 401(k) vendor rep, and she agreed to partner with us to put together a presentation.

We covered everything

Since this would be our first financial planning session, we wanted to focus on the basics:

- weekly and monthly budgeting
- reducing credit card debt by paying more than the minimum balance on statements
- committing to setting aside a certain amount each paycheck for a savings account, and
- participating in our company's 401(k) plan and, for those who already did, striving to increase their contribution.

Employees received an invite to the session that listed the topics that'd be covered. We also encouraged them to come prepared with questions.

The majority of employees did attend. Some shared their own tips, like having money automatically deducted into a separate savings account.

Afterward, four people said they were signing up for the 401(k) plan at the next enrollment period.

The presentation was so successful that we're planning follow-up sessions on our flexible spending account and how to calculate retirement needs.

(An office manager for a document management firm in Maryland)

5. Benefits strategy that allows us to retain top talent

We couldn't compete with the big guys when it came to salaries.

But we refused to let that keep us from bringing in top talent. So we decided to look at the different aspects of our company that stood out – and really play them up.

We knew we had a very solid benefits package. Problem was, people didn't find out how rich our benefits were until after they were hired.

A recruiting tool

To change that, we started highlighting the "hidden paycheck" we offered: our benefits.

Instead of waiting until somebody was hired to get into benefits details, we started talking up our offerings throughout the actual hiring process.

Our strategy worked, and we attracted some top-caliber employees.

And the type of people we were bringing in seemed more focused on a long-term future with the company than before.

Reason: Our benefits reflect our values, and prospective employees see we're very dedicated to the health and well-being of our workforce.

Retention-focused

We were spending a significant amount of time using our benefits to bring in the right people.

But what about the employees we already had? We figured we could bolster our retention rate if we ramped up our regular benefits communications.

Finger on the pulse

To make sure our offerings remained in line with what our staffers wanted, we started:

- conducting employee exit interviews
- surveying current employees about their benefits
- benchmarking our offerings against the competition and sharing the results with employees, and
- sending out total-compensation statements annually.

In addition, we routinely conduct thorough examinations of all of our existing benefits to see what is – and isn't – working for us. And we make it a point to listen to employees' suggestions and, whenever possible, make the changes.

Major improvements

Emphasizing our benefits throughout the hiring process has allowed us to consistently bring in top performers.

Offering regular benefits communications – and changing our package to fit employees' needs – is what keeps them here.

By shifting the focus to our benefits, we've experienced a huge improvement in recruiting and retention.

(A senior director of HR for a law firm in Washington, D.C.)

6. *Providing investment advice has huge impact on 401(k) participation*

We had a great 401(k) plan. But quite a few employees either weren't participating or weren't taking advantage of the full company match.

We wanted to help employees do a better job of planning for retirement.

That meant one thing: employee investment education.

Dollars and sense

So we partnered with an independent investment firm, whose only motive was to help advise employees.

Since the firm didn't stand to gain from the advice it provided, employees would know they could trust its guidance.

In the know

The next step was to tell employees the new service was available to them. Together with the investment firm, we created an info packet and mailed it to each employee.

This was followed up with small group meetings held in our office, where the investment reps explained to employees the importance of asset allocation and taking advantage of the full company match.

But this was just scratching the surface.

Investment issues can get complicated, and our staffers had a range of investment goals.

Getting the most

To get the most from the advice service, the employees would need one-on-one sessions with the reps.

And to make scheduling the sessions as convenient as possible, they could arrange to meet with an investment rep in our office before, during or after work.

This way, employees could get the help without it affecting their workloads or after-hours commitments.

There was also an option to get individual recommendations over the phone.

These one-on-one sessions really had an impact. Employees got the info they needed to make the best decisions for themselves and their families.

Result: The number of employees receiving the maximum company match jumped dramatically.

As an added bonus, the number of employees enrolled in Roth 401(k) accounts almost doubled.

More to come

But we didn't stop there. Unless future financial planning is kept top of mind, it's easy for employees to get distracted with day-to-day issues.

So there needs to be an ongoing marketing effort. We're regularly sending out reminders about the service and how it can benefit employees and their families when it'll matter most – in their retirement.

(A benefits manager for an office supply firm in Milwaukee)

D. Statutes and Regulations

1. Fair Labor Standards Act (Selected Sections)

§ 201. Short title

This chapter may be cited as the "Fair Labor Standards Act of 1938."

§ 206. Minimum wage

(a) Employees engaged in commerce; home workers in Puerto Rico and Virgin Islands; employees in American Samoa; seamen on American vessels; agricultural employees

Every employer shall pay to each of his employees who in any workweek is engaged in commerce or in the production of goods for commerce, or is employed in an enterprise engaged in commerce or in the production of goods for commerce, wages at the following rates:

(1) except as otherwise provided in this section, not less than—

(A) $5.85 an hour, beginning on the 60th day after May 25, 2007;

(B) $6.55 an hour, beginning 12 months after that 60th day; and

(C) $7.25 an hour, beginning 24 months after that 60th day;

(2) if such employee is a home worker in Puerto Rico or the Virgin Islands, not less than the minimum piece rate prescribed by regulation or order; or, if no such minimum piece rate is in effect, any piece rate adopted by such employer which shall yield, to the proportion or class of employees prescribed by regulation or order, not less than the applicable minimum hourly wage rate. Such minimum piece rates or employer piece rates shall be commensurate with, and shall be paid in lieu of, the minimum hourly wage rate applicable under the provisions of this section. The Administrator, or his authorized representative, shall have power to make such regulations or orders as are necessary or appropriate to carry out any of the provisions of this paragraph, including the power without limiting the generality of the foregoing, to define any operation or occupation which is performed by such home work employees in Puerto Rico or the Virgin Islands; to establish minimum piece rates for any operation or occupation so defined; to prescribe the method and procedure for ascertaining and promulgating minimum piece rates; to prescribe standards for employer piece rates, including the proportion or class of employees who shall receive not less than the minimum hourly wage rate; to define the term "home worker"; and to prescribe the conditions under which employers, agents, contractors, and subcontractors shall cause goods to be produced by home workers;

(3) if such employee is employed as a seaman on an American vessel, not less than the rate which will provide to the employee, for the period covered by the wage payment, wages equal to compensation at the hourly rate prescribed by paragraph (1) of this subsection for all hours during such period when he was actually on duty (including periods aboard ship when the employee was on watch or was, at the direction of a superior

officer, performing work or standing by, but not including off-duty periods which are provided pursuant to the employment agreement); or

(4) if such employee is employed in agriculture, not less than the minimum wage rate in effect under paragraph (1) after December 31, 1977.

(b) Additional applicability to employees pursuant to subsequent amendatory provisions

Every employer shall pay to each of his employees (other than an employee to whom subsection (a)(5) of this section applies) who in any workweek is engaged in commerce or in the production of goods for commerce, or is employed in an enterprise engaged in commerce or in the production of goods for commerce, and who in such workweek is brought within the purview of this section by the amendments made to this chapter by the Fair Labor Standards Amendments of 1966, title IX of the Education Amendments of 1972 [20 U.S.C. 1681 et seq.], or the Fair Labor Standards Amendments of 1974, wages at the following rate: Effective after December 31, 1977, not less than the minimum wage rate in effect under subsection (a)(1) of this section.

(c) Repealed. Pub. L. 104–188, [title II], §?2104(c), Aug. 20, 1996, 110 Stat. 1929

(d) Prohibition of sex discrimination

(1) No employer having employees subject to any provisions of this section shall discriminate, within any establishment in which such employees are employed, between employees on the basis of sex by paying wages to employees in such establishment at a rate less than the rate at which he pays wages to employees of the opposite sex in such establishment for equal work on jobs the performance of which requires equal skill, effort, and responsibility, and which are performed under similar working conditions, except where such payment is made pursuant to

(i) a seniority system;

(ii) a merit system;

(iii) a system which measures earnings by quantity or quality of production; or

(iv) a differential based on any other factor other than sex: Provided, That an employer who is paying a wage rate differential in violation of this subsection shall not, in order to comply with the provisions of this subsection, reduce the wage rate of any employee.

(2) No labor organization, or its agents, representing employees of an employer having employees subject to any provisions of this section shall cause or attempt to cause such an employer to discriminate against an employee in violation of paragraph (1) of this subsection.

(3) For purposes of administration and enforcement, any amounts owing to any employee which have been withheld in violation of this subsection shall be deemed to be unpaid minimum wages or unpaid overtime compensation under this chapter.

(4) As used in this subsection, the term "labor organization" means any

organization of any kind, or any agency or employee representation committee or plan, in which employees participate and which exists for the purpose, in whole or in part, of dealing with employers concerning grievances, labor disputes, wages, rates of pay, hours of employment, or conditions of work.

(e) Employees of employers providing contract services to United States

(1) Notwithstanding the provisions of section 213 of this title (except subsections (a)(1) and (f) thereof), every employer providing any contract services (other than linen supply services) under a contract with the United States or any subcontract thereunder shall pay to each of his employees whose rate of pay is not governed by the Service Contract Act of 1965 (41 U.S.C. 351–357) or to whom subsection (a)(1) of this section is not applicable, wages at rates not less than the rates provided for in subsection (b) of this section.

(2) Notwithstanding the provisions of section 213 of this title (except subsections (a)(1) and (f) thereof) and the provisions of the Service Contract Act of 1965 [41 U.S.C. 351 et seq.] every employer in an establishment providing linen supply services to the United States under a contract with the United States or any subcontract thereunder shall pay to each of his employees in such establishment wages at rates not less than those prescribed in subsection (b) of this section, except that if more than 50 per centum of the gross annual dollar volume of sales made or business done by such establishment is derived from providing such linen supply services under any such contracts or subcontracts, such employer shall pay to each of his employees in such establishment wages at rates not less than those prescribed in subsection (a)(1) of this section.

(f) Employees in domestic service

Any employee—

(1) who in any workweek is employed in domestic service in a household shall be paid wages at a rate not less than the wage rate in effect under subsection (b) of this section unless such employee's compensation for such service would not because of section 209(a)(6) of the Social Security Act [42 U.S.C. 409 (a)(6)] constitute wages for the purposes of title II of such Act [42 U.S.C. 401 et seq.], or

(2) who in any workweek—

(A) is employed in domestic service in one or more households, and

(B) is so employed for more than 8 hours in the aggregate, shall be paid wages for such employment in such workweek at a rate not less than the wage rate in effect under subsection (b) of this section.

(g) Newly hired employees who are less than 20 years old

(1) In lieu of the rate prescribed by subsection (a)(1) of this section, any employer may pay any employee of such employer, during the first 90 consecutive calendar days after such employee is initially employed by such employer, a wage which is not less than $4.25 an hour.

(2) No employer may take any action to displace employees (including

partial displacements such as reduction in hours, wages, or employment benefits) for purposes of hiring individuals at the wage authorized in paragraph (1).

(3) Any employer who violates this subsection shall be considered to have violated section 215 (a)(3) of this title.

(4) This subsection shall only apply to an employee who has not attained the age of 20 years.

§ 207. Maximum hours

(a) Employees engaged in interstate commerce; additional applicability to employees pursuant to subsequent amendatory provisions

(1) Except as otherwise provided in this section, no employer shall employ any of his employees who in any workweek is engaged in commerce or in the production of goods for commerce, or is employed in an enterprise engaged in commerce or in the production of goods for commerce, for a workweek longer than forty hours unless such employee receives compensation for his employment in excess of the hours above specified at a rate not less than one and one-half times the regular rate at which he is employed.

(2) No employer shall employ any of his employees who in any workweek is engaged in commerce or in the production of goods for commerce, or is employed in an enterprise engaged in commerce or in the production of goods for commerce, and who in such workweek is brought within the purview of this subsection by the amendments made to this chapter by the Fair Labor Standards Amendments of 1966—

(A) for a workweek longer than forty-four hours during the first year from the effective date of the Fair Labor Standards Amendments of 1966,

(B) for a workweek longer than forty-two hours during the second year from such date, or

(C) for a workweek longer than forty hours after the expiration of the second year from such date,

unless such employee receives compensation for his employment in excess of the hours above specified at a rate not less than one and one-half times the regular rate at which he is employed.

(b) Employment pursuant to collective bargaining agreement; employment by independently owned and controlled local enterprise engaged in distribution of petroleum products

No employer shall be deemed to have violated subsection (a) of this section by employing any employee for a workweek in excess of that specified in such subsection without paying the compensation for overtime employment prescribed therein if such employee is so employed—

(1) in pursuance of an agreement, made as a result of collective bargaining by representatives of employees certified as bona fide by the National Labor Relations Board, which provides that no employee shall

be employed more than one thousand and forty hours during any period of twenty-six consecutive weeks; or

(2) in pursuance of an agreement, made as a result of collective bargaining by representatives of employees certified as bona fide by the National Labor Relations Board, which provides that during a specified period of fifty-two consecutive weeks the employee shall be employed not more than two thousand two hundred and forty hours and shall be guaranteed not less than one thousand eight hundred and forty-hours (or not less than forty-six weeks at the normal number of hours worked per week, but not less than thirty hours per week) and not more than two thousand and eighty hours of employment for which he shall receive compensation for all hours guaranteed or worked at rates not less than those applicable under the agreement to the work performed and for all hours in excess of the guaranty which are also in excess of the maximum workweek applicable to such employee under subsection (a) of this section or two thousand and eighty in such period at rates not less than one and one-half times the regular rate at which he is employed; or

(3) by an independently owned and controlled local enterprise (including an enterprise with more than one bulk storage establishment) engaged in the wholesale or bulk distribution of petroleum products if—

(A) the annual gross volume of sales of such enterprise is less than $1,000,000 exclusive of excise taxes,

(B) more than 75 per centum of such enterprise's annual dollar volume of sales is made within the State in which such enterprise is located, and

(C) not more than 25 per centum of the annual dollar volume of sales of such enterprise is to customers who are engaged in the bulk distribution of such products for resale, and such employee receives compensation for employment in excess of forty hours in any workweek at a rate not less than one and one-half times the minimum wage rate applicable to him under section 206 of this title, and if such employee receives compensation for employment in excess of twelve hours in any workday, or for employment in excess of fifty-six hours in any workweek, as the case may be, at a rate not less than one and one-half times the regular rate at which he is employed.

(c) , (d) Repealed. Pub. L. 93–259, §19(e), Apr. 8, 1974, 88 Stat. 66

(e) "Regular rate" defined

As used in this section the "regular rate" at which an employee is employed shall be deemed to include all remuneration for employment paid to, or on behalf of, the employee, but shall not be deemed to include—

(1) sums paid as gifts; payments in the nature of gifts made at Christmas time or on other special occasions, as a reward for service, the amounts of which are not measured by or dependent on hours worked, production, or efficiency;

(2) payments made for occasional periods when no work is performed

due to vacation, holiday, illness, failure of the employer to provide sufficient work, or other similar cause; reasonable payments for traveling expenses, or other expenses, incurred by an employee in the furtherance of his employer's interests and properly reimbursable by the employer; and other similar payments to an employee which are not made as compensation for his hours of employment;

(3) Sums paid in recognition of services performed during a given period if either, (a) both the fact that payment is to be made and the amount of the payment are determined at the sole discretion of the employer at or near the end of the period and not pursuant to any prior contract, agreement, or promise causing the employee to expect such payments regularly; or (b) the payments are made pursuant to a bona fide profit-sharing plan or trust or bona fide thrift or savings plan, meeting the requirements of the Administrator set forth in appropriate regulations which he shall issue, having due regard among other relevant factors, to the extent to which the amounts paid to the employee are determined without regard to hours of work, production, or efficiency; or (c) the payments are talent fees (as such talent fees are defined and delimited by regulations of the Administrator) paid to performers, including announcers, on radio and television programs;

(4) contributions irrevocably made by an employer to a trustee or third person pursuant to a bona fide plan for providing old-age, retirement, life, accident, or health insurance or similar benefits for employees;

(5) extra compensation provided by a premium rate paid for certain hours worked by the employee in any day of workweek because such hours are hours worked in excess of eight in a day or in excess of the maximum workweek applicable to such employee under subsection (a) of this section or in excess of the employee's normal working hours or regular working hours, as the case may be;

(6) extra compensation provided by a premium rate paid for work by the employee on Saturdays, Sundays, holidays, or regular days of rest, or on the sixth or seventh day of the workweek, where such premium rate is not less than one and one-half times the rate established in good faith for like work performed in nonovertime hours on other days;

(7) extra compensation provided by a premium rate paid to the employee, in pursuance of an applicable employment contract or collective-bargaining agreement, for work outside of the hours established in good faith by the contract or agreement as the basic, normal, or regular workday (not exceeding eight hours) or workweek (not exceeding the maximum workweek applicable to such employee under subsection (a) of this section,[2] where such premium rate is not less than one and one-half times the rate established in good faith by the contract or agreement for like work performed during such workday or workweek; or

(8) any value or income derived from employer-provided grants or rights provided pursuant to a stock option, stock appreciation right, or bona fide employee stock purchase program which is not otherwise excludable

under any of paragraphs (1) through (7) if—

(A) grants are made pursuant to a program, the terms and conditions of which are communicated to participating employees either at the beginning of the employee's participation in the program or at the time of the grant;

(B) in the case of stock options and stock appreciation rights, the grant or right cannot be exercisable for a period of at least 6 months after the time of grant (except that grants or rights may become exercisable because of an employee's death, disability, retirement, or a change in corporate ownership, or other circumstances permitted by regulation), and the exercise price is at least 85 percent of the fair market value of the stock at the time of grant;

(C) exercise of any grant or right is voluntary; and

(D) any determinations regarding the award of, and the amount of, employer-provided grants or rights that are based on performance are—

(i) made based upon meeting previously established performance criteria (which may include hours of work, efficiency, or productivity) of any business unit consisting of at least 10 employees or of a facility, except that, any determinations may be based on length of service or minimum schedule of hours or days of work; or

(ii) made based upon the past performance (which may include any criteria) of one or more employees in a given period so long as the determination is in the sole discretion of the employer and not pursuant to any prior contract.

(f) Employment necessitating irregular hours of work

No employer shall be deemed to have violated subsection (a) of this section by employing any employee for a workweek in excess of the maximum workweek applicable to such employee under subsection (a) of this section if such employee is employed pursuant to a bona fide individual contract, or pursuant to an agreement made as a result of collective bargaining by representatives of employees, if the duties of such employee necessitate irregular hours of work, and the contract or agreement

(1) specifies a regular rate of pay of not less than the minimum hourly rate provided in subsection (a) or (b) of section 206 of this title (whichever may be applicable) and compensation at not less than one and one-half times such rate for all hours worked in excess of such maximum workweek, and

(2) provides a weekly guaranty of pay for not more than sixty hours based on the rates so specified.

(g) Employment at piece rates

No employer shall be deemed to have violated subsection (a) of this section by employing any employee for a workweek in excess of the maximum workweek applicable to such employee under such subsection if, pursuant to an agreement or understanding arrived at between the employer and the employee before performance of the work, the amount paid to the employee for the number of hours worked by him in such workweek in excess of the maximum workweek applicable to such employee under such subsection—

(1) in the case of an employee employed at piece rates, is computed at piece rates not less than one and one-half times the bona fide piece rates applicable to the same work when performed during nonovertime hours; or

(2) in the case of an employee performing two or more kinds of work for which different hourly or piece rates have been established, is computed at rates not less than one and one-half times such bona fide rates applicable to the same work when performed during nonovertime hours; or

(3) is computed at a rate not less than one and one-half times the rate established by such agreement or understanding as the basic rate to be used in computing overtime compensation thereunder: Provided, That the rate so established shall be authorized by regulation by the Administrator as being substantially equivalent to the average hourly earnings of the employee, exclusive of overtime premiums, in the particular work over a representative period of time;

and if

(i) the employee's average hourly earnings for the workweek exclusive of payments described in paragraphs (1) through (7) of subsection (e) of this section are not less than the minimum hourly rate required by applicable law, and

(ii) extra overtime compensation is properly computed and paid on other forms of additional pay required to be included in computing the regular rate.

(h) Credit toward minimum wage or overtime compensation of amounts excluded from regular rate

(1) Except as provided in paragraph (2), sums excluded from the regular rate pursuant to subsection (e) of this section shall not be creditable toward wages required under section 206 of this title or overtime compensation required under this section.

(2) Extra compensation paid as described in paragraphs (5), (6), and (7) of subsection (e) of this section shall be creditable toward overtime compensation payable pursuant to this section.

(i) Employment by retail or service establishment

No employer shall be deemed to have violated subsection (a) of this section by employing any employee of a retail or service establishment for a workweek in excess of the applicable workweek specified therein, if

(1) the regular rate of pay of such employee is in excess of one and one-half times the minimum hourly rate applicable to him under section 206 of this title, and

(2) more than half his compensation for a representative period (not less

than one month) represents commissions on goods or services. In determining the proportion of compensation representing commissions, all earnings resulting from the application of a bona fide commission rate shall be deemed commissions on goods or services without regard to whether the computed commissions exceed the draw or guarantee.

(j) Employment in hospital or establishment engaged in care of sick, aged, or mentally ill

No employer engaged in the operation of a hospital or an establishment which is an institution primarily engaged in the care of the sick, the aged, or the mentally ill or defective who reside on the premises shall be deemed to have violated subsection (a) of this section if, pursuant to an agreement or understanding arrived at between the employer and the employee before performance of the work, a work period of fourteen consecutive days is accepted in lieu of the workweek of seven consecutive days for purposes of overtime computation and if, for his employment in excess of eight hours in any workday and in excess of eighty hours in such fourteen-day period, the employee receives compensation at a rate not less than one and one-half times the regular rate at which he is employed.

(k) Employment by public agency engaged in fire protection or law enforcement activities

No public agency shall be deemed to have violated subsection (a) of this section with respect to the employment of any employee in fire protection activities or any employee in law enforcement activities (including security personnel in correctional institutions) if—

(1) in a work period of 28 consecutive days the employee receives for tours of duty which in the aggregate exceed the lesser of

(A) 216 hours, or

(B) the average number of hours (as determined by the Secretary pursuant to section 6(c)(3) of the Fair Labor Standards Amendments of 1974) in tours of duty of employees engaged in such activities in work periods of 28 consecutive days in calendar year 1975; or

(2) in the case of such an employee to whom a work period of at least 7 but less than 28 days applies, in his work period the employee receives for tours of duty which in the aggregate exceed a number of hours which bears the same ratio to the number of consecutive days in his work period as 216 hours (or if lower, the number of hours referred to in clause (B) of paragraph (1)) bears to 28 days,

compensation at a rate not less than one and one-half times the regular rate at which he is employed.

(l) Employment in domestic service in one or more households

No employer shall employ any employee in domestic service in one or more households for a workweek longer than forty hours unless such employee receives compensation for such employment in accordance with subsection (a) of this section.

(m) Employment in tobacco industry

For a period or periods of not more than fourteen workweeks in the aggregate in any calendar year, any employer may employ any employee for a workweek in excess of that specified in subsection (a) of this section without paying the compensation for overtime employment prescribed in such subsection, if such employee—

(1) is employed by such employer—

(A) to provide services (including stripping and grading) necessary and incidental to the sale at auction of green leaf tobacco of type 11, 12, 13, 14, 21, 22, 23, 24, 31, 35, 36, or 37 (as such types are defined by the Secretary of Agriculture), or in auction sale, buying, handling, stemming, redrying, packing, and storing of such tobacco,

(B) in auction sale, buying, handling, sorting, grading, packing, or storing green leaf tobacco of type 32 (as such type is defined by the Secretary of Agriculture), or

(C) in auction sale, buying, handling, stripping, sorting, grading, sizing, packing, or stemming prior to packing, of perishable cigar leaf tobacco of type 41, 42, 43, 44, 45, 46, 51, 52, 53, 54, 55, 61, or 62 (as such types are defined by the Secretary of Agriculture); and

(2) receives for—

(A) such employment by such employer which is in excess of ten hours in any workday, and

(B) such employment by such employer which is in excess of forty-eight hours in any workweek,

compensation at a rate not less than one and one-half times the regular rate at which he is employed.

An employer who receives an exemption under this subsection shall not be eligible for any other exemption under this section.

(n) Employment by street, suburban, or interurban electric railway, or local trolley or motorbus carrier

In the case of an employee of an employer engaged in the business of operating a street, suburban or interurban electric railway, or local trolley or motorbus carrier (regardless of whether or not such railway or carrier is public or private or operated for profit or not for profit), in determining the hours of employment of such an employee to which the rate prescribed by subsection (a) of this section applies there shall be excluded the hours such employee was employed in charter activities by such employer if

(1) the employee's employment in such activities was pursuant to an agreement or understanding with his employer arrived at before engaging in such employment, and

(2) if employment in such activities is not part of such employee's regular employment.

(o) Compensatory time

(1) Employees of a public agency which is a State, a political subdivision of a State, or an interstate governmental agency may receive, in

accordance with this subsection and in lieu of overtime compensation, compensatory time off at a rate not less than one and one-half hours for each hour of employment for which overtime compensation is required by this section.

(2) A public agency may provide compensatory time under paragraph (1) only—

    (A) pursuant to—

        (i) applicable provisions of a collective bargaining agreement, memorandum of understanding, or any other agreement between the public agency and representatives of such employees; or

        (ii) in the case of employees not covered by subclause (i), an agreement or understanding arrived at between the employer and employee before the performance of the work; and

    (B) if the employee has not accrued compensatory time in excess of the limit applicable to the employee prescribed by paragraph (3).

In the case of employees described in clause (A)(ii) hired prior to April 15, 1986, the regular practice in effect on April 15, 1986, with respect to compensatory time off for such employees in lieu of the receipt of overtime compensation, shall constitute an agreement or understanding under such clause (A)(ii). Except as provided in the previous sentence, the provision of compensatory time off to such employees for hours worked after April 14, 1986, shall be in accordance with this subsection.

    (3)

    (A) If the work of an employee for which compensatory time may be provided included work in a public safety activity, an emergency response activity, or a seasonal activity, the employee engaged in such work may accrue not more than 480 hours of compensatory time for hours worked after April 15, 1986. If such work was any other work, the employee engaged in such work may accrue not more than 240 hours of compensatory time for hours worked after April 15, 1986. Any such employee who, after April 15, 1986, has accrued 480 or 240 hours, as the case may be, of compensatory time off shall, for additional overtime hours of work, be paid overtime compensation.

    (B) If compensation is paid to an employee for accrued compensatory time off, such compensation shall be paid at the regular rate earned by the employee at the time the employee receives such payment.

(4) An employee who has accrued compensatory time off authorized to be provided under paragraph (1) shall, upon termination of employment, be paid for the unused compensatory time at a rate of compensation not less than—

    (A) the average regular rate received by such employee during the last 3 years of the employee's employment, or

    (B) the final regular rate received by such employee,

    whichever is higher

(5) An employee of a public agency which is a State, political subdivision

of a State, or an interstate governmental agency—

(A) who has accrued compensatory time off authorized to be provided under paragraph (1), and

(B) who has requested the use of such compensatory time,

shall be permitted by the employee's employer to use such time within a reasonable period after making the request if the use of the compensatory time does not unduly disrupt the operations of the public agency.

(6) The hours an employee of a public agency performs court reporting transcript preparation duties shall not be considered as hours worked for the purposes of subsection (a) of this section if—

(A) such employee is paid at a per-page rate which is not less than—

(i) the maximum rate established by State law or local ordinance for the jurisdiction of such public agency,

(ii) the maximum rate otherwise established by a judicial or administrative officer and in effect on July 1, 1995, or

(iii) the rate freely negotiated between the employee and the party requesting the transcript, other than the judge who presided over the proceedings being transcribed, and

(B) the hours spent performing such duties are outside of the hours such employee performs other work (including hours for which the agency requires the employee's attendance) pursuant to the employment relationship with such public agency.

For purposes of this section, the amount paid such employee in accordance with subparagraph (A) for the performance of court reporting transcript preparation duties, shall not be considered in the calculation of the regular rate at which such employee is employed.

(7) For purposes of this subsection—

(A) the term "overtime compensation" means the compensation required by subsection (a), and

(B) the terms "compensatory time" and "compensatory time off" mean hours during which an employee is not working, which are not counted as hours worked during the applicable workweek or other work period for purposes of overtime compensation, and for which the employee is compensated at the employee's regular rate.

(p) Special detail work for fire protection and law enforcement employees; occasional or sporadic employment; substitution

(1) If an individual who is employed by a State, political subdivision of a State, or an interstate governmental agency in fire protection or law enforcement activities (including activities of security personnel in correctional institutions) and who, solely at such individual's option, agrees to be employed on a special detail by a separate or independent employer in fire protection, law enforcement, or related activities, the hours such individual was employed by such separate and independent

employer shall be excluded by the public agency employing such individual in the calculation of the hours for which the employee is entitled to overtime compensation under this section if the public agency—

(A) requires that its employees engaged in fire protection, law enforcement, or security activities be hired by a separate and independent employer to perform the special detail,

(B) facilitates the employment of such employees by a separate and independent employer, or

(C) otherwise affects the condition of employment of such employees by a separate and independent employer.

(2) If an employee of a public agency which is a State, political subdivision of a State, or an interstate governmental agency undertakes, on an occasional or sporadic basis and solely at the employee's option, part-time employment for the public agency which is in a different capacity from any capacity in which the employee is regularly employed with the public agency, the hours such employee was employed in performing the different employment shall be excluded by the public agency in the calculation of the hours for which the employee is entitled to overtime compensation under this section.

(3) If an individual who is employed in any capacity by a public agency which is a State, political subdivision of a State, or an interstate governmental agency, agrees, with the approval of the public agency and solely at the option of such individual, to substitute during scheduled work hours for another individual who is employed by such agency in the same capacity, the hours such employee worked as a substitute shall be excluded by the public agency in the calculation of the hours for which the employee is entitled to overtime compensation under this section.

(q) Maximum hour exemption for employees receiving remedial education

Any employer may employ any employee for a period or periods of not more than 10 hours in the aggregate in any workweek in excess of the maximum workweek specified in subsection (a) of this section without paying the compensation for overtime employment prescribed in such subsection, if during such period or periods the employee is receiving remedial education that is—

(1) provided to employees who lack a high school diploma or educational attainment at the eighth grade level;

(2) designed to provide reading and other basic skills at an eighth grade level or below; and

(3) does not include job specific training.

§ 213. Exemptions

(a) Minimum wage and maximum hour requirements

The provisions of sections 206 (except subsection (d) in the case of paragraph (1) of this subsection) and 207 of this title shall not apply with respect to—

(1) any employee employed in a bona fide executive, administrative, or professional capacity (including any employee employed in the capacity of academic administrative personnel or teacher in elementary or secondary schools), or in the capacity of outside salesman (as such terms are defined and delimited from time to time by regulations of the Secretary, subject to the provisions of subchapter II of chapter 5 of title 5, except that an employee of a retail or service establishment shall not be excluded from the definition of employee employed in a bona fide executive or administrative capacity because of the number of hours in his workweek which he devotes to activities not directly or closely related to the performance of executive or administrative activities, if less than 40 per centum of his hours worked in the workweek are devoted to such activities); or

(2) Repealed. Pub. L. 101–157, § 3(c)(1), Nov. 17, 1989, 103 Stat. 939.

(3) any employee employed by an establishment which is an amusement or recreational establishment, organized camp, or religious or non-profit educational conference center, if

(A) it does not operate for more than seven months in any calendar year, or

(B) during the preceding calendar year, its average receipts for any six months of such year were not more than 331/3 per centum of its average receipts for the other six months of such year, except that the exemption from sections 206 and 207 of this title provided by this paragraph does not apply with respect to any employee of a private entity engaged in providing services or facilities (other than, in the case of the exemption from section 206 of this title, a private entity engaged in providing services and facilities directly related to skiing) in a national park or a national forest, or on land in the National Wildlife Refuge System, under a contract with the Secretary of the Interior or the Secretary of Agriculture; or

(4) Repealed. Pub. L. 101–157, § 3(c)(1), Nov. 17, 1989, 103 Stat. 939.

(5) any employee employed in the catching, taking, propagating, harvesting, cultivating, or farming of any kind of fish, shellfish, crustacea, sponges, seaweeds, or other aquatic forms of animal and vegetable life, or in the first processing, canning or packing such marine products at sea as an incident to, or in conjunction with, such fishing operations, including the going to and returning from work and loading and unloading when performed by any such employee; or

(6) any employee employed in agriculture

(A) if such employee is employed by an employer who did not, during any calendar quarter during the preceding calendar year, use more than five hundred man-days of agricultural labor,

(B) if such employee is the parent, spouse, child, or other member of his employer's immediate family,

(C) if such employee

(i) is employed as a hand harvest laborer and is paid on a piece rate basis in an operation which has been, and is customarily and generally recognized as having been, paid on a piece rate basis in the region of employment,

(ii) commutes daily from his permanent residence to the farm on which he is so employed, and

(iii) has been employed in agriculture less than thirteen weeks during the preceding calendar year,

(D) if such employee (other than an employee described in clause (C) of this subsection)

(i) is sixteen years of age or under and is employed as a hand harvest laborer, is paid on a piece rate basis in an operation which has been, and is customarily and generally recognized as having been, paid on a piece rate basis in the region of employment,

(ii) is employed on the same farm as his parent or person standing in the place of his parent, and

(iii) is paid at the same piece rate as employees over age sixteen are paid on the same farm, or

(E) if such employee is principally engaged in the range production of livestock; or

(7) any employee to the extent that such employee is exempted by regulations, order, or certificate of the Secretary issued under section 214 of this title; or

(8) any employee employed in connection with the publication of any weekly, semiweekly, or daily newspaper with a circulation of less than four thousand the major part of which circulation is within the county where published or counties contiguous thereto; or

(9) Repealed. Pub. L. 93–259, § 23(a)(1), Apr. 8, 1974, 88 Stat. 69.

(10) any switchboard operator employed by an independently owned public telephone company which has not more than seven hundred and fifty stations; or

(11) Repealed. Pub. L. 93–259, § 10(a), Apr. 8, 1974, 88 Stat. 63.

(12) any employee employed as a seaman on a vessel other than an American vessel; or

(13) , (14) Repealed. Pub. L. 93–259, §§ 9(b)(1), 23 (b)(1), Apr. 8, 1974, 88 Stat. 63, 69.

(15) any employee employed on a casual basis in domestic service employment to provide babysitting services or any employee employed in domestic service employment to provide companionship services for individuals who (because of age or infirmity) are unable to care for themselves (as such terms are defined and delimited by regulations of the Secretary); or

(16) a criminal investigator who is paid availability pay under section 5545a of title 5; or

(17) any employee who is a computer systems analyst, computer programmer, software engineer, or other similarly skilled worker, whose primary duty is—

(A) the application of systems analysis techniques and procedures, including consulting with users, to determine hardware, software, or system functional specifications;

(B) the design, development, documentation, analysis, creation, testing, or modification of computer systems or programs, including prototypes, based on and related to user or system design specifications;

(C) the design, documentation, testing, creation, or modification of computer programs related to machine operating systems; or

(D) a combination of duties described in subparagraphs (A), (B), and (C) the performance of which requires the same level of skills, and

who, in the case of an employee who is compensated on an hourly basis, is compensated at a rate of not less than $27.63 an hour.

(b) Maximum hour requirements

The provisions of section 207 of this title shall not apply with respect to—

(1) any employee with respect to whom the Secretary of Transportation has power to establish qualifications and maximum hours of service pursuant to the provisions of section 31502 of title 49; or

(2) any employee of an employer engaged in the operation of a rail carrier subject to part A of subtitle IV of title 49; or

(3) any employee of a carrier by air subject to the provisions of title II of the Railway Labor Act [45 U.S.C. 181 et seq.]; or

(4) Repealed. Pub. L. 93–259, § 11(c), Apr. 8, 1974, 88 Stat. 64.

(5) any individual employed as an outside buyer of poultry, eggs, cream, or milk, in their raw or natural state; or

(6) any employee employed as a seaman; or

(7) Repealed. Pub. L. 93–259, § 21(b)(3), Apr. 8, 1974, 88 Stat. 68.

(8) Repealed. Pub. L. 95–151, § 14(b), Nov. 1, 1977, 91 Stat. 1252.

(9) any employee employed as an announcer, news editor, or chief engineer by a radio or television station the major studio of which is located

(A) in a city or town of one hundred thousand population or less, according to the latest available decennial census figures as compiled by the Bureau of the Census, except where such city or town is part of a standard metropolitan statistical area, as defined and designated by the Office of Management and Budget, which has a total population in excess of one hundred thousand, or

(B) in a city or town of twenty-five thousand population or less, which is part of such an area but is at least 40 airline miles from the principal city in such area; or

(10)

(A) any salesman, partsman, or mechanic primarily engaged in selling or servicing automobiles, trucks, or farm implements, if he is employed by a nonmanufacturing establishment primarily engaged in the business of selling such vehicles or implements to ultimate purchasers; or

(B) any salesman primarily engaged in selling trailers, boats, or aircraft, if he is employed by a nonmanufacturing establishment primarily engaged in the business of selling trailers, boats, or aircraft to ultimate purchasers; or

(11) any employee employed as a driver or driver's helper making local deliveries, who is compensated for such employment on the basis of trip rates, or other delivery payment plan, if the Secretary shall find that such plan has the general purpose and effect of reducing hours worked by such employees to, or below, the maximum workweek applicable to them under section 207 (a) of this title; or

(12) any employee employed in agriculture or in connection with the operation or maintenance of ditches, canals, reservoirs, or waterways, not owned or operated for profit, or operated on a sharecrop basis, and which are used exclusively for supply and storing of water, at least 90 percent of which was ultimately delivered for agricultural purposes during the preceding calendar year; or

(13) any employee with respect to his employment in agriculture by a farmer, notwithstanding other employment of such employee in connection with livestock auction operations in which such farmer is engaged as an adjunct to the raising of livestock, either on his own account or in conjunction with other farmers, if such employee

(A) is primarily employed during his workweek in agriculture by such farmer, and

(B) is paid for his employment in connection with such livestock auction operations at a wage rate not less than that prescribed by section 206 (a)(1) of this title; or

(14) any employee employed within the area of production (as defined by the Secretary) by an establishment commonly recognized as a country elevator, including such an establishment which sells products and services used in the operation of a farm, if no more than five employees are employed in the establishment in such operations; or

(15) any employee engaged in the processing of maple sap into sugar (other than refined sugar) or syrup; or

(16) any employee engaged

(A) in the transportation and preparation for transportation of fruits or vegetables, whether or not performed by the farmer, from the farm to a place of first processing or first marketing within the same State, or

(B) in transportation, whether or not performed by the farmer, between the farm and any point within the same State of persons employed or to be employed in the harvesting of fruits or vegetables; or

(17) any driver employed by an employer engaged in the business of operating taxicabs; or

(18) , (19) Repealed. Pub. L. 93–259, §§ 15(c), 16 (b), Apr. 8, 1974, 88 Stat. 65.

(20) any employee of a public agency who in any workweek is employed in fire protection activities or any employee of a public agency who in any workweek is employed in law enforcement activities (including security personnel in correctional institutions), if the public agency employs during the workweek less than 5 employees in fire protection or law enforcement activities, as the case may be; or

(21) any employee who is employed in domestic service in a household and who resides in such household; or

(22) Repealed. Pub. L. 95–151, § 5, Nov. 1, 1977, 91 Stat. 1249.

(23) Repealed. Pub. L. 93–259, § 10(b)(3), Apr. 8, 1974, 88 Stat. 64.

(24) any employee who is employed with his spouse by a nonprofit educational institution to serve as the parents of children—

(A) who are orphans or one of whose natural parents is deceased, or

(B) who are enrolled in such institution and reside in residential facilities of the institution,

while such children are in residence at such institution, if such employee and his spouse reside in such facilities, receive, without cost, board and lodging from such institution, and are together compensated, on a cash basis, at an annual rate of not less than $10,000; or

(25) , (26) Repealed. Pub. L. 95–151, §§ 6(a), 7 (a), Nov. 1, 1977, 91 Stat. 1249, 1250.

(27) any employee employed by an establishment which is a motion picture theater; or

(28) any employee employed in planting or tending trees, cruising, surveying, or felling timber, or in preparing or transporting logs or other forestry products to the mill, processing plant, railroad, or other transportation terminal, if the number of employees employed by his employer in such forestry or lumbering operations does not exceed eight;

(29) any employee of an amusement or recreational establishment located in a national park or national forest or on land in the National Wildlife Refuge System if such employee

(A) is an employee of a private entity engaged in providing services or facilities in a national park or national forest, or on land in the National Wildlife Refuge System, under a contract with the Secretary of the Interior or the Secretary of Agriculture, and

(B) receives compensation for employment in excess of fifty-six hours in any workweek at a rate not less than one and one-half times the regular rate at which he is employed; or

(30) a criminal investigator who is paid availability pay under section 5545a of title 5.

(c) Child labor requirements

(1) Except as provided in paragraph (2) or (4), the provisions of section 212 of this title relating to child labor shall not apply to any employee employed in agriculture outside of school hours for the school district where such employee is living while he is so employed, if such employee—

(A) is less than twelve years of age and

(i) is employed by his parent, or by a person standing in the place of his parent, on a farm owned or operated by such parent or person, or

(ii) is employed, with the consent of his parent or person standing in the place of his parent, on a farm, none of the employees of which are (because of subsection (a)(6)(A) of this section) required to be paid at the wage rate prescribed by section 206 (a)(5) [1] of this title,

(B) is twelve years or thirteen years of age and

(i) such employment is with the consent of his parent or person standing in the place of his parent, or

(ii) his parent or such person is employed on the same farm as such employee, or

(C) is fourteen years of age or older.

(2) The provisions of section 212 of this title relating to child labor shall apply to an employee below the age of sixteen employed in agriculture in an occupation that the Secretary of Labor finds and declares to be particularly hazardous for the employment of children below the age of sixteen, except where such employee is employed by his parent or by a person standing in the place of his parent on a farm owned or operated by such parent or person.

(3) The provisions of section 212 of this title relating to child labor shall not apply to any child employed as an actor or performer in motion pictures or theatrical productions, or in radio or television productions.

(4)

(A) An employer or group of employers may apply to the Secretary for a waiver of the application of section 212 of this title to the employment for not more than eight weeks in any calendar year of individuals who are less than twelve years of age, but not less than ten years of age, as hand harvest laborers in an agricultural operation which has been, and is customarily and generally recognized as being, paid on a piece rate basis in the region in which such individuals would be employed. The Secretary may not grant such a waiver unless he finds, based on objective data submitted by the applicant, that—

(i) the crop to be harvested is one with a particularly short harvesting season and the application of section 212 of this title would cause severe economic disruption in the industry of the employer or group of employers applying for the waiver;

(ii) the employment of the individuals to whom the waiver would apply would not be deleterious to their health or well-being;

(iii) the level and type of pesticides and other chemicals used would not have an adverse effect on the health or well-being of the individuals to whom the waiver would apply;

(iv) individuals age twelve and above are not available for such employment; and

(v) the industry of such employer or group of employers has traditionally and substantially employed individuals under twelve years of age without displacing substantial job opportunities for individuals over sixteen years of age.

(B) Any waiver granted by the Secretary under subparagraph (A) shall require that—

(i) the individuals employed under such waiver be employed outside of school hours for the school district where they are living while so employed;

(ii) such individuals while so employed commute daily from their permanent residence to the farm on which they are so employed; and

(iii) such individuals be employed under such waiver

(I) for not more than eight weeks between June 1 and October 15 of any calendar year, and

(II) in accordance with such other terms and conditions as the Secretary shall prescribe for such individuals' protection.

(5)

(A) In the administration and enforcement of the child labor provisions of this chapter, employees who are 16 and 17 years of age shall be permitted to load materials into, but not operate or unload materials from, scrap paper balers and paper box compactors—

(i) that are safe for 16- and 17-year-old employees loading the scrap paper balers or paper box compactors; and

(ii) that cannot be operated while being loaded.

(B) For purposes of subparagraph (A), scrap paper balers and paper box compactors shall be considered safe for 16- or 17-year-old employees to load only if—

(i)

(I) the scrap paper balers and paper box compactors meet the American National Standards Institute's Standard ANSI Z245.5–1990 for scrap paper balers and Standard ANSI Z245.2–1992 for paper box compactors; or

(II) the scrap paper balers and paper box compactors meet an applicable standard that is adopted by the American National Standards Institute after August 6, 1996, and that is certified by the Secretary to be at least as protective of the safety of minors as the standard described in subclause (I);

(ii) the scrap paper balers and paper box compactors include an on-off switch incorporating a key-lock or other system and the control of the system is maintained in the custody of employees who are 18 years of age or older;

(iii) the on-off switch of the scrap paper balers and paper box compactors is maintained in an off position when the scrap paper balers and paper box compactors are not in operation; and

(iv) the employer of 16- and 17-year-old employees provides notice, and posts a notice, on the scrap paper balers and paper box compactors stating that—

(I) the scrap paper balers and paper box compactors meet the applicable standard described in clause (i);

(II) 16- and 17-year-old employees may only load the scrap paper balers and paper box compactors; and

(III) any employee under the age of 18 may not operate or unload the scrap paper balers and paper box compactors.

The Secretary shall publish in the Federal Register a standard that is adopted by the American National Standards Institute for scrap paper balers or paper box compactors and certified by the Secretary to be protective of the safety of minors under clause (i)(II).

(C)

(i) Employers shall prepare and submit to the Secretary reports—

(I) on any injury to an employee under the age of 18 that requires medical treatment (other than first aid) resulting from the employee's contact with a scrap paper baler or paper box compactor during the loading, operation, or unloading of the baler or compactor; and

(II) on any fatality of an employee under the age of 18 resulting from the employee's contact with a scrap paper baler or paper box compactor during the loading, operation, or unloading of the baler or compactor.

(ii) The reports described in clause (i) shall be used by the Secretary to determine whether or not the implementation of subparagraph (A) has had any effect on the safety of children.

(iii) The reports described in clause (i) shall provide—

(I) the name, telephone number, and address of the employer and the address of the place of employment where the incident occurred;

(II) the name, telephone number, and address of the employee who suffered an injury or death as a result of the incident;

(III) the date of the incident;

(IV) a description of the injury and a narrative describing how the incident occurred; and

(V) the name of the manufacturer and the model number of the scrap paper baler or paper box compactor involved in the incident.

(iv) The reports described in clause (i) shall be submitted to the Secretary promptly, but not later than 10 days after the date on which an incident relating to an injury or death occurred.

(v) The Secretary may not rely solely on the reports described in clause (i) as the basis for making a determination that any of the employers described in clause (i) has violated a provision of section 212 of this title relating to oppressive child labor or a regulation or order issued pursuant to section 212 of this title. The Secretary shall, prior to making such a determination, conduct an investigation and inspection in accordance with section 212 (b) of this title.

(vi) The reporting requirements of this subparagraph shall expire 2 years after August 6, 1996.

(6) In the administration and enforcement of the child labor provisions of this chapter, employees who are under 17 years of age may not drive automobiles or trucks on public roadways. Employees who are 17 years of age may drive automobiles or trucks on public roadways only if—

(A) such driving is restricted to daylight hours;

(B) the employee holds a State license valid for the type of driving involved in the job performed and has no records of any moving violation at the time of hire;

(C) the employee has successfully completed a State approved driver education course;

(D) the automobile or truck is equipped with a seat belt for the driver and any passengers and the employee's employer has instructed the employee that the seat belts must be used when driving the automobile or truck;

(E) the automobile or truck does not exceed 6,000 pounds of gross vehicle weight;

(F) such driving does not involve—

(i) the towing of vehicles;

(ii) route deliveries or route sales;

(iii) the transportation for hire of property, goods, or passengers;

(iv) urgent, time-sensitive deliveries;

(v) more than two trips away from the primary place of employment in any single day for the purpose of delivering goods of the employee's employer to a customer (other than urgent, time-sensitive deliveries);

(vi) more than two trips away from the primary place of employment in any single day for the purpose of transporting passengers (other than employees of the employer);

(vii) transporting more than three passengers (including employees of the employer); or

(viii) driving beyond a 30 mile radius from the employee's place of employment; and

(G) such driving is only occasional and incidental to the employee's employment.

For purposes of subparagraph (G), the term "occasional and incidental" is no more than one-third of an employee's worktime in any workday and no more than 20 percent of an employee's worktime in any workweek.

(7)

(A)

(i) Subject to subparagraph (B), in the administration and enforcement of the child labor provisions of this chapter, it shall not be considered oppressive child labor for a new entrant into the workforce to be employed inside or outside places of business where machinery is used to process wood products.

(ii) In this paragraph, the term "new entrant into the workforce" means an individual who—

(I) is under the age of 18 and at least the age of 14, and

(II) by statute or judicial order is exempt from compulsory school attendance beyond the eighth grade.

(B) The employment of a new entrant into the workforce under subparagraph (A) shall be permitted—

(i) if the entrant is supervised by an adult relative of the entrant or is supervised by an adult member of the same religious sect or division as the entrant;

(ii) if the entrant does not operate or assist in the operation of power-driven woodworking machines;

(iii) if the entrant is protected from wood particles or other flying debris within the workplace by a barrier appropriate to the potential hazard of such wood particles or flying debris or by maintaining a sufficient distance from machinery in operation; and

(iv) if the entrant is required to use personal protective equipment to prevent exposure to excessive levels of noise and saw dust.

(d) Delivery of newspapers and wreathmaking

The provisions of sections 206, 207, and 212 of this title shall not apply with respect to any employee engaged in the delivery of newspapers to the consumer or to any homeworker engaged in the making of wreaths composed principally of natural holly, pine, cedar, or other evergreens (including the harvesting of the evergreens or other forest products used in making such wreaths).

(e) Maximum hour requirements and minimum wage employees

The provisions of section 207 of this title shall not apply with respect to employees for whom the Secretary of Labor is authorized to establish minimum wage rates as provided in section 206 (a)(3) [1] of this title, except with respect to employees for whom such rates are in effect; and with respect to such employees the Secretary may make rules and regulations providing reasonable limitations and allowing reasonable variations, tolerances, and exemptions to and from any or all of the provisions of section 207 of this title if he shall find, after a public hearing on the matter, and taking into account the factors set forth in section 206 (a)(3) [1] of this title, that economic conditions warrant such action.

(f) Employment in foreign countries and certain United States territories

The provisions of sections 206, 207, 211, and 212 of this title shall not apply with respect to any employee whose services during the workweek are performed in a workplace within a foreign country or within territory under the jurisdiction of the United States other than the following: a State of the United States; the District of Columbia; Puerto Rico; the Virgin Islands; outer Continental Shelf lands defined in the Outer Continental Shelf Lands Act (ch. 345, 67 Stat. 462) [43 U.S.C. 1331 et seq.]; American Samoa; Guam; Wake Island; Eniwetok Atoll; Kwajalein Atoll; and Johnston Island.

(g) Certain employment in retail or service establishments, agriculture

The exemption from section 206 of this title provided by paragraph (6) of subsection (a) of this section shall not apply with respect to any employee employed by an establishment

(1) which controls, is controlled by, or is under common control with, another establishment the activities of which are not related for a common business purpose to, but materially support the activities of the establishment employing such employee; and

(2) whose annual gross volume of sales made or business done, when combined with the annual gross volume of sales made or business done by each establishment which controls, is controlled by, or is under common control with, the establishment employing such employee, exceeds $10,000,000 (exclusive of excise taxes at the retail level which are separately stated).

(h) Maximum hour requirement: fourteen workweek limitation

The provisions of section 207 of this title shall not apply for a period or periods of not more than fourteen workweeks in the aggregate in any calendar year to any employee who—

(1) is employed by such employer—

(A) exclusively to provide services necessary and incidental to the ginning of cotton in an establishment primarily engaged in the ginning of cotton;

(B) exclusively to provide services necessary and incidental to the receiving, handling, and storing of raw cotton and the compressing of raw cotton when performed at a cotton warehouse or compress-warehouse facility, other than one operated in conjunction with a cotton mill, primarily engaged in storing and compressing;

(C) exclusively to provide services necessary and incidental to the receiving, handling, storing, and processing of cottonseed in an establishment primarily engaged in the receiving, handling, storing, and processing of cottonseed; or

(D) exclusively to provide services necessary and incidental to the processing of sugar cane or sugar beets in an establishment primarily engaged in the processing of sugar cane or sugar beets; and

(2) receives for—

(A) such employment by such employer which is in excess of ten hours in any workday, and

(B) such employment by such employer which is in excess of forty-eight hours in any workweek,

compensation at a rate not less than one and one-half times the regular rate at which he is employed.

Any employer who receives an exemption under this subsection shall not be eligible for any other exemption under this section or section 207 of this title.

(i) Cotton ginning

The provisions of section 207 of this title shall not apply for a period or periods of not more than fourteen workweeks in the aggregate in any period of fifty-two consecutive weeks to any employee who—

(1) is engaged in the ginning of cotton for market in any place of employment located in a county where cotton is grown in commercial quantities; and

(2) receives for any such employment during such workweeks—

(A) in excess of ten hours in any workday, and

(B) in excess of forty-eight hours in any workweek,

compensation at a rate not less than one and one-half times the regular rate at which he is employed. No week included in any fifty-two week period for purposes of the preceding sentence may be included for such purposes in any other fifty-two week period.

(j) Processing of sugar beets, sugar beet molasses, or sugar cane

The provisions of section 207 of this title shall not apply for a period or periods of not more than fourteen workweeks in the aggregate in any period of fifty-two consecutive weeks to any employee who—

(1) is engaged in the processing of sugar beets, sugar beet molasses, or sugar cane into sugar (other than refined sugar) or syrup; and

(2) receives for any such employment during such workweeks—

(A) in excess of ten hours in any workday, and

(B) in excess of forty-eight hours in any workweek,

compensation at a rate not less than one and one-half times the regular rate at which he is employed. No week included in any fifty-two week period for purposes of the preceding sentence may be included for such purposes in any other fifty-two week period.

2. Lilly Ledbetter Fair Pay Act of 2009

SECTION 1. SHORT TITLE.

This Act may be cited as the 'Lilly Ledbetter Fair Pay Act of 2009'.

SEC. 2. FINDINGS.

Congress finds the following:

(1) The Supreme Court in Ledbetter v. Goodyear Tire & Rubber Co., 550 U.S. 618 (2007), significantly impairs statutory protections against discrimination in compensation that Congress established and that have been bedrock principles of American law for decades. The Ledbetter decision undermines those statutory protections by unduly restricting the time period in which victims of discrimination can challenge and recover for discriminatory compensation decisions or other practices, contrary to the intent of Congress.

(2) The limitation imposed by the Court on the filing of discriminatory compensation claims ignores the reality of wage discrimination and is at odds with the robust application of the civil rights laws that Congress intended.

(3) With regard to any charge of discrimination under any law, nothing in this Act is intended to preclude or limit an aggrieved person's right to introduce evidence of an unlawful employment practice that has occurred outside the time for filing a charge of discrimination.

(4) Nothing in this Act is intended to change current law treatment of when pension distributions are considered paid.

SEC. 3. DISCRIMINATION IN COMPENSATION BECAUSE OF RACE, COLOR, RELIGION, SEX, OR NATIONAL ORIGIN.

Section 706(e) of the Civil Rights Act of 1964 (42 U.S.C. 2000e-5(e)) is amended by adding at the end the following:

(3)(A) For purposes of this section, an unlawful employment practice occurs, with respect to discrimination in compensation in violation of this title, when a discriminatory compensation decision or other practice is adopted, when an individual becomes subject to a discriminatory compensation decision or other practice, or when an individual is affected by application of a discriminatory compensation decision or other practice, including each time wages, benefits, or other compensation is paid, resulting in whole or in part from such a decision or other practice.

(B) In addition to any relief authorized by section 1977A of the Revised Statutes (42 U.S.C. 1981a), liability may accrue and an aggrieved person may obtain relief as provided in subsection (g)(1), including recovery of back pay for up to two years preceding the filing of the charge, where the unlawful employment practices that have occurred during the charge filing period are similar or related to unlawful employment practices with regard to discrimination in compensation that occurred outside the time for filing a charge.

SEC. 4. DISCRIMINATION IN COMPENSATION BECAUSE OF AGE.

Section 7(d) of the Age Discrimination in Employment Act of 1967 (29 U.S.C. 626(d)) is amended--

(1) in the first sentence--

(A) by redesignating paragraphs (1) and (2) as subparagraphs (A) and (B), respectively; and

(B) by striking '(d)' and inserting '(d)(1)';

(2) in the third sentence, by striking 'Upon' and inserting the following: (2) 'Upon'; and (3) by adding at the end the following:

(3) For purposes of this section, an unlawful practice occurs, with respect to discrimination in compensation in violation of this Act, when a discriminatory compensation decision or other practice is adopted, when a person becomes subject to a discriminatory compensation decision or other practice, or when a person is affected by application of a discriminatory compensation decision or other practice, including each time wages, benefits, or other compensation is paid, resulting in whole or in part from such a decision or other practice.

SEC. 5. APPLICATION TO OTHER LAWS.

(a) Americans With Disabilities Act of 1990- The amendments made by section 3 shall apply to claims of discrimination in compensation brought under title I and section 503 of the Americans with Disabilities Act of 1990 (42 U.S.C. 12111 et seq., 12203), pursuant to section 107(a) of such Act (42 U.S.C. 12117(a)), which adopts the powers, remedies, and procedures set forth in section 706 of the Civil Rights Act of 1964 (42 U.S.C. 2000e-5).

(b) Rehabilitation Act of 1973- The amendments made by section 3 shall apply to claims of discrimination in compensation brought under sections 501 and 504 of the Rehabilitation Act of 1973 (29 U.S.C. 791, 794), pursuant to--

(1) sections 501(g) and 504(d) of such Act (29 U.S.C. 791(g), 794(d)), respectively, which adopt the standards applied under title I of the Americans with Disabilities Act of 1990 for determining whether a violation has occurred in a complaint alleging employment discrimination; and

(2) paragraphs (1) and (2) of section 505(a) of such Act (29 U.S.C. 794a(a)) (as amended by subsection (c)).

(c) Conforming Amendments-

(1) REHABILITATION ACT OF 1973- Section 505(a) of the

Rehabilitation Act of 1973 (29 U.S.C. 794a(a)) is amended--

(A) in paragraph (1), by inserting after '(42 U.S.C. 2000e-5 (f) through (k))' the following: '(and the application of section 706(e)(3) (42 U.S.C. 2000e-5(e)(3)) to claims of discrimination in compensation)'; and

(B) in paragraph (2), by inserting after '1964' the following: '(42 U.S.C. 2000d et seq.) (and in subsection (e)(3) of section 706 of such Act (42 U.S.C. 2000e-5), applied to claims of discrimination in compensation)'.

(2) CIVIL RIGHTS ACT OF 1964- Section 717 of the Civil Rights Act of 1964 (42 U.S.C. 2000e-16) is amended by adding at the end the following:

(f) Section 706(e)(3) shall apply to complaints of discrimination in compensation under this section.

(3) AGE DISCRIMINATION IN EMPLOYMENT ACT OF 1967- Section 15(f) of the Age Discrimination in Employment Act of 1967 (29 U.S.C. 633a(f)) is amended by striking 'of section' and inserting 'of sections 7(d)(3) and'.

SEC. 6. EFFECTIVE DATE.

This Act, and the amendments made by this Act, take effect as if enacted on May 28, 2007 and apply to all claims of discrimination in compensation under title VII of the Civil Rights Act of 1964 (42 U.S.C. 2000e et seq.), the Age Discrimination in Employment Act of 1967 (29 U.S.C. 621 et seq.), title I and section 503 of the Americans with Disabilities Act of 1990, and sections 501 and 504 of the Rehabilitation Act of 1973, that are pending on or after that date.

3. Employee Retirement Income Security Act (Selected Sections)

§ 1021. Duty of disclosure and reporting

(a) Summary plan description and information to be furnished to participants and beneficiaries

The administrator of each employee benefit plan shall cause to be furnished in accordance with section 1024 (b) of this title to each participant covered under the plan and to each beneficiary who is receiving benefits under the plan—

(1) a summary plan description described in section 1022 (a)(1) [1] of this title; and

(2) the information described in subsection (f) and sections 1024 (b)(3) and 1025 (a) and (c) of this title.

(b) Reports to be filed with Secretary of Labor

The administrator shall, in accordance with section 1024 (a) of this title, file with the Secretary—

(1) the annual report containing the information required by section 1023 of this title; and

(2) terminal and supplementary reports as required by subsection (c) of this section.

(c) Terminal and supplementary reports

(1) Each administrator of an employee pension benefit plan which is winding up its affairs (without regard to the number of participants remaining in the plan) shall, in accordance with regulations prescribed by the Secretary, file such terminal reports as the Secretary may consider necessary. A copy of such report shall also be filed with the Pension Benefit Guaranty Corporation.

(2) The Secretary may require terminal reports to be filed with regard to any employee welfare benefit plan which is winding up its affairs in accordance with regulations promulgated by the Secretary.

(3) The Secretary may require that a plan described in paragraph (1) or (2) file a supplementary or terminal report with the annual report in the year such plan is terminated and that a copy of such supplementary or terminal report in the case of a plan described in paragraph (1) be also filed with the Pension Benefit Guaranty Corporation.

(d) Notice of failure to meet minimum funding standards

(1) In general

If an employer maintaining a plan other than a multiemployer plan fails to make a required installment or other payment required to meet the minimum funding standard under section 1082 of this title to a plan before the 60th day following the due date for such installment or other payment, the employer shall notify each participant and beneficiary (including an alternate payee as defined in section 1056 (d)(3)(K) of this title) of such plan of such failure. Such notice shall be made at such time and in such manner as the Secretary may prescribe.

(2) Subsection not to apply if waiver pending

This subsection shall not apply to any failure if the employer has filed a waiver request under section 1083 of this title with respect to the plan year to which the required installment relates, except that if the waiver request is denied, notice under paragraph (1) shall be provided within 60 days after the date of such denial.

(3) Definitions

For purposes of this subsection, the terms "required installment" and "due date" have the same meanings given such terms by section 1083 (j) of this title.

(e) Notice of transfer of excess pension assets to health benefits accounts

(1) Notice to participants

Not later than 60 days before the date of a qualified transfer by an employee pension benefit plan of excess pension assets to a health benefits account, the administrator of the plan shall notify (in such manner as the Secretary may prescribe) each participant and beneficiary under the plan of such transfer. Such notice shall include information with respect to the amount of excess pension assets, the portion to be transferred, the amount of health benefits liabilities expected to be provided with the assets transferred, and the amount of pension benefits of the participant which will be nonforfeitable immediately after the transfer.

(2) Notice to Secretaries, administrator, and employee organizations

(A) In general

Not later than 60 days before the date of any qualified transfer by an employee pension benefit plan of excess pension assets to a health benefits account, the employer maintaining the plan from which the transfer is made shall provide the Secretary, the Secretary of the Treasury, the administrator, and each employee organization representing participants in the plan a written notice of such transfer. A copy of any such notice shall be available for inspection in the principal office of the administrator.

(B) Information relating to transfer

Such notice shall identify the plan from which the transfer is made, the amount of the transfer, a detailed accounting of assets projected to be held by the plan immediately before and immediately after the transfer, and the current liabilities under the plan at the time of the transfer.

(C) Authority for additional reporting requirements

The Secretary may prescribe such additional reporting requirements as may be necessary to carry out the purposes of this section.

(3) Definitions

For purposes of paragraph (1), any term used in such paragraph which is also used in section 420 of title 26 (as in effect on August 17, 2006) shall have the same meaning as when used in such section.

(f) Defined benefit plan funding notices

(1) In general

The administrator of a defined benefit plan to which subchapter III applies shall for each plan year provide a plan funding notice to the Pension Benefit Guaranty Corporation, to each plan participant and beneficiary, to each labor organization representing such participants or beneficiaries, and, in the case of a multiemployer plan, to each employer that has an obligation to contribute to the plan.

(2) Information contained in notices

(A) Identifying information

Each notice required under paragraph (1) shall contain identifying information, including the name of the plan, the address and phone number of the plan administrator and the plan's principal administrative officer, each plan sponsor's employer identification number, and the plan number of the plan.

(B) Specific information

A plan funding notice under paragraph (1) shall include—

(i)

(I) in the case of a single-employer plan, a statement as to whether the plan's funding target attainment percentage (as defined in section 1083 (d)(2) of this title) for the plan year to which the notice relates, and for the 2 preceding plan years, is at least 100 percent (and, if not, the actual percentages), or

(II) in the case of a multiemployer plan, a statement as to whether the plan's funded percentage (as defined in section 1085 (i) of this title) for the plan year to which the notice relates, and for the 2 preceding plan years, is at least 100 percent (and, if not, the actual percentages),

(ii)

(I) in the case of a single-employer plan, a statement of—

(aa) the total assets (separately stating the prefunding balance and the funding standard carryover balance) and liabilities of the plan, determined in the same manner as under section 1083 of this title, for the plan year to which the notice relates and for the 2 preceding plan years, as reported in the annual report for each such plan year, and

(bb) the value of the plan's assets and liabilities for the plan year to which the notice relates as of the last day of the plan year to which the notice relates determined using the asset valuation under subclause (II) of section 1306 (a)(3)(E)(iii) of this title and the interest rate under section 1306 (a)(3)(E)(iv) of this title, and

(II) in the case of a multiemployer plan, a statement, for the plan year to which the notice relates and the preceding 2 plan years, of the value of the plan assets (determined both in the same manner as under section 1084 of this title and under the rules of subclause (I)(bb)) and the value of the plan liabilities (determined in the same manner as under section 1084 of this title except that the method specified in section 1085 (i)(8) of this title shall be used),

(iii) a statement of the number of participants who are—

(I) retired or separated from service and are receiving benefits,

(II) retired or separated participants entitled to future benefits, and

(III) active participants under the plan,

(iv) a statement setting forth the funding policy of the plan and the asset allocation of investments under the plan (expressed as percentages of total assets) as of the end of the plan year to which the notice relates,

(v) in the case of a multiemployer plan, whether the plan was in critical or endangered status under section 1085 of this title for such plan year and, if so—

(I) a statement describing how a person may obtain a copy of the plan's funding improvement or rehabilitation plan, as appropriate, adopted under section 1085 of this title and the actuarial and financial data that demonstrate any action taken by the plan toward fiscal improvement, and

(II) a summary of any funding improvement plan, rehabilitation plan, or modification thereof adopted under section 1085 of this title during the plan year to which the notice relates,

(vi) in the case of any plan amendment, scheduled benefit increase or reduction, or other known event taking effect in the current plan year and having a material effect on plan liabilities or assets for the year (as defined in regulations by the Secretary), an explanation of the amendment, schedule increase or reduction, or event, and a projection to the end of such plan year of the effect of the amendment, scheduled increase or reduction, or event on plan liabilities,

(vii)

(I) in the case of a single-employer plan, a summary of the rules governing termination of single-employer plans under subtitle C of subchapter III, or

(II) in the case of a multiemployer plan, a summary of the rules governing reorganization or insolvency, including the limitations on benefit payments,

(viii) a general description of the benefits under the plan which are eligible to be guaranteed by the Pension Benefit Guaranty Corporation, along with an explanation of the limitations on the guarantee and the circumstances under which such limitations apply,

(ix) a statement that a person may obtain a copy of the annual report of the plan filed under section 1024 (a) of this title upon request, through the Internet website of the Department of Labor, or through an Intranet website maintained by the applicable plan sponsor (or plan administrator on behalf of the plan sponsor), and

(x) if applicable, a statement that each contributing sponsor, and each member of the contributing sponsor's controlled group, of the single-employer plan was required to provide the information under section 1310 of this title for the plan year to which the notice relates.

(C) Other information

Each notice under paragraph (1) shall include—

(i) in the case of a multiemployer plan, a statement that the plan administrator shall provide, upon written request, to any labor organization representing plan participants and beneficiaries and any employer that has an obligation to contribute to the plan, a copy of the annual report filed with the Secretary under section 1024 (a) of this title, and

(ii) any additional information which the plan administrator elects to include to the extent not inconsistent with regulations prescribed by the Secretary.

(3) Time for providing notice

(A) In general

Any notice under paragraph (1) shall be provided not later than 120 days after the end of the plan year to which the notice relates.

(B) Exception for small plans

In the case of a small plan (as such term is used under section 1083 (g)(2)(B) of this title) any notice under paragraph (1) shall be provided upon filing of the annual report under section 1024 (a) of this title.

(4) Form and manner

Any notice under paragraph (1)—

(A) shall be provided in a form and manner prescribed in regulations of the Secretary,

(B) shall be written in a manner so as to be understood by the average plan participant, and

(C) may be provided in written, electronic, or other appropriate form to the extent such form is reasonably accessible to persons to whom the notice is required to be provided.

(g) Reporting by certain arrangements

The Secretary may, by regulation, require multiple employer welfare arrangements providing benefits consisting of medical care (within the meaning of section 1191b (a)(2) of this title) which are not group health plans to report, not more frequently than annually, in such form and such manner as the Secretary may require for the purpose of determining the extent to which the requirements of part 7 are being carried out in connection with such benefits.

(h) Simple retirement accounts

(1) No employer reports

Except as provided in this subsection, no report shall be required under this section by an employer maintaining a qualified salary reduction arrangement under section 408 (p) of title 26.

(2) Summary description

The trustee of any simple retirement account established pursuant to a qualified salary reduction arrangement under section 408 (p) of title 26 shall provide to the employer maintaining the arrangement each year a description containing the following information:

(A) The name and address of the employer and the trustee.

(B) The requirements for eligibility for participation.

(C) The benefits provided with respect to the arrangement.

(D) The time and method of making elections with respect to the arrangement.

(E) The procedures for, and effects of, withdrawals (including rollovers) from the arrangement.

(3) Employee notification

The employer shall notify each employee immediately before the period for which an election described in section 408 (p)(5)(C) of title 26 may be made of the employee's opportunity to make such election. Such notice shall include a copy of the description described in paragraph (2).

(i) Notice of blackout periods to participant or beneficiary under individual account plan

(1) Duties of plan administrator

In advance of the commencement of any blackout period with respect to an individual account plan, the plan administrator shall notify the plan participants and beneficiaries who are affected by such action in accordance with this subsection.

(2) Notice requirements

(A) In general

The notices described in paragraph (1) shall be written in a manner calculated to be understood by the average plan participant and shall include—

(i) the reasons for the blackout period,

(ii) an identification of the investments and other rights affected,

(iii) the expected beginning date and length of the blackout period,

(iv) in the case of investments affected, a statement that the participant or beneficiary should evaluate the appropriateness of their current investment decisions in light of their inability to direct or diversify assets credited to their accounts during the blackout period, and

(v) such other matters as the Secretary may require by regulation.

(B) Notice to participants and beneficiaries

Except as otherwise provided in this subsection, notices described in paragraph (1) shall be furnished to all participants and beneficiaries under the plan to whom the blackout period applies at least 30 days in advance of the blackout period.

(C) Exception to 30-day notice requirement

In any case in which—

(i) a deferral of the blackout period would violate the requirements of subparagraph (A) or (B) of section 1104 (a)(1) of this title, and a fiduciary of the plan reasonably so determines in writing, or

(ii) the inability to provide the 30-day advance notice is due to events that were unforeseeable or circumstances beyond the reasonable control of the plan administrator, and a fiduciary of the plan reasonably so determines in writing, subparagraph (B) shall not apply, and the notice shall be furnished to all participants and beneficiaries under the plan to whom the blackout period applies as soon as reasonably possible under the circumstances unless such a notice in advance of the termination of the blackout period is impracticable.

(D) Written notice

The notice required to be provided under this subsection shall be in writing, except that such notice may be in electronic or other form to the extent that such form is reasonably accessible to the recipient.

(E) Notice to issuers of employer securities subject to blackout period

In the case of any blackout period in connection with an individual account plan, the plan administrator shall provide timely notice of such blackout period to the issuer of any employer securities subject to such blackout period.

(3) Exception for blackout periods with limited applicability

In any case in which the blackout period applies only to 1 or more participants or beneficiaries in connection with a merger, acquisition, divestiture, or similar transaction involving the plan or plan sponsor and occurs solely in connection with becoming or ceasing to be a participant or beneficiary under the plan by reason of such merger, acquisition, divestiture, or transaction, the requirement of this subsection that the notice be provided to all participants and beneficiaries shall be treated as met if the notice required under paragraph (1) is provided to such participants or beneficiaries to whom the blackout period applies as soon as reasonably practicable.

(4) Changes in length of blackout period

If, following the furnishing of the notice pursuant to this subsection, there is a change in the beginning date or length of the blackout period (specified in such notice pursuant to paragraph (2)(A)(iii)), the administrator shall provide affected participants and beneficiaries notice of the change as soon as reasonably practicable. In relation to the extended blackout period, such notice shall meet the requirements of paragraph (2)(D) and shall specify any material change in the matters referred to in clauses (i) through (v) of paragraph (2)(A).

(5) Regulatory exceptions

The Secretary may provide by regulation for additional exceptions to the requirements of this subsection which the Secretary determines are in the interests of participants and beneficiaries.

(6) Guidance and model notices

The Secretary shall issue guidance and model notices which meet the requirements of this subsection.

(7) Blackout period

For purposes of this subsection—

(A) In general

The term "blackout period" means, in connection with an individual account plan, any period for which any ability of participants or beneficiaries under the plan, which is otherwise available under the terms of such plan, to direct or diversify assets credited to their accounts, to obtain loans from the plan, or to obtain distributions from the plan is temporarily suspended, limited, or restricted, if such suspension, limitation, or restriction is for any period of more than 3 consecutive business days.

(B) Exclusions

The term "blackout period" does not include a suspension, limitation, or restriction—

(i) which occurs by reason of the application of the securities laws (as defined in section 78c (a)(47) of title 15),

(ii) which is a change to the plan which provides for a regularly scheduled suspension, limitation, or restriction which is disclosed to participants or beneficiaries through any summary of material modifications, any materials describing specific investment alternatives under the plan, or any changes thereto, or

(iii) which applies only to 1 or more individuals, each of whom is the participant, an alternate payee (as defined in section 1056 (d)(3)(K) of this title), or any other beneficiary pursuant to a qualified domestic relations order (as defined in section 1056 (d)(3)(B)(i) of this title).

(8) Individual account plan

(A) In general

For purposes of this subsection, the term "individual account plan" shall have the meaning provided such term in section 1002 (34) of this title, except that such term shall not include a one-participant retirement plan.

(B) One-participant retirement plan

For purposes of subparagraph (A), the term "one-participant retirement plan" means a retirement plan that on the first day of the plan year—

(i) covered only one individual (or the individual and the individual's spouse) and the individual (or the individual and the individual's spouse) owned 100 percent of the plan sponsor (whether or not incorporated), or

(ii) covered only one or more partners (or partners and their spouses) in the plan sponsor.

(j) Notice of funding-based limitation on certain forms of distribution

The plan administrator of a single-employer plan shall provide a written notice to plan participants and beneficiaries within 30 days—

(1) after the plan has become subject to a restriction described in paragraph (1) or (3) of section 1056 (g) of this title),[2]

(2) in the case of a plan to which section 1056 (g)(4) of this title applies, after the valuation date for the plan year described in section 1056 (g)(4)(A) of this title for which the plan's adjusted funding target

attainment percentage for the plan year is less than 60 percent (or, if earlier, the date such percentage is deemed to be less than 60 percent under section 1056 (g)(7) of this title), and

(3) at such other time as may be determined by the Secretary of the Treasury.

The notice required to be provided under this subsection shall be in writing, except that such notice may be in electronic or other form to the extent that such form is reasonably accessible to the recipient. The Secretary of the Treasury, in consultation with the Secretary, shall have the authority to prescribe rules applicable to the notices required under this subsection.

(k) Multiemployer plan information made available on request

(1) In general

Each administrator of a multiemployer plan shall, upon written request, furnish to any plan participant or beneficiary, employee representative, or any employer that has an obligation to contribute to the plan—

(A) a copy of any periodic actuarial report (including any sensitivity testing) received by the plan for any plan year which has been in the plan's possession for at least 30 days,

(B) a copy of any quarterly, semi-annual, or annual financial report prepared for the plan by any plan investment manager or advisor or other fiduciary which has been in the plan's possession for at least 30 days, and

(C) a copy of any application filed with the Secretary of the Treasury requesting an extension under section 1084 of this title or section 431 (d) of title 26 and the determination of such Secretary pursuant to such application.

(2) Compliance

Information required to be provided under paragraph (1)—

(A) shall be provided to the requesting participant, beneficiary, or employer within 30 days after the request in a form and manner prescribed in regulations of the Secretary,

(B) may be provided in written, electronic, or other appropriate form to the extent such form is reasonably accessible to persons to whom the information is required to be provided, and

(C) shall not—

(i) include any individually identifiable information regarding any plan participant, beneficiary, employee, fiduciary, or contributing employer, or

(ii) reveal any proprietary information regarding the plan, any contributing employer, or entity providing services to the plan.

Subparagraph (C)(i) shall not apply to individually identifiable information with respect to any plan investment manager or adviser, or with respect to any other person (other than an employee of the plan) preparing a financial report required to be included under paragraph (1)(B).

(3) Limitations

In no case shall a participant, beneficiary, or employer be entitled under this subsection to receive more than one copy of any report or application described in paragraph (1) during any one 12-month period. The administrator may make a reasonable charge to cover copying, mailing, and other costs of furnishing copies of information pursuant to paragraph (1). The Secretary may by regulations prescribe the maximum amount which will constitute a reasonable charge under the preceding sentence.

(l) Notice of potential withdrawal liability

(1) In general

The plan sponsor or administrator of a multiemployer plan shall, upon written request, furnish to any employer who has an obligation to contribute to the plan a notice of—

(A) the estimated amount which would be the amount of such employer's withdrawal liability under part 1 of subtitle E of subchapter III if such employer withdrew on the last day of the plan year preceding the date of the request, and

(B) an explanation of how such estimated liability amount was determined, including the actuarial assumptions and methods used to determine the value of the plan liabilities and assets, the data regarding employer contributions, unfunded vested benefits, annual changes in the plan's unfunded vested benefits, and the application of any relevant limitations on the estimated withdrawal liability.

For purposes of subparagraph (B), the term "employer contribution" means, in connection with a participant, a contribution made by an employer as an employer of such participant.

(2) Compliance

Any notice required to be provided under paragraph (1)—

(A) shall be provided in a form and manner prescribed in regulations of the Secretary to the requesting employer within—

(i) 180 days after the request, or

(ii) subject to regulations of the Secretary, such longer time as may be necessary in the case of a plan that determines withdrawal liability based on any method described under paragraph (4) or (5) of section 1391 (c) of this title; and

(B) may be provided in written, electronic, or other appropriate form to the extent such form is reasonably accessible to employers to whom the information is required to be provided.

(3) Limitations

In no case shall an employer be entitled under this subsection to receive more than one notice described in paragraph (1) during any one 12-month period. The person required to provide such notice may make a reasonable charge to cover copying, mailing, and other costs of furnishing such notice pursuant to paragraph (1). The Secretary may by regulations prescribe the maximum amount which will constitute a reasonable charge under the preceding sentence.

(m) Notice of right to divest

Not later than 30 days before the first date on which an applicable individual of an applicable individual account plan is eligible to exercise the right under section 1054 (j) of this title to direct the proceeds from the divestment of employer securities with respect to any type of contribution, the administrator shall provide to such individual a notice—

(1) setting forth such right under such section, and

(2) describing the importance of diversifying the investment of retirement account assets.

The notice required by this subsection shall be written in a manner calculated to be understood by the average plan participant and may be delivered in written, electronic, or other appropriate form to the extent that such form is reasonably accessible to the recipient.

(n) Cross reference

For regulations relating to coordination of reports to the Secretaries of Labor and the Treasury, see section 1204 of this title.

§ 1104. Fiduciary duties

(a) Prudent man standard of care

(1) Subject to sections 1103 (c) and (d), 1342, and 1344 of this title, a fiduciary shall discharge his duties with respect to a plan solely in the interest of the participants and beneficiaries and—

(A) for the exclusive purpose of:

(i) providing benefits to participants and their beneficiaries; and

(ii) defraying reasonable expenses of administering the plan;

(B) with the care, skill, prudence, and diligence under the circumstances then prevailing that a prudent man acting in a like capacity and familiar with such matters would use in the conduct of an enterprise of a like character and with like aims;

(C) by diversifying the investments of the plan so as to minimize the risk of large losses, unless under the circumstances it is clearly prudent not to do so; and

(D) in accordance with the documents and instruments governing the plan insofar as such documents and instruments are consistent with the provisions of this subchapter and subchapter III of this chapter.

(2) In the case of an eligible individual account plan (as defined in section 1107 (d)(3) of this title), the diversification requirement of paragraph (1)(C) and the prudence requirement (only to the extent that it requires diversification) of paragraph (1)(B) is not violated by acquisition or holding of qualifying employer real property or qualifying employer securities (as defined in section 1107 (d)(4) and (5) of this title).

(b) Indicia of ownership of assets outside jurisdiction of district courts

Except as authorized by the Secretary by regulations, no fiduciary may maintain the indicia of ownership of any assets of a plan outside the jurisdiction of the district courts of the United States.

(c) Control over assets by participant or beneficiary

(1)

(A) In the case of a pension plan which provides for individual accounts and permits a participant or beneficiary to exercise control over the assets in his account, if a participant or beneficiary exercises control over the assets in his account (as determined under regulations of the Secretary)—

(i) such participant or beneficiary shall not be deemed to be a fiduciary by reason of such exercise, and

(ii) no person who is otherwise a fiduciary shall be liable under this part for any loss, or by reason of any breach, which results from such participant's or beneficiary's exercise of control, except that this clause shall not apply in connection with such participant or beneficiary for any blackout period during which the ability of such participant or beneficiary to direct the investment of the assets in his or her account is suspended by a plan sponsor or fiduciary.

(B) If a person referred to in subparagraph (A)(ii) meets the requirements of this subchapter in connection with authorizing and implementing the blackout period, any person who is otherwise a fiduciary shall not be liable under this subchapter for any loss occurring during such period.

(C) For purposes of this paragraph, the term "blackout period" has the meaning given such term by section 1021 (i)(7) of this title.

(2) In the case of a simple retirement account established pursuant to a qualified salary reduction arrangement under section 408 (p) of title 26, a participant or beneficiary shall, for purposes of paragraph (1), be treated as exercising control over the assets in the account upon the earliest of—

(A) an affirmative election among investment options with respect to the initial investment of any contribution,

(B) a rollover to any other simple retirement account or individual retirement plan, or

(C) one year after the simple retirement account is established.

No reports, other than those required under section 1021 (g) of this title, shall be required with respect to a simple retirement account established pursuant to such a qualified salary reduction arrangement.

(3) In the case of a pension plan which makes a transfer to an individual retirement account or annuity of a designated trustee or issuer under section 401 (a)(31)(B) of title 26, the participant or beneficiary shall, for purposes of paragraph (1), be treated as exercising control over the assets in the account or annuity upon—

(A) the earlier of—

(i) a rollover of all or a portion of the amount to another individual retirement account or annuity; or

(ii) one year after the transfer is made; or

(B) a transfer that is made in a manner consistent with guidance provided by the Secretary.

(4)

(A) In any case in which a qualified change in investment options occurs in connection with an individual account plan, a participant or beneficiary shall not be treated for purposes of paragraph (1) as not exercising control over the assets in his account in connection with such change if the requirements of subparagraph (C) are met in connection with such change.

(B) For purposes of subparagraph (A), the term "qualified change in investment options" means, in connection with an individual account plan, a change in the investment options offered to the participant or beneficiary under the terms of the plan, under which—

(i) the account of the participant or beneficiary is reallocated among one or more remaining or new investment options which are offered in lieu of one or more investment options offered immediately prior to the effective date of the change, and

(ii) the stated characteristics of the remaining or new investment options provided under clause (i), including characteristics relating to risk and rate of return, are, as of immediately after the change, reasonably similar to those of the existing investment options as of immediately before the change.

(C) The requirements of this subparagraph are met in connection with a qualified change in investment options if—

(i) at least 30 days and no more than 60 days prior to the effective date of the change, the plan administrator furnishes written notice of the change to the participants and beneficiaries, including information comparing the existing and new investment options and an explanation that, in the absence of affirmative investment instructions from the participant or beneficiary to the contrary, the account of the participant or beneficiary will be invested in the manner described in subparagraph (B),

(ii) the participant or beneficiary has not provided to the plan administrator, in advance of the effective date of the change, affirmative investment instructions contrary to the change, and

(iii) the investments under the plan of the participant or beneficiary as in effect immediately prior to the effective date of the change were the product of the exercise by such participant or beneficiary of control over the assets of the account within the meaning of paragraph (1).

(5) Default investment arrangements.—

(A) In general.— For purposes of paragraph (1), a participant or beneficiary in an individual account plan meeting the notice requirements of subparagraph (B) shall be treated as exercising control over the assets in the account with respect to the amount of contributions and earnings which, in the absence of an investment election by the participant or beneficiary, are invested by the plan in accordance with regulations prescribed by the Secretary. The regulations under this subparagraph shall provide guidance on the appropriateness of designating default investments that include a mix of asset classes consistent with capital preservation or long-term capital appreciation, or a blend of both.

(B) Notice requirements.—

(i) In general.— The requirements of this subparagraph are met if each participant or beneficiary—

(I) receives, within a reasonable period of time before each plan year, a notice explaining the employee's right under the plan to designate how contributions and earnings will be invested and explaining how, in the absence of any investment election by the participant or beneficiary, such contributions and earnings will be invested, and

(II) has a reasonable period of time after receipt of such notice and before the beginning of the plan year to make such designation.

(ii) Form of notice.— The requirements of clauses (i) and (ii) of section 401 (k)(12)(D) of title 26 shall apply with respect to the notices described in this subparagraph.

(d) Plan terminations

(1) If, in connection with the termination of a pension plan which is a single-employer plan, there is an election to establish or maintain a qualified replacement plan, or to increase benefits, as provided under section 4980 (d) of title 26, a fiduciary shall discharge the fiduciary's duties under this subchapter and subchapter III of this chapter in accordance with the following requirements:

(A) In the case of a fiduciary of the terminated plan, any requirement—

(i) under section 4980 (d)(2)(B) of title 26 with respect to the transfer of assets from the terminated plan to a qualified replacement plan, and

(ii) under section 4980 (d)(2)(B)(ii) or 4980 (d)(3) of title 26 with respect to any increase in benefits under the terminated plan.

(B) In the case of a fiduciary of a qualified replacement plan, any requirement—

(i) under section 4980 (d)(2)(A) of title 26 with respect to participation in the qualified replacement plan of active participants in the terminated plan,

(ii) under section 4980 (d)(2)(B) of title 26 with respect to the receipt of assets from the terminated plan, and

(iii) under section 4980 (d)(2)(C) of title 26 with respect to the allocation of assets to participants of the qualified replacement plan.

(2) For purposes of this subsection—

(A) any term used in this subsection which is also used in section 4980 (d) of title 26 shall have the same meaning as when used in such section, and

(B) any reference in this subsection to title 26 shall be a reference to title 26 as in effect immediately after the enactment of the Omnibus Budget Reconciliation Act of 1990.

§ 1321. Coverage

(a) Plans covered

Except as provided in subsection (b) of this section, this subchapter applies to any plan (including a successor plan) which, for a plan year—

(1) is an employee pension benefit plan (as defined in paragraph (2) of section 1002 of this title) established or maintained—

(A) by an employer engaged in commerce or in any industry or activity affecting commerce, or

(B) by any employee organization, or organization representing employees, engaged in commerce or in any industry or activity affecting commerce, or

(C) by both, which has, in practice, met the requirements of part I of subchapter D of chapter 1 of title 26 (as in effect for the preceding 5 plan years of the plan) applicable to the plans described in paragraph (2) for the preceding 5 plan years; or

(2) is, or has been determined by the Secretary of the Treasury to be, a plan described in section 401 (a) of title 26, or which meets, or has been determined by the Secretary of the Treasury to meet, the requirements of section 404 (a)(2) of title 26.

For purposes of this subchapter, a successor plan is considered to be a continuation of a predecessor plan. For this purpose, unless otherwise specifically indicated in this subchapter, a successor plan is a plan which covers a group of employees which includes substantially the same employees as a previously established plan, and provides substantially the same benefits as that plan provided.

(b) Plans not covered

This section does not apply to any plan—

(1) which is an individual account plan, as defined in paragraph (34) of section 1002 of this title,[1]

(2) established and maintained for its employees by the Government of the United States, by the government of any State or political subdivision thereof, or by any agency or instrumentality of any of the foregoing, or to

which the Railroad Retirement Act of 1935 or 1937 [45 U.S.C. 231 et seq.] applies and which is financed by contributions required under that Act, or which is described in the last sentence of section 1002 (32) of this title [2]

(3) which is a church plan as defined in section 414 (e) of title 26, unless that plan has made an election under section 410 (d) of title 26, and has notified the corporation in accordance with procedures prescribed by the corporation, that it wishes to have the provisions of this part apply to it,[1]

(4)

    (A) established and maintained by a society, order, or association described in section 501 (c)(8) or (9) of title 26, if no part of the contributions to or under the plan is made by employers of participants in the plan, or

    (B) of which a trust described in section 501 (c)(18) of title 26 is a part;

(5) which has not at any time after September 2, 1974, provided for employer contributions;

(6) which is unfunded and which is maintained by an employer primarily for the purpose of providing deferred compensation for a select group of management or highly compensated employees;

(7) which is established and maintained outside of the United States primarily for the benefit of individuals substantially all of whom are nonresident aliens;

(8) which is maintained by an employer solely for the purpose of providing benefits for certain employees in excess of the limitations on contributions and benefits imposed by section 415 of title 26 on plans to which that section applies, without regard to whether the plan is funded, and, to the extent that a separable part of a plan (as determined by the corporation) maintained by an employer is maintained for such purpose, that part shall be treated for purposes of this subchapter, as a separate plan which is an excess benefit plan;

(9) which is established and maintained exclusively for substantial owners;

(10) of an international organization which is exempt from taxation under the International Organizations Immunities Act [22 U.S.C. 288 et seq.];

(11) maintained solely for the purpose of complying with applicable workmen's compensation laws or unemployment compensation or disability insurance laws;

(12) which is a defined benefit plan, to the extent that it is treated as an individual account plan under paragraph (35)(B) of section 1002 of this title; or

(13) established and maintained by a professional service employer which does not at any time after September 2, 1974, have more than 25 active participants in the plan.

(c) Definitions

    (1) For purposes of subsection (b)(1) of this section, the term "individual

account plan" does not include a plan under which a fixed benefit is promised if the employer or his representative participated in the determination of that benefit.

(2) For purposes of this paragraph and for purposes of subsection (b)(13) of this section—

   (A) the term "professional service employer" means any proprietorship, partnership, corporation, or other association or organization

      (i) owned or controlled by professional individuals or by executors or administrators of professional individuals,

      (ii) the principal business of which is the performance of professional services, and

   (B) the term "professional individuals" includes but is not limited to, physicians, dentists, chiropractors, osteopaths, optometrists, other licensed practitioners of the healing arts, attorneys at law, public accountants, public engineers, architects, draftsmen, actuaries, psychologists, social or physical scientists, and performing artists.

(3) In the case of a plan established and maintained by more than one professional service employer, the plan shall not be treated as a plan described in subsection (b)(13) of this section if, at any time after September 2, 1974, the plan has more than 25 active participants.

(d) Substantial owner defined

For purposes of subsection (b)(9), the term "substantial owner" means an individual who, at any time during the 60-month period ending on the date the determination is being made—

   (1) owns the entire interest in an unincorporated trade or business,

   (2) in the case of a partnership, is a partner who owns, directly or indirectly, more than 10 percent of either the capital interest or the profits interest in such partnership, or

   (3) in the case of a corporation, owns, directly or indirectly, more than 10 percent in value of either the voting stock of that corporation or all the stock of that corporation.

For purposes of paragraph (3), the constructive ownership rules of section 1563 (e) of title 26 (other than paragraph (3)(C) thereof) shall apply, including the application of such rules under section 414 (c) of title 26.

CHAPTER THREE

Setting and Communicating Rules and Policies

I. EMPLOYEE HANDBOOKS

A. Overview

Employee handbooks and manuals are usually intended only as a guide for both employer and employee. Yet, these documents can modify at-will employment if they do not clearly state that they are nothing more than a guide.

Courts generally require employers to conspicuously state that the handbook does not create an employment contract to avoid having the handbook construed as a contract. Language in the handbook indicating that the handbook does not create a contract should stand out from the rest of the manual. This can be done by using bold and/or capital letters and presenting the language in a separate paragraph.

Handbooks should be written in clear, understandable language and should take a positive tone. Although there is no fixed format, subject-matter areas typically addressed in handbooks include:

- hours of operation
- how salaries are set, paid, and changed
- benefits, such as vacation and insurance
- attendance requirements
- conduct standards and discipline
- drug, tobacco and alcohol use
- employee safety
- discrimination and harassment, and
- complaint reporting and resolution.

Handbooks should be periodically reviewed for currency and continuing accuracy. In addition, it is important that employees acknowledge their receipt of your handbook in writing.

B. Judicial Decisions

♦   After 28 years, and two years shy of qualifying for a "Class C" pension, a West Virginia employee was fired. He claimed that the firing was for financial reasons and that it **violated the company's well-established policy of making major employment decisions on the basis of seniority** (because several less-senior employees continued working for the company in jobs that he could perform). He also asserted that the company's handbook created an implied contract that the company violated. A federal court ruled against him, finding that the handbook did not alter the at-will nature of the relationship. Thus, even if the company violated its own internal policy regarding seniority, the employment remained at will, and the court refused to enforce the internal policy. The employee also failed to show that there was a substantial public policy against firing employees to save on pension obligations so as to override the at-will doctrine. *Veltri v. Graybar Electric Co., Inc.,* No. 5:09CV101, 2010 WL 2365446 (N.D. W.Va. 6/9/10).

♦   After 16 years as a driver for a company in Illinois, an employee was informed that his position was being eliminated due to budgetary issues. The employee sued for breach of contract, alleging he was wrongfully discharged because a less-senior employee was retained. **He asserted that the employee manual's seniority provisions required the company to terminate the other employee first.** The Appellate Court of Illinois disagreed. The manual did not constitute a contract between the parties. It contained a disclaimer stating that the manual was intended to serve as a general outline of company policy, and that it did not create a contract, express or implied. Thus, the seniority provisions of the manual did not require the company to terminate the other employee first. *Ivory v. Specialized Assistance Services, Inc.,* 365 Ill.App.3d 544, 850 N.E.2d 230 (Ill. App. Ct. 2006).

♦   A Massachusetts investment company employee was recruited to be a sales rep for the company, making him eligible for incentive compensation. Company policy at that time did not provide for the loss of incentive compensation upon termination. Later, the company issued a new handbook, which changed that policy, eliminating incentive compensation upon termination. The employee was then let go in a sales group restructuring. He received severance pay of $137,933, including a bonus of over $58,000. He nevertheless sued, claiming he was due incentive compensation after his discharge. The Appeals Court of Massachusetts disagreed. **The new handbook modified the incentive compensation agreement between the parties**, and the company properly fired him as part of a cost-cutting measure because he remained an at-will employee. *York v. Zurich Scudder Investments, Inc.,* 849 N.E.2d 892 (Mass. App. Ct. 2006).

♦   An airline in North Carolina hired a pilot and gave him a handbook addressing seniority, progressive discipline, and other terms and conditions of employment. It provided a three-step warning process for most offenses. When the pilot became unavailable for an assignment, he was not given progressive discipline, but was instead sent a termination letter. He sued the airline for breach of contract, alleging that it should have taken the seniority and progressive discipline provisions of the handbook into account. A federal court ruled for the airline, deciding that the handbook did not modify the at-will employment relationship. **The seniority and progressive discipline provisions did not imply that the airline could not fire the pilot** for an unspecified major infraction. Further, the pilot signed a document acknowledging that the employment was at will. He had been properly fired. *Norman v. Tradewinds Airlines, Inc.,* 286 F.Supp.2d 575 (M.D.N.C. 2003).

♦   A Michigan employer maintained an employment handbook declaring that employees would not be discharged without good cause. The employer later added disclaimer language to the handbook, stating that it did not constitute a contract of employment and that the employment relationship was at will. One longtime human resources employee, who had been hired prior to adoption of the handbook, claimed that her supervisor gave her a poor work evaluation after she refused to wear a dress to a company function. She was eventually laid off in a reduction in force while her male supervisor and several other younger, less senior males were retained. She sued the employer and supervisor for breach of contract and employment discrimination. The case reached the Supreme Court of Michigan, which noted that **the handbook policy did not overcome the presumption of employment at will**. It contained a specific disclaimer that no just-cause employment contract existed. The employee's discrimination claims also failed because she failed to prove that discrimination was a motivating factor in her layoff. The reduction in force had been based on economic factors. *Lytle v. Malady,* 579 N.W.2d 906 (Mich. 1998).

♦   A Wyoming mining company distributed employee handbooks to four supervisors, which stated that they could be terminated only for cause. The handbooks established 90-day probationary periods, after which an employee became "permanent," and stated that layoffs would generally be made in the reverse order of seniority. The employer later issued a series of handbooks that qualified these provisions by specifying that employment remained at will. It laid off the four supervisory employees while retaining some less experienced employees with better performance ratings. The supervisors sued for breach of contract, breach of an implied covenant of good faith and fair dealing and reliance upon the earlier handbooks. A federal court granted pretrial judgment to the employer, and the supervisors appealed. The Tenth Circuit observed that the handbooks were sufficiently ambiguous to prevent pretrial judgment on the issue of whether they reasonably created an expectation that there would be no dismissals without cause and that the company would perform layoffs by seniority. The case required a trial. *McIlravy v. Kerr-McGee Corp.,* 119 F.3d 876 (10th Cir. 1997).

♦   A company hired a pension benefits manager as a salaried employee and gave her a copy of the employee handbook, which contained a termination section for hourly and nonexempt employees (which she was not). The handbook noted that warnings normally were given before an employee was fired. When the manager was terminated without warning for what her supervisors perceived was poor performance, she sued for breach of contract, among other claims. The case reached the South Carolina Court of Appeals, which noted that the handbook did not apply to the manager. And even if it did, **nothing in the handbook outlined progressive disciplinary procedures in mandatory terms**. Finally, even if the company gave other salaried employees a warning before firing them, it was not required to do the same for the manager. At-will employment was presumed and no disclaimer was needed in the handbook. *Grant v. Mount Vernon Mills, Inc.,* 370 S.C. 138, 634 S.E.2d 15 (S.C. Ct. App. 2006).

♦   A company in Vermont had a personnel manual that described progressive discipline and just cause termination policies for employee misconduct. It stated that two written warnings would be given before termination. When the company experienced an economic slowdown, it attempted to reorganize, and one employee resisted changes a new manager tried to institute. She received a letter of reprimand from the company's president, but the letter stated that it was not a disciplinary warning. A month later she was fired. She sued, claiming breach of an implied contract that she would only be fired for just cause after progressive discipline. The Vermont Supreme Court held that **the letter of reprimand established the company's intent to abide by its progressive discipline policy**. Even though the employee could have been laid off for economic reasons without progressive discipline, she was fired for insubordination. *Havill v. Woodstock Soapstone Co.*, 865 A.2d 335 (Vt. 2004).

♦   A 55-year-old manager of a company in Massachusetts claimed that he was improperly fired. He asserted that he should have been progressively disciplined under the employee handbook and the "Guide to Corporate Conduct." He claimed that the real reason for the termination was age discrimination. The company argued that the manager attempted to misuse company property for his personal benefit; that he retaliated against another employee who refused to cooperate in that misuse; and that he had an abusive management style. The First Circuit Court of Appeals held that **the manager was not entitled to progressive discipline**. Nothing in the handbook or the guide promised progressive discipline. And even if the company generally applied progressive discipline to its employees, there was never any such policy for management. *Joyal v. Hasbro, Inc.*, 380 F.3d 14 (1st Cir. 2004).

♦   An Iowa healthcare center administrator had a poor working relationship with her supervisor. She believed that the supervisor wanted her to withhold information from an auditor. The supervisor allegedly told the center's owners that she would quit unless they fired the administrator. The center fired the administrator without warning for lack of leadership and inability to provide continuity. She obtained unemployment compensation benefits and then sued the center and its owners for breach of contract and intentional interference with her employment contract. The court awarded compensatory and punitive damages to the administrator and held that the owners were jointly liable for compensatory damages and individually responsible for punitive damages. The Supreme Court of Iowa affirmed, finding that the language of the center's employee handbook was sufficiently definite to create an employment contract. The administrator had a **right to receive notice of any deficiencies in her performance under the handbook's progressive disciplinary policy**. Because the employer had failed to follow these procedures, the breach of contract action was appropriate. Corporate officers or directors may be held personally liable if they fail to act in good faith to protect the interests of the corporation. Here, the employment contract had been terminated because of the administrator's failure to perform an illegal act in violation of public policy, and the owners were liable for the damage award. *Jones v. Lake Park Care Center, Inc.*, 569 N.W.2d 369 (Iowa 1997).

♦   A New Jersey maintenance mechanic worked for a large manufacturing company that had distributed an employment manual containing a four-step disciplinary policy. The company found some of its property in the mechanic's locker and fired him for theft, one of several grounds listed for immediate dismissal. The mechanic sued the employer, claiming that it had violated the disciplinary procedure in the manual. The court granted the employer pretrial judgment, finding that the manual did not create an implied employment contract. The appeals court reversed. The Supreme Court of New Jersey stated that **an employment manual that fails to include a clear and prominent disclaimer may create an enforceable contract** even when the employment is otherwise terminable at will. If the manual is sufficiently definite to raise the reasonable expectations of employees concerning job security provisions, the provisions may be construed as contractual promises. The case was reversed and remanded to the trial court to decide whether the manual created a reasonable expectation of job security that formed an implied employment contract. The jury was then to determine whether the mechanic was guilty of stealing or unauthorized possession of company property. *Witkowski v. Thomas J. Lipton, Inc.,* 136 N.J. 385, 643 A.2d 546 (N.J. 1994).

♦   A South Dakota FedEx driver complained that he experienced offensive and harassing conduct. Shortly thereafter, his supervisors investigated his delivery records due to suspicious delays and gaps in delivery times and found that he had scanned at least one package as delivered prior to delivery in order to meet scheduled delivery times. He was fired and sued for wrongful discharge. The company asserted that its **handbook expressly identified him as an at-will employee and that there was no public policy exception allowing him to succeed in his lawsuit.** The case reached the Eighth Circuit, which agreed that his discharge was permissible. The handbook clearly made his employment at will, and any harassment he endured was not actionable under Title VII or state law. The termination did not violate a substantial public policy. *Semple v. Federal Express Corp.,* 566 F.3d 788 (8th Cir. 2009).

♦   A Texas nurse fell while moving a patient. A month later she spoke with a co-worker about receiving medical treatment. The co-worker told her she would have to undergo a drug screening as part of any treatment at the company's facilities. She chose not to undergo the drug screen, which raised suspicions and resulted in the company requesting a for-cause drug screen. She eventually agreed to the drug screen, but resigned before the results came back (positive for marijuana and a narcotic). She then sued the company for negligence, and also asserted that it owed her $2,458 for the cash value of her accrued time off pursuant to the employee handbook. The Texas Court of Appeals held that the company was not negligent and noted that **the handbook clearly identified itself as a "guide" rather than a contract.** Thus, the paid time-off policy was voluntary and could be changed at any time. *Drake v. Wilson N. Jones Medical Center,* 259 S.W.3d 386 (Tex. Ct. App. 2008).

♦   A company in Indiana created an employee handbook with a chapter on family and medical care leave even though it did not have enough employees to be eligible for coverage under the FMLA. The handbook offered similar benefits to those available under the FMLA. When an employee took unpaid leave and was replaced by another employee, he sued the company for violating the FMLA as well as for promissory estoppel (alleging that he reasonably relied, to his detriment, on a promise to provide benefits). A federal court granted pretrial judgment to the company, but the Seventh Circuit reversed. It found questions of fact over whether the handbook created a binding contract, and also determined that **the handbook gave rise to a cause of action for promissory estoppel**. It remanded the case for further proceedings. *Peters v. Gilead Sciences, Inc.,* 533 F.3d 594 (7th Cir. 2008).

♦ A Hispanic field supervisor for a company with an office in Wyoming lost out on a promotion and had a new manager remove from the office some of the equipment he used to provide oilfield services. He suspected his days were numbered and quit, then sued for racial harassment and breach of contract, among other claims. He asserted that the employee manual created a contract that promised continued employment and **cited the job security provision of the manual**, wherein the company stated that it made "every effort to provide continuous employment." It also stated: "An individual employee can increase his job security by increasing his knowledge and skills. The more knowledge and skill you acquire, the more productive you are likely to be, and naturally the more productive, the better your chance for stable employment." However, the Tenth Circuit noted that those provisions did not promise continued employment. The court allowed the racial harassment claim to proceed but not the breach of contract action. *Herrera v. Lufkin Industries, Inc.,* 474 F.3d 675 (10th Cir. 2007).

♦ The director of a shelter for battered women in South Carolina called the executive director to inform her that no one was operating the hotline but refused to tell the executive director who had given her that information. The executive director suspended her for insubordination, doubled her duties, then fired her when she refused to accept them. She sued for breach of contract, claiming the employee handbook altered the at-will nature of the employment and that she had been fired in violation of its nondiscrimination provision. The handbook stated that the shelter reserved the right to terminate an employee at any time if the executive director believed it was in the shelter's best interests. The Supreme Court of South Carolina ruled that **the handbook did not create contractual rights because of the disclaimer**. The director was not fired in violation of the nondiscrimination provision. *Hessenthaler v. Tri-County Sister Help, Inc.,* 616 S.E.2d 694 (S.C. 2005).

♦ An Indiana employee of United Parcel Service (UPS) was demoted. He sued for breach of contract, maintaining that the employee handbook stated that company policy was that employees would not be demoted without just cause. The company asserted that it had placed a disclaimer in the handbook stating that the handbook did not create a contract of employment. The disclaimer further stated that the handbook gave the employee no rights. The case reached the Seventh Circuit Court of Appeals, which held in favor of UPS. It rejected the notion (adopted by Oklahoma and Alaska) that in addition to stating that the handbook did not create a contract, it also had to state that the employee could be terminated at the will of the employer. Here, **the disclaimer was sufficient to inform the employee that the handbook did not create a contract**. Nor could the employee use the doctrine of promissory estoppel (detrimental reliance) because it was not reasonable for him to rely on the statement that he would not be demoted without cause. *Workman v. United Parcel Service,* 234 F.3d 998 (7th Cir. 2000).

♦   A nurse who worked in the intensive care unit of a Wisconsin hospital was discharged after telling a supervisor that she was not going to return to work following a lunch-time doctor's appointment. Prior to the appointment, the nurse had received five disciplinary warnings. She sued for wrongful discharge/breach of contract in a state court, which dismissed her claims. The Court of Appeals of Wisconsin affirmed, noting that although the handbook in place at the time the nurse was hired provided that discipline could only be for just cause upon completion of the probationary period, the updated handbook contained a specific disclaimer that it did not create any employment contractual rights. Here, the nurse had signed an acknowledgement form for the earlier handbook, which stated that she understood it to be "a working guide of policies, rights and responsibilities for [hospital] employees." The form also stated that the handbook did not "replace or supercede original hospital policies," and that hospital **policies, practices and procedures were subject to change at the sole discretion of management**. This language did not alter the at-will relationship. Moreover, the updated handbook clearly reserved the hospital's right to amend or delete any provisions at any time, without advance notice. *Helland v. Froedtert Memorial Lutheran Hospital,* 601 N.W.2d 318 (Wis. Ct. App. 1999).

♦   A hospital implemented a new employee handbook that changed the discipline procedure. Under the old handbook, discharge could only be for cause, and the third reprimand an employee received would result in automatic dismissal. Under the new handbook, a "flexible" progressive disciplinary procedure was established. Shortly after the new handbook was in place, a nurse's supervisor filled out three performance reports based on three different complaints from patients' family members. She then recommended termination, stating that "the third reprimand results in automatic dismissal." The nurse sued for wrongful discharge. The Vermont Supreme Court ruled for the nurse. **Because the supervisor's report recommending termination mirrored language used in the old handbook, there was an ambiguity as to which handbook ought to be used.** Further, the new handbook was unclear as to what the progressive disciplinary procedure was. Finally, the new handbook had been in effect only four months when the nurse was fired. *Trombley v. Southwestern Vermont Medical Center,* 738 A.2d 103 (Vt. 1999).

♦   An Arizona resort distributed an employment manual reciting that it maintained an at-will relationship with its employees. The manual prohibited the use, possession or sale of illegal drugs and called for immediate termination in such a case. Each employee had to sign an acknowledgment of the employer's drug-free workplace policy and agree to take a drug test at any time subject to discipline including discharge. When the employer's general manager learned that five employees had recently used drugs on company grounds, he attempted to transport them to a test site. Four refused to take the test. The manager fired them, and they sued for breach of contract, invasion of privacy, and other alleged legal violations. The court ruled for the employer, and the employees appealed to the Court of Appeals of Arizona, asserting that their firing violated public policy (the state constitution's personal right to privacy). The court disagreed, stating that while the government was required to refrain from invasions of personal privacy, the constitution did not protect individuals from the actions of private actors. The court also rejected the breach of contract claims since **the employment manual conspicuously notified employees that the employment relationship was at will**. The court affirmed the judgment. *Hart v. Seven Resorts Inc.,* 947 P.2d 846 (Ariz. Ct. App. 1997).

♦   An Iowa grocery store's management received reports that the night stock crew was eating food without paying for it. A private investigator interviewed the employees, and the leader of the night crew wrote out a statement indicating that during his employment he had eaten about $20 worth of food that he would be willing to pay for. He was fired anyway. He then filed a breach of contract lawsuit. The court ruled for the grocery store. The crew leader appealed to the Supreme Court of Iowa, claiming that the employee handbook created an express contract of employment. The grocery store argued that the employment was at will and that the crew leader was subject to discharge at any time for any reason, or no reason at all. Here, **throughout the handbook, the employer had placed clauses that retained its right to terminate the employment relationship at any time**. Further, the crew leader had signed a receipt for a copy of the handbook that stated: "I recognize that either [the store] or I may terminate the employment relationship at any time for any reason." Thus, the handbook did not create a contract and the court upheld the ruling for the store. *French v. Foods, Inc.,* 495 N.W.2d 768 (Iowa 1993).

C. Q&As

1. *What should we add to our employee handbook to make sure we're in compliance with the Genetic Information Nondiscrimination Act (GINA)?*

A new section and specific safe-harbor language, says Philip Miles *(pkmiles@mqblaw.com)* of McQuaide Blasko.

First, you likely already have an anti-discrimination policy protecting race, gender, disability, etc. Add "genetic information" to that list.

Second, insert the following safe-harbor language into the section on "genetic information" in your handbook:

"The Genetic Information Nondiscrimination Act of 2008 (GINA) prohibits employers and other entities covered by GINA Title II from requesting or requiring genetic info of employees or their family members. In order to comply with this law, we are asking that you not provide any genetic information to your employer."

That will protect you when you lawfully request medical info from a worker (e.g., for an FMLA certification request).

2.   We update our handbook often, which means we're left with obsolete copies when we make a change. How can we avoid that?

Issue them in three-ring binders, says George Lenard *(gll@hdfh.com)* of George's Employment Blawg.

Putting each policy or section on a fresh page makes it easy to swap out pages. Some other things to keep in mind:

*   Get fresh employee acknowledgments each time you update the handbook.
*   Use a footer on each page with the effective date of the policy.
*   Keep an archive so if you need to prove what version of a changed policy was in effect on a particular date, you can.

D.   Real-Life Success Stories

1.   *Stemmed the flow of staffer policy queries*

We were spending way too much time answering policy-related questions from managers and employees.

Don't get us wrong – we prefer workers and supervisors to come to us with questions they have rather than do something that could get us into legal trouble.

At the same time, most of the questions we were fielding could easily be answered by something that was already on every staff member's desk: our company handbook.

Our goal was simple: Get workers to check the handbook before they come to us for clarification.

Steer them in the right direction

So we decided to show everyone the way.

Now, when workers or managers come to us, we still answer their questions – but we take it a step further, too.

We take out our company handbook and show them where the information can be found in the future.

That's helped jog workers' memories without us having to come out and say, "Please check your handbook first."

So far, the approach has worked well. How do we know? Simple – we've been answering far fewer questions recently.

(A senior VP for a bank in Texas)

2. *Extra handbook copies got staff up-to-date*

Some of our employees kept coming to us with questions because they weren't keeping up to date on our policies and procedures.

Many of them had been here for years and were used to the way things were run when they first started.

But no matter how long a new policy had been in place, they would still come to HR insisting we had gotten it wrong – and we'd have to take the time to explain policies again.

Some even brought outdated versions of our handbook that they saw as proof they were right.

We needed a way to gently remind employees that policy changes were an ongoing process and to check their handbooks before coming to HR.

A teachable moment

After we had a day off due to weather conditions, a number of employees came to us asking whether they would be paid for the time.

We used the issue as a jumping-off point to remind staff that our weather closure policy changed some time ago. We then handed out an extra copy of the most recent handbook to each employee and reminded them to replace their old copies.

Employees now know that the most recent handbook is the final word on any policy dispute.

And now that everyone has an extra copy of the up-to-date version, we've been getting fewer questions and arguments from staff.

(An office manager for a doctor's office in Pennsylvania)

3. Got managers' input on consistent policies

We knew how important it is for managers to apply policies and discipline consistently.

But some of our managers weren't getting the message – especially when it came to small stuff like dress codes, time sheets and requesting vacation.

We knew that in these times, even small procedural inconsistencies can open the door to discrimination claims – or at least internal griping.

And our managers varied widely in how they handled these small chores. Some were very formal, others extremely informal.

It was time to set down some ground rules.

'You helped write this'

We started to work on written procedures for these "small" issues – making sure our managers were smack-dab in the middle of the process.

That way, if there were any problems with enforcement, I could tell the manager, "You helped write this."

When they were finished, we sent the procedures to every employee and posted them on our intranet.

It let employees know that everyone has to follow the same rules. And it gave us tools to use when it came time to discipline someone.

Most importantly, though, it's helped managers achieve our goal: consistency.

(A controller for a risk management firm in Maryland)

II. ELECTRONIC COMMUNICATIONS

A. Overview

Email, Facebook and smartphones aren't going away anytime soon. Unfortunately, employees don't always put aside their personal electronic gadgets – and their interest in non-work-related Internet sites – aside when they get to work. The increasing prevalence of electronic forms of communication makes it more important than ever for employers to have clear, specific policies regulating employee use of email, the Internet, blogs, cell phones, smartphones, camera phones and social media sites.

Solid electronic communications policies improve employee productivity and properly safeguard sensitive company information.

B. Q&As

1. We're going to start searching applicants' social media profiles. Should we do it ourselves or hire a third party to conduct it?

Do it in-house, says Nicholas Walker *(clientservices@ogletreedeakins.com)* of the labor and employment law firm Ogletree Deakins.

The Fair Credit Reporting Act comes into play here. The bill governs "employment background checks for the purposes of hiring" and applies if "an employer uses a third-party screening company to prepare the check."

Under the law, if you hire a third party, you'll need to tell applicants of the investigation, get the candidates' OK to conduct the search, and notify them if the report is used to make an adverse decision.

2. Can we request that candidates give us their social media passwords as part of the application process?

You probably shouldn't, says Molly DiBianca *(mdibianca@ycst.com)* of the Delaware Employment Law Blog. You could instead gain that info by:
- requiring candidates to grant your online "friend" request for 24 to 48 hours, or
- asking candidates to log in to their social media pages during the interview in the presence of an HR staffer.

3. Can we require employees to turn over to us Twitter accounts they've set up and used in the company's name?

Yes, says Focal PLLC technology and Internet lawyer Venkat Balasubramani *(venkat@focallaw.com)* on his Spam Notes blog.

However, given the uncertainty over who owns what, set up a policy. Make it clear that it's legal to request that, upon termination, workers:
- stop using the account immediately
- give the password of the account to the company, and
- turn over the account to you.

4. *Is there ever an instance where a company can be held liable for what a worker says online?*

Yes, says Rich Meneghello *(rmeneghello@laborlawyers.com)* of Fisher & Phillips.

If workers use social media to comment on their company's products in inappropriate ways, they can run into trouble with the Federal Trade Commission.

What the feds don't want is firms secretly building up their own online reputation via reviews and ratings – in other words, workers going online and covertly giving company products rave reviews.

If the government discovers this, a firm can then be on the hook for a violation.

To avoid this, you have two options: Prohibit postings about company products entirely, or tightly regulate them. If you allow comments, update your social media policy to require online posters to reveal their relationship to the company and say their comments are their own personal opinion.

5. *An employee came to us saying a co-worker had posted nasty comments about her on his Facebook page, calling her an "incompetent nitwit" and worse. Should we do anything about it?*

You should probably get involved, says industrial psychologist Dennis Davis (760-599-0998) of Ogletree Deakins who spoke at the Labor & Employment Law Advanced Practices (LEAP) symposium.

Even if you can't control what people post on private social networking sites, you should step in if cyber-bullying affects staffers' ability to do their jobs.

If a worker is so distraught that she can't function normally at work, it's time to call the offenders in, make them see the consequences of their actions and ask them to stop.

6. *We're putting together a policy for Internet usage, but we're in a dilemma – we have some employees who use social media for their jobs while others don't. How can we be sure we get the most comprehensive policy?*

Create two separate policies, says consultant Briana Marrah *(Brianam@ parkerlepla.com)*.

Draw up a policy that handles general Internet behavior – confidentiality, cyberbullying, etc. – and distribute it to staff.

Then create one that covers on-site social media use – what is and isn't appropriate behavior for company representatives. Give that one to staff who use social media in their daily work.

7. *We ask candidates to sign off on a background check which includes a look into their social networking profiles (if they're public). Can we have staff sign off on a similar notice so we can monitor their online activity?*

You don't have to, says Molly DiBianca *(mdibianca@ycst.com)* of the Delaware Employment Law Blog.

You likely won't run into legal trouble looking at staffers' social networking profiles since you don't need consent to search what's publicly available.

But there's a lot to be gained from being transparent with staff. Disclosure may be a better option. Consider explaining:

- what interests you're trying to protect (like confidentiality)
- which online activities pose the biggest risk to the company (for example, discriminatory remarks), and
- the lengths and limits of the monitoring efforts.

8. *Personal Internet use at our office has gotten out of hand, and senior management is considering banning it. Should we do this?*

Banning personal use of the Internet is impractical and hard to enforce – once you allow one exception, you're sunk, says Rich Paul *(rpaul@paulplevin)*.

Instead, have managers walk around to see what people are doing on work time, then adjust policies accordingly. Or target byte-hogging activities like streaming video or audio, or personal use at peak times of system use.

C. Real-Life Success Stories

1. *Social media nightmare raised staff awareness*

One of our worst nightmares had come true – a young employee had said something inappropriate about his manager on Facebook.

What's worse: The manager was the one who discovered it because he was friends with the staffer online.

The manager sent the worker an email saying it probably wasn't a great idea to make comments like that online, but the damage was done.

We already were working on social media training sessions, but the incident lit a big fire under us.

Mandatory training session

So HR and upper management arranged a mandatory 45-minute training session for all employees.

The CEO introduced the meeting before turning it over to the communications director, who made a PowerPoint presentation on our social networking policy, splicing in pictures and videos from YouTube.

Finally, HR spoke about the legal ramifications of social networks, citing recent examples that had made headlines.

Employee feedback was good – afterward staffers also gave examples of friends who'd gotten in trouble for posting things online.

Now we know our employees – especially the younger generation – are on the right page regarding social networking.

(An HR director for a church in Houston)

III. DRESS CODES

A. Overview

As a general rule, employers are free to set dress code policies for their employees, and many employers do so to create a desired atmosphere or project a particular image. Dress codes may also derive from a need to comply with applicable health or safety standards.

Federal law does not specifically address dress codes, and employers have a good deal of discretion in this area. The main land mine for employers to avoid when it comes to dress codes is the claim that a code requirement unlawfully discriminates based on race, religion or some other protected characteristic.

Here are a few brief examples of the types of claims that can arise:

- An employee claims that a dress code rule requiring a neat appearance shouldn't apply to him because his disheveled look is caused by his psychiatric disability.
- A female employee claims that a rule requiring women to wear skirts unlawfully discriminates against females on the basis of gender.
- An employee challenges a rule against facial hair, claiming his religion requires him to wear a beard.

Before finalizing dress code requirements, employers should carefully consider whether any of the requirements would negatively impact employees based on a protected characteristic such as race, religion, gender or disability.

Dress codes should be communicated clearly and applied evenhandedly.

B. Judicial Decisions

♦   A Nevada casino instituted a "Personal Best" program under which female bartenders and beverage servers had to wear makeup and nail polish, while male bartenders and beverage servers had to keep their hair short and have clean, trimmed fingernails. A female bartender with excellent performance reviews refused to comply with the makeup policy and never applied for a position that did not require makeup. She was fired, and then sued the casino under Title VII, alleging sex discrimination. A federal court and the Ninth Circuit ruled against her. The policy did not burden female servers more than males. **Different grooming standards are discriminatory only when they impose a greater burden on one sex than the other.** Accordingly, the casino could legally enforce its personal appearance policy. *Jespersen v. Harrah's Operating Co.*, 392 F.3d 1076 (9th Cir. 2004).

♦   A front desk clerk at an Iowa hotel wore men's button-down shirts and had a masculine, "Ellen DeGeneres kind of look." She received praise and raises, but when the director of operations saw her at the front desk during the day shift, **he decided she didn't have that "Midwestern girl look" and sought to transfer her to the night shift**. Her manager refused to transfer her and was then asked to resign. The director then told the clerk she would have to interview with him to keep her shift, but three days later, he fired her. She sued for gender discrimination under Title VII, and the Eighth Circuit held that she deserved a trial. Here, the hotel did not claim poor performance until after it fired her, and she had no history of discipline. Also, the hotel didn't follow its written termination procedures. *Lewis v. Heartland Inns of America, LLC,* 591 F.3d 1033 (8th Cir. 2010).

♦   A salon in New York **fired an openly gay assistant stylist** because she got an "extremely unprofessional-looking haircut at a barbershop," which amounted to insubordination. She claimed that she was really fired because she did not conform to gender stereotypes of how a woman should look. When she sued the salon under Title VII, she lost. A federal court and the Second Circuit held that the salon did not violate Title VII. The salon could require her to have her hair cut by its stylists as a means of advertising its techniques. Title VII does not protect against sexual orientation discrimination and this was not gender stereotyping. *Dawson v. Bumble & Bumble,* 398 F.3d 211 (2d Cir. 2005).

♦   A temporary placement agency refused to refer a Muslim woman to a client that ran a commercial printing operation because the woman wore a khimar (a scarf that covers the head and can extend to the waist) and the client's dress code policy prohibited workers from wearing headwear or loose clothing that could get caught in the machines. The woman filed a religious discrimination complaint with the EEOC, which sued the temp agency for violating Title VII. A Minnesota federal court and the Eighth Circuit ruled for the temp agency, noting that **the client's legitimate and facially neutral safety policy** justified the refusal to refer the woman for employment. *EEOC v. Kelly Services, Inc.,* 598 F.3d 1022 (8th Cir. 2010).

♦   A Jiffy Lube technician in Massachusetts practiced Rastafarianism, which prohibited him from cutting his hair or shaving. When a new grooming policy took effect, requiring employees who had customer contact to be clean-shaven and to keep their hair neatly trimmed, he asked for an accommodation so he could continue to work with customers rather than simply working in the lower bay. The company's vice president refused to discuss the matter and assigned him to the lower bay. He quit and then sued for religious discrimination. A state court granted pretrial judgment to the company, but the Supreme Judicial Court of Massachusetts reversed. Here, because **the company failed to engage in the interactive process**, it could not show that exempting the technician from the policy was the only possible accommodation and that doing so would impose an undue hardship on its business. The case required a trial. *Brown v. F.L. Roberts & Co., Inc.,* 896 N.E.2d 1279 (Mass. 2008).

♦   A cashier in Massachusetts with multiple body piercings and tattoos claimed that she was **required by her religion – the Church of Body Modification – to display her body piercings to the public.** Her employer had a dress code policy that forbade the wearing of any facial jewelry except earrings. It rejected her suggested accommodation that she cover her eyebrow piercings with a flesh-colored Band-Aid and fired her for unexcused absences as well as failure to comply with the dress code. During Equal Employment

Opportunity Commission mediation, the employer offered to let her return to work with her jewelry covered, but she then took the position that she should be exempted from the dress code for religious reasons. When she sued under Title VII, a federal court ruled against her and the First Circuit Court of Appeals affirmed the ruling. Granting such an exemption would be an undue hardship to the employer because it would adversely affect the employer's public image. *Cloutier v. Costco Wholesale Corp.*, 390 F.3d 126 (1st Cir. 2004).

C. Q&As

1. *We have a dress code in place, but employees frequently violate it – and our supervisors aren't cracking down on it. What should we do?*

Explain to your managers that you've been too tolerant about the dress code, but you now expect them to start enforcing it, says Marie McIntyre *(www.yourofficecoach.com)*, author of "Secrets to Winning at Office Politics."

Next, inform the entire staff that the dress code will begin to be enforced starting next week. On the first day of enforcement, instruct managers to hand out warning notices to anyone who is inappropriately dressed. Use your disciplinary policy to deal with habitual violators.

2. *One of our new workers is just out of college, and she hasn't quite figured out how to dress appropriately for the workplace. Any tips for getting the message across when we talk to her?*

Don't sound overly critical by saying "You aren't dressing right for the workplace," says Liz Reyer *(liz@deliverchange.com)*.

Your best bet is to assume she wants to do the right thing. Stick to phrases such as "Expectations in the workplace may be different than what you're used to."

If she takes an "I've got to be me" path, note the possible effect on her career in business.

Even better: Rehearse with a friend, going over how you'll respond to different reactions like tears, anger or stony silence.

IV. DRUG AND ALCOHOL POLICIES

A. Overview

Employers clearly have a legitimate interest in keeping illegal drugs and alcohol out of the workplace. At the same time, care must be taken when crafting drug and alcohol policies to avoid pitfalls that can lead to legal claims of privacy violations or disability discrimination.

Although a federal law called the Drug-Free Workplace Act of 1988 sets rules in this subject-matter area for federal contractors and grantees, for most private employers there is no federal statute regulating drug testing of employees. Nonetheless, many private employers are subject to state or local laws that address the topic.

Drug and alcohol policies should unequivocally ban the unlawful use, possession and sale of drugs in the workplace. It is important to make it clear in your policy that illegal drug use includes both drugs that are defined as illegal under the law and legal drugs, such as prescription medications, that are illegally obtained.

Special care must be taken if the policy includes provisions relating to drug testing. Such testing may be required with respect to job applicants, after there has been a workplace accident, on the basis of reasonable suspicion, or on a random basis.

Alcoholism can be a disability under the federal Americans with Disabilities Act. However, the ADA permits employers to hold alcoholic employees to the same performance standards as other employees, even if an employee's unsatisfactory job performance is caused by alcoholism.

Drug and alcohol policies must be drafted and implemented in a way that is mindful of another federal law: the Family and Medical Leave Act. Under the FMLA, covered employers must provide eligible employees with up to 12 workweeks of unpaid leave over a 12-month period when the employee cannot work due to a serious health condition – which can include a period of incapacity related to treatment for substance abuse.

B. Judicial Decisions

1. Pre-Employment Testing

Employers often present job applicants with conditional offers of employment, contingent upon the successful completion of a drug screening test. This is perfectly legal as long as it is not done as a pretext to discriminate against certain applicants.

♦   A Massachusetts job applicant was given a conditional job offer and required to pass a drug screen, which included a test for nicotine. As part of its wellness plan, the company had a policy of not hiring smokers. The applicant submitted a urine sample and began working for the company pending the test results. When his urine tested positive for nicotine, he was told he would not be permanently hired. He sued, asserting that he had been "fired" in violation of his ERISA rights. A federal court ruled against him, noting that he was not an employee who "may become eligible to receive a benefit from an employee benefit plan." **His "regular" employment was clearly contingent on passing the background check and urinalysis screening.** He also could not claim a violation of his privacy rights because he smoked in public and received a warning after his supervisor noticed his cigarettes on his dashboard. *Rodrigues v. EG Systems d/b/a Scotts Lawnservice,* 639 F.Supp.2d 131 (D. Mass. 2009).

♦   A North Carolina applicant with depression, bipolar disorder and ADHD received a conditional offer of employment, contingent on passing a drug test. He did not mention that he was taking medication for his condition and tested positive for amphetamines. When the job offer was withdrawn, he did not contact the company's medical review officer to provide proof that he was taking legal medication. Instead, he sued under the ADA. A federal court ruled for the company, noting that **its drug-free workplace policy did not improperly prohibit employees' use of prescription drugs**. In fact, several other applicants had contacted the medical review officer after testing positive for amphetamines, and provided documentation that they were taking prescription medication. They were subsequently hired. Thus, the company did not discriminate against the applicant. *Meyer v. Qualex, Inc.,* 388 F.Supp.2d 630 (E.D.N.C. 2005).

♦   After Wal-Mart offered a West Virginia applicant a job, it required her to give a urine sample. The test came back negative for drugs and the employee began working. She later quit and sued the company for invasion of privacy. The case reached the Supreme Court of Appeals of West Virginia, which noted that an employer may not require an employee to submit to drug testing unless it has a reasonable good-faith suspicion of drug use, or the employee's job responsibilities involve public safety or the safety of others. However, **in the pre-employment context, the individual has a lower expectation of privacy**. Background checks, references and medical examinations all contribute to that lower expectation. The urine sample requirement did not violate the employee's privacy rights. *Baughman v. Wal-Mart Stores,* 592 S.E.2d 824 (W.Va. 2003).

♦   A manager accepted a conditional offer of employment that required him to pass a drug test prior to beginning the job. He succeeded in delaying the test until four days after his eventual date of hire and then submitted a test indicating marijuana use. The employer withdrew its offer of employment, and the manager sued, claiming that he could not be tested for drugs without individualized suspicion of drug use. The Court of Appeal of California noted that the state **approved of drug testing without individualized suspicion for job applicants**. Suspicionless testing is appropriate in such cases, because prospective employers have not had the opportunity to observe them and may have a need to evaluate their drug usage. In contrast, an employer generally should not have to resort to suspicionless testing of current employees. In this case, the manager had not performed any work for the new employer and was properly viewed as a job applicant. An applicant could not avoid drug testing by delaying a test beyond the date of hire. *Pilkington Barnes Hind v. Superior Court (Visbal),* 77 Cal.Rptr.2d 596 (Cal. Ct. App. 1998).

♦   An electrical contractor hired employees for construction projects in North and South Carolina. A labor organization charged that the contractor violated federal labor law at the North Carolina site by refusing to hire, threatening and interrogating union-affiliated applicants, and for devising and enforcing a drug testing policy to discourage union activities. The union also claimed that the contractor failed to offer work to 16 union-affiliated employees at the South Carolina site based on their union activities or sympathies. The National Labor Relations Board (NLRB) affirmed the findings of an administrative law judge (ALJ) in favor of the union and ordered the contractor to reinstate two union-affiliated employees who had been fired for refusing to take a drug test. The contractor appealed. The Fourth Circuit rejected the contractor's claim that the ALJ was biased and held that the contractor had committed unfair labor practices. However, the drug testing policy had been **legitimately enacted in response to information that employees of other contractors at the two work sites were using drugs**. The drug testing policy had been uniformly applied to all new employees. The court reversed the NLRB's decision concerning the drug testing policy. *Eldeco, Inc. v. NLRB*, 132 F.3d 1007 (4th Cir. 1997).

2. Employee Testing

Employees may also remain subject to drug testing throughout their employment. Some employer policies rely on random testing (usually for "safety-sensitive" positions), while other policies require reasonable cause or suspicion before testing an employee.

Where an employee has a history of drug use or alcohol abuse but is currently clean and sober, that past history generally cannot be used against the employee.

Absent a last chance agreement (an agreement wherein an employee who has tested positive agrees to be tested in the future in order to save his or her job, with any further positive result allowing the employer to fire him or her), testing targeted to employees with only a past history of drug or alcohol use can be a violation of the Americans with Disabilities Act.

♦ When a railway engineer reported for work in Indiana, he was informed that he had been selected for random drug testing. He was unable to provide a sample and was given a second opportunity some time later. On the second try, he provided an insufficient sample. According to then-existing Federal Railroad Administration regulations, he was to be afforded two hours to produce an adequate sample. Failure to produce would result in dismissal, unless the failure was medically excusable. When he again **failed to produce a sample**, he was removed from service. A doctor's exam found no medical explanation for his failure to provide a sample. An arbitration panel upheld his dismissal, finding that the railway's actions were not "unjust." A federal court and the Seventh Circuit affirmed. A court's role is not to judge whether the arbitrator's contract interpretation is right or wrong but solely to review whether the arbitrator interpreted the contract at all. If so, that interpretation is conclusive. *Lyons v. Norfolk & Western Railway Co.*, 163 F.3d 466 (7th Cir. 1999).

3. Privacy Claims

It is not uncommon for invasion of privacy and defamation claims to arise as a result of drug testing policies. Although such claims usually fail, they can succeed where the employer goes out of its way to publicize the results of a test, or where it breaches its own policy of confidentiality.

♦ A temporary employee of a nonprofit agency in New Jersey was taking six different medications for degenerative disc disease. When he applied for a permanent job with the agency, he was required to provide a urine sample, which came back positive for morphine. After the agency fired him, he sued for invasion of privacy, negligence and wrongful discharge. The case reached the Superior Court of New Jersey, Appellate Division, which ruled in favor of the agency. **The employee had no reasonable expectation of privacy with regard to the drug testing**, and the actions taken by the agency and its laboratory did not amount to negligence even though it used an older opiate cutoff level that might pick up on innocent activity, like eating a poppy seed muffin. Here, the employee's level was above what might be expected from such an occurrence. Also, it was not unlawful for the agency to perceive that the employee was taking illegal drugs. *Vargo v. National Exchange Carriers Ass'n, Inc.*, 870 A.2d 679 (N.J. Super. Ct. App. Div. 2005).

◆ A Texas employer periodically tested its employees for use of illegal controlled substances and randomly tested an employee who yielded a positive result for a cocaine metabolite. He told his supervisor that the result was due to his consumption of herbal teas and offered to have the teas tested by an independent laboratory. A doctor hired by the employer stated that tea could not have caused a positive drug test, and the employee was fired. He sued the employer and physician for discrimination, false light invasion of privacy, negligence, and intentional infliction of emotional distress. The court stated that **Texas does not recognize claims for false light invasion of privacy** because of concerns that doing so would duplicate other claims, including defamation. It dismissed the negligence claims since the employee had sought to impose upon the employer a duty of good faith and fair dealing, which was nonexistent in Texas. In the absence of any evidence of outrageous conduct by the employer, there was also no basis for the intentional infliction of emotional distress claim, and the court granted a partial dismissal of the case. Only the discrimination claims remained. *Quintanilla v. K-Bin, Inc.*, 993 F.Supp. 560 (S.D. Tex. 1998).

◆ A hotel employee signed a consent form required by her employer under which she agreed to participate in a random drug and alcohol testing program. She tested positive for illegal drug use and requested another test from a different laboratory. The employer declined the request but offered to retest the original sample, which the employee refused. The employer then discharged her, and she sued it for wrongful discharge and invasion of privacy. A state court dismissed her lawsuit, and the court of appeals affirmed. The employee appealed to the Supreme Court of Tennessee, arguing that Tennessee public policy protected her against wrongful discharge because the employer had violated a clear mandate of public policy. The court **rejected her claim that the state constitutional guarantee of privacy restricted the right of a private employer to fire an at-will employee who tested positive for drug use**. Privacy standards applicable to public employers were inapplicable in private employment cases and to the extent that public policy existed concerning drug screening, it favored drug-free workplaces. The court affirmed the ruling for the employer. *Stein v. Davidson Hotel Co.*, 945 S.W.2d 714 (Tenn. 1997).

♦ A Texas employer required its employees to participate in random drug testing. The testing laboratory informed the employer's vice president that one employee tested positive for drug use, and the vice president told the employee's supervisors not to assign him hazardous work. The confirming test result was negative, and the supervisors apologized to the employee for telling him he had failed the drug test. The employee was fired the next year for an unrelated matter, and he sued the employer for negligent and intentional infliction of emotional distress, breach of contract, defamation and invasion of privacy. The court ruled for the employer, and the Court of Appeals of Texas affirmed. Although it agreed with the employee that the employer had breached its own policy of confidentiality in reporting lab results, its report was not false. **Truth was a complete defense to the slander cause of action.** The employee's breach of contract claim also failed, because the employment relationship was at will. The employee was unable to show that the employer's conduct had been intentional, reckless, extreme or outrageous. Accordingly, it did not support a claim for emotional distress. *Washington v. Naylor Industrial Services, Inc.,* 893 S.W.2d 309 (Tex. Ct. App. 1995).

♦ A Massachusetts tool grinder was never under any reasonable suspicion that she ingested illegal drugs. However, one of the company's owners became concerned about drug use by employees and decided to initiate a drug testing policy. When the tool grinder refused to take the test because she found the testing procedure degrading, the company fired her. She sued, alleging a violation of her statutory right to privacy and wrongful termination in violation of public policy. The Supreme Judicial Court of Massachusetts ruled for the employer. Although submission to urinalysis involves a significant invasion of privacy, especially when employees are required to submit to a visual inspection to ensure that they are not concealing vials of urine, the company had a legitimate business interest in protecting its employees and customers, and the owner had a strong basis for suspecting that employees were using drugs. Further, the owner had promised that anyone who tested positive would not be fired, but would be retested in 30 days and given an opportunity to undergo counseling at company expense. Thus, **the drug testing policy was reasonable and did not violate the tool grinder's right to privacy.** *Folmsbee v. Tech Tool Grinding & Supply, Inc.,* 630 N.E.2d 586 (Mass. 1994).

4. Consent

Employees can be required to consent to drug testing as a condition of employment.

♦ A full-time warehouse employee for a Minnesota company also served as a part-time driver. When he was selected for random drug testing, he refused to take the test. After he was suspended and fired, he sued under state and federal drug testing laws. A federal court ruled for the company, and the Eighth Circuit Court of Appeals affirmed. **Even though the employee was only a part-time driver, he was still subject to random testing under the federal law,** and the refusal to take that test could be treated as a positive test justifying his discharge. Also, state law did not prevent the company from firing him for refusing to take a federally mandated test. *Belde v. Ferguson Enterprises, Inc.,* 460 F.3d 976 (8th Cir. 2006).

♦ An employee attempted to steal a surge protector and made several misrepresentations to different employees in his effort to conceal the theft. His behavior prompted the employer to conduct a fitness-for-duty evaluation, which included a drug test. He tested positive and was offered enrollment in an employee assistance plan. However, he was fired after submitting another positive result in a random drug test. He sued for violations of the state workplace drug testing law. The court found that the employer lacked probable cause to suspect the employee of drug use. It also refused to include testimony suggesting that the employer could have fired the employee solely on the basis of the theft incident. The employer appealed. The Supreme Court of Connecticut held that **private sector employees could waive their statutory rights by giving their consent to be tested**. Waiver rights were necessary to ensure that employees maintained the option of entering employee assistance programs and retaining their employment, and to remove an employer's incentive to simply fire employees in response to their drug problems. The trial court had improperly excluded testimony concerning the employee's state of mind at the time of the waiver, and a new trial was required at which evidence concerning the theft incident would be considered. *Poulos v. Pfizer, Inc.,* 244 Conn. 598, 711 A.2d 688 (Conn. 1998).

♦ A California employer maintained a drug testing policy under which employees could be tested where reasonable cause or suspicion of drug or alcohol use was present. **Employees consented in writing to testing as a condition of employment.** The policy stated that disciplinary action, including discharge, could be imposed for refusing to consent to a test. The employer hired an executive secretary, then discharged her eight months later when she refused to take a drug test after two co-workers observed her slumping over her desk. She sued the employer for wrongful discharge, intentional infliction of emotional distress and violation of the California Constitution, which has been interpreted by state courts as creating a right of action against private employers for invasion of privacy. The Court of Appeal of California stated that employee drug testing claims under the state constitution required balancing the employee's reasonable privacy expectations against the employer's legitimate business interests. The employee had presented evidence that the employer had no reasonable cause to suspect her of drug abuse, and had offered an alternative explanation for the discharge (retaliation against her for refusing to work uncompensated overtime). A trial was required on the wrongful discharge and invasion of privacy claims. However, the trial court had properly dismissed the claim for intentional infliction of emotional distress. *Kraslawsky v. Upper Deck Co.,* 65 Cal.Rptr.2d 297 (Cal. Ct. App. 1997).

5. Adequacy of Testing

The employer should put in place procedures that ensure the testing will be accurate so that any challenge to the procedures will be unsuccessful. The lab used to test the samples should comply with the guidelines of the U.S. Department of Health and Human Services.

♦ An Oklahoma UPS driver was subject to the federal Omnibus Transportation Employee Testing Act, which requires drug and alcohol testing of employees in "safety sensitive" jobs in various transportation industries. After he swerved onto the shoulder of a highway, overturning the two trailers he was pulling, he was ordered to submit to a drug test. When his tests came back positive, he was fired. He sued under Oklahoma's drug testing law, **claiming he did not receive proper notice of the first test as required by federal DOT regulations**. He sought reinstatement, back pay and lost benefits – remedies not available under the federal law. The Tenth Circuit ruled against him, noting that he was not entitled to get his job back or any monetary compensation. Here, the driver was required to be tested by federal law; therefore, the Oklahoma statute exempted him from its protections. *Williams v. United Parcel Service, Inc.,* 527 F.3d 1135 (10th Cir. 2008).

♦ A Kentucky truck driver was fired after testing positive for drugs. However, **the testing was not conducted in a manner required by federal regulations** and the results were inaccurate due to the improper handling of the sample and the driver's use of legal over-the-counter medications. He submitted to a later, more accurate test, which demonstrated that the earlier test had indicated a false positive. After he had trouble finding another job due to disclosures by his former employer that he had tested positive for drugs, he sued for wrongful termination and defamation. A trial court dismissed the lawsuit, and the Kentucky Court of Appeals agreed that his wrongful discharge claim could not stand because he was an at-will employee and there was no public policy against firing someone based on a violation of federal regulations. However, he did state a claim for defamation based on the release of the drug test information. That part of the lawsuit required a trial. *Shrout v. The TFE Group,* 161 S.W.3d 351 (Ky. Ct. App. 2005).

♦ A Texas truck driver was required to submit to random drug testing pursuant to Department of Transportation (DOT) regulations. He tested positive for THC (marijuana) in two different urine samples and was fired after the second test. He sued the company for violating five of the DOT collection protocols. A jury found that the company was negligent in collecting his urine sample and awarded him more than $800,000 in damages, as well as exemplary damages of $100,000 after finding that the company acted with malice. The court of appeals affirmed, but the Supreme Court of Texas reversed. It found no basis for holding an employer liable for firing an at-will employee for a positive drug test. Under the at-will employment doctrine, an employer does not have to determine if a termination was based on correct information. **The court refused** to adopt a new theory of negligent drug testing. *Mission Petroleum Carriers, Inc. v. Solomon,* 106 S.W.3d 705 (Tex. 2003).

♦   A North Carolina employer asked an employee to submit to random drug screening. The employee tested positive for drug use and was fired. He filed a wrongful discharge action against the employer, asserting that the laboratory used for the testing was not approved by the state as required by law. The court granted pretrial judgment to the employer, but the court of appeals reversed, holding that state law established procedures required of employers to conduct drug screening on employees to protect them from unreliable or inadequate testing. It agreed with the employee that the law was an express policy declaration by the state and that any discharge inconsistent with the law violated a public policy exception to the presumption of employment at will. The employer here had violated public policy by utilizing an unapproved laboratory. On further appeal, the North Carolina Supreme Court reversed, holding that **the employer's failure to use an approved laboratory for the drug testing did not give rise to a claim for wrongful discharge**. There must be more than a statutory violation; there must also be an unlawful reason or purpose that violates public policy. Here, there was no evidence of such a purpose. *Garner v. Rentenbach Constructors, Inc.,* 515 S.E.2d 438 (N.C. 1999).

6. Collective Bargaining Agreements

In unionized workplaces, collective bargaining agreements generally define the nature of drug testing policies and limits. They also generally provide a disciplinary procedure and a grievance process for employees who wish to challenge positive test results.

♦   A New Jersey brewery worker submitted a hair for drug testing and was fired when a positive result came back. He and his wife sued the brewery, alleging that although the drug test reading was below the "minimum detection level," and thus was not reliable, the brewery nonetheless discharged him. They asserted breach of contract and intentional infliction of emotional distress, among other claims. A federal court ruled against them, noting that the breach of contract action was preempted by Section 301 of the LMRA because a collective bargaining agreement was in place at the time of the firing and any resolution of the claim would demand the interpretation of the agreement. Further, the emotional distress claim could not survive because the brewery's action in firing the worker was not so extreme and outrageous that it went beyond all possible bounds of decency. *Brandt v. Anheuser-Busch, Inc.,* 2007 WL 1175751 (D.N.J. 2007).

♦   An employee of an aircraft manufacturing corporation was fired after his second positive drug test. He sued the company and the union under Section 301 of the LMRA, alleging wrongful discharge by the company and breach of the duty of fair representation by the union. A Connecticut federal court and the Second Circuit ruled against him. **Firing the employee for the second positive drug test did not violate the collective bargaining agreement.** Further, the union's decision not to arbitrate the employee's claim was not irrational or arbitrary so as to constitute a breach of the duty of fair representation. *Verrilli v. Sikorsky Aircraft Corp.*, 221 Fed.Appx. 8 (2d Cir. 2007).

◆ A West Virginia truck driver, who was subject to Department of Transportation regulations requiring random drug testing for workers engaged in "safety-sensitive" tasks, tested positive for marijuana on two occasions. Both times, his employer sought to discharge him, but the union went to arbitration on both occasions and obtained awards that ordered his reinstatement. The employer then sued to nullify the arbitrator's award. A federal court enforced the award, and the Fourth Circuit affirmed. The U.S. Supreme Court also affirmed. It held that **public policy did not require the courts to prevent the driver's reinstatement despite the positive drug tests**. Federal law encourages rehabilitation where possible. Here, the arbitration award did not condone the driver's conduct or ignore the risk to public safety that drug use by truck drivers may pose, but punished the driver by placing conditions on his reinstatement. He had to pay both parties' arbitration costs, undergo further substance abuse treatment and testing, and provide a signed letter of resignation in the event he failed any more drug tests. *Eastern Associated Coal Corp. v. UMW of America*, 531 U.S. 57, 121 S.Ct. 462, 148 L.Ed.2d 354 (2000).

◆ An electrical contractor in Illinois agreed to abide by the collective bargaining agreement between a contractors association and the International Brotherhood of Electrical Workers. **The bargaining agreement contained a drug testing provision for all employees of each participating firm.** When the contractor refused to implement the drug testing rule for employees other than electricians represented by the union, an arbitration board ordered the electricians' union not to refer any of its members to the contractor for employment. The contractor sued, and a federal court held the board's order invalid, but the Seventh Circuit Court of Appeals reversed. It held that the contractor had agreed to be bound by the bargaining agreement, and that federal labor law allowed bargaining agreements to reach beyond the certified unit of workers. Thus, the contractor could not test only the electricians. However, if the separate bargaining agreement between the contractor and the operating engineers' union had its own drug testing rules, the contractor would have to abide by those rules for those employees. *Lid Electric, Inc. v. IBEW, Local 134*, 362 F.3d 940 (7th Cir. 2004).

◆ A bus driver for the New York City Transit Authority was randomly called to the office for a drug test. She was unable to provide an adequate sample of at least 45 ml of urine and was required to drink 40 ounces of liquid within a three-hour period. She still could not provide an adequate sample and was referred to a doctor, who could find no medical reason for the failure. This was deemed a "refusal" to provide a sample and resulted in the employee's suspension. The transit authority also told her it intended to fire her. Doctors later found that she had slow urine flow and urgency incontinence, but that she should have been able to provide a sample within the three-hour period. Her union filed a grievance, and an arbitration panel determined that she should not be disciplined. The Supreme Court, Appellate Division, held that **Department of Transportation regulations specified removal from a safety-sensitive position (like driving a bus) where an employee "refuses" to provide a sample**. However, the Court of Appeals reversed, ruling that the appellate division improperly substituted its factual finding for that of a majority of the arbitration panel. *Dowleyne v. NYCTA,* 816 N.E.2d 191 (N.Y. 2004).

♦ A collective bargaining agreement provided that where a company had reasonable cause to believe that an employee was working while under the influence of drugs, the employee would be required to submit to a blood or urine test or be fired. After the company received anonymous phone calls accusing an employee of drug trafficking, it used a machine to sweep the employee's car and work area for drug residue. Cocaine was detected in both places. The company asked the employee to take a drug test. He refused and was fired. The union took the case to arbitration, where the arbitrator determined that the company **could require the drug test only if there was reasonable cause to believe the employee was on drugs at the time** he was asked to submit to the test. Since the company did not believe the employee was on drugs at the moment it asked him to take the drug test, it could not fire him for refusing to submit. The Seventh Circuit Court of Appeals affirmed the arbitrator's order that the employee be reinstated. Although it would not have read the bargaining agreement so literally, it refused to overturn the ruling because the ruling was not arbitrary and capricious. *Int'l Truck and Engine Corp. v. United Steel Workers of America, Local 3740,* 294 F.3d 860 (7th Cir. 2002).

V. LEAVES OF ABSENCE

A. Overview

The Family and Medical Leave Act of 1993 (FMLA), 29 U.S.C. §§ 2601-2654, grants eligible employees the right to take up to 12 weeks of unpaid leave per year under specified circumstances related to family healthcare and childbirth, and (with the passage of amendments in 2008) for military caregiver leave or in exigent circumstances relating to the National Guard or Reserves. Employees become eligible by working:
1)   for an employer with at least 50 employees,
2)   for the employer for at least 12 months, and
3)   at least 1,250 hours in the previous year.

Eligible employees are expressly authorized by the act to take leave upon the birth of a child by the employee or the employee's spouse, or by the placement of a child for adoption or foster care with the employee.

The act also applies when the employee is needed to care for a child, spouse or parent who has a serious health condition, and when the employee is unable to perform employment duties because of her own serious health condition.

Under the FMLA regulations, a serious health condition is one requiring an overnight stay in a hospital, hospice or residential medical care facility or a period of incapacity requiring more than <u>three calendar days' absence</u> and two visits to a healthcare provider.

Under the new regulations, the first healthcare provider visit must occur within seven days of the first day of incapacity and the second visit must occur within 30 days. For chronic health conditions, the employee must make at least two visits to a healthcare provider per year.

A serious health condition can also involve a period of incapacity due to pregnancy, a chronic serious health condition (like asthma, diabetes or epilepsy) or a permanent or long-term condition like Alzheimer's, a severe stroke or the terminal stages of a disease.

B. Judicial Decisions

1. What Is a "Serious Health Condition"?

♦   A Pennsylvania medical receptionist was diagnosed with a urinary tract infection and low back pain. She got a prescription for antibiotics from her doctor, who also provided a note stating that it was likely she'd be able to return to work within a day or two, though it was possible she wouldn't be able to return to work after three days. She stayed out for a week and was fired for performance reasons. When she sued under the FMLA, she presented her doctor's note and her testimony that she was incapacitated. A federal court ruled that she failed to prove she had a "serious health condition" under the act. However, the Third Circuit held that her testimony, combined with the doctor's note, was sufficient to prove she had a serious health condition. The court remanded the case for a determination of whether she provided sufficient notice of her need for leave and whether she was improperly fired. *Schaar v. Lehigh Valley Health Services, Inc.,* 598 F.3d 156 (3d Cir. 2010).

♦   While riding his bike, a UPS employee in Michigan was hit by a car. He refused medical treatment at the scene, but went to the emergency room that night. Doctors noted contusions on his back and legs and prescribed pain medication, but he didn't fill the prescription. He returned to the ER the next night with back pain, but again refused to fill the prescription for pain medication. He called his supervisor to report that he'd been struck by a car and submitted vague doctors' reports that contained no details. After UPS fired him for unexcused absenteeism, he sued under the FMLA. The Sixth Circuit ruled against him, finding that **his contusions and sore back did not amount to a serious health condition**. *Stimpson v. UPS,* 351 Fed.Appx. 42 (6th Cir. 2009).

♦   A janitor for a property management company in Illinois notified his employer that he was having medical problems, including a weak bladder. He also told his supervisor he was having a biopsy to determine whether he had prostate cancer. After the biopsy, he returned to work with a temporary restriction on heavy lifting and a treatment plan, which his supervisor allegedly ignored. He said he was going home because he felt sick. The next day he was fired. After being diagnosed with prostate cancer, he sued under the FMLA and ADA. His FMLA suit was allowed to move forward. **Even though he didn't**

know of his diagnosis until after he was fired, he was entitled to FMLA protection. However, he could not show that he was disabled under the ADA. *Burnett v. LFW Inc.,* 472 F.3d 471 (7th Cir. 2006).

♦   When a company refused to allow an employee time off to care for his 13-year-old son who had severe attention deficit disorder, the employee sued under the FMLA. A Michigan federal court ruled in favor of the company, and the Sixth Circuit Court of Appeals affirmed. Here, the son did not qualify as having a serious health condition because even though he saw his doctor every six months to monitor his medication, he was not incapacitated during the requested leave time. He was able to attend school and do the same activities most children do; he simply had to be watched all the time. *Perry v. Jaguar of Troy,* 353 F.3d 510 (6th Cir. 2003).

♦   A clerical worker at a Florida hospital was disciplined three times for unscheduled absences and was given a final written warning threatening suspension and possible termination. Later, she slipped and fell at work, fracturing an elbow and ankle. She returned to work on her doctor's recommendation after he put her arm in a sling. She left work early on several days and took two days off the following week without informing her supervisor. The following Monday she was fired. She sued the hospital under the FMLA, and a federal court ruled against her. The Eleventh Circuit affirmed. Here, the employee did not have a "serious health condition" under the FMLA because **her injury did not require her to miss three consecutive full calendar days of work.** Even though the several partial days and two non-consecutive days she took off added up to more than three days away from work during a 10-day period, she was not protected by the FMLA. The regulations clearly require some fraction more than three consecutive calendar days to constitute the period of incapacity. And she did not meet that requirement. The termination was justified. *Russell v. North Broward Hospital,* 346 F.3d 1335 (11th Cir. 2003).

♦   While unloading his truck, a driver experienced chest pains and, after another employee relieved him, drove himself to the hospital where he underwent an EKG. When no apparent heart damage was found, the driver was released under a "personal discharge plan" that warned he should not return to work until after a stress test was performed – 10 days later. He called several management employees to inform them he could not yet return to work. He forwarded the discharge plan to the company and passed the stress test. When he attempted to return to work, he was informed that he had been fired for violating the company's collective bargaining provisions concerning absences. He sued under the FMLA, and a trial court awarded him over $59,000 along with a reinstatement order. The Michigan Court of Appeals affirmed. Here, the driver's telephone notice regarding the reason he could not return to work was sufficient to trigger the protections of the FMLA. Also, he provided the discharge plan to the company within the 15-day period in the statute for requests for medical certification. Finally, **even though he did not actually have a serious health condition under the FMLA**, his absence qualified under the statute because a doctor concluded that an extended absence from work was needed following his emergency room visit. *Woodman v. Miesel Sysco Food Service Co.,* 657 N.W.2d 122 (Mich. Ct. App. 2003).

♦   A California truck driver's sister was murdered by her ex-husband. The truck driver moved to Reno temporarily to be with his father, who had fallen into a depression. He drove his father to counseling sessions and did household chores. While on leave, he agreed with the company's HR manager that he would resign from his job and would be rehired if he returned to work within six months. When he sought reinstatement, the company cited union-related restrictions and refused to reinstate him with seniority. It did, however, give him a position as a probationary truck driver. He sued under the FMLA, and a federal court granted pretrial judgment to the company. The Ninth Circuit reversed, finding an issue of fact as to whether the leave of absence qualified as FMLA leave. Here, if the father had a "serious health condition" and if the truck driver cared for him within the meaning of the FMLA, then he should have been reinstated to his position with seniority. *Scamihorn v. General Truck Drivers,* 282 F.3d 1078 (9th Cir. 2002).

♦   A West Virginia employee with a history of absenteeism was warned about her poor attendance. Subsequently, she came down with the flu and missed a week of work. She saw her doctor twice during the week and requested FMLA leave when she returned to work. Her employer denied her request and fired her for excessive absenteeism. When she sued under the FMLA, a federal court ruled in her favor. The Fourth Circuit affirmed, holding that **an employee with the flu could be suffering from a "serious health condition"** where the employee cannot work for at least three consecutive days and receives continuing treatment from her doctor. The court noted that "treatment" includes examinations and evaluations of the seriousness of the illness. Here, even though the employee's second visit to the doctor was to evaluate her condition, this constituted continuing treatment for a serious health condition. *Miller v. AT&T Corp.,* 250 F.3d 820 (4th Cir. 2001).

2. Notice

The FMLA requires employees to give employers sufficient notice, usually 30 days, to prevent unduly disrupting employer operations. However, lesser notice may be sufficient when a 30-day notice is impossible.

Under the new regulations, employees have to follow the employer's usual and customary call-in procedures for reporting an absence unless unusual circumstances exist to excuse that lack.

The FMLA also requires employers to give notice to employees who request leave. Under the new regulations, the notice has to be given within five business days and must contain the following:

1)   a statement that the leave will be counted against the employee's annual FMLA entitlement,

2)   any requirements for the employee to furnish medical certification of a serious health condition,

3) a statement of the employee's right to substitute paid leave and whether the employer will require the substitution of paid leave,

4) any requirement for the employee to make any premium payments to maintain health benefits,

5) any requirement for the employee to present a fitness-for-duty certificate to be restored to employment,

6) if the employee is a "key employee," a statement explaining that status and the potential consequence that restoration may be denied following the leave,

7) a statement of the employee's right to restoration to the same or an equivalent job upon return from leave, and

8) a statement of the employee's potential liability for payment of health insurance premiums paid by the employer during the leave if the employee fails to return to work after the leave.

◆   An assembly line worker at a Ford plant in Indiana requested leave for stress. Her doctor faxed a form to the plant's clinic stating that she needed until August 28, then referred her to a psychiatrist, who could not see her until August 29. She asked her doctor to let the plant clinic know she needed more time off, but she did not notify the clinic herself. When the clinic didn't hear from her, it sent her a "quit notice" via certified mail, which she waited a few days to pick up. After her termination, she sued under the FMLA but lost. A federal court and the Seventh Circuit ruled that she could be fired for violating the FMLA's "two-day" rule, which required her to give notice of unforeseeable need for leave within two days. Although that rule has since been replaced by **a rule requiring employees to comply with the employer's usual and customary policy on notice of need for leave**, the two-day rule applied here. And the employee failed to show that extraordinary circumstances prevented her from complying. *Brown v. Automotive Components Holdings, LLC*, 622 F.3d 685 (7th Cir. 2010).

◆   A Texas medical center employee with a seizure disorder had a history of FMLA-approved absences and unexcused absences. One day, her mother found her hallucinating at home and contacted her supervisor. She was told to take the employee to the emergency room. The employee was later transferred to a behavior center, where she was diagnosed with bipolar disorder. When she sought to obtain additional FMLA leave, she learned that she had been fired for failing to contact the medical center's third-party administrator within two days of her release from the hospital. She sued. A federal court granted pretrial judgment to the medical center, but the Fifth Circuit reversed, finding issues of fact over **whether the center's strict notice policy should be set aside** because her mother tried to comply with it by speaking with her supervisor. *Saenz v. Harlingen Medical Center, LP*, 613 F.3d 576 (5th Cir. 2010).

◆   An Arkansas steel mill employee with two unexcused absences sought a day off for his ex-father-in-law's funeral on the following Wednesday. He was told to swap with another employee on Sunday, but instead he called up on Sunday, intoxicated and emotional, and said he was "through" with the company. He then called his supervisor on Monday and claimed he'd had a nervous breakdown. But because he had previously been dishonest, his supervisor thought he was making an excuse not to come to work. He stayed away all week. The next week he called an HR manager and claimed an alcohol problem and depression. The manager referred him to the Employee Assistance Program, and he underwent treatment, after which he was demoted because of his unexcused absences. When he sued under the FMLA, he lost. A federal court and the Eighth Circuit ruled that **his shifting explanations for why he couldn't work did not provide sufficient notice of his need for FMLA leave.** *Scobey v. Nucor Steel-Arkansas,* 580 F.3d 781 (8th Cir. 2009).

♦ A service manager for a New Jersey company had a chronic heart condition, which his employer knew about. About two weeks after he returned from quintuple bypass surgery, he received a written warning about his job performance. He later told a supervisor that his doctor had found more blockages, that he was going to have to undergo medical monitoring, and that he might need more surgery. A week later he was fired for performance-related reasons. When he sued under the FMLA, a federal court granted pretrial judgment to the company. However, the Third Circuit reversed, finding issues of fact that required a trial. Here, **the employee's statement to his supervisor was sufficient to provide notice of his need for FMLA leave.** *Sarnowski v. Air Brooke Limousine, Inc.,* 510 F.3d 398 (3d Cir. 2007).

♦ An Illinois employee with a previously unblemished record got dizzy and felt her neck muscles tighten when a stray dog entered the facility where she worked. She began yelling to her supervisor that "f——— animals shouldn't be in the workplace." Two hours later she went home ill. She called in sick the next day, but the following day, she charged into the company president's office and began screaming and cursing at him for allowing a dog to enter the facility. She then missed three more days, and when she returned to work, she found the contents of her desk moved to another room to accommodate her fear of animals. She called the police, believing she was being harassed, then went home early. She went to a doctor but did not provide written or oral notice of her need for FMLA leave. After she was fired, she sued. A federal court granted pretrial judgment to the employer, but the Seventh Circuit reversed, finding issues of fact that required a trial. **Her unusual behavior may have provided the employer with constructive notice of her need for FMLA leave.** *Stevenson v. Hyre Electric,* 505 F.3d 720 (7th Cir. 2007).

♦ A Maryland employee missed two-and-a-half days of work because of illness. She saw a doctor and returned to work with medical reports diagnosing her with a possible peptic ulcer. She worked four days. On the fifth day she told her supervisor she was sick and had to leave early for a doctor's appointment. She was absent for the next eight days, but failed to inform her superiors that she would be gone, instead telling three co-workers to inform her supervisor that she was sick. She was fired, then provided documentation of her absence, and was offered a lower-paying position. She turned it down, then sued under the FMLA. A federal court ruled against her, noting that **her minimal notice to**

the employer did not satisfy the requirements of the FMLA. *Rodriguez v. Smithfield Packing Co.,* 545 F.Supp.2d 508 (D. Md. 2008).

♦   A Louisiana employee called her supervisor on a Monday to tell him she was sick. She also told him she was pregnant, but did not say that the sickness was related to pregnancy complications. When she called back on Tuesday, she was told to get a medical release. She told her supervisor she had a doctor's appointment on Wednesday, meaning more than a week later. However, her supervisor thought she meant the next day. She had no further contact with her employer for 10 days. When she was fired for violating the "no call/no show" policy, she sued under the FMLA. A federal court and the Fifth Circuit ruled against her. **She failed to give her supervisor enough information to put the employer on notice that she had a "serious health condition."** *Willis v. Coca-Cola Enterprises,* 445 F.3d 413 (5th Cir. 2006).

♦   An attendance-challenged Wisconsin employee in danger of being fired left work early because she was sick. She submitted a form from the company's health center stating that she should be off work for three days. Several months later, after more absences, she was fired. She was diagnosed with a head tumor and sued under the FMLA, claiming the three-day absence should not have been counted against her. A federal court and the Seventh Circuit ruled against her. **The note from the health center did not inform the company that she had a serious health condition**, and she did not tell the company she was taking prescribed antibiotics. *Phillips v. Quebecor World RAI, Inc.,* 450 F.3d 308 (7th Cir. 2006).

♦   After learning that she needed surgery, a pharmaceutical sales rep in Minnesota sought and obtained FMLA leave. However, the company sent her confusing notices as to when the leave started. One notice put the start date at August 2; another put it at August 20. Nevertheless, the company gave her more than 12 weeks leave, ultimately filling her position with someone else and firing her six months later. When she sued under the FMLA, she lost. The Eighth Circuit noted that **the ambiguities and contradictions in the company's notices did not create an FMLA claim.** *Grosenick v. SmithKline Beecham Corp.,* 454 F.3d 832 (8th Cir. 2006).

♦   A Florida employee asked for two weeks off to assist her pregnant daughter in Colorado because her daughter's husband had broken his collarbone. Even though she had already used her vacation time, the store manager granted her request. She asked the personnel office about FMLA leave, but did not assert that her daughter was suffering from any complications of pregnancy. The personnel office instructed her to obtain a doctor's note, but the doctor's note did not indicate there was any problem with the pregnancy either. Based on the note, the store manager denied her request for an additional two weeks' leave. She stayed with her daughter for four weeks and was fired. When she sued under the FMLA, she lost. The Eleventh Circuit noted that **she never gave the manager any indication that her daughter had a serious health condition**, so the store had no duty to inquire further. *Cruz v. Publix Super Markets, Inc.,* 428 F.3d 1379 (11th Cir. 2005).

♦   A union employee in New Jersey signed a last chance agreement after problems with absenteeism. Shortly thereafter, he got in a car accident. He was eligible for leave under the FMLA and requested such leave, but his employer did not provide him with the required notice of his entitlement to 12 weeks' leave. He decided to have surgery to correct the shoulder problem from the accident and was out for more than 12 weeks. The employer fired him after his 12 weeks of leave expired, and he sued under the FMLA. A federal court granted pretrial judgment to the employer, but the Third Circuit reversed in part. Here, **the employee was claiming that he was prejudiced by the lack of notice**: specifically, he said he would have reconsidered the surgery if he knew he only had 12 weeks of leave. This issue required a trial. *Conoshenti v. Public Service Electric & Gas Co.*, 364 F.3d 135 (3d Cir. 2004).

C. Q&As

1.   *We require all staff returning from FMLA leave to be able to handle the workload they had before they left. Is that legal?*

No, says Sindy Warren *(swarren@warrenhays.com)* of HR consulting firm Warren & Hays. Telling staffers they need to return for "full duty" can violate the ADA.

Advise returning staff that they must be able to do the essential functions of the job – with or without accommodation.

2.   *Our office was closed one day last week due to snow, and we had an employee out on FMLA leave that day. How does that affect the worker's FMLA time?*

It comes down to how the worker's FMLA time was going to be used that week, says Bill Pokorny *(wrp@franczek.com)*.

If the worker is out on extended FMLA leave, then count the snow day against the worker's leave bank.

But if the staffer is on intermittent leave and worked part of the week, only count the day as leave if he or she was expected to work that day.

3.   *We know we must give staff 15 days to return FMLA medical certification. When does that 15-day clock start ticking?*

It starts on the day the worker receives the certification, says Bill Pokorny *(wrp@franczek.com)*.

Follow this four-step process:
1.   Send the request in writing. State a response is due within 15 days by providing a date: "assuming this request is received on [date], it's due on [date]." Keep a record of when the request is sent.
2.   Get delivery confirmation and keep it with a copy of the request.
3.   Count the 15 days from the date of delivery to the worker.
4.   If the worker doesn't return the certification, consider a follow-up

request before denying leave. Tell the employee he or she must explain why the certification wasn't provided within the initial 15-day period.

4. Do we have to pay the doctor's fees for filling out FMLA certification forms, or do employees cover the cost?

Employees are on the hook for the initial certification, says Christine Walters *(christine@fivel.net)*, an independent consultant for FiveL Company *(www.FiveL.net)* who recently spoke at the annual SHRM conference in San Diego.

Companies that ask staffers to get a second or third opinion, however, are required by law to pay those fees.

D. Real-Life Success Stories

1. Paper trail prevents any FMLA issues

Our FMLA leave process needed some tightening up. Our goal was to keep the communication lines open with workers – and to create a solid paper trail in case of a problem.

First, we made it a point to distribute and personally go over all of the FMLA info with any employee requesting leave.

Next, I put my name and a confidential HR fax number on top of any forms that had to be returned to us. It ensured the doctor's office could never say it didn't know our contact or fax number.

After receiving the doctor's return-to-work forms, I'd mark my Outlook calendar to revisit the case 15 days before a worker's return date.

Then a letter would be sent to the employee informing him or her of the status of the claim.

I'd also let the person know when the doctor said he or she could return to work and when the next scheduled work day would be.

If the return date wasn't feasible, staffers had to submit a revised return-to-work form before the scheduled return date.

Tried and tested

The updated process did the trick when we had to fire someone for failing to return to work from FMLA leave. We attached our documentation with the unemployment protest, and the person was denied unemployment benefits from our company.

(An HR manager for an auto dealership in the Northeast)

2. Gave managers a tool to clarify procedures

Our supervisors just weren't equipped to handle the kind of FMLA and workers' comp issues they were being confronted with.

Some of them just picked up the phone and called us. No problem – that's what we're here for.

But the others didn't call – they just sort of muddled through.

That meant we weren't getting the necessary paperwork.

Some of our records were in bad shape. We never seemed to have the documentation we needed to handle FMLA and workers' comp claims.

We needed a simple resource to guide managers when these kinds of issues came up.

Step-by-step instructions

What we needed was an operating manual. So we came up with one.

It wasn't anything fancy – just a loose-leaf notebook with separators for the issues they might have to face.

Every problem had a checklist of steps to take: fill out this form, tell employees what they should know (sample language included), and then send us an email.

The manual didn't smooth out all the bumps, but it sure helped.

We still get some phone calls. But because the manual answers most of our managers' questions, the problems are usually solved quickly.

And our records have never been in better shape.

(A personnel coordinator for a rehabilitation center in California)

3. Took mystery out of FMLA designations

We never had a major problem with FMLA abuse, but day-to-day administration was a real pain.

A lot of employees didn't grasp how we calculated intermittent FMLA leave or how our rolling calendars worked.

Others were confused by our policy of requiring paid-time off (PTO) to be used up first.

Result: Several workers who were out on FMLA called to say they were uncertain how much leave time they had left. We knew this could spell trouble.

Info at their fingertips

So as a safeguard, when employees took time off, we sent notices to their homes. In them, we noted when there were overlaps of PTO and FMLA.

We also enclosed info about our FMLA designation procedures, taken from employee handbooks.

At a glance, recipients could check our rolling leave calendar, which events qualified for FMLA, medical certification requirements and the procedures for disputing an FMLA designation.

Result: Employees liked the notices because they didn't have to dig out their handbooks for the info.

We liked it because there were no surprises with FMLA.

No one could cry ignorance about remaining leave. And if we made a calculation mistake, we fixed it fast.

(A senior systems analyst for a medical facility in Illinois)

E. Statutes and Regulations

Family and Medical Leave Act

An Act

To grant family and temporary medical leave under certain circumstances.

Be it enacted by the Senate and House of Representatives of the United States of America in Congress assembled,

SECTION 1. SHORT TITLE; TABLE OF CONTENTS.

(a) SHORT TITLE. – This Act may be cited as the "Family and Medical Leave Act of 1993".

(b) TABLE OF CONTENTS. – The table of contents is as follows:

TITLE I – GENERAL REQUIREMENTS FOR LEAVE

TITLE II – LEAVE FOR CIVIL SERVICE EMPLOYEES

TITLE III – COMMISSION ON LEAVE

TITLE IV – MISCELLANEOUS PROVISIONS

SEC. 2. FINDINGS AND PURPOSES.

(a) FINDINGS. – Congress finds that –

(1) the number of single-parent households and two-parent households in which the single parent or both parents work is increasing significantly;

(2) it is important for the development of children and the family unit that fathers and mothers be able to participate in early childrearing and the care of family members who have serious health conditions;

(3) the lack of employment policies to accommodate working parents can force individuals to choose between job security and parenting;

(4) there is inadequate job security for employees who have serious health conditions that prevent them from working for temporary periods;

(5) due to the nature of the roles of men and women in our society, the primary responsibility for family caretaking often falls on women, and such responsibility affects the working lives of women more than it affects the working lives of men; and

(6) employment standards that apply to one gender only have serious potential for encouraging employers to discriminate against employees and applicants for employment who are of that gender.

(b) PURPOSES. – It is the purpose of this Act –

(1) to balance the demands of the workplace with the needs of families, to promote the stability and economic security of families, and to promote national interests in preserving family integrity;

(2) to entitle employees to take reasonable leave for medical reasons, for the birth or adoption of a child, and for the care of a child, spouse, or parent who has a serious health condition;

(3) to accomplish the purposes described in paragraphs (1) and (2) in a manner that accommodates the legitimate interests of employers;

(4) to accomplish the purposes described in paragraphs (1) and (2) in a manner that, consistent with the Equal Protection Clause of the Fourteenth Amendment, minimizes the potential for employment discrimination on the basis of sex by ensuring generally that leave is available for eligible medical reasons (including maternity-related

disability) and for compelling family reasons, on a gender-neutral basis; and

(5) to promote the goal of equal employment opportunity for women and men, pursuant to such clause.

TITLE I – GENERAL REQUIREMENTS FOR LEAVE

SEC. 101. DEFINITIONS.

(1) COMMERCE. – The terms "commerce" and "industry or activity affecting commerce" mean any activity, business, or industry in commerce or in which a labor dispute would hinder or obstruct commerce or the free flow of commerce, and include "commerce" and any "industry affecting commerce", as defined in paragraphs (1) and (3) of section 501 of the Labor Management Relations Act, 1947 (29 U.S.C. 142 (1) and (3)).

(2) ELIGIBLE EMPLOYEE. –

(A) IN GENERAL. – The term "eligible employee" means an employee who has been employed

(i) for at least 12 months by the employer with respect to whom leave is requested under section 102; and

(ii) for at least 1,250 hours of service with such employer during the previous 12-month period.

(B) EXCLUSIONS. – The term "eligible employee" does not include

(i) any Federal officer or employee covered under subchapter V of chapter 63 of title 5, United States Code (as added by title II of this Act); or

(ii) any employee of an employer who is employed at a worksite at which such employer employs less than 50 employees if the total number of employees employed by that employer within 75 miles of that worksite is less than 50.

(C) DETERMINATION. – For purposes of determining whether an employee meets the hours of service requirement specified in subparagraph (A)(ii), the legal standards established under section 7 of the Fair Labor Standards Act of 1938 (29 U.S.C. 207) shall apply.

(D) AIRLINE FLIGHT CREWS.—

(i) DETERMINATION.—For purposes of determining whether an employee who is a flight attendant or flight crewmember (as such terms are defined in regulations of the Federal Aviation Administration) meets the hours of service requirement specified in subparagraph (A)(ii), the employee will be considered to meet the requirement if—

(I) the employee has worked or been paid for not less than 60 percent of the applicable total monthly guarantee, or the equivalent, for the previous 12-month period, for or by the employer with respect to whom leave is requested under section 102; and

(II) the employee has worked or been paid for not less than 504 hours (not counting personal commute time or time spent on vacation leave or medical or sick leave) during the previous 12-month period, for or by that employer.

(ii) FILE.—Each employer of an employee described in clause (i) shall maintain on file with the Secretary (in accordance with such regulations as the Secretary may prescribe) containing information specifying the applicable monthly guarantee with respect to each category of employee to which such guarantee applies.

(iii) DEFINITION.—In this subparagraph, the term 'applicable monthly guarantee' means—

(I) for an employee described in clause (i) other than an employee on reserve status, the minimum number of hours for which an employer has agreed to schedule such employee for any given month; and

(II) for an employee described in clause (i) who is on reserve status, the number of hours for which an employer has agreed to pay such employee on reserve status for any given month, as established in the applicable collective bargaining agreement or, if none exists, in the employer's policies.

(3) EMPLOY; EMPLOYEE; STATE. – The terms "employ", "employee", and "State" have the same meanings given such terms in subsections (c), (e), and (g) of section 3 of the Fair Labor Standards Act of 1938 (29 U.S.C. 203(c), (e), and (g)).

(4) EMPLOYER. –

(A) IN GENERAL. – The term "employer"

(i) means any person engaged in commerce or in any industry or activity affecting commerce who employs 50 or more employees for each working day during each of 20 or more calendar workweeks in the current or preceding calendar year;

(ii) includes –

(I) any person who acts, directly or indirectly, in the interest of an employer to any of the employees of such employer; and

(II) any successor in interest of an employer; and

(iii) includes any "public agency", as defined in section 3(x) of the Fair Labor Standards Act of 1938 (29 U.S.C. 203(x)).

(B) PUBLIC AGENCY. – For purposes of subparagraph (A)(iii), a public agency shall be considered to be a person engaged in commerce or in an industry or activity affecting commerce.

(5) EMPLOYMENT BENEFITS. – The term "employment benefits" means all benefits provided or made available to employees by an employer, including group life insurance, health insurance, disability insurance, sick leave, annual leave, educational benefits, and pensions, regardless of whether such benefits are provided by a practice or written policy of an employer or through an "employee benefit plan", as defined in section 3(3) of the Employee Retirement Income Security Act of 1974

(29 U.S.C. 1002(3)).

(6) HEALTH CARE PROVIDER. – The term "health care provider" means –

(A) a doctor of medicine or osteopathy who is authorized to practice medicine or surgery (as appropriate) by the State in which the doctor practices; or

(B) any other person determined by the Secretary to be capable of providing health care services.

(7) PARENT. – The term "parent" means the biological parent of an employee or an individual who stood in loco parentis to an employee when the employee was a son or daughter.

(8) PERSON. – The term "person" has the same meaning given such term in section 3(a) of the Fair Labor Standards Act of 1938 (29 U.S.C. 203(a)).

(9) REDUCED LEAVE SCHEDULE. – The term "reduced leave schedule" means a leave schedule that reduces the usual number of hours per workweek, or hours per workday, of an employee.

(10) SECRETARY. – The term "Secretary" means the Secretary of Labor.

(11) SERIOUS HEALTH CONDITION. The term "serious health condition" means an illness, injury, impairment, or physical or mental condition that involves

(A) inpatient care in a hospital, hospice, or residential medical care facility; or

(B) continuing treatment by a health care provider.

(12) SON OR DAUGHTER. – The term "son or daughter" means a biological, adopted, or foster child, a stepchild, a legal ward, or a child of a person standing in loco parentis, who is –

(A) under 18 years of age; or

(B) 18 years of age or older and incapable of self-care because of a mental or physical disability.

(13) SPOUSE. – The term "spouse" means a husband or wife, as the case may be.

(14) COVERED ACTIVE DUTY.—The term 'covered active duty' means –

(A) in the case of a member of a regular component of the Armed Forces, duty during the deployment of the member with the Armed Forces to a foreign country; and

(B) in the case of a member of the reserve component of the Armed Forces, duty during the deployment of the member with the Armed Forces to a foreign country under a call or order to active duty under a provision of law referred to in section 101(a)(13)(B) of title 10, United States Code.

(15) COVERED SERVICEMEMBER.—The term "covered servicemember" means—

(A) a member of the Armed Forces (including a member of the

National Guard or Reserves) who is undergoing medical treatment, recuperation, or therapy, is otherwise in outpatient status, or is otherwise on the temporary disability retired list, for a serious injury of illness; or

(B) a veteran who is undergoing medical treatment, recuperation, or therapy, for a serious injury or illness and who was a member of the Armed Forces (including a member of the National Guard or Reserves) at any time during the period of 5 years preceding the date on which the veteran undergoes that medical treatment, recuperation, or therapy.

(16) OUTPATIENT STATUS.—The term "outpatient status", with respect to a covered servicemember, means the status of a member of the Armed Forces assigned to—

(A) a military medical treatment facility as an outpatient; or

(B) a unit established for the purpose of providing command and control of members of the Armed Forces receiving medical care as outpatients.

(17) NEXT OF KIN.—The term "next of kin", used with respect to an individual, means the nearest blood relative of that individual.

(18) SERIOUS INJURY OR ILLNESS.—The term 'serious injury or illness'—

(A) in the case of a member of the Armed Forces (including a member of the National Guard or Reserves), means an injury or illness that was incurred by the member in line of duty on active duty in the Armed Forces (or existed before the beginning of the member's active duty and was aggravated by service in line of duty on active duty in the Armed Forces) and that may render the member medically unfit to perform the duties of the member's office, grade, rank, or rating; and

(B) in the case of a veteran who was a member of the Armed Forces (including a member of the National Guard or Reserves) at any time during a period described in paragraph (15)(B), means a qualifying (as defined by the Secretary of Labor) injury or illness that was incurred by the member in line of duty on active duty in the Armed Forces (or existed before the beginning of the member's active duty and was aggravated by service in line of duty on active duty in the Armed Forces) and that manifested itself before or after the member became a veteran.

(19) VETERAN.—The term 'veteran' has the meaning given the term in section 101 of title 38, United States Code.

SEC. 102. LEAVE REQUIREMENT .

(a) IN GENERAL. –

(1) ENTITLEMENT TO LEAVE. – Subject to section 103, an eligible employee shall be entitled to a total of 12 workweeks of leave during any 12-month period for one or more of the following:

(A) Because of the birth of a son or daughter of the employee and in order to care for such son or daughter.

(B) Because of the placement of a son or daughter with the employee for adoption or foster care.

(C) In order to care for the spouse, or a son, daughter, or parent, of the employee, if such spouse, son, daughter, or parent has a serious health condition.

(D) Because of a serious health condition that makes the employee unable to perform the functions of the position of such employee.

(E) Because of any qualifying exigency (as the Secretary shall, by regulation, determine) arising out of the fact that the spouse, or a son, daughter, or parent of the employee is on covered active duty (or has been notified of an impending call or order to covered active duty) in the Armed Forces.

(2) EXPIRATION OF ENTITLEMENT. – The entitlement to leave under subparagraphs (A) and (B) of paragraph (1) for a birth or placement of a son or daughter shall expire at the end of the 12-month period beginning on the date of such birth or placement.

(3) SERVICEMEMBER FAMILY LEAVE.—Subject to section 103, an eligible employee who is the spouse, son, daughter, parent, or next of kin of a covered servicemember shall be entitled to a total of 26 workweeks of leave during a 12-month period to care for the servicemember. The leave described in this paragraph shall only be available during a single 12-month period.

(4) COMBINED LEAVE TOTAL.—During the single 12-month period described in paragraph (3), an eligible employee shall be entitled to a combined total of 26 workweeks of leave under paragraphs (1) and (3). Nothing in this paragraph shall be construed to limit the availability of leave under paragraph (1) during any other 12-month period.

(5) CALCULATION OF LEAVE FOR AIRLINE FLIGHT CREWS.— The Secretary may provide, by regulation, a method for calculating the leave described in paragraph (1) with respect to employees described in section 101(2)(D).

(b) LEAVE TAKEN INTERMITTENTLY OR ON A REDUCED LEAVE SCHEDULE.

(1) IN GENERAL. – Leave under subparagraph (A) or (B) of subsection (a)(1) shall not be taken by an employee intermittently or on a reduced leave schedule unless the employee and the employer of the employee agree otherwise. Subject to paragraph (2), subsection (e)(2), and subsection (b)(5) or (f) (as appropriate) of section 103, leave under subparagraph (C) or (D) of subsection (a)(1) or under subsection (a)(3) may be taken intermittently or on a reduced leave schedule when medically necessary. Subject to subsection (e)(3) and section 103(f), leave under subsection (a)(1)(E) may be taken intermittently or on a reduced leave schedule. The taking of leave intermittently or on a reduced leave schedule pursuant to this paragraph shall not result in a reduction in the total amount of leave to which the employee is entitled

under subsection (a) beyond the amount of leave actually taken.

(2) ALTERNATIVE POSITION. – If an employee requests intermittent leave, or leave on a reduced leave schedule, under subparagraph (C) or (D) of subsection (a)(1) or under subsection (a)(3), that is foreseeable based on planned medical treatment, the employer may require such employee to transfer temporarily to an available alternative position offered by the employer for which the employee is qualified and that –

(A) has equivalent pay and benefits; and

(B) better accommodates recurring periods of leave than the regular employment position of the employee.

(c) UNPAID LEAVE PERMITTED. – Except as provided in subsection (d), leave granted under subsection (a) may consist of unpaid leave. Where an employee is otherwise exempt under regulations issued by the Secretary pursuant to section 13(a)(1) of the Fair Labor Standards Act of 1938 (29 U.S.C. 213(a)(1)), the compliance of an employer with this title by providing unpaid leave shall not affect the exempt status of the employee under such section.

(d) RELATIONSHIP TO PAID LEAVE. –

(1) UNPAID LEAVE. – If an employer provides paid leave for fewer than 12 workweeks (or 26 workweeks in the case of leave provided under subsection (a)(3)), the additional weeks of leave necessary to attain the 12 workweeks (or 26 workweeks, as appropriate) of leave required under this title may be provided without compensation.

(2) SUBSTITUTION OF PAID LEAVE. –

(A) IN GENERAL. – An eligible employee may elect, or an employer may require the employee, to substitute any of the accrued paid vacation leave, personal leave, or family leave of the employee for leave provided under subparagraph (A), (B), (C), or (E) of subsection (a)(1) for any part of the 12-week period of such leave under such subsection.

(B) SERIOUS HEALTH CONDITION. – An eligible employee may elect, or an employer may require the employee, to substitute any of the accrued paid vacation leave, personal leave, or medical or sick leave of the employee for leave provided under subparagraph (C) or (D) of subsection (a)(1) for any part of the 12-week period of such leave under such subsection, except that nothing in this title shall require an employer to provide paid sick leave or paid medical leave in any situation in which such employer would not normally provide any such paid leave. An eligible employee may elect, or an employer may require the employee, to substitute any of the accrued paid vacation leave, personal leave, family leave, or medical or sick leave of the employee for leave provided under subsection (a)(3) for any part of the 26-week period of such leave under such subsection, except that nothing in this title requires an employer to provide paid sick leave or paid medical leave in any situation in which the employer would not normally provide any such paid leave.

(e) FORESEEABLE LEAVE. –

(1) REQUIREMENT OF NOTICE. – In any case in which the necessity for leave under subparagraph (A) or (B) of subsection (a)(1) is foreseeable based on an expected birth or placement, the employee shall provide the employer with not less than 30 days' notice, before the date the leave is to begin, of the employee's intention to take leave under such subparagraph, except that if the date of the birth or placement requires leave to begin in less than 30 days, the employee shall provide such notice as is practicable.

(2) DUTIES OF EMPLOYEE. – In any case in which the necessity for leave under subparagraph (C) or (D) of subsection (a)(1) or under subsection (a)(3) is foreseeable based on planned medical treatment, the employee –

(A) shall make a reasonable effort to schedule the treatment so as not to disrupt unduly the operations of the employer, subject to the approval of the health care provider of the employee or the health care provider of the son, daughter, spouse, parent, or covered servicemember of the employee, as appropriate; and

(B) shall provide the employer with not less than 30 days' notice, before the date the leave is to begin, of the employee's intention to take leave under such subparagraph, except that if the date of the treatment requires leave to begin in less than 30 days, the employee shall provide such notice as is practicable.

(3) NOTICE FOR LEAVE DUE TO COVERED ACTIVE DUTY OF FAMILY MEMBER. – In any case in which the necessity for leave under subsection (a)(1)(E) is foreseeable, whether because the spouse, or a son, daughter, or parent, of the employee is on covered active duty, or because of notification of an impending call or order to covered active duty, the employee shall provide such notice to the employer as is reasonable and practicable.

(f) SPOUSES EMPLOYED BY THE SAME EMPLOYER. –

(1) IN GENERAL. – In any case in which a husband and wife entitled to leave under subsection (a) are employed by the same employer, the aggregate number of workweeks of leave to which both may be entitled may be limited to 12 workweeks during any 12-month period, if such leave is taken –

(A) under subparagraph (A) or (B) of subsection (a)(1); or

(B) to care for a sick parent under subparagraph (C) of such subsection.

(2) SERVICEMEMBER FAMILY LEAVE. –

(A) IN GENERAL. – The aggregate number of workweeks of leave to which both that husband and wife may be entitled under subsection (a) may be limited to 26 workweeks during the single 12-month period described in subsection (a)(3) if the leave is –

(i) leave under subsection (a)(3); or

(ii) a combination of leave under subsection (a)(3) and leave described in paragraph (1).

(B) BOTH LIMITATIONS APPLICABLE. – If the leave taken by the husband and wife includes leave described in paragraph (1), the limitation in paragraph (1) shall apply to the leave described in paragraph (1).

SEC. 103. CERTIFICATION.

(a) IN GENERAL. – An employer may require that a request for leave under subparagraph (C) or (D) of paragraph (1) or paragraph (3) of section 102(a) be supported by a certification issued by the health care provider of the eligible employee or of the son, daughter, spouse, or parent of the employee, or of the next of kin of an individual in the case of leave taken under such paragraph (3), as appropriate. The employee shall provide, in a timely manner, a copy of such certification to the employer.

(b) SUFFICIENT CERTIFICATION. – Certification provided under subsection (a) shall be sufficient if it states

(1) the date on which the serious health condition commenced;

(2) the probable duration of the condition;

(3) the appropriate medical facts within the knowledge of the health care provider regarding the condition;

(4)(A) for purposes of leave under section 102(a)(1)(C), a statement that the eligible employee is needed to care for the son, daughter, spouse, or parent and an estimate of the amount of time that such employee is needed to care for the son, daughter, spouse, or parent; and

(B) for purposes of leave under section 102(a)(1)(D), a statement that the employee is unable to perform the functions of the position of the employee;

(5) in the case of certification for intermittent leave, or leave on a reduced leave schedule, for planned medical treatment, the dates on which such treatment is expected to be given and the duration of such treatment;

(6) in the case of certification for intermittent leave, or leave on a reduced leave schedule, under section 102(a)(1)(D), a statement of the medical necessity for the intermittent leave or leave on a reduced leave schedule, and the expected duration of the intermittent leave or reduced leave schedule; and

(7) in the case of certification for intermittent leave, or leave on a reduced leave schedule, under section 102(a)(1)(C), a statement that the employee's intermittent leave or leave on a reduced leave schedule is necessary for the care of the son, daughter, parent, or spouse who has a serious health condition, or will assist in their recovery, and the expected duration and schedule of the intermittent leave or reduced leave schedule.

(c) SECOND opinion. –

(1) IN GENERAL. – In any case in which the employer has reason to

doubt the validity of the certification provided under subsection (a) for leave under subparagraph (C) or (D) of section 102(a)(1), the employer may require, at the expense of the employer, that the eligible employee obtain the opinion of a second health care provider designated or approved by the employer concerning any information certified under subsection (b) for such leave.

(2) LIMITATION. – A health care provider designated or approved under paragraph (1) shall not be employed on a regular basis by the employer.

(d) RESOLUTION OF CONFLICTING OPINIONS. –

(1) IN GENERAL. – In any case in which the second opinion described in subsection (c) differs from the opinion in the original certification provided under subsection (a), the employer may require, at the expense of the employer, that the employee obtain the opinion of a third health care provider designated or approved jointly by the employer and the employee concerning the information certified under subsection (b).

(2) FINALITY. – The opinion of the third health care provider concerning the information certified under subsection (b) shall be considered to be final and shall be binding on the employer and the employee.

(e) SUBSEQUENT RECERTIFICATION. – The employer may require that the eligible employee obtain subsequent recertifications on a reasonable basis.

(f) CERTIFICATION RELATED TO COVERED ACTIVE DUTY OR CALL TO COVERED ACTIVE DUTY.—An employer may require that a request for leave under section 102(a)(1)(E) be supported by a certification issued at such time and in such manner as the Secretary may by regulation prescribe. If the Secretary issues a regulation requiring such certification, the employee shall provide, in a timely manner, a copy of such certification to the employer.

SEC. 104. EMPLOYMENT AND BENEFITS PROTECTION.

(a) RESTORATION TO POSITION. –

(1) IN GENERAL. – Except as provided in subsection (b), any eligible employee who takes leave under section 102 for the intended purpose of the leave shall be entitled, on return from such leave –

(A) to be restored by the employer to the position of employment held by the employee when the leave commenced; or

(B) to be restored to an equivalent position with equivalent employment benefits, pay, and other terms and conditions of employment.

(2) LOSS OF BENEFITS. – The taking of leave under section 102 shall not result in the loss of any employment benefit accrued prior to the date on which the leave commenced.

(3) LIMITATIONS. – Nothing in this section shall be construed to

entitle any restored employee to –

(A) the accrual of any seniority or employment benefits during any period of leave; or

(B) any right, benefit, or position of employment other than any right, benefit, or position to which the employee would have been entitled had the employee not taken the leave.

(4) CERTIFICATION. – As a condition of restoration under paragraph (1) for an employee who has taken leave under section 102(a)(1)(D), the employer may have a uniformly applied practice or policy that requires each such employee to receive certification from the health care provider of the employee that the employee is able to resume work, except that nothing in this paragraph shall supersede a valid State or local law or a collective bargaining agreement that governs the return to work of such employees.

(5) CONSTRUCTION. – Nothing in this subsection shall be construed to prohibit an employer from requiring an employee on leave under section 102 to report periodically to the employer on the status and intention of the employee to return to work.

(b) EXEMPTION CONCERNING CERTAIN HIGHLY COMPENSATED EMPLOYEES. –

(1) DENIAL OF RESTORATION. – An employer may deny restoration under subsection (a) to any eligible employee described in paragraph (2) if –

(A) such denial is necessary to prevent substantial and grievous economic injury to the operations of the employer;

(B) the employer notifies the employee of the intent of the employer to deny restoration on such basis at the time the employer determines that such injury would occur; and

(C) in any case in which the leave has commenced, the employee elects not to return to employment after receiving such notice.

(2) AFFECTED EMPLOYEES. – An eligible employee described in paragraph (1) is a salaried eligible employee who is among the highest paid 10 percent of the employees employed by the employer within 75 miles of the facility at which the employee is employed.

(c) MAINTENANCE OF HEALTH BENEFITS. –

(1) COVERAGE. – Except as provided in paragraph (2), during any period that an eligible employee takes leave under section 102, the employer shall maintain coverage under any "group health plan" (as defined in section 5000(b)(1) of the Internal Revenue Code of 1986) for the duration of such leave at the level and under the conditions coverage would have been provided if the employee had continued in employment continuously for the duration of such leave.

(2) FAILURE TO RETURN FROM LEAVE. – The employer may recover the premium that the employer paid for maintaining coverage for the employee under such group health plan during any period of

unpaid leave under section 102 if –

(A) the employee fails to return from leave under section 102 after the period of leave to which the employee is entitled has expired; and

(B) the employee fails to return to work for a reason other than –

(i) the continuation, recurrence, or onset of a serious health condition that entitles the employee to leave under subparagraph (C) or (D) of section 102(a)(1) or under section 102(a)(3); or

(ii) other circumstances beyond the control of the employee.

(3) CERTIFICATION. –

(A) ISSUANCE. – An employer may require that a claim that an employee is unable to return to work because of the continuation, recurrence, or onset of the serious health condition described in paragraph (2)(B)(i) be supported by –

(i) a certification issued by the health care provider of the son, daughter, spouse, or parent of the employee, as appropriate, in the case of an employee unable to return to work because of a condition specified in section 102(a)(1)(C); or

(ii) a certification issued by the health care provider of the eligible employee, in the case of an employee unable to return to work because of a condition specified in section 102(a)(1)(D); or

(iii) a certification issued by the health care provider of the servicemember being cared for by the employee, in the case of an employee unable to return to work because of a condition specified in section 102(a)(3).

(B) COPY. – The employee shall provide, in a timely manner, a copy of such certification to the employer.

(C) SUFFICIENCY OF CERTIFICATION. –

(i) LEAVE DUE TO SERIOUS HEALTH CONDITION OF EMPLOYEE. – The certification described in subparagraph (A)(ii) shall be sufficient if the certification states that a serious health condition prevented the employee from being able to perform the functions of the position of the employee on the date that the leave of the employee expired.

(ii) LEAVE DUE TO SERIOUS HEALTH CONDITION OF FAMILY MEMBER. – The certification described in subparagraph (A)(i) shall be sufficient if the certification states that the employee is needed to care for the son, daughter, spouse, or parent who has a serious health condition on the date that the leave of the employee expired.

SEC. 105. PROHIBITED ACTS.

(a) INTERFERENCE WITH RIGHTS. –

(1) EXERCISE OF RIGHTS. – It shall be unlawful for any employer to interfere with, restrain, or deny the exercise of or the attempt to exercise, any right provided under this title.

(2) DISCRIMINATION. – It shall be unlawful for any employer to discharge or in any other manner discriminate against any individual for opposing any practice made unlawful by this title.

(b) INTERFERENCE WITH PROCEEDINGS OR INQUIRIES. – It shall be unlawful for any person to discharge or in any other manner discriminate against any individual because such individual –

(1) has filed any charge, or has instituted or caused to be instituted any proceeding, under or related to this title;

(2) has given, or is about to give, any information in connection with any inquiry or proceeding relating to any right provided under this title; or

(3) has testified, or is about to testify, in any inquiry or proceeding relating to any right provided under this title.

SEC. 106. INVESTIGATIVE AUTHORITY.

(a) IN GENERAL. – To ensure compliance with the provisions of this title, or any regulation or order issued under this title, the Secretary shall have, subject to subsection (c), the investigative authority provided under section 11(a) of the Fair Labor Standards Act of 1938 (29 U.S.C. 211(a)).

(b) OBLIGATION TO KEEP AND PRESERVE RECORDS. – Any employer shall make, keep, and preserve records pertaining to compliance with this title in accordance with section 11(c) of the Fair Labor Standards Act of 1938 (29 U.S.C. 211(c)) and in accordance with regulations issued by the Secretary.

(c) REQUIRED SUBMISSIONS GENERALLY LIMITED TO AN ANNUAL BASIS. – The Secretary shall not under the authority of this section require any employer or any plan, fund, or program to submit to the Secretary any books or records more than once during any 12-month period, unless the Secretary has reasonable cause to believe there may exist a violation of this title or any regulation or order issued pursuant to this title, or is investigating a charge pursuant to section 107(b).

(d) SUBPOENA POWERS. – For the purposes of any investigation provided for in this section, the Secretary shall have the subpoena authority provided for under section 9 of the Fair Labor Standards Act of 1938.

SEC. 107. ENFORCEMENT.

(a) CIVIL ACTION BY EMPLOYEES. –

(1) LIABILITY. – Any employer who violates section 105 shall be liable to any eligible employee affected –

(A) for damages equal to –

(i) the amount of –

(I) any wages, salary, employment benefits, or other compensation denied or lost to such employee by reason of the violation; or

(II) in a case in which wages, salary, employment benefits, or other compensation have not been denied or lost to the employee, any actual monetary losses sustained by the employee as a direct result of the violation, such as the cost of providing care, up to a sum equal to 12 weeks (or 26 weeks, in a case involving leave under section 102(a)(3)) of wages or salary for the employee;

(ii) the interest on the amount described in clause (i) calculated at the prevailing rate; and

(iii) an additional amount as liquidated damages equal to the sum of the amount described in clause (i) and the interest described in clause (ii), except that if an employer who has violated section 105 proves to the satisfaction of the court that the act or omission which violated section 105 was in good faith and that the employer had reasonable grounds for believing that the act or omission was not a violation of section 105, such court may, in the discretion of the court, reduce the amount of the liability to the amount and interest determined under clauses (i) and (ii), respectively; and

(B) for such equitable relief as may be appropriate, including employment, reinstatement, and promotion.

(2) RIGHT OF ACTION. – An action to recover the damages or equitable relief prescribed in paragraph (1) may be maintained against any employer (including a public agency) in any Federal or State court of competent jurisdiction by any one or more employees for and in behalf of –

(A) the employees; or

(B) the employees and other employees similarly situated.

(3) FEES AND COSTS. – The court in such an action shall, in addition to any judgment awarded to the plaintiff, allow a reasonable attorney's fee, reasonable expert witness fees, and other costs of the action to be paid by the defendant.

(4) LIMITATIONS. – The right provided by paragraph (2) to bring an action by or on behalf of any employee shall terminate –

(A) on the filing of a complaint by the Secretary in an action under subsection (d) in which restraint is sought of any further delay in the payment of the amount described in paragraph (1)(A) to such employee by an employer responsible under paragraph (1) for the payment; or

(B) on the filing of a complaint by the Secretary in an action under subsection (b) in which a recovery is sought of the damages described in paragraph (1)(A) owing to an eligible employee by an employer liable under paragraph (1), unless the action described in subparagraph (A) or (B) is dismissed without prejudice on motion of the Secretary.

(b) ACTION BY THE SECRETARY. –

(1) ADMINISTRATIVE ACTION. – The Secretary shall receive, investigate, and attempt to resolve complaints of violations of section 105 in the same manner that the Secretary receives, investigates, and attempts to resolve complaints of violations of sections 6 and 7 of the

Fair Labor Standards Act of 1938 (29 U.S.C. 206 and 207).

(2) CIVIL ACTION. – The Secretary may bring an action in any court of competent jurisdiction to recover the damages described in subsection (a)(1)(A).

(3) SUMS RECOVERED. – Any sums recovered by the Secretary pursuant to paragraph (2) shall be held in a special deposit account and shall be paid, on order of the Secretary, directly to each employee affected. Any such sums not paid to an employee because of inability to do so within a period of 3 years shall be deposited into the Treasury of the United States as miscellaneous receipts.

(c) LIMITATION. –

(1) IN GENERAL. – Except as provided in paragraph (2), an action may be brought under this section not later than 2 years after the date of the last event constituting the alleged violation for which the action is brought.

(2) WILLFUL VIOLATION. – In the case of such action brought for a willful violation of section 105, such action may be brought within 3 years of the date of the last event constituting the alleged violation for which such action is brought.

(3) COMMENCEMENT. – In determining when an action is commenced by the Secretary under this section for the purposes of this subsection, it shall be considered to be commenced on the date when the complaint is filed.

(d) ACTION FOR INJUNCTION BY SECRETARY. – The district courts of the United States shall have jurisdiction, for cause shown, in an action brought by the Secretary –

(1) to restrain violations of section 105, including the restraint of any withholding of payment of wages, salary, employment benefits, or other compensation, plus interest, found by the court to be due to eligible employees; or

(2) to award such other equitable relief as may be appropriate, including employment, reinstatement, and promotion.

(e) SOLICITOR OF LABOR. – The Solicitor of Labor may appear for and represent the Secretary on any litigation brought under this section.

SEC. 108. SPECIAL RULES CONCERNING EMPLOYEES OF LOCAL EDUCATIONAL AGENCIES.

(a) APPLICATION. –

(1) IN GENERAL. – Except as otherwise provided in this section, the rights (including the rights under section 104, which shall extend throughout the period of leave of any employee under this section), remedies, and procedures under this title shall apply to –

(A) any "local educational agency" (as defined in section 1471(12) of the Elementary and Secondary Education Act of 1965 (20 U.S.C. 2891(12))) and an eligible employee of the agency; and

(B) any private elementary or secondary school and an eligible employee of the school.

(2) DEFINITIONS. – For purposes of the application described in paragraph (1):

(A) ELIGIBLE EMPLOYEE. – The term "eligible employee" means an eligible employee of an agency or school described in paragraph (1).

(B) EMPLOYER. – The term "employer" means an agency or school described in paragraph (1).

(b) LEAVE DOES NOT VIOLATE CERTAIN OTHER FEDERAL LAWS. – A local educational agency and a private elementary or secondary school shall not be in violation of the Individuals with Disabilities Education Act (20 U.S.C. 1400 et seq.), section 504 of the Rehabilitation Act of 1973 (29 U.S.C. 794), or title VI of the Civil Rights Act of 1964 (42 U.S.C. 2000d et seq.), solely as a result of an eligible employee of such agency or school exercising the rights of such employee under this title.

(c) INTERMITTENT LEAVE OR LEAVE ON A REDUCED SCHEDULE FOR INSTRUCTIONAL EMPLOYEES. –

(1) IN GENERAL. – Subject to paragraph (2), in any case in which an eligible employee employed principally in an instructional capacity by any such educational agency or school requests leave under subparagraph (C) or (D) of section 102(a)(1) or under section 102(a)(3) that is foreseeable based on planned medical treatment and the employee would be on leave for greater than 20 percent of the total number of working days in the period during which the leave would extend, the agency or school may require that such employee elect either –

(A) to take leave for periods of a particular duration, not to exceed the duration of the planned medical treatment; or

(B) to transfer temporarily to an available alternative position offered by the employer for which the employee is qualified, and that –

(i) has equivalent pay and benefits; and

(ii) better accommodates recurring periods of leave than the regular employment position of the employee.

(2) APPLICATION. – The elections described in subparagraphs (A) and (B) of paragraph (1) shall apply only with respect to an eligible employee who complies with section 102(e)(2).

(d) RULES APPLICABLE TO PERIODS NEAR THE CONCLUSION OF AN ACADEMIC TERM. – The following rules shall apply with respect to periods of leave near the conclusion of an academic term in the case of any eligible employee employed principally in an instructional capacity by any such educational agency or school:

(1) LEAVE MORE THAN 5 WEEKS PRIOR TO END OF TERM. – If the eligible employee begins leave under section 102 more than 5 weeks prior to the end of the academic term, the agency or school

may require the employee to continue taking leave until the end of such term, if –

(A) the leave is of at least 3 weeks duration; and

(B) the return to employment would occur during the 3-week period before the end of such term.

(2) LEAVE LESS THAN 5 WEEKS PRIOR TO END OF TERM. – If the eligible employee begins leave under subparagraph (A), (B), or (C) of section 102(a)(1) or under section 102(a)(3) during the period that commences 5 weeks prior to the end of the academic term, the agency or school may require the employee to continue taking leave until the end of such term, if –

(A) the leave is of greater than 2 weeks duration; and

(B) the return to employment would occur during the 2-week period before the end of such term.

(3) LEAVE LESS THAN 3 WEEKS PRIOR TO END OF TERM. – If the eligible employee begins leave under subparagraph (A), (B), or (C) of section 102(a)(1) or under section 102(a)(3) during the period that commences 3 weeks prior to the end of the academic term and the duration of the leave is greater than 5 working days, the agency or school may require the employee to continue to take leave until the end of such term.

(e) RESTORATION TO EQUIVALENT EMPLOYMENT POSITION. – For purposes of determinations under section 104(a)(1)(B) (relating to the restoration of an eligible employee to an equivalent position), in the case of a local educational agency or a private elementary or secondary school, such determination shall be made on the basis of established school board policies and practices, private school policies and practices, and collective bargaining agreements.

(f) REDUCTION OF THE AMOUNT OF LIABILITY. – If a local educational agency or a private elementary or secondary school that has violated this title proves to the satisfaction of the court that the agency, school, or department had reasonable grounds for believing that the underlying act or omission was not a violation of this title, such court may, in the discretion of the court, reduce the amount of the liability provided for under section 107(a)(1)(A) to the amount and interest determined under clauses (i) and (ii), respectively, of such section.

SEC. 109. NOTICE.

(a) IN GENERAL. – Each employer shall post and keep posted, in conspicuous places on the premises of the employer where notices to employees and applicants for employment are customarily posted, a notice, to be prepared or approved by the Secretary, setting forth excerpts from, or summaries of, the pertinent provisions of this title and information pertaining to the filing of a charge.

(b) PENALTY. – Any employer that willfully violates this section may be assessed a civil money penalty not to exceed $100 for each separate offense.

CHAPTER FOUR

Personnel Development and Retention

I. TOPIC OVERVIEW

In a climate where finding qualified people is getting more and more difficult, retention efforts become more important than ever before.

And there's another reason it's crucial to hang on to top employees: Turnover's expensive.

First, there are the separation costs:

- administrative: HR's time handling paperwork and exit interviews, IT time removing network user privileges, Payroll's paperwork, etc.
- possible severance payment, and
- a potential increase in unemployment insurance costs.

Then there are the vacancy costs (set against the savings of the departed employee's salary and benefits):

- additional overtime to cover the departed employee's duties, and
- temporary employees, if necessary.

Finally, the replacement costs:

- job advertising
- HR interviewing/screening time
- testing
- training, and
- lower-than-normal productivity as the new hire gets up to speed.

Final tally? Some experts claim turnover ends up costing 150% of each departing employee's yearly compensation.

II. EMPLOYEE ENGAGEMENT

"Employee engagement" is one of those terms that's commonly bandied about in meetings, but it's a concept not easy to nail down. Nonetheless, it's a vital factor in what makes employees decide to stick with their employers for the long haul.

Here's a pretty commonly accepted checklist of the factors that, when taken together, add up to engagement. The Top Ten:

- interesting, challenging work
- opportunities for advancement and learning
- collegial workforce
- fair compensation
- a respected manager
- recognition for accomplishment
- feeling a valued member of a team
- a substantial benefits package
- the feeling their work "makes a difference," and
- overall pride in the company's mission and its products.

Top performers are a special breed.

They're engaged by the same factors as their not-quite-so-accomplished cohorts, but they're truly interested in three specific job conditions:

- They want to be fairly compensated
- They want to be provided with challenging work, and
- They want to be recognized and rewarded for their efforts.

Think that third factor isn't important? Check this out: One study said 79% of employees who quit their jobs cited a lack of recognition as a key reason for leaving.

A. The Basics of Retention

Yes, money matters.

It's true, people will cite any number of reasons for showing up on the job every day. They love the work. They love their co-workers. They get a sense of fulfillment from what they do. They enjoy the challenge. Their work helps the planet. They need to get out of the house. And on and on.

But there's only one genuine reason people work: They get paid. That paycheck underwrites the American Dream. It pays the mortgage, feeds the kids and the dog, pays college tuitions and funds retirements.

Or at least it used to. The recent economy has shaken employees' faith in their economic futures. That makes the paycheck – both its size and its reliability – a huge morale/retention factor.

Used to be, the experts pooh-poohed the effects of salary hikes: "The boost in motivation and loyalty doesn't last past one or two paychecks. Then it's just back to business as usual."

That may well be true in the long run. But all the signals say it's not so today. Fair compensation – pay and benefits – is the no-brainer of retention today.

Companies that offer competitive comp levels can enhance retention with other management techniques. But if they're not competitive in salary and benefits, it's going to be tough to hang on to their best people.

B. Flexible Hours and Telecommuting

Two other retention-builders that have become increasingly common over the past several years: flex time and telecommuting.

Flexible schedules can benefit both employees and employers, if done correctly.

Working staggered hours can help workers with families maintain the work/life balance they need – a giant morale builder. And in some instances, flexible hours allow companies to be operating additional hours in the day. That can mean more sales and better customer service.

Telecommuting can also be a win/win. To begin with, it saves employers the cost of office space and utilities. Companies can bring on new workers who live in another part of the country without having to pick up massive relocation costs. And in today's wired world, instant communication's no problem.

The details of telecommuting carry some pitfalls, of course – employers have to figure out who owns the equipment (and who's responsible for paying for repairs when things break), specific work hours and chain of command.

But many firms find telecommuters are not only more productive, but they actually put in longer hours than their office-bound colleagues. Apparently, when the commute's a matter of steps to a home office – and they're not subject to the normal workplace interruptions – employees find they can better concentrate on day-to-day duties.

C. Bonuses

Pay-for-performance plans certainly aren't new. But in an uncertain economy, more and more employers are adopting the concept as a technique to give workers an opportunity to increase salary levels.

Nowadays, most employers tie bonuses to special achievements and behaviors – not subjective judgments on workers' performance, but specific criteria that reflect the company goals and the employee's contribution to the bottom line.

Typical types of bonus programs:
- individual incentives
- team incentives
- a share in the gains from improvements in production and quality, and
- a share of the company's overall profits.

One form of incentive that was common during the pre-recession years seems to have pretty much fallen by the wayside: retention bonuses.

While that may seem counterintuitive for companies worried about keeping their best performers, that particular perk has faded for a good reason: It usually wasn't based on hard performance numbers.

Today's companies are focused on each employee's contribution – in hard cash. Rewarding someone for simply hanging around another year just won't fly in the current business atmosphere.

D. Perks

Little things do mean a lot. Employee love perks – because they're not really about the perk itself but the recognition that goes along with it. These kinds of low-cost rewards can be almost anything.

Here's a decidedly non-exhaustive sampling:

- Tickets to sporting events and shows
- Free beverages and snacks
- Small plaques bearing the employee's name and the date
- Gift certificates for meals
- Yoga classes
- Community service days
- Free lunch once a week
- Free car washes
- Health club membership discounts
- Continental breakfasts, and
- Holiday family parties or picnics.

There's one more perk that pleases everybody: time off. An extra day off to reward an outstanding job goes a very long way toward lifting an employee's opinion of his or her company.

E. Q&As

1. *One of our managers is looking for ways to make his off-site staff feel more like part of the team. How can he do that best?*

Think of ways to increase day-to-day contact between on-site and off-site staff, says Paul Schneider, senior product manager at GeoLearning.

Here are three ways:

- **Schedule regular check-in appointments.** Formalize it so supervisors check in at the same time every day, week, etc.
- **Have remote employees visit the office.** Whether it's every week or every six months, this interaction helps build rapport and strengthen connections.
- **Schedule a team outing when remote staff are in the office or in town.** Face-to-face contact helps build relationships and makes it easier to continue them over a distance.

F. Real-Life Success Stories

1. 'Reminder training' fixed phone issues

Some of our workers were getting a little too comfortable talking on the phone at work on personal calls.

We were never too strict about proper phone etiquette, but employees typically understood what was OK to discuss and what wasn't.

But sure enough, workers started taking more and more personal calls at their desks – and some of the topics weren't appropriate for the professional environment.

That began to have a negative effect on productivity and attention to detail, for both the offending employees and the ones distracted by the calls.

We weren't sure if it was a generational problem or what, but it was time for HR to step in.

What is and isn't appropriate

So we decided to hold a quick refresher course on phone etiquette.

The training wasn't an all-day affair, but we included a quick PowerPoint presentation, a video and, most importantly, role playing.

Our goal: Remind staffers about the basics of proper phone etiquette – especially for the business environment.

Now, we estimate that probably 90% of employees are more respectful on the phone.

We know that because we haven't received any complaints since the training.
(An HR manager for a financial organization in Atlanta)

2. From on-site, trained off-site staffers

We needed a way to get our staff on the same page regarding training.

A number of workers were on the road a lot or frequently out of the office. That was just the nature of our business.

But those workers still needed to be updated on healthcare changes and take part in our annual harassment training.

We needed a way to get workers up to speed – and fast.

The answer turned out to be right under our noses.

Group presentation from afar

We set up a way for employees to get the same presentation on the road.

We emailed the presentation that we used for in-house training to staff not in the office.

Then we conference-called a group of workers and took them through the presentation. They followed along on their computers while listening on the phone.

The presentation lasted about 15 minutes, and had 10 employees on the call. Most importantly, we saved questions until the end so staff could hear each question asked.

That eliminated the need to answer the same question repeatedly.

The feedback's been great. Workers get all the info they need without having to come into the office.

Best of all: Now we use that format for all necessary off-site training.

(An HR specialist from Atlanta)

3.   Small group training aided hiring process

We're a small firm, and it's easy for our managers to get busy and forget things. Where we saw the biggest issues: the hiring process.

Example: Sometimes managers forgot to include specific qualifications for candidates when they posted a new position online. The result? Almost 200 resumes for HR and managers to comb through.

We wanted supervisors to buy in to the fact that even though we're all busy, a little effort up front can save a ton of time later – especially in hiring.

We'd done group manager training before, but we wanted something else.

'We're here to help'

So we drew up a presentation and scheduled time to speak with each department head and the managers below him or her in small groups.

We gave them concrete examples of how their mistakes had cost us time and money, and how much time they could save by doing one or two small things.

Afterward, we opened the floor to questions – not just issues limited to the presentation, but any issues on supervisors' minds.

The response was unanimous – managers got a lot out of the session.

Now we schedule time to meet and present different topics to each department several times a year.

The best part: Managers very rarely make mistakes during the hiring process anymore.

(An HR manager for a bank in Oklahoma City)

4.   Manager mistakes prompted HR training

Some of our managers were giving employees wrong information on HR matters.

We trusted our supervisors, but they sometimes made mistakes when staff questioned them on tricky HR areas like FMLA, COBRA, etc.

We couldn't have issues like that – they were lawsuits waiting to happen.

First we brought in an external consultant at the company's expense to educate managers.

But after a couple of sessions, we realized we could do just as good a job in-house – and save the company money in the process.

Managers trust info from us

We already held supervisor training once every quarter, so we decided to tie our managerial education efforts to the training sessions.

At each session, we educate managers on a new HR topic – FMLA, ADA, etc. – and throw out questions they may field from staff.

Hearing the info from someone in the company makes a big difference.

We're able to relate the big legal issues to our own company policies – something the external consultant wasn't able to do as well.

Plus, we know they're more likely to listen if the training comes from us.

How do we know it's working? Since we started, we haven't had any manager miscommunication issues.

(An HR coordinator for an industrial manufacturer in Delaware)

5. Setting benchmarks on day one prepared staff

Our new hires were suffering from information overload – to the point where they would lose sight of the big picture.

With orientation, training and meetings, the one thing they weren't getting in the early going was a better idea of where they fit in the company.

A new evaluation system

We decided to set up a one-on-one meeting between each new hire and a supervisor.

The supervisor would provide several benchmarks that the employee would be responsible for meeting within their first year on the job.

To challenge new hires to take an active role in their development, we also added a twist.

We collaboratively developed a list of key goals for becoming a better worker and asked staff to select a handful of these goals to be evaluated on after their first year.

Once employees selected their goals, they would bring them back to their supervisors, who would approve them.

These goals were then locked into a computer system for employees to be evaluated on in a year's time.

By having new hires get involved in developing their skills early on,we've had tremendous success.

Not only do they get a sense right away of what to expect, they also get an early start in developing their skills and setting personal goals.

(A senior VP of HR for a real estate company in Maryland)

6. Bringing the classroom to them saved us big

Regular training is one of the most important parts of our company, but the costs – both in work hours and money – were astronomical.

Getting everyone we needed in the same room was a cost and logistical nightmare.

Or, we had to spend on time and expenses for our trainers to travel around to all our locations.

When they got there, we needed to pull groups of staff from their regular duties to attend training, which decreased productivity.

These sessions were essential, but we couldn't help feeling like there was a more efficient way to conduct them.

Put it on your calendar

We decided on a web-based solution that allowed employees to access training at their convenience.

This solved many of our biggest headaches.

First, we didn't rack up travel expenses for our training staff.

Second, we didn't have to sacrifice productivity because our staff could get training during off-hours.

And we're now able to add an online final exam to the training – something we couldn't fit into the schedule before.

Online lessons turned out to be a real time- and money-saver, and the tests gave us a way to tell what our employees actually learned.

(A Sr. VP for a bank in New York)

7. Mentoring program had unexpected twists

In a tight economy, we weren't too worried about retention. But we knew that once the job market opens up, turnover could be a problem.

So the question was, what steps do we take to make sure we keep our best people – without breaking the bank?

We decided that a mentoring program was our best bet.

And we staked a lot on mentoring.

We had special training for mentors, adjusted schedules to make room for one-on-one time, and made sure our best people got the opportunity to take part in the program.

A closer look showed ...

The program went along fine – no big surprises. Then we began to notice something unexpected.

We'd thought the mentoring program would largely improve the morale and commitment of mentees. But what we saw was that the morale of *mentors* had improved dramatically.

Being a mentor renewed employees' enthusiasm for the company and gave them a real sense of accomplishment.

So we recast the program. We started to make mentors of the people we really wanted to keep, regardless of how long they'd been with us.

The program's given them a real sense of connection with the company. And they're staying for the long run.

(An HR manager for a law firm in Delaware)

8. New training modules helped plug the gaps in our training process

We needed to fix some flaws in the way we trained new employees and managers.

It wasn't like our process was broken. Employees would work side-by-side with a current employee or manager until they understood what was expected of them in their new position. Overall, it worked pretty well.

But we worried that staffers might not get all the information they needed about our company and our policies – just in case the employees doing the training overlooked something important.

That meant we needed to compile a formalized training program to supplement new staff members' side-by-side work.

Tools on the intranet

So we devised a new tool: training modules hosted on our company intranet.

HR and management wrote small training modules for each level of employment at our company.

The modules were basically small PowerPoint presentations that covered all aspects of our company, but were also tailored to each department. Each module ended with a small quiz on the material in each section.

Employees were asked to complete a certain number of training modules by specific dates in their employment.

The best part: Workers didn't have to stay after work or come in early to complete them. They could do them whenever they had a free couple of minutes during the day.

The modules have been a great idea, and we rarely have to bug new employees to finish completing them.

We've also seen a decrease in turnover and positive results in production, as well.

We still use the side-by-side training process. There's definitely value in a hands-on approach.

But now we're certain that all new staff members get the information they need to become vital members of our company.

A helpful guide

The training modules were such a success with new hires that we wondered if we could create a similar tool for hiring managers.

So we created a hiring guide. It included tips for the entire hiring process, including:
- specific traits we were looking for in new hires
- the right – and wrong – questions to ask applicants, and
- tips on thorough documentation.

Now we knew our managers would have all the necessary info they needed to go through the hiring process smoothly – and legally.

Revamped and revitalized

It's important for our staff to have info on everything from hiring guidelines to harassment policy to sick leave. And now that we've revamped our hiring and training processes, we're certain they'll get that info.

(An HR director for a bank in Missouri)

9. Cut training costs by staying closer to home

Our management training costs were through the roof.

We couldn't afford an in-house trainer, so we had to send supervisors off-site to get the education they needed.

But that was ineffective as well – managers would be gone for days or a week, and that hurt performance on-site.

Then we thought: Maybe we didn't have to send the managers away. Maybe they could stay closer to home.

Don't go anywhere

Maybe having our own training staff was too expensive. But we could still train managers on-site.

We had two approaches:

- **Bring them to us.** Instead of sending managers away, we brought the instructors to us. And to our surprise, it was actually cheaper than sending our managers off-site.
- **Video conferencing.** For training that couldn't be done entirely on-site, we had a different solution – video conferencing. Managers could get training via video conferencing on our company computer system.

The result? Our training costs are down, and our managers don't have to lose valuable time traveling.

Best of all: We've gotten a very positive response from our managers about the new training setup.

(An HR manager for a cleaning services firm in Missouri)

10. Found tailored training – and cut our costs

Our training costs were going up.

In the past, we'd brought in specialized training consultants. But they were as expensive as they sounded.

And in today's economy, we simply couldn't afford to pay for that type of training anymore.

At the same time, depriving employees of proper training might hurt the company in the long term.

There had to be a way to get worthwhile training without breaking the bank.

Sidestepped the status quo

So we shopped around, looking at options we'd skimmed over in the past, or ones we'd deemed "too risky." We tried to find the perfect balance between cost and quality.

And after a long search, we found it.

We brought in a woman who, instead of relying on cookie-cutter, generalized training materials, has designed a program that suits our company's needs.

She's been able to give our employees quality, personalized training on par with what we've received in the past from big name (and big money) companies.

The sessions have been consistently well-received by our workers.

Now we've got our training under control, and it doesn't cost an arm and a leg to train our employees.

(An HR director for a research center in Boston)

III. MANAGERS' ROLE IN RETENTION

There's no dearth of opinions about how managers should motivate, nurture and reward employees – and make them want to stay with their employer.

But many of these theories stress the nuts and bolts of manager behavior – as in, "You need to praise at least three employees in your department every day." That approach tends to overlook the key issue: What do employees want from their job on an emotional level?

Here's a rundown of the things the experts say resonate most with employees – and make them want to stick around:

- **Clear expectations.** Pretty simple: Workers want to know exactly what they're responsible for, and what they'll be judged on.
- **A sense of control.** Employees aren't robots. They need to feel they have the power to decide how their jobs can be completed – and the freedom to suggest how tasks can be simplified or streamlined.
- **Feeling they're "in the loop."** Employees not only wish to know – and have input on – what's going on in their department, but what's happening in the business as a whole. And they want to be secure in their understanding of how what they do on a day-to-day basis fits into the overall operation – today and in the future.
- **Room to grow.** These include potential promotions, extra training, learning new skills and the possibility of using those new skills in a different area of the company.
- **Recognition.** Everyone wants to believe their extra effort won't go unnoticed – or unrewarded.
- **Leadership.** Employees want to be led by people they trust. And the people they trust are those who value workers' contributions, recognize and accept differences in people and act with employees' best interests in mind.

A. "Emotional Intelligence"

You've heard the phrase – it's been brought up about as often as the term "engagement" over the last couple years – and while it grates on the nerves of many managers, it's nonetheless an important concept. It merely signifies the change in how today's great managers handle their employees.

The days of "my way or the highway" are gone. Now, managers need to have real relationships with their people. They need to know what makes each employee unique – his or her talents, weaknesses, sense of humor, family situation … the whole picture.

Then great managers use all that data to put each employee in a position to thrive.

It's been said that great managers handle employees like they're playing a game of chess. Mediocre managers play checkers.

The connection: In checkers, all the game pieces are the same. They all move the same way. Chess is far more complex. The pieces are different. They can move in all sorts of different ways.

In other words, checkers is the outdated "straight-ahead, bodies-in-predetermined slots" approach to management. Chess is today's approach. It allows managers to respond to changing conditions, moving the right pieces to the best situations. And it also requires managers to think several moves ahead.

In order to make those moves, of course, the manager has to know the players. And people don't always fit into narrow categories like chess pieces do.

Bottom line: Managers have to discover the best roles for each unique employee to play. Doing so:

- takes advantage of the individual's strengths and minimizes the time wasted in trying to cover up for the person's weak points
- makes the individual more accountable
- builds stronger teams – every member knows his/her role, and depends on teammates to play theirs
- encourages a healthy exchange of diverse viewpoints.

Three key things managers need to know about employees:

- what they're best at
- the "triggers" that allow them to perform at their best
- how they process new information.

That last one is critical. Research shows that people tend to learn in three basic ways. Management gurus identify these types as: analyzers, doers and watchers.

The analyzers need solid study materials before they jump into a task for the first time.

Doers want a hands-on approach. They should start with the basics of a particular job, and then gradually move into the task's more difficult phases.

Watchers want to do just that – watch and learn. Best bet: Let them shadow top performers for a time. That way, they won't just learn the job – they'll see the job done at its highest level.

B. New Responsibilities

Unlike managers from other eras, today's managers have to perform their "due diligence" to uncover what makes each of his or her employees tick. Here are a few exercises that can help:

- **Cataloging motivation.** Managers should compose a checklist of the things they think motivate employees, leaving room for write-in candidates. Managers check off the items that motivate them, and then distribute the checklist to each of their employees.

Then the manager analyzes the overall results. This often reveals a number of things that are common to most workers – recognition, perks, interesting and fulfilling work, etc. – but it can also reveal some special tweaks that might boost the engagement levels of specific individuals.

This analysis is valuable in another way – it often indicates to managers how different their own motivators are from their employees'. Finally, the manager meets with each employee to discuss the worker's specific responses to the checklist – and then devises a plan tailored to meet his or her motivational factors.

Reality check: No, managers won't be able to make every employee's job perfect. But it is possible to adjust job duties and assignments to better fit employee needs. And specific motivators – like more flexible schedules for those with family responsibilities – can be worked into reward programs. For example, their jobs might be redesigned to be more fulfilling.

Managers might find more means to provide recognition, if that is important to them. Or they could develop a personnel policy that rewards employees with more family time, etc.

- **Establish a genuine bond.** Employees who feel their manager genuinely cares about them as a human being tend to be a lot more loyal than those who work for a supervisor who's distant and aloof.

  Managers should make a genuine effort to know employees' backgrounds, family information, their interests outside of work ... a well-rounded picture of their lives.

  It's not a matter of sitting the person down and giving them the third degree – the smart manager will pick up most of the information in informal day-to-day conversation, and can gently probe for details in an appropriate moment.

- **Recognize blind spots.** Sometimes, employees' and managers' personalities clash. This is a tricky area for managers – they must guard against treating the disliked employee differently than his peers.

  The best practice in this scenario is for the manager to recognize his or her blind spot in this particular case, and discuss it with a trusted supervisor. The objective is to figure out a way to establish a positive working relationship with the employee.

  Admitting the problem and then talking it out with a trusted colleague often goes a long way toward defusing the situation.

- **Put the insight to work.** Knowing employees' strengths and motivators is a big piece of the puzzle. But that knowledge needs to be put to use on a day-to-day basis.

Here's a rundown of some key behaviors managers should try to adopt:

- **Delegate – and then get out of the way.** Obviously, a big part of a manager's job is handing out tasks. But too many managers then hover over employees, getting so tied up in job details it makes it difficult for employees to get things done.

  Managers need to leave it up to their employees to decide how they will carry out their assignments. There are a couple big payoffs in this hands-off approach.

  First, it can free up a great deal of time for managers and supervisors. And it also allows employees to take a stronger role in their jobs, which usually translates into great employee satisfaction and motivation.

- **Speak up – right away.** Far too often, managers don't respond immediately when they spot an employee who's putting in extra effort, or doing a job particularly well. But research shows that this kind of "spontaneous" positive feedback is a great morale builder.

  Many companies offer "spot rewards" – small things like movie tickets or inexpensive gift certificates that managers can hand out at random times during the workday when an employee's exhibiting exemplary behavior. This, too, has been found to be a good morale builder and productivity booster.

- **Tell workers how what they're doing right now benefits the overall operation.** Employees get a genuine sense of fulfillment when they realize how their work fits into overall company success. When they hear that the widget they're assembling is going to be shipped to a key customer overseas, that point really hits home.
- **Celebrate achievements.** This is a little bit different from the "speak up when you see something good" rule. Too often, managers are overfocused on getting things done. They tend to put too much emphasis on end results. But a lot of significant achievements are made on the road to that end product. Problem solving, process streamlining and overcoming unexpected hurdles are all worth recognizing as well.

IV. EMPLOYEE TRAINING

Another key to retention is employee training and education. No question, employees are less likely to leave if they have the opportunity to learn new skills and keep up within their industry.

Training can also:

- increase productivity – thereby offering employees greater opportunities to earn performance bonuses
- improve job satisfaction
- reward long-term employees
- aid in the recruiting process, and
- lessen the burden of close supervision by managers.

Some training isn't optional – topics like discrimination and sexual harassment are not just essential in today's workplace, they're actually required under some state laws.

Training's an essential part of any successful business. But when the economy slows and money gets tight, many companies trim back their educational initiatives.

That's a mistake. Employees can't reach their full potential – not to mention optimum productivity – unless they're properly trained. And that means their employer's overall profitability will inevitably suffer.

A. Key Questions

When starting up an overall training initiative, employers need to ask themselves a set of key questions:

- In what crucial areas are employees missing important skills and knowledge?
- Which employees – individuals and departments – need the additional skills?
- Do the skills they'll learn fit with the organization's overall objectives?

- What form of training will best transfer the new knowledge and skills to specific jobs?

It's important for the company to explain to employees exactly what the training session will involve – and what's expected of the employee in terms of passing exams, hands-on demonstrations of skills, etc.

That will give workers a chance to ask questions about the process, which will likely eliminate the pre-training anxiety many employees experience.

It's also crucial to make it clear that training is part of every employee's job – and a key part, at that. All trainees are expected to make every effort to take the educational program seriously. That means completing assignments on time and participating fully in discussion sessions.

After the classroom work's done, all employees will be expected to apply their new knowledge and skills when they return to their regular duties.

Here, too, managers need to play an active role. Supervisors need to understand what the training will cover and how it will improve their department's operation.

Supervisors should meet with their employees prior to training sessions to not simply explain what's going to happen, but how they expect employees to use their new skills once training's over.

A cautionary note: Managers sometimes grouse about employee training programs, complaining that productivity is negatively affected by their workers being off the job.

That's a syndrome company leaders need to nip in the bud. If employees feel their manager doesn't care about the training program, it's not likely workers are going to go into the process whole-heartedly.

And that would be a waste of resources, time, and a missed opportunity to increase overall productivity.

B. Real-Life Success Stories

1. Tackled turnover with attention to detail

Turnover is a big problem in our profession, and at our firm things were no different.

We'd hire new people who'd stay for a few years to gain experience and then leave to work in industry.

We knew one of the biggest reasons they left was lack of flexibility – long hours, the seasonality of the work, etc. Historically, we accepted that cycle as inevitable.

But when turnover hit 24%, we realized we had to do something to retain our top talent – so we focused our efforts on flexibility.

Extra push from supervisors

We determined one area we could address was vacation time – our people rarely used all the vacation they earned.

So we devised a plan to help prevent staffers from leaving days on the table.

We set up a system where supervisors were notified when their staff were about to lose vacation.

Those managers then sit down with their people to talk about upcoming deadlines to see when our people can take time off.

That extra push from supervisors has gone a long way.

Employees now feel encouraged to take vacation – and that's given them some much-needed flexibility in their positions.

(A managing director for an accounting firm in New York)

2.   *Exit interviews reveal money isn't everything*

When staff members started jumping ship to work for the competition, we knew we had a problem.

Our first thought: Workers wanted more pay.

But we were wrong. Exit interviews revealed instead that employees no longer felt the same sense of engagement working on projects as they had in the past.

If those employees felt this way, others probably did, too.

Maybe we needed to give employees a little more control and input into new projects.

More chances to lead

Our solution: We created a leadership team every time we were about to begin a new project.

This gave employees – who maybe felt like they hadn't been able to put in their two cents up to that point – a real chance to be heard.

Employees loved the fact that they had more opportunities to lead the projects they were involved in.

It was a small change that made a big difference in employee morale.

Now, staff members have found a new sense of engagement.

And we're no longer losing our best and brightest workers to the competition.

(An HR director for a software company in Illinois)

3.   *We solved turnover problems by giving staff a good reason to stay*

We were worried about our turnover rate.

The majority of our jobs are entry-level, and we usually offer workers their first official positions.

At the same time, we know it's not likely these people will stay with us for a career, and our turnover rate reflected that – which didn't mean it hurt any less.

As a result, we had to spend more time training employees, not to mention the constant efforts to hire new staff members.

But most of all it hurt our relationships with customers, who didn't like always having to deal with different workers.

We tried bumping up workers' pay, and even though it helped, it didn't seem like it was enough.

We had to figure out what was a reasonable amount of time to keep these workers. After some research, we came up with an unusual idea.

Offered incentives

We decided to train employees for their next jobs while they were working for us – even though their next job likely wouldn't be at our company.

We knew it sounded counterintuitive, but we arranged it so the process worked in our favor.

In order to get the paid training, staffers had to work with us for two full years.

We figured if we could get employees to stay with us for that long, the training would be well worth it.

The training consisted of one-on-one meetings with upper management to create a detailed career plan for our workers.

In the process, we found out that many of our staffers were interested in using the knowledge and skills they learned while working for us.

Once we'd created a customized career plan for employees, we helped them get there.

Provided training

Our company would pay for employees to get the training they needed to reach their goals with classes online or at local community colleges.

At around $75 to $100 per class, the cost wasn't a great expense.

In addition to the classes, we'd offer assignments that were different from employees' normal duties.

Example: Staff members could design an advertising campaign to help develop their marketing skills.

Lastly, we held monthly performance reviews with employees just to make sure everything was running smoothly.

Boosted retention

Our retention strategy isn't for all companies, but it definitely worked for us.

How do we know? Last year, our turnover rate was zero.

And even though we expect employees to seek greener pastures after the two-year mark, we're confident new hires will show the same loyalty.

As an added bonus, retaining employees has boosted our customers' loyalty as well.

(Owner of a maid service in Ohio)

4.   New program advanced employees from within

We were worried about losing some of our best employees to the competition.

These were the people we saw as prime candidates for promotion to leadership positions.

We knew that if they didn't advance their careers with us, they'd be less inclined to stick around.

They needed more training – but outside courses were expensive.

We needed to transition employees to leadership positions so we could retain up-and-coming talent.

Leadership training

We began offering classes that provided leadership training to select employees from our company.

Employees who are serious about advancing their skills can submit applications for classes specially designed for various career tracks.

If their application is accepted, we provide the training necessary to advance their careers free of charge.

Graduating from these classes gives employees the skills that make them attractive candidates for promotions down the line.

And because training is free, our employees stick with the company to advance their careers.

Thanks to our leadership training, we've been able to advance candidates from within and retain employees who might have otherwise left.

(A director of talent and HR for a food services firm in South Dakota)

5. Retention program had a two-pronged payoff

High turnover was costing us money and frustrating our seasoned veterans.

We'd hire new people, and our longtime workers would bend over backward to help the newbies learn the ropes.

And then some of the new folks – too many – would move on. The veterans were starting to grouse about going out of their way to help new employees only to see them quit after just a few months.

So we had a double problem. We needed to cut our new-hire turnover rate and improve morale for our seasoned vets.

We'd already instituted a successful referral program with a monetary bonus. Would a similar program help us retain workers?

90-day survey

When a new worker hit the 90-day mark in their employment, we asked them: "What one worker has gone above and beyond to help you in your first three months?"

We then treated both the mentor and the new worker to a luncheon hosted by upper management. And quarterly, HR rewarded the most helpful staffer with a bonus.

Now our staff is more motivated than ever to help new workers, which has cut turnover rates and helped boost enthusiasm of our veterans.

(An HR director for a special needs center in Pennsylvania)

CHAPTER FIVE

Discipline and Termination

I. DISCIPLINE

A. Overview

The success of any organization depends in large part on its ability to effectively address subpar employee performance and employee misconduct. There are several tools available to help employees meet this critical goal.

An important key to minimizing disciplinary issues is to clearly communicate expectations and requirements to employees. These expectations and requirements are typically communicated to employees by way of job descriptions and employee handbooks.

But no matter how clearly expectations are set forth, at one time or another most managers will find themselves in the often-dreaded position of needing to correct a deficiency. Managers must be trained to deal with subpar performance quickly and effectively.

Most disciplinary policies provide for progressive disciplinary measures. A typical progression is as follows:

- oral warning
- written warning
- suspension
- termination.

From the first stage of the disciplinary process to the last, concrete and detailed documentation is an absolute must.

B. Progressive Discipline

Progressive discipline has three basic goals:
1. to bring employee performance or behavior into compliance with company standards and expectations
2. to encourage other employees to succeed – under the standards of ethics and behavior the company has established, and
3. create a comprehensive paper trail to outline the good-faith process the company went through to handle the problem, in case termination is the final outcome.

A typical progressive discipline structure looks something like this:

Step One: counseling. This is where the manager first brings the problem to the employee's attention. It's also where the supervisor can learn if there are unknown factors contributing to the problem. The supervisor gives the employee a clear explanation as to how the problem can be fixed. Ideally, the staffer gets the message and things improve.

Step Two: verbal reprimand. The initial counseling session didn't have the desired effect, and the manager is forced to revisit the topic. A memo detailing the verbal conversation is placed in the employee's file.

Step Three: written warning. If a situation continues to deteriorate, this step formalizes the manager's concern about the employee's performance or behavior, and outlines the potential consequences that could follow if the situation doesn't change.

Step Four: dismissal. After a specified period of time, if the problem is not satisfactorily addressed, the company and employee part ways.

These steps can be flexible and tailored to the needs of different kinds of work, different companies or even different departments within an organization.

For instance, an employer could repeat Step Three several times if it's determined to be in the company's best interest because some types of jobs are far more difficult to fill.

The types of problems progressive discipline is best designed to handle fall into two categories: performance and behavior.

Performance problems sometimes have a behavior component (a sub-par salesperson is chronically late for work, for instance), but behavior problems normally fall into the category of breaking specific company rules.

Unionized workplaces generally have specific standards for how behavior issues are handled, and although non-union businesses aren't required to follow a strict protocol in these matters, it's worthwhile to take a look at the process in strict technical terms.

Here are some of the formal standards of a typical progressive discipline policy in a collective bargaining agreement (CBA):

Did the employee have adequate warning?

Did the employee know – or should he or she have known – that the behavior could result in disciplinary action?

Both the company and the manager are responsible for communicating the rules employees are required to follow. If workers aren't told the rules, they can't be punished for violating them.

Naturally, there are some actions employees can be expected to understand without being told: Things like drinking on the job, stealing, fighting, insubordination or acting in an unsafe manner are regarded as unacceptable in general.

Was the rule reasonable?

Written rules usually pass this test. Where some companies run into trouble is when managers issue their own on-the-spot requirements of employees – for example, modifying safety procedures in order to boost production rates.

Did the violation actually occur?

Prior to taking the disciplinary action, did the manager establish that the employee actually violated the rule? Mere allegations of rule-breaking generally aren't sufficient to punish an employee.

Was the investigation fair?

Did the supervisor conduct a thorough investigation of the facts and circumstances before starting the disciplinary process? Did the manager actively seek information – not simply wait for people to volunteer information?

The good and the bad

Like every effort designed to deal with the spectrum of human behavior, there are advantages and disadvantages to adopting a progressive discipline policy.

The advantages

Thorough documentation of how the company responded to specific workforce problems is a great advantage to having a progressive discipline policy, but it isn't the only one.

Handled correctly, these policies also:

- give managers an established, structured, consistent and repeatable method of correcting employee performance and behavior problems
- help managers spur better employee performance and productivity
- demonstrate, when coupled with rewards for good behavior and performance, a company's commitment to treating employees fairly, and
- cut down on turnover by rehabilitating problem employees who might otherwise have been terminated.

The disadvantages

Like every employment policy, progressive discipline has its pitfalls. The four major ones are:

- management needs to write a formal policy and include it in all company documentation for employees, like employee handbooks
- all managers have to be properly trained in the policy
- administering the plan adds new managerial burdens of documentation and follow-up, and
- in some cases the process might alter – or at least suspend – the at-will status of the employee involved until all the steps have run their course.

Performance problems

In progressive discipline for behavior problems like rule-breaking or safety violations, the process is comparatively simple: The employee needs to put a halt to the specific behavior, or suffer the consequences.

Progressive discipline for performance deficiencies, however, isn't always so clear-cut. The amount of time and effort a manager is willing to put into improving an employee's performance can vary widely, depending on the nature of the performance issue and the perceived value of the employee.

Usually, progressive discipline is addressed through a performance improvement plan, or PIP, as they're commonly known.

The basic components of a PIP:

- **The deficiency statement.** This is a rundown of just where the employee's performance hasn't been up to standards.
  Managers should determine if the problem is performance (a lack of mastery of skills or tasks) or a behavior problem (an ability to perform the tasks, but a disruptive presence in the workforce).

- **The overall action plan.** This section defines what skills or behaviors need improvement and specific duties where improvement is necessary. Also included should be a rundown of any special training that will be provided, either by the manager or other individuals.

- **Specific goals.** Most PIPs include both short- and long-term performance targets.

- **The time frame.** When does the manager expect to see improvement in the specified areas?

- **Specific measurements.** What's going to be an acceptable standard of improvement?

- **Specific consequences.** If the employee's performance – or behavior – doesn't improve within the time limits, what happens next?

- **Feedback sessions.** The manager should schedule periodic update sessions during the PIP time frame.
  It's very difficult for a PIP to be successful if the parties don't get together regularly to check on how things are going – and make whatever mid-course corrections are needed.

An overall look at the process

Here's an overview of the progressive discipline process.

Timing

Timing is critical in three different areas in the disciplinary process:

Acting on rules or conduct violations. Although there's no hard and fast rule, managers should start the disciplinary process on conduct or rules violations within 10 days of learning of the alleged offense.

If more time's needed to complete an investigation, the company should inform the employee that an investigation is under way and provide a date when the disciplinary decision will be made.

Setting time frames for correcting problems. Some problems can be solved almost immediately – tardiness, for instance – so it doesn't make sense to drag out the process past a couple of weeks.

Other issues, like performance difficulties, may require periods as long as three to six months, or more.

Tread carefully when giving feedback to employees who've successfully corrected the problem addressed by the disciplinary action.

While positive feedback is certainly appropriate, it's important for the employee to know that although they've done well, the manager's still concerned about the potential of the problem reappearing.

Managers should stress the importance of maintaining an acceptable performance level.

Time between disciplinary actions. Some companies wipe the slate clean if an employee isn't involved in a disciplinary action for a specific period of time – the most common standard is two or three years.

What's the appropriate level of discipline?

Sometimes managers treat two employees differently for the same workplace violation.

For example, a top performer may be given a slap on the wrist for insubordination while an average performer is given a stern written warning.

Big mistake. That's the kind of thing that can lead to discrimination claims.

The safe route: Managers should base the disciplinary measure on the offense rather than the employee.

Before deciding what level of discipline to impose, managers should consider things like:

• the seriousness of the offense
• the employee's previous disciplinary record, and
• the discipline other employees have been handed for similar offenses.

Managers should also review the employee's recent performance reviews, and attendance and safety records.

Gauging the violation

Here's a general rundown of how serious certain workplace violations are usually considered to be:

Minor: Absenteeism and leaving work without permission, tardiness, personal appearance or hygiene

Mid-level: Fudging work records (if the action doesn't result in a loss for the company), minor insubordination, and

Serious (the ones that could warrant immediate termination): Theft, violence, sexual harassment, discrimination.

Documentation tips

No surprise here: Documentation is the bedrock on which progressive discipline is built.

Managers need to confirm all disciplinary actions – from a memo confirming an initial verbal warning to the final termination decision (if the process gets that far).

Documentation of disciplinary action must be kept in the employee's personnel file and the employee must receive a copy. If it's a union situation, it's likely the shop steward and others should be given the documentation as well.

A disciplinary record should cover three distinct phases:

The present. This is a rundown of the issue that's at the center of the discipline action. It should include specifics of the problem (or offense, if it's a case of rule-breaking), a breakdown of the negative effect on the overall operation, and disciplinary action being taken as a result of the employee's actions.

The past. This section reviews the employee's work record, outlines any history of related offenses, and summarizes previous disciplinary actions taken.

The future. This section lays down the expected standard of behavior or performance, how this standard can be achieved, and the consequences of continued failure to meet expectations.

All this documentation should be witnessed and signed by the manager and the employee.

To sum up, here's a general checklist of what disciplinary documentation should include:

- a description of the performance issue or rule violation
- an outline of the results of any investigation
- a description of the discipline being imposed
- a timeline for meeting the standards outlined by the manager
- a description of the consequences of not meeting expectations
- the supervisor's signature (if it is a high level of discipline, a second signature such as from the human resource department or another level of management, should be included)
- the employee's signature acknowledging that the reasons for discipline have been explained and that he or she has been given an opportunity to respond, and
- the date.

C. Q&As

1.   Can we ban weapons in the workplace?

It depends on what state you live in, says Christopher McFadden of Ford & Harrison.

In most states, you're permitted to ban staffers from bringing weapons into work or on to work premises.

But in some states, staffers generally are permitted to bring guns to work, as long as they leave them locked in their cars. Takeaway: Check your local laws before you ban weapons outright at your workplace.

D.   Real-Life Success Stories

1.   We convinced managers to improve documentation

We were struck by *the* classic HR problem – our managers weren't documenting properly.

No matter how often we told supervisors to dot their i's and cross their t's, they'd still neglect to write down details about employee performance.

Like any HR pro worth his or her salt, we know that lack of documentation could come back to bite us if we ever ended up in court.

But we needed managers to see that, too.

That's when it hit us. They could see – we just had to show them.

Real-life court cases to the rescue

So we started writing "Why they won" and "Why they lost" stories based on recent court decisions that succeeded or failed based on quality of documentation.

It didn't take long – quick Google searches turned up tons of cases.

And we didn't get bogged down in the legalities of the decisions – we just wanted supervisors to see the consequences of poor documentation.

It turned out to be a huge success, and managers tell us they learned a lot.

More importantly, they've gotten much better at documentation – which will prove invaluable if we ever end up in court.

(An HR director from Texas)

II. TERMINATION

A. Overview

Terminating employees is an unfortunate but often necessary part of running a business. When termination becomes necessary, you'll want to take steps that will help the termination process go smoothly. You'll also want to do all that you can to avoid a lawsuit against you by a terminated employee.

A critical key to implementing smooth termination decisions is the ability to recognize legal reasons for discharge. To stay out of legal trouble, you must be able to distinguish a legal basis for a decision to terminate an employee from a prohibited one.

The most common legitimate reasons to terminate an employee are:

- poor job performance
- misconduct, and
- insubordination.

It's just as important for supervisors to recognize prohibited grounds for termination as it is for them to recognize permissible grounds for termination. Here are some of the more common prohibited grounds for discharging an employee:

- retaliation
- breach of contract, and
- unlawful discrimination.

In most cases, a key to proving a termination was made for a permissible reason is the production of supporting documentation. Written documentation should clearly describe the problem, disciplinary or remedial actions taken, and any other information reflecting a failure on the part of the employee to respond to help or discipline. As a general rule, news of termination should not come as a complete shock to the employee. Instead, there should be a detailed record of the employee's history of problems – a record that the employee is well aware of. This record will help the termination process go more smoothly and protect employers from claims that the termination was motivated by an improper reason.

In the hit movie "Up in the Air," George Clooney plays a professional "terminator," a hired gun who travels around the country firing people for big corporations.

In real life, HR people aren't that lucky to have someone else do the dirty deed for them – they have to do it themselves, and usually without any help. Even the managers who decide the employee must go often get weak-kneed in the end.

All terminations are difficult, and it's no surprise many HR pros get knots in their stomachs when they let someone go. You never know how the person is going to react – and if he or she will hire a lawyer to sue you for wrongful termination over some imagined injustice.

With the right preparation, firings can go easier – and the chances of wrongful termination suits can be substantially reduced.

Here's a 10-point plan for "firing without fear" covering the periods before, during and after a termination:

1. **Set expectations.** Clear expectations should be set out for performance in job descriptions and employee handbooks. Adherence to those high expectations should be monitored through honest performance reviews.

   The goal: No surprises at the end. The employee should know what's coming.

2. **Track performance, discipline.** Aside from the performance review, all incidents when employees failed to meet expectations should be tracked, and any needed discipline should be swiftly meted out.

   Again, the goal is no surprises at the end.

3. **Train supervisors.** Supervisors should be trained to give both good and bad feedback and document everything.

   Supervisors often shy away from confrontation, but confrontation to address unacceptable behavior can be very constructive.

4. **Set protocols for terminations.** Make sure in every case progressive discipline policies have been followed.

   Consider all possible claims the employee may make for wrongful termination – and what the company's defenses would be.

5. **State the case – in writing.** Keep it short and sweet.

   The more you say, the more cause you may give a plaintiff's attorney to poke holes in your case.

6. **Don't argue.** Don't let yourself get drawn into arguments – the decision is final.

   You can show sympathy for the terminated employee, but not empathy. There's a subtle difference.

7. **Let employees say goodbye.** Unless they become violent, it's best to let them say goodbye to colleagues.

8. **Treat them with dignity.** Showing some respect will deflect any claims for intentional infliction of emotional distress.

9. **Give them time to pack up.** Giving them time to clear their desk and pack up personal belongings also helps show respect.

10. **Communicate with staff.** Tell remaining staff how tasks will be redistributed. You may say you wish the departed employee well.

Preventing workplace violence

It's unlikely any terminations you've had to carry out have resulted in a worker's death.

But the infrequent occurrences of workplace violence that do happen are a reminder of just how important it is to handle terminations properly by emotionally engaging your workers.

The goal of every termination, according to communications expert Joseph Grenny, is to have staff leave feeling like they were treated fairly and with respect. Research shows doing so significantly decreases the likelihood of a violent reaction or future litigation.

Here are five steps to ensure staff leave a termination feeling that way:

1. **Manage your own emotions.** It's easy to see a worker like someone who stole from a company as morally deficient.

   But the best HR pros realize that all people – even intelligent HR pros – make mistakes.

   A soon-to-be-fired worker has just made one too many. Keeping that in mind helps prevent you from vilifying the employee.

2. **Get your motives right.** It's not easy to fire someone, so your natural tendency is to make the termination as brief as possible.

   But that's a mistake.

   You're trying to do right by the company and the worker. Rushing through the discussion, no matter how uncomfortable it is, will only make staffers feel tossed aside.

3. **Be firm and compassionate.** Many HR pros believe there's no room for sympathy in a termination talk. Grenny says that's untrue.

   Yes, you need to be firm in the belief that the decision you're making is the right one.

   But nothing is compromised by saying, "I know this is going to be tough for you and your family."

   Recognizing the personal side of the termination shows you realize the impact the termination will have.

4. **Don't start at the end.** Starting the conversation with your conclusion – "We're going to fire you because you stole from the company" – is a surefire way to rile up a worker.

   Instead, start with facts stripped of provocative language: "We have some evidence that's troubling. We'd like to share it and hear your reaction."

5. **Let employees speak.** Some workers may calmly nod and agree with you during the talk, which you might interpret as a good sign.

   But there's no way to know what the worker is feeling inside – so you need to draw those feelings out.

   Example: "I'm having a hard time believing anything other than you stole something. Is there a different way I should be seeing this? Is there any other info you want to bring forward now?"

This doesn't deny the facts, but letting staff speak lets them air their concerns, feel listened to and could allow them to blow off some steam – which might be just enough for staff to feel like they were treated fairly.

Common firing mistakes

There are a handful of firing mistakes that many companies commonly make. A selection:

Not firing bad employees. Sure, everybody knows that keeping marginal people around holds back productivity, and it certainly doesn't help morale.

But there aren't any legal ramifications, right?

Wrong. If a company allows a sub-par performer to stay on the job for an extended period of time, it's possible the employer will set a "customary practice" precedent.

And some judges have ruled such customary practice is an implied contract – meaning the employer officially recognizes that poor performance is acceptable.

Making an employee so miserable that he or she eventually quits. Instead of firing the person, a manager sets out to make his or her job unbearable.

This is an incredibly risky way to get rid of a problem employee – often riskier than an outright firing.

"Constructive discharge" – the practice of putting an employee in a spot where he or she has no rational choice but to quit – is the basis of many a successful retaliation charge.

Asking an employee to resign. This sometimes seems the humane way to go, but it can lead to serious problems down the road.

For instance: Handling reference requests on the departed employee, especially if the employee has indicated a potential to be violent or disruptive.

Relying on a probationary period as blanket protection for firing. The idea of probationary periods began in union and government operations.

Originally, it was a guarantee that the new employee couldn't file a grievance if they were let go before the end of probation.

Private sector firms adopted the practice, many assuming it was a "safety valve" to allow them to shed new hires that didn't work out.

But legally, it just doesn't work that way. Probationary employees have exactly the same legal protections their longer-tenured colleagues enjoy.

And if their termination doesn't conform with the law, they can bring suit just like everybody else.

Little things mean a lot

Another common problem area for managers is the employee who's constantly making small mistakes – a little late arriving at work, a little slow completing her duties, a little sloppy in her work.

They're not a big deal, but they're irritating, and they send the wrong message to the offender's co-workers.

But managers are loathe to take action – you can't fire somebody for being five minutes late, can you? And anybody could make a clerical error now and then.

They key here is the cumulative effect of the employee's actions. Fixing one small mistake may be no big deal. Fixing 20 small mistakes starts to take a quantifiable chunk of worker time.

Grounds for firing this employee? An "unproductive work pattern." And companies can make it stick through solid documentation.

Documentation: Build a solid foundation

There's just no overstating the importance of documentation when a company embarks on the process of firing an employee.

Documentation is the written record of how a company came to the termination decision. It offers a chronology of what the employee did, how the manager responded, and when. Done correctly, it provides a clear road map of how both employee and employer made their way to the eventual destination – the employee's termination.

Documentation is also the foundation of a company's defense, should the employee bring suit. It's proof that an employer didn't act arbitrarily.

Oftentimes, a good documentary record can short-stop a lawsuit on its own. An employee's attorney, presented with a thorough and thoughtful written record, may well decide that filing suit just isn't worth it.

And if a case does make it to court, an employer is better positioned to obtain a favorable outcome if the jury's presented with written proof that the employer engaged in ongoing communications about performance problems and set clear expectations for the employee.

Handling verbal warnings

Managers are often confused about how they handle informal verbal warnings to employees.

It's a bit of a judgment call. A non-specific, "Bob, you need to dial up your attention to detail" probably isn't worth the time it'd take to make a written record.

But the following statement probably is: "Bob, today is the third day in a row you forgot to put the extra washer on the thingamajig. You know that step's been added to the assembly process, and I've mentioned it to you several times. I'm going to be monitoring your attention to detail, and if you continue to make the same mistake, I may have to move on to the next disciplinary step."

After that encounter, it makes sense for the manager to write down – as precisely as possible – exactly what he or she told the employee, date it and put it in the worker's file. At this point, it's probably not necessary to get the employee to sign off on the document.

If the employee then fails to rise to improve, the manager then begins the formal progressive discipline process.

And in the first writeup, the manager should refer to earlier verbal coaching: "As we've discussed on several occasions, your attention to detail ... "

If the employee claims he wasn't given prior notice that his performance or behavior was unacceptable, the manager has the earlier notes to fall back on.

The nuts and bolts of paperwork

There's effective documentation and ineffective documentation.

Managers may well think an employee's performance is irresponsible, dishonest, selfish, boorish and all sorts of other unpleasant things. But saying so in disciplinary documentation serves no purpose.

If the narrative is long on emotion and personality judgments and short on facts, it's probably not going to stand up legally.

Effective documentation is about behavior, work outcomes or the impact of the employees' behavior on the overall operation.

So managers need to remember the old Jack Webb mantra from *Dragnet*: Just the facts, ma'am.

When they write up an employee, managers need to ask themselves a couple of key questions:

1. *Have I described what happened, and its effect on our operation?*
2. *Have I avoided interpreting the employee's behavior?*

A couple of examples:

Weak: "Bob was irresponsible by not paying attention to detail in the thingamajig assembly process."

Stronger: "Bob failed to install one of the washers involved in the thingamajig assembly process. When his mistake was discovered, we had to stop the line, disassemble 14 units, add the washer and reassemble the units. The rebuilds halted production for a total of two hours."

Getting employees to sign off

Ideally, managers want employees to sign all written disciplinary documents. But employees often refuse.

What's the answer? Managers have a few options.

*   *"Agree/don't agree" check boxes.* The employee puts a tick mark in the appropriate box, and then signs on the dotted line.
*   *The "I refuse to sign" technique.* The manager just asks the employee to turn the memo over, write, "I refuse to sign," and then initial it.

Both approaches achieve the desired result: Solid evidence that the employee has received the disciplinary document and understands its contents.

Whether they agree with what's in the document doesn't matter. The important part: The manager can prove they've received it.

One possible script

An example of an appropriately handled termination conversation:

Manager: *Bob, I've asked you to meet with the HR director and me today* *because you must be aware that for sometime now, we've not been happy with the quality of your work.*

We've met with you several times over the past few months, pinpointing the areas you needed to improve. Unfortunately, we haven't seen the improvement we needed to see.

For that reason, we've decided to end your employment here.

Bob: *I'm fired?*

Manager: *That's right. We've tried to give you a chance to improve. We gave you at least two written warnings and several verbal warnings. But you didn't make the kind of progress we needed to see.*

Bob: *Wait a minute. My supervisor said I did a great job on that project we finished last month.*

Manager: *I'm not prepared to discuss details of your work record here, Bob. I'm sorry, but our decision's made.*

Bob: *You're firing me and keeping that idiot Kenny? He's certainly screwed up a lot more than I have. How come you're not getting rid of him?*

Manager: *Bob, I'm not going to talk about any other employees. We're here to talk about your performance. And we've decided it's no longer acceptable. We're letting you go.*

Bob: *A few months ago, I mentioned I might be interested in another assignment, and you said then it could be possible. What about that? Could I get a transfer to a different position?*

Manager: *Bob, I'm sorry. We all like you here, but it's time to move on. We don't take this kind of thing lightly at our company. It's a difficult decision for all of us. But the decision has been made. We truly wish you the best.*

After the departure

Unfortunately, the termination tale doesn't end after the fired employee goes through the door. Two main issues remain.

What to tell the fired employee's co-workers

Employees aren't stupid; the fired employee's colleagues are almost certainly going to know their co-worker was in trouble. But that doesn't mean they won't have questions.

Some of this interest in the firing will be prurient, but much of it will spring from uncertainty.

They want to know their job's still OK.

Managers should simply state that the terminated employee's no longer with the company. No details on the firing need be offered, but the managers can offer a general statement about how things will continue into the future.

If people press for details, managers can simply say, "I'm sorry, but I can't discuss it. It's confidential."

Handling reference requests

This can be a trouble spot for companies. The best policy when a potential employer calls for a reference for an employee who was fired? Say as little as possible and stick to facts that can be proven.

Many employers only allow the HR department to respond to requests for references. And HR only gives out dates of employment, job title, and final salary.

Many firms keep a record of all reference requests. Some only provide references in writing, so there's an accurate record of the information released.

Many employers are acting pro-actively in this area – requiring former employees to sign a release giving the company permission to provide prospective employers with information about the person's work history.

B. Q&As

1. *We just had to let someone go. What, if anything, should we say to the remaining employees?*

Pick and choose what you say carefully, says Jerry Huffman *(504-524-8556)* of Curry & Friend in New Orleans.

Don't go into too much detail, but you can't pretend the person was never there. Just say so-and-so has left the firm, wish him or her well and announce how the work will be redistributed.

Saying nothing will just fuel idle speculation and let people fill in their own reasons.

C. Checklists

☑ CHECKLIST

A pre-termination checklist

Sometimes the choice to fire an employee is a no-brainer. But more often than not, a termination decision isn't always black and white.

Throw in the always present legal risks involved, and what may have seemed like an easy decision can get complicated very quickly.

Well, good news: Here's a checklist to help you decide when a worker's behavior is grounds for termination, courtesy of Hunter Lott, a nationally known staffing and management consultant who operates the HR site *PleaseSueMe.com*:

❑ Was a specific policy violated and does the violation warrant termination?
❑ Show me the policy!
❑ Have other employees been held accountable to the same policy?
❑ Prove the employee knowingly violated the policy!
❑ Do we have confirmation that the employee did indeed violate the policy?

❑ How did the employee react when confronted with the violation?

❑ Has the employee complained of harassment or unfair treatment?

❑ Has the employee recently filed a worker's compensation claim?

❑ Is the employee about to vest in certain benefits or become involved in union activities?

❑ Has the employee returned from, or applied for, military/medical leave?

❑ Has the employee recently complained of company wrongdoing or of a safety issue?

❑ Are there any current grievances or complaints pending?

❑ Were any promises made verbally, or in writing, to this employee by senior management?

❑ Were any requested accommodations denied to this employee?

❑ Is there evidence of discrimination based on age, sex, race, religion, national origin, disability or any other legally protected characteristic?

Once you've considered all these issues, your company can make an informed decision about whether or not termination's a good idea, says Lott.

Just because some problems may come up through this process – say, for instance, the employee has made a recent complaint about his supervisor – you don't have to reverse the termination decision. But it's likely you will have to have strong documentation that explains the circumstances and management's rationale for its actions.

III. JUDICIAL DECISIONS

♦   A company hired a pension benefits manager as a salaried employee and gave her a copy of the employee handbook, which contained a termination section for hourly and nonexempt employees (which she was not). The handbook noted that warnings normally were given before an employee was fired. When the manager was terminated without warning for what her supervisors perceived was poor performance, she sued for breach of contract, among other claims. The case reached the South Carolina Court of Appeals, which noted that the handbook did not apply to the manager. And even if it did, **nothing in the handbook outlined progressive disciplinary procedures in mandatory terms**. Finally, even if the company gave other salaried employees a warning before firing them, it was not required to do the same for the manager. At-will employment was presumed and no disclaimer was needed in the handbook. *Grant v. Mount Vernon Mills, Inc.,* 370 S.C. 138, 634 S.E.2d 15 (S.C. Ct. App. 2006).

♦   A company in Vermont had a personnel manual that described progressive discipline and just cause termination policies for employee misconduct. It stated that two written warnings would be given before termination. When the company experienced an economic slowdown, it attempted to reorganize, and one employee resisted changes a new manager tried to institute. She received a letter of reprimand from the company's president, but the letter stated that it was not a disciplinary warning. A month later she was fired. She sued, claiming breach of an implied contract that she would only be fired for just cause after progressive discipline. The Vermont Supreme Court held that the **letter of reprimand established the company's intent to abide by its progressive discipline policy**. Even though the employee could have been laid off for economic reasons without progressive discipline, she was fired for insubordination. *Havill v. Woodstock Soapstone Co.*, 865 A.2d 335 (Vt. 2004).

♦   A 55-year-old manager of a company in Massachusetts claimed that he was improperly fired. He asserted that he should have been progressively disciplined under the employee handbook and the "Guide to Corporate Conduct." He claimed that the real reason for the termination was age discrimination. The company argued that the manager attempted to misuse company property for his personal benefit; that he retaliated against another employee who refused to cooperate in that misuse; and that he had an abusive management style. The First Circuit Court of Appeals held that **the manager was not entitled to progressive discipline**. Nothing in the handbook or the guide promised progressive discipline. And even if the company generally applied progressive discipline to its employees, there was never any such policy for management. *Joyal v. Hasbro, Inc.*, 380 F.3d 14 (1st Cir. 2004).

♦   An Iowa healthcare center administrator had a poor working relationship with her supervisor. She believed that the supervisor wanted her to withhold information from an auditor. The supervisor allegedly told the center's owners that she would quit unless they fired the administrator. The center fired the administrator without warning for lack of leadership and inability to provide continuity. She obtained unemployment compensation benefits and then sued the center and its owners for breach of contract and intentional interference with her employment contract. The court awarded compensatory and punitive damages to the administrator and held that the owners were jointly liable for compensatory damages and individually responsible for punitive damages. The Supreme Court of Iowa affirmed, finding that the language of the center's employee handbook was sufficiently definite to create an employment contract. The administrator had a **right to receive notice of any deficiencies in her performance under the handbook's progressive disciplinary policy**. Because the employer had failed to follow these procedures, the breach of contract action was appropriate. Corporate officers or directors may be held personally liable if they fail to act in good faith to protect the interests of the corporation. Here, the employment contract had been terminated because of the administrator's failure to perform an illegal act in violation of public policy, and the owners were liable for the damage award. *Jones v. Lake Park Care Center, Inc.*, 569 N.W.2d 369 (Iowa 1997).

♦   A Utah metallurgical engineer worked for over 15 years for a mining company in several different positions. He eventually got a substandard rating and was told that he had one last chance to redeem himself. The company then fired him for inadequate performance without providing progressive discipline, notice, a hearing or other protections. He claimed that the company policy in effect at the time of his hiring was applicable and required a written warning and a suspension or hearing for disciplinary purposes. He claimed that the policy constituted a contract that replaced the presumption of at-will employment. He sued the company in a Utah trial court, which held for the company. The engineer appealed.

The Court of Appeals of Utah observed that employment in the state is presumed to be at will and that overcoming this presumption requires showing a definite communication by the employer to the employee that a contract exists under different terms. The company policy referred to by the engineer had been **replaced with a policy that did not call for progressive discipline or other protections**. The most recent employee policy was applicable, not the original one. The current handbook language called for hearings for disciplinary offenses, but not in cases of insufficient performance, which was the cause of termination here. The court affirmed the decision for the employer. *Sorenson v. Kennecott-Utah Copper Corp.*, 873 P.2d 1141 (Utah App. 1994).

◆   A Michigan hospital fired an ICU nurse for putting other staff in life-threatening danger. It believed she was trying to discharge the current on a defibrillator before telling other members of the hospital's ICU department to stand clear. An arbitrator found that the nurse was not going to discharge the current, but was just attempting to turn on the defibrillator. As such, the arbitrator concluded **her mistake, although negligent, was not "gross neglect,"** as the hospital claimed. The collective bargaining agreement in place identified two levels of discipline, the first warranting suspension for careless conduct and the second warranting discharge for gross neglect or abuse of a patient. In light of a previous reprimand, the arbitrator ordered the nurse to be reinstated with a six-month suspension. The hospital appealed, and the U.S. Court of Appeals, Sixth Circuit, held that the arbitrator did not exceed his authority. Nor did the arbitrator's order violate Michigan's public policy of ensuring safe and competent nursing care. The arbitrator did not order the hospital to reinstate her to the same department but gave it the flexibility of placing her in a less dangerous position and providing whatever training it deemed appropriate. *MidMichigan Regional Medical Center v. Professional Employees Local 79*, 183 F.3d 497 (6th Cir. 1999).

◆   A New Jersey maintenance mechanic worked for a large manufacturing company that had distributed an employment manual containing a four-step disciplinary policy. The company found some of its property in the mechanic's locker and fired him for theft, one of several grounds listed for immediate dismissal. The mechanic sued the employer, claiming that it had violated the disciplinary procedure in the manual. The court granted the employer pretrial judgment, finding that the manual did not create an implied employment contract. The appeals court reversed. The Supreme Court of New Jersey stated that **an employment manual that fails to include a clear and prominent disclaimer may create an enforceable contract** even when the employment is otherwise terminable at will. If the manual is sufficiently definite to raise the reasonable expectations of employees concerning job security provisions, the provisions may be construed as contractual promises. The case was reversed and remanded to the trial court to decide whether the manual created a reasonable expectation of job security that formed an implied employment contract. The jury was then to determine whether the mechanic was guilty of stealing or unauthorized possession of company property. *Witkowski v. Thomas J. Lipton, Inc.*, 136 N.J. 385, 643 A.2d 546 (N.J. 1994).

CHAPTER SIX

Discrimination

I. TOPIC OVERVIEW

A number of federal laws prohibit employers from discriminating against applicants and employees on the basis of particular characteristics or attributes, such as race and disability. These laws create what are known as "protected classes" and bar employers from discriminating against any individual who fits within one or more of them. Although employers are not required to hire or retain unqualified individuals who happen to fall within a protected class, they are prohibited from discriminating against applicants and employees on the basis of a protected characteristic. The smallest employers are exempted from complying with these federal anti-discrimination laws, but those with at least 15 employees are subject to most of the federal legislation in this area. The task of enforcing these federal mandates falls primarily with the federal Equal Employment Opportunity Commission, which has regional offices nationwide. Enforcement is also accomplished via private lawsuits. State laws provide a corresponding measure of protection from discrimination for applicants and employees. While state-law provisions are sometimes co-extensive with federal ones, they can also provide a greater measure of protection by establishing protected classes that do not exist under federal law and/or by expanding the scope of available relief.

II. AGE DISCRIMINATION

A. Overview

The federal law addressing age discrimination in the workplace is known as the Age Discrimination in Employment Act (ADEA). This law bars employers who retain at least 20 employees from discriminating against any applicant or employee who is 40 years of age or older. The prohibition is not limited solely to decisions related to hiring and firing. Instead, it applies to any decision that affects a term, condition or privilege of employment. For example, a covered employer's decisions relating to compensation, benefits, job assignments, promotion, training and layoff are also covered.

B. Retaliation and Harassment

Under the ADEA, it is unlawful for a covered employer to retaliate against an individual who files an age discrimination charge or opposes an employment practice that discriminates based on age. In addition, covered employers can't retaliate against an individual for participating in an ADEA investigation, proceeding or lawsuit. Employers can be held liable if an employee age 40 or older is harassed at work on the basis of his age.

C. Exceptions/Exclusions

1. Adverse Actions

The ADEA does not completely prohibit covered employers from taking what is known as "adverse actions" against any employee who has reached age 40. An "adverse action" is an employment decision that negatively affects an employee. If all adverse actions were prohibited, an employee who has reached age 40 could never be disciplined for misconduct or terminated for poor performance. The ADEA does not insulate over-40 employees in this way. Instead, it prohibits employers from subjecting employees to adverse actions simply because they are age 40 or older.

2. BFOQ

The ADEA does not prevent employers from making job decisions based on age when age is a bona fide occupational qualification (BFOQ). This BFOQ exception is a narrow one, and it does not apply unless the employer can show that the age limit is "reasonably necessary to the essence of the business." In addition, the employer must show either that all or most people over 40 would not be able to do the job safely and efficiently or that it is not feasible to assess qualifications individually.

3. Foreign Employment

When a covered employer's employee is in a workplace in a foreign country, the covered employer is not required to meet ADEA requirements when doing so would violate the laws of the country where the workplace is located.

4. Seniority Systems and Benefit Plans

The ADEA doesn't prohibit covered employers from observing the terms of a bona fide seniority system or employee benefit plan.

D. The Older Workers Benefits Protection Act (OWBPA)

The OWBPA was passed as an amendment to the ADEA. It specifically provides that it is not a violation of the ADEA for a covered employer to observe the terms of a bona fide seniority system or employee benefit plan. In addition, the OWBPA sets requirements that must be met for an employee's waiver or release of his claims under the ADEA to be valid. A waiver or release of rights under the ADEA must:

* be in writing
* be written so it is understandable to the person signing it
* refer specifically to ADEA claims or rights
* not attempt to waive future claims or rights
* provide the signer with consideration
* advise the signer to consult an attorney before signing
* give the signer 21 days to think about whether to sign the waiver, and
* give the signer at least seven days to revoke the waiver after signing it.

E. Judicial Decisions

The following case summaries provide examples of issues that can arise under the ADEA and how they were resolved by the U.S. Supreme Court. They are lessons learned by employers.

♦ A group of night watchmen in New York sued under the ADEA after they were removed from their positions and assigned to less desirable jobs as night porters and light-duty cleaners. The employer asserted that they should have arbitrated their claims as required by the collective bargaining agreement in place. The case reached the U.S. Supreme Court, which agreed with the employer that **the watchmen had to arbitrate their claims under the ADEA**. The union and the employer bargained in good faith and agreed that employment-related discrimination claims would be subject to arbitration. And the ADEA does not preclude the arbitration of such claims. As a result, the employees had to arbitrate their claims. They still could sue their union for breach of the duty of fair representation; they could also sue the union directly under the ADEA; and they could still bring individual claims to the EEOC or the NLRB. *14 Penn Plaza LLC v. Pyett,* 129 S.Ct. 1456, 173 L.Ed.2d 398 (U.S. 2009).

◆ A 54-year-old claims administration director for a financial services company in Iowa was reassigned to a job as a claims project coordinator. The employer transferred many of his duties to a newly created position and gave the job to a woman in her early 40s whom the coordinator had previously supervised. He sued the company under the ADEA, presenting evidence that he was reassigned in part because of his age. The company claimed the reassignment was part of corporate restructuring. The case reached the U.S. Supreme Court, which held that **an employee can win an ADEA claim by only proving that age was the sole motivating factor for the adverse action.** *Gross v. FBL Financial Services, Inc.,* 129 S.Ct. 2343, 174 L.Ed.2d 119 (U.S. 2009).

◆ An atomic power laboratory in New York was ordered to reduce its work force and had to cut 31 jobs. It did so in part by ranking employees on job performance, flexibility and criticality. The flexibility factor assessed whether the employees' skills were transferable to other assignments. The criticality factor assessed the importance of the employees' skills to the lab. When 30 of the 31 people laid off were age 40 or older, an ADEA lawsuit ensued. A jury ruled that the layoff process had a disparate impact on older employees, but the Second Circuit reversed, finding the employees should have been required to prove that the selection process was unreasonable. The Supreme Court vacated and remanded the case. Here, **the burden should have been on the employer to prove that its layoff process used reasonable factors other than age.** *Meacham v. Knolls Atomic Power Laboratory,* 554 U.S. 84, 128 S.Ct. 2395, 171 L.Ed.2d 283 (2008).

◆ After an older employee in Kansas was fired as part of a reduction in force, she sued for age discrimination. When she sought to introduce testimony from five other employees who claimed that their supervisors discriminated against them because of age, the court refused to allow the "me too" testimony. The Tenth Circuit reversed, but the Supreme Court reversed the court of appeals. It held that such **"me too" testimony can be admitted if it is relevant and not unduly prejudicial.** This is a fact-based inquiry that is best left to the trial court to ascertain. *Sprint/United Management Co. v. Mendelsohn,* 552 U.S. 379, 128 S.Ct. 1140, 170 L.Ed.2d 1 (2008).

◆ A group of senior, longtime police officers with a Mississippi city challenged the city's revised pay policy because it gave proportionately higher raises to officers with less than five years' tenure. They claimed that the revised policy had a disparate (discriminatory) impact on them. The U.S. Supreme Court held that **the officers could sue for disparate impact discrimination under the ADEA.** To win, the officers would have to identify a "specific test, requirement, or practice with the pay plan that ha[d] an adverse impact on older workers." The city claimed that the differential was justified by the need to make junior officers' salaries competitive with comparable positions in the market. Here, the Court determined that the policy was based on reasonable factors other than age and therefore did not violate the ADEA. *Smith v. City of Jackson,* 544 U.S. 228, 125 S.Ct. 1536, 161 L.Ed.2d 410 (2005).

♦ A company and a union entered into a collective bargaining agreement, which eliminated the company's obligation to provide health benefits to subsequently retired employees, except for current workers at least 50 years old. Employees ages 40 to 49 filed charges with the EEOC, claiming that the bargaining agreement violated the ADEA. When the company and union refused to settle, the employees sued in an Ohio federal court, which dismissed the action on the grounds that the ADEA did not cover "reverse age discrimination." The case reached the U.S. Supreme Court, which held that the ADEA was never intended to prevent an employer from favoring an older worker over a younger one. Rather, Congress was concerned with discrimination against older workers. **Reverse age discrimination is not barred by the ADEA.** *General Dynamics Land Systems, Inc. v. Cline,* 540 U.S. 581, 124 S.Ct. 1236, 157 L.Ed.2d 1094 (2004).

♦ The Supreme Court held that in a lawsuit brought under the ADEA, once the employee presented a *prima facie* case of discrimination and showed that the employer's asserted nondiscriminatory reason for its adverse action was false, **intentional discrimination could be inferred** without further evidence of discrimination. This reaffirmed the holding of *St. Mary's Honor Center v. Hicks,* 509 U.S. 502 (1993), a Title VII case that set forth the same standard. The case involved a supervisor in the "hinge room" of a manufacturer of toilet seats and covers. After he was fired for failing to keep accurate records, he sued under the ADEA and presented evidence that his recordkeeping had been proper. The district court had properly let the case go to the jury without further evidence of discrimination, and the jury's award of $98,000 should not have been overturned by the court of appeals. *Reeves v. Sanderson Plumbing Products,* 530 U.S. 133, 120 S.Ct. 2097, 147 L.Ed.2d 105 (2000).

♦ The OWBPA imposes specific requirements on employers who discharge employees and seek **a waiver or release of potential claims** against them under the ADEA. The requirements apply where an employee is offered a severance package. A valid OWBPA waiver must provide at least 20 days' notice to the employee to consider the waiver, written advice to consult an attorney prior to executing the waiver, a seven-day period after signing the waiver to revoke consent, and specifically refer to rights or claims arising under the ADEA. A Louisiana employer presented an employee with a severance agreement and waiver after she received a poor performance rating. The employer gave her only 14 days to consider the waiver, failed to allow seven days after signing the release during which to change her mind, and made no reference to ADEA claims. The employee signed the release, waiving all claims against the employer in return for $6,258. She then sued the employer for constructive discharge in violation of the ADEA. The court granted the employer pretrial judgment, ruling that she had ratified the defective release by retaining the severance pay.

The Fifth Circuit affirmed the district court judgment, but the U.S. Supreme Court found that the employee's **retention of the severance pay did not effectively waive the ADEA claim.** The OWBPA amended the ADEA with specific statutory commands forbidding the waiver of an ADEA claim unless the statutory requirements are met. The Court reversed and remanded the case, since the release did not comply with OWBPA standards and was unenforceable. The failure to tender back the severance pay award did not excuse the employer's failure to comply with the OWBPA. *Oubre v. Entergy Operations, Inc.,* 522 U.S. 422, 118 S.Ct. 838, 139 L.Ed.2d 849 (1998).

♦   A 56-year-old North Carolina employee was fired by his employer after 12 years of work and replaced by a 40-year-old man. The discharged employee sued under the ADEA. The U.S. Supreme Court agreed to review the question of whether the employee was barred from proving age discrimination under the ADEA solely because he had been replaced by a worker who was 40 years old and also within the class of persons protected by the ADEA. It stated that, in age discrimination cases, it was **not necessary that the employee be replaced by someone outside the protected class.** Under that logic, a 40-year-old worker replaced by a 39-year-old worker would be entitled to ADEA protection while the 56-year-old employee in this case would gain no relief despite being replaced by an individual who was 16 years younger. Because the ADEA prohibits discrimination on the basis of age, the replacement of an employee by a substantially younger employee was a far more reliable indicator of age discrimination. *O'Connor v. Consolidated Coin Caterers Corp.,* 517 U.S. 308, 116 S.Ct. 1307, 134 L.Ed.2d 433 (1996).

♦   A 62-year-old secretary at a Tennessee publishing company had access to company financial records and made copies of documents when she became concerned that the company would fire her because of her age. The company dismissed the secretary under a work force reduction plan. She sued under the ADEA, seeking back pay and other relief. When the company learned that she had copied financial documents, it filed a motion for pretrial judgment, which the court granted on the basis of the secretary's misconduct. The Sixth Circuit affirmed, but the U.S. Supreme Court reversed. It rejected the reasoning of the lower courts that the secretary's misconduct constituted proper grounds for termination based on the **after-acquired evidence.** Employee wrongdoing remained relevant and would preclude reinstatement or front pay as an appropriate remedy in this case. However, the district court could not impose an absolute rule barring the secretary's recovery of back pay. The remedy should calculate back pay from the date of the unlawful discharge to the date the company discovered the wrongdoing. *McKennon v. Nashville Banner Publishing Co.,* 513 U.S. 352, 115 S.Ct. 879, 130 L.Ed.2d 852 (1995).

♦   A Massachusetts manufacturing employee was fired at age 62, a few weeks before his pension benefits were due to vest. He sued under the ADEA and the Employee Retirement Income Security Act. The case reached the U.S. Supreme

Court, which noted that when **an employer's decision is wholly motivated by factors other than age**, no ADEA violation occurs. This was true even when the motivating factor was correlated with age (such as pension status). Because age and years of service may be analytically distinct, an employer could take account of one while ignoring the other. The Court remanded the case to the court of appeals to determine if the jury had sufficient evidence to find a violation of the ADEA. *Hazen Paper Co. v. Biggins,* 507 U.S. 604, 113 S.Ct. 1701, 123 L.Ed.2d 338 (1993).

◆   An airline company required all cockpit crew members (pilots, copilots and flight engineers) to retire at the age of 60. A Federal Aviation Administration regulation prohibited persons from serving as pilots or copilots after turning 60, but there was no similar provision for flight engineers. A group of flight engineers and pilots who wished to become flight engineers sued the airline in a California federal court, contending that the mandatory retirement provision violated the ADEA. The airline argued that the **age 60 limit was a bona fide occupational qualification** (BFOQ) reasonably necessary to the safe operation of the airline. A jury held for the employees, and the Ninth Circuit affirmed. The U.S. Supreme Court stated that the BFOQ exception to the ADEA's prohibition on age discrimination was intended to be extremely narrow. Thus, even if it was "rational" for the airline to set age 60 as the limit for flight engineers, the airline still had to show that it had reasonable cause to believe that all or substantially all flight engineers over 60 would be unable to safely perform their job duties, or that it would be highly impractical to deal with older employees on an individual basis to determine whether they had the necessary qualifications for the job. Because the airline had not shown this, the Court affirmed the lower court decisions in favor of the employees. *Western Air Lines, Inc. v. Criswell,* 472 U.S. 400, 105 S.Ct. 2743, 86 L.Ed.2d 321 (1985).

F. Checklists

☑ CHECKLIST

Waiver or Release of Rights Under ADEA

❑ The waiver is in writing.
❑ The waiver is written in plain language that is understandable to the person who is signing it.
❑ The waiver refers specifically to ADEA claims and rights.
❑ The waiver does not attempt to waive future claims or rights.
❑ The waiver provides the signer with consideration (something he/she receives in exchange for signing the waiver).
❑ The waiver advises the signer to consult an attorney before signing it.
❑ The waiver gives the signer 21 days to think about the waiver before signing it.
❑ The waiver gives the signer at least seven days to revoke the waiver after signing it.

If the waiver is sought in connection with a termination program that is offered to a group or class of employees, the employer must also:

❑ Give the employee 45 days to think about it before signing it.
❑ Identify the group of employees covered by the program, as well as time limits and eligibility factors.
❑ Identify the job titles and ages of eligible employees.
❑ Identify the ages of employees who are not eligible or selected.

G. Statutes and Regulations

The ADEA is a federal law that is located in the United States Code at 29 U.S.C. § 621 *et seq.* The statute is enforced primarily by the Equal Employment Opportunity Commission, which has promulgated implementing regulations. These regulations are located in the Code of Federal Regulations at 29 C.F.R. Part 1625.

III. DISABILITY DISCRIMINATION

A. Overview

The Americans with Disabilities Act prohibits covered entities from discriminating against qualified applicants and employees on the basis of disability. Discrimination is prohibited with respect to the full range of employment actions, including recruiting, hiring, pay, promotion and any other privilege or benefit of employment. The law applies to employers who retain at least 15 employees and defines discrimination to include a failure to accommodate the known disability of an applicant or employee. Employers must provide what is known as "reasonable accommodation" to applicants and employees, unless doing so would result in what is known as "undue hardship." The statute also specifically prohibits employers from discriminating against non-disabled applicants and employees based on their relationship or association with an individual who has a disability.

B. What's a "Disability"?

Generally an applicant or employee is not covered by the ADA unless he or she has a disability. But the term "disability" has a very specific meaning under the statute, which is not meant to apply to people with relatively minor ailments. Instead, an individual has a "disability" under the ADA if he has a physical or mental impairment that substantially limits at least one major life activity, such as seeing or hearing. The ADA's definition of disability also includes having a record of a substantially limiting impairment and being regarded as having a substantially limiting impairment. These parts of the definition are meant to protect people from being discriminated against based on false perceptions or stereotypes. A number of conditions and characteristics are specifically excluded from the definition of disability, including homosexuality, bisexuality, sexual behavior disorders, kleptomania and pyromania. People who are currently engaged in illegal drug use are generally not covered by the ADA. In determining whether an individual is disabled under the ADA, the positive effects of what are known as "mitigating measures" generally are not to be taken into account. For example, an individual who uses a hearing aid may be disabled, even though the aid enables him to hear. Other examples of mitigating measures include prosthetic devices and medication.

C. Reasonable Accommodation and Undue Hardship

Generally, a reasonable accommodation by an employer is a change that enables a disabled employee to do his job. Reasonable accommodations come in many forms, including modifications or adjustments to the work environment, modification of work schedules, reassignment to a vacant position, and acquisition of new equipment. The ADA does not require employers to provide the best available accommodation or the accommodation preferred by the employer. Instead, employers can meet their responsibility to provide a reasonable accommodation by providing any accommodation that is effective. An accommodation is not required if it would cause the employer undue hardship. This means an employer is not required to take an action that would result in significant difficulty or expense, taking into account the nature and cost of the accommodation, the employer's financial resources, the employer's type of operation, and the impact that providing the accommodation would have on the employer's operations.

D. Direct Threat

An employer is not required to employ an individual who would pose a direct threat to the health or safety of others in the workplace. When determining whether an applicant or employee poses a direct threat, employers must take into account whether the provision of a reasonable accommodation will eliminate the threat. Employers must make this assessment on an individualized basis and must take into account the duration of the risk, the nature and severity of the harm posed, and the likelihood that it will occur. In the case of *Chevron U.S.A. Inc. v. Echazabal,* the United States Supreme Court upheld the Equal Employment Opportunity Commission's conclusion that an individual can be disqualified as a "direct threat" even if the only danger he poses is to himself. Before this ruling, there was some dispute as to whether an individual was disqualified under this exception only if he posed a threat to others.

E. Association Discrimination

A little-known but important provision of the ADA prohibits employers from discriminating against non-disabled individuals based on their relationship or association with a person who has a disability. This provision is unusual because it allows people who are not disabled to file a claim of discrimination under the ADA. The relationship need not be familial. It can also be of a business or social nature. To be able to file a claim under this provision, the applicant or employee must be qualified for the job. In addition, the ADA's requirement to provide reasonable accommodation does not apply with respect to non-disabled individuals who sue under this provision. For example, employers are not required by the ADA to provide time off to a non-disabled employee so he can care for a disabled family member.

F. Medical Examinations and Inquiries

Before a job offer has been made, employers cannot conduct medical examinations or ask applicants disability-related questions. This includes questions about a job applicant's workers' compensation history. At the pre-offer stage, employers should focus on asking questions relating to the applicant's ability to perform the job. Once an offer of employment has been made, employers can make medical inquiries and require applicants to submit to a medical examination, as long as it subjects all new employees in the same job category to the same requirements. Employers cannot subject current employees to medical examinations or inquiries unless they are "job-related and consistent with business necessity." This means the employer has a reasonable belief that the employee will be unable to perform his job because of a medical condition or will pose a direct threat.

G. Judicial Decisions

The following case summaries provide examples of issues that can arise under the ADA and how they were resolved by the U.S. Supreme Court. They are lessons learned by employers.

♦   An Arizona employee tested positive for cocaine during a drug test at work and was allowed to resign rather than face termination. Two years later, the employee sought to be rehired to the same position. He attached to his application glowing reference letters from his pastor and his Alcoholics Anonymous counselor. The company refused to rehire him, and he sued under the ADA. He asserted that the no-rehire policy violated the ADA by discriminating against him **because of a record of a disability or because he was regarded as disabled**. A federal court granted pretrial judgment to the company, but the Ninth Circuit reversed. It stated that the no-rehire policy violated the ADA as applied to former employees whose only work-related offense was testing positive because of their addiction. On further appeal, the U.S. Supreme Court held that the employer could legitimately refuse to rehire an employee who was discharged for violating workplace conduct rules. The employer's neutral no-rehire policy satisfied its obligation under McDonnell Douglas to provide a legitimate, nondiscriminatory reason for refusing to rehire the employee. The only remaining question was whether the stated reason for the refusal to rehire was in fact the real reason. The Court remanded the case. *Raytheon Co. v. Hernandez,* 540 U.S. 44, 124 S.Ct. 513, 157 L.Ed.2d 357 (2003). On remand, the Ninth Circuit Court of Appeals held that a trial was required because the company gave inconsistent reasons for why it refused to rehire the employee. *Hernandez v. Hughes Missile Systems Co. (Raytheon),* 362 F.3d 564 (9th Cir. 2004).

♦   A bookkeeper at a medical clinic in Oregon sued the clinic under the ADA after she was fired. The clinic sought to have the case dismissed, alleging that it did not have **the necessary 15 employees to qualify it as a covered employer under the ADA** because the four physician-shareholders who owned the clinic could not be counted as employees. A federal court agreed with the clinic and dismissed the case, but the Ninth Circuit reversed. The case reached the U.S. Supreme Court, which adopted the Equal Employment Opportunity Commission's standard for determining when a director-shareholder should be counted as an employee under the ADA. The standard provides six factors for ascertaining whether the organization has control over the individual. The Court reversed and remanded the case for a determination of whether the doctor-shareholders should be counted as employees. *Clackamas Gastroenterology Associates, P.C. v. Wells,* 538 U.S. 440, 123 S.Ct. 1673, 155 L.Ed.2d 615 (2003).

♦   The U.S. Supreme Court held that a gas company could reject an applicant for a position in a California refinery where the applicant suffered from hepatitis C and could die from prolonged exposure to chemicals in the refinery. Here, the gas company made an offer of employment, then conducted a medical exam that found the hepatitis. When it revoked the offer, the applicant sued under the ADA, claiming that since he was not a direct threat to anyone else in the workplace, the company could not refuse to hire him. The Supreme Court stated that **the "direct threat" defense could be applied to prevent harm to the individual seeking a job**. It was not limited to preventing harm to "others" in the workplace. If a person's disability would create a direct threat of harm to himself in the workplace, the employer need not hire the person, even if the individual is willing to take the risk. *Chevron U.S.A. v. Echazabal,* 536 U.S. 73, 122 S.Ct. 2045, 153 L.Ed.2d 82 (2002).

♦   A 10-year customer service employee for an airline was placed in a mail room position after he injured his back handling cargo. He obtained the position by invoking his seniority rights. A few years later, he learned that two senior employees were going to bid on the mail room position. He asked the airline to make an exception to its seniority policy to accommodate his back injury by allowing him to stay in the mail room. After allowing the employee to stay in the mail room for five months, the airline decided not to make an exception to its seniority policy, and the employee lost his job. He sued the airline under the ADA, and a California federal court ruled that requiring the airline to accommodate the employee would cause an undue hardship. The Ninth Circuit reversed, and the airline appealed. The U.S. Supreme Court held that as a general rule, an accommodation under the ADA is not reasonable if it conflicts with an employer's **seniority rules**. However, employees may present evidence of special circumstances that make a "seniority rule exception" reasonable in a particular case. The Court remanded the case. *US Airways, Inc. v. Barnett,* 535 U.S. 391, 122 S.Ct. 1516, 152 L.Ed.2d 589 (2002).

♦ An employee at a Kentucky manufacturing plant had a severe case of carpal tunnel syndrome and tendonitis that prevented her from gripping tools and raising her arms over her head for extended periods of time. She was assigned to modified-duty positions for two years, but she eventually became unable to perform two of the essential functions of the job. She began missing work and was eventually fired for poor attendance. When she sued under the ADA, a federal court found that she was not disabled under the statute. The Sixth Circuit reversed, but the U.S. Supreme Court reversed the court of appeals. It held that the ADA requires a person to be substantially limited in a "major" life activity, and that **the employee's inability to perform a manufacturing job did not qualify her as disabled under the act**. If the employee was substantially limited in the ability to perform the types of tasks that are centrally important to people's daily lives (like household chores, bathing and brushing her teeth), then she would be disabled under the ADA. The Court remanded the case. *Toyota Motor Manufacturing v. Williams,* 534 U.S. 184, 122 S.Ct. 681, 151 L.Ed.2d 615 (2002).

♦ Twin sisters with uncorrected vision of 20/200 or worse, but corrected vision of 20/20 or better, applied to United Air Lines for positions as global airline pilots. United rejected them because they did not meet its minimum requirement of at least 20/100 uncorrected vision. They sued under the ADA. A Colorado federal court dismissed their lawsuit, and the case reached the U.S. Supreme Court, which found that the sisters had not shown they were disabled under the ADA. First, because the ADA defines a disability as an impairment that "substantially limits" a major life activity, and because the sisters, with glasses or contacts, had 20/20 vision, **they were not presently substantially limited**. The sisters also failed to show that they were regarded as disabled by United. Even though it regarded them as unable to perform in the particular position of global airline pilot, it did not regard them as substantially limited in the major life activity of working. Other jobs were still available to them, including jobs such as regional pilots or pilot instructors. *Sutton v. United Air Lines, Inc.,* 527 U.S. 471, 119 S.Ct. 2139, 144 L.Ed.2d 450 (1999).

♦ The U.S. Supreme Court held that a mechanic with high blood pressure that was controllable with medication was not disabled under the ADA, because **his high blood pressure did not substantially limit him in the major life activity of working**. Further, he was not regarded as disabled. Rather, he was regarded as unqualified to work in the single position of United Parcel Service mechanic because he could not obtain a Department of Transportation health certification. *Murphy v. United Parcel Service,* 527 U.S. 516, 119 S.Ct. 2133, 144 L.Ed.2d 484 (1999).

♦ An Oregon truck driver with monocular vision was fired because he did not meet the visual acuity standards of the Federal Motor Carrier Safety Regulations. The U.S. Supreme Court noted that the driver was not necessarily disabled within the meaning of the ADA. Even though he had monocular vision, his brain had developed subconscious mechanisms for coping with his visual impairment. This was a mitigating measure (like glasses or medication) that had to be taken into account when determining whether he was substantially limited in one or more major life activities. An employer who requires as a job qualification that an employee **meet a federal safety regulation** does not have to justify enforcing the regulation simply because the government has waived the safety standard experimentally in an individual case. *Albertsons, Inc. v. Kirkingburg,* 527 U.S. 555, 119 S.Ct. 2162, 144 L.Ed.2d 518 (1999).

◆   A Texas employee suffered a stroke and applied for Social Security benefits, alleging that she was disabled and unable to work. When her condition improved, she returned to work. However, her employer fired her less than a week later. She sued in a Texas federal court under the ADA asserting that a reasonable accommodation would allow her to perform her job. The court ruled that she could not assert she was disabled in her application for and receipt of Social Security benefits, and later claim that she could perform the essential functions of her job. The case reached the U.S. Supreme Court, which held that **the pursuit and receipt of Social Security Disability Insurance benefits does not automatically bar a person from litigating a claim under the ADA.** However, to survive a motion to dismiss, the person must present a sufficient explanation of the seeming contradiction that she is disabled under the Social Security Act (SSA) while not disabled under the ADA. Because the SSA does not take into account a reasonable accommodation when it determines whether a person is disabled for Social Security purposes, qualifying for such benefits might not bar an ADA claim. *Cleveland v. Policy Management Systems Corp.,* 526 U.S. 795, 119 S.Ct. 1597, 143 L.Ed.2d 966 (1999).

◆   The U.S. Supreme Court held that **asymptomatic HIV is a physical impairment that substantially limits the major life activity of reproduction.** Accordingly, a dentist's patient was disabled within the meaning of the ADA. The question then became whether the patient's HIV infection posed a significant threat to the health and safety of others that might justify the dentist's refusal to treat her in his office. *Bragdon v. Abbott,* 524 U.S. 624, 118 S.Ct. 2196, 141 L.Ed.2d 540 (1998).

H. Checklists

☑ CHECKLIST

Determining Whether an Individual Poses a Direct Threat to Health or Safety Under the ADA

❑ Can the threat be reduced or eliminated by providing a reasonable accommodation?
❑ What is the duration of the risk?
❑ What is the nature and severity of the potential harm posed by the individual?
❑ What is the likelihood that the harm will occur?

❏ Is the potential harm imminent?
❏ Have medical analyses been taken into account?

I. Quiz

REASONABLE ACCOMMODATION QUIZ – TEST YOUR KNOWLEDGE

This true-false quiz is based on an EEOC Enforcement Guidance titled Reasonable Accommodation and Undue Hardship Under the Americans with Disabilities Act.

1. An employee's request for reasonable accommodation must be in writing.
2. A request for a reasonable accommodation can be made by another individual on behalf of an employee with a disability.
3. When an employee asks for a reasonable accommodation, an employer can never require the employee to submit documentation supporting the request.
4. If an employee suggests an accommodation that meets his needs and does not pose an undue hardship, the employer must provide it.
5. An employer may be required to change an employee's supervisor as a reasonable accommodation.
6. An employer might be required to allow an employee to work at home as a reasonable accommodation.
7. Job restructuring, a part-time schedule and reassignment are all potential reasonable accommodations.
8. Employers can ask job applicants whether they will need a reasonable accommodation to complete the job application process.
9. Employers must provide reasonable accommodations for training programs.
10. Employers can't penalize employees who take a leave of absence as a reasonable accommodation under the ADA.

Answers:
1. *False.* Individuals may make a request for accommodation in writing, but they are also free to request an accommodation orally or in any other way.
2. *True.* A request for accommodation can also be made by a disabled individual's family member, friend, health professional or other representative.
3. *False.* This is a tricky one. There are situations in which an employer can't ask for documentation in response to a request for reasonable accommodation. Specifically, an employer can't ask for documentation if both the disability and the need for accommodation are obvious, or if the individual has already provided information showing he has a disability and needs an accommodation. But when the disability and the need for accommodation are not obvious, the

employer can ask for documentation from a healthcare or rehabilitation professional.

4. *False.* The employer's obligation is to provide an effective accommodation, not to provide the accommodation of the employee's choosing. If there is an effective alternative to the employee's specific request, the employer can provide it.

5. *False.* An employer does not have to change an employee's supervisor as a reasonable accommodation.

6. *True.* An employer may be required to permit an employee to work at home as a reasonable accommodation, as long as doing so would be effective and would not cause an undue hardship.

7. *True.* These are just a few examples of accommodations that may be required in specific situations.

8. *True.* Employers should tell applicants what is involved with the hiring process and can ask applicants whether any accommodation will be needed.

9. *True.* This obligation applies to in-house programs as well as to programs that are provided by outside entities.

10. *True.* This would be retaliation and would make the leave ineffective.

J. Statutes and Regulations

The Americans with Disabilities Act is a federal law that is located in the United States Code at 42 U.S.C. § 12101 *et seq.* It is enforced primarily by the Equal Employment Opportunity Commission. The federal regulation implementing the ADA is located in the Code of Federal Regulations at 29 C.F.R. Part 1630.

IV. SEX DISCRIMINATION

A. Overview

Title VII of the Civil Rights Act of 1964 is a federal law that prohibits employers who retain at least 15 employees from discriminating against applicants and employees on the basis of sex. This prohibition of discrimination extends to all aspects of the employment relationship, including but not limited to hiring, promotion, compensation, training and termination. Under Title VII, sex-based discrimination includes sexual harassment and discrimination based on pregnancy, childbirth or any related medical condition. In addition to intentional discrimination, Title VII also limits the ability of employers to adopt job policies that have the effect of excluding people on the basis of sex. This is called disparate impact discrimination. Another federal law called the Equal Pay Act generally requires that men and women be paid equally when they perform equal work.

B. Intentional Discrimination/Disparate Impact

It is important to remember that Title VII prohibits two separate and distinct forms of discrimination based on sex: intentional discrimination and discrimination that results from the application of neutral policies that have the effect of unfairly excluding people on the basis of sex. Intentional discrimination, also known as disparate treatment, occurs when an employer takes action against an employee or applicant based on sex. Disparate impact claims involve employment policies or practices that are applied neutrally but have a negative impact on one sex. For example, a minimum height requirement for all police officer applicants might be challenged by female applicants under a disparate impact theory. Disparate impact claims can be defended by showing the qualification or requirement at issue is related to the job and necessary for business reasons. The most important thing to remember about disparate impact claims is that employers can be found liable even though there was no intent to discriminate.

C. Bona Fide Occupational Qualification

Employers can sometimes defend claims of sex discrimination by showing that a challenged classification is what is known under the law as a bona fide occupational qualification. This means that the qualification at issue is reasonably necessary to the normal operation of the employer's business. For example, a federal appeals court held that sex was a bona fide occupational qualification for corrections officers at a women's prison. It is important to remember that the bona fide occupational qualification exception to the Title VII rule against discriminating on the basis of sex is very narrow. It does not allow employers to make employment decisions based on stereotypical characterizations of males or females, or based on preferences of customers or co-workers.

D. Pregnancy

An amendment to Title VII called the Pregnancy Discrimination Act prohibits employers from discriminating against employees based on pregnancy, childbirth and related medical conditions. The law recognizes that pregnancy creates limitations and simply requires employers to treat pregnant women in the same way they would treat other applicants or employees with similar medical conditions. Employers cannot refuse to hire a woman because she is pregnant. Employers can't require employees to take a specified amount of time off before returning to work after giving birth. Nor can they prevent a pregnant employee from remaining at work, as long as the employee can still perform her job.

E. Judicial Decisions

The following case summaries provide examples of issues that can arise relating to sex and pregnancy discrimination and how they were resolved by the courts. They are lessons learned by employers.

1. Sex

♦ One of the few female area managers for an Alabama plant worked for the company from 1979 until 1998. For most of that time, she and all other salaried employees received or were denied raises based on their supervisors' evaluations of their job performance. Initially, her salary was in line with the salaries of male area managers, but over time her pay slipped in comparison. She alleged that the pay disparity began in the 1980s as retaliation because she rejected a supervisor's sexual advances. She also claimed that another supervisor gave her a poor evaluation because of her gender. However, she didn't complain to the EEOC until March 1998. When she finally sued under Title VII, the case reached the U.S. Supreme Court. Over a vigorous dissent, the Court held that she waited too long to sue. **She could not prove that the most current raises she received were the result of any discriminatory intent.** She should have filed an EEOC charge within 180 days after each of the earlier poor evaluations. *Ledbetter v. Goodyear Tire & Rubber Co., Inc.,* 550 U.S. 618, 127 S.Ct. 2162, 167 L.Ed.2d 982 (2007).

♦ A Caesars Palace (Las Vegas) employee claimed she was disciplined and finally fired because of her gender. She was the only woman who worked in the hotel and casino's warehouse. Although her work was regarded as "excellent," she had a number of problems with her co-workers and supervisors. When she complained about being singled out because she was a woman, the human resources (HR) department refused to intervene. At trial, she recounted several incidents of discrimination where she was formally reprimanded for rules infractions while similarly situated male employees were not. Caesars maintained that she was fired because of the disciplinary problems. She countered that, although she was not a perfect employee, her gender was the "real" reason or motivating factor for her discharge. The jury awarded $264,000 to the employee. The Ninth Circuit and the Supreme Court affirmed. **A plaintiff in a discrimination case need not have direct proof of bias to qualify for a "mixed motive" jury instruction.** Title VII provides that "a plaintiff need only 'demonstrate' that an employer used a forbidden consideration with respect to 'any employment practice.'" *Desert Palace Inc. d/b/a Caesars Palace Hotel & Casino v. Costa,* 539 U.S. 90, 123 S.Ct. 2148, 156 L.Ed.2d 84 (2003).

♦ A female lower-level director of the American Dental Association sought a promotion to the position of legislative director. She competed for the position with a male lower-level director; both had received "distinguished" performance ratings. After she was rejected, she sued in a federal court for gender discrimination, claiming that the male candidate had been pre-selected. A jury found discrimination and awarded her $52,718 in back pay. However, the district court judge refused to allow the jury to consider punitive damages. The case reached the U.S. Supreme Court, which clarified when employers may be liable for punitive damages under Title VII. A plaintiff need not prove that the employer engaged in some extraordinarily egregious behavior independent of the employer's state of mind. Instead, the employer must act with **malice or reckless indifference** to the plaintiff's federally protected rights. In other words, the terms "malice" and "reckless indifference" pertain to "the employer's knowledge that it may be acting in violation of federal law." **Punitive damages** are not warranted where the employer is unaware of the relevant federal prohibition, or where the employer discriminates with the distinct belief the discrimination is lawful, such as where it reasonably believes a bona fide occupational qualification is satisfied. *Kolstad v. American Dental Ass'n*, 527 U.S. 526, 119 S.Ct. 2118, 144 L.Ed.2d 494 (1999).

◆   An employee of an Illinois educational materials company filed a sex discrimination complaint against her employer with the Equal Employment Opportunity Commission (EEOC) asserting that she should have received a promotion. The employer then fired her. The EEOC sued the employer on her behalf for retaliation under Title VII. The employer sought to dismiss the case, stating that it did not have 15 employees during 20 weeks in the past two years and therefore did not come within the coverage of the act. The case reached the U.S. Supreme Court, which held that the appropriate test is whether the parties have an employment relationship on the day in question. **Since the employer had employment relationships with 15 or more employees for 38 weeks of the calendar year in question, it was an "employer" under Title VII.** *Walters v. Metropolitan Educ. Enterprises, Inc.*, 519 U.S. 202, 117 S.Ct. 660, 136 L.Ed.2d 644 (1997).

◆   A senior manager at a nationwide professional accounting firm was refused admission as a partner. She sued the firm under Title VII, charging that it had discriminated against her on the basis of sex in its partnership decisions. The district court found that the firm had discriminated against the manager, but held that it could avoid equitable relief if it could prove by clear and convincing evidence that it would have made the same decision absent a discriminatory motive. The U.S. Court of Appeals, D.C. Circuit, affirmed. The U.S. Supreme Court held that under Title VII, the employer could avoid liability if it showed by a mere preponderance of the evidence that it would have made the same decision even if it had not taken the manager's gender into account. This preserved the employer's right to freedom of choice. The court then reversed and remanded the case for a determination of whether the same decision would have been made absent the discrimination. *Price Waterhouse v. Hopkins*, 490 U.S. 228, 109 S.Ct. 1775, 104 L.Ed.2d 268 (1989).

Under the Civil Rights Act of 1991, if it is shown that **discrimination is a contributing factor in the employment decision**, then (assuming that the employer can show that it would have made the same decision absent the discrimination) courts will be prohibited from ordering certain injunctive relief – like reinstatement. However, money damages may still be available.

♦ A Humane Society employee in New York claimed that she was subjected to a hostile work environment because her married, female boss was having an affair with the organization's largest donor. She asserted that the donor kept intimidating her with how she ought to do her job and that her boss sided with the donor. When she revealed to her boss that she was aware of the affair, she was fired. She sued under Title VII and lost because **she could not show that she was treated any differently than a male employee in the same position would have been treated.** *Foster v. Humane Society of Rochester and Monroe County,* 724 F.Supp.2d 382 (W.D.N.Y. 2010).

♦ A temporary employee for a company in Pennsylvania applied for a permanent position but did not get it. The company ended her temporary assignment and she found another job eight months later that paid less. When she sued for gender discrimination, a jury ruled in her favor and a trial court awarded her over $164,000 in compensatory damages ($63,000 in back pay and $101,000 in front pay). However, the Third Circuit vacated the award, finding that it had been improperly calculated. The lower court should not have relied on her testimony as to what sort of raises she would have gotten had she been hired. On remand, she would get the chance to receive both back pay and front pay if she could show that her new pay was not substantially equivalent to her old pay. *Donlin v. Philips Lighting North America Corp.,* 581 F.3d 73 (3d Cir. 2009).

♦ An investor analyst in Missouri claimed that his supervisor subjected him to humiliating and undeserved criticism, forcing him to resign. He said she made the workplace so intolerable that he had no choice but to leave. When he sued for sex discrimination under Title VII, he lost. The Eighth Circuit held that he presented **no evidence that he was singled out because of his gender.** *Hawks v. J.P. Morgan Chase Bank,* 591 F.3d 1043 (8th Cir. 2010).

♦ A UPS driver in Arkansas used her seniority to obtain a higher-paying "feeder driver" position. However, on her second day on the new job, she caused an accident. She was told that she was no longer qualified for the feeder job and that she should report to her old job as a regular driver. She filed a grievance with her union, and a week later filed a complaint with the EEOC, claiming race and gender discrimination. Meanwhile, another supervisor determined that she should not have been disqualified from the feeder job because of the accident. Upon learning of the EEOC charge, UPS postponed reinstating her to the feeder job. Two months later, UPS and the union reached a settlement reinstating her to the feeder job with full back pay, seniority and all benefits. She nevertheless sued under Title VII and lost. The Eighth Circuit held that **the demotion was not an adverse action because UPS corrected it in a timely manner.** *Jackson v. United Parcel Service, Inc.,* 548 F.3d 1137 (8th Cir. 2008).

♦ An employee in Maine applied for a promotion to a managerial position. She was already performing many of the job's tasks, had stellar performance reviews, and had been encouraged to apply for the job by superiors. However, her immediate supervisor told her that she decided not to promote her, saying it was nothing she did or didn't do; it was just that she had a lot on her plate with her kids. The employee had an 11-year-old son and triplets in kindergarten. When she sued under Title VII, a federal court granted pretrial judgment to the company. The First Circuit reversed, finding issues of fact that required a trial. Here, **a jury could find that she was denied a promotion because she was a woman with young children.** *Chadwick v. WellPoint, Inc.,* 561 F.3d 38 (1st Cir. 2009).

♦ A Colorado woman applied for a job at a power plant and reached the interview stage. An all-male panel interviewed her, and she did not get the job. She sued for discrimination under Title VII and lost because the subjective interview process was not discriminatory. **The panel asked the same questions of every applicant** and ranked them using predetermined criteria from an HR interview guide. The questions were meant to elicit information about job competencies, technical knowledge, initiative and comfort taking risks, adaptability, communication skills and ability to work on a team. Also, another female interviewee scored second highest and was offered a job. *Turner v. Public Service Co. of Colorado,* 563 F.3d 1136 (10th Cir. 2009).

♦ A casino sales manager in Nevada claimed that she was reprimanded for making two phone calls to her children, while a male employee who also called his children was not reprimanded. Also, **her supervisor allegedly said that mothers can't perform as well as men or women without children** and that they should stay at home. After she complained about him, she was fired. She sued for discrimination and retaliation under Title VII. The casino claimed it had a valid reason for her termination – poor performance – and a federal court granted it pretrial judgment. However, the Ninth Circuit reversed, finding issues of fact that required a trial. *Gerving v. Opbiz, LLC d/b/a Aladdin Resort and Casino,* 324 Fed.Appx. 692 (9th Cir. 2009).

♦ An Ohio moving and storage **company decided to lay off people in departments staffed predominantly by women**. Of the 13 employees laid off, only one was male. Four of the laid-off women sued for discrimination, alleging that the company's reduction in force had a disparate impact (or discriminatory effect) on female employees. A federal court and the Sixth Circuit ruled in the company's favor, noting that the employees failed to prove that the company's asserted reasons for laying people off from the heavily female departments were pretextual. Those departments were more strongly affected by declining business. *Shollenbarger v. Planes Moving & Storage,* 297 Fed.Appx. 483 (6th Cir. 2008).

♦ A New Mexico car dealership disciplined a female manager for unsatisfactory performance because she was chronically late for work, made personal phone calls and frequently wasn't in the office such that the dealership had to assign someone else as her backup. However, the dealership didn't discipline a male manager who was also often tardy. When the EEOC sued on her behalf, the Tenth Circuit ruled in favor of the dealership. Here, the two employees were not similarly situated because **the female's problems affected**

productivity while the male's did not. No one had to do extra work for him. Thus, the dealership did not violate Title VII. *EEOC v. PVNF, LLC,* 487 F.3d 790 (10th Cir. 2007).

◆ A department director had to decide which of two managers to keep in a reduction in force. He interviewed the managers for about an hour each, then spoke to their subordinates and supervisors. Afterward, he chose to retain the male, and the female sued for sex discrimination under Title VII. A Maryland federal court ruled for the company, and the Fourth Circuit upheld that decision. **Even though the selection process was informal, the company had established criteria for the decision** and the male candidate had seemed to be more committed to the position. By contrast, the female stated that she did not see herself with the company in five years. *Luh v. J.M. Huber Corp.,* 211 Fed.Appx. 143 (4th Cir. 2006).

◆ A company told a South Dakota employee it was eliminating her position around the same time she informed it she was pregnant. The company then moved up her evaluation and told her she would have to relocate or leave the company. Two weeks later she had a miscarriage. When she refused the transfer, she was fired. She sued for sex discrimination under Title VII and lost because **the transfer offer was not an adverse action**. Further, the Eighth Circuit held that the company had no liability for causing her miscarriage through the stress of the relocation situation. *Reynolds v. Ethicon Endo-Surgery, Inc.,* 454 F.3d 868 (8th Cir. 2006).

◆ An HR manager for a company in Rhode Island counseled a district manager about his treatment of women after **an investigation revealed that he treated women worse than he treated men**. About a year later, the company hired a woman to manage one of its stores. She worked there for less than a year, then quit and sued the company for sex discrimination. A trial court dismissed the lawsuit, but the Supreme Court of Rhode Island reinstated it. Even though the district manager never referred to her gender when he yelled at her, the company could still be liable for sex discrimination where the HR manager's notes revealed the company's awareness of a potential problem. *DeCamp v. Dollar Tree Stores, Inc.,* 875 A.2d 13 (R.I. 2005).

◆ The CEO of the Wisconsin Health Fund became romantically interested in a dentist who worked for the fund and decided to promote her to the position of director of the dental clinic. To do so, he had to fire the current director of the clinic – a male with an MBA as well as a dental degree. After being fired, the male clinic director sued the health fund for sex discrimination under Title VII. A federal district court and the Seventh Circuit Court of Appeals ruled against him. **Favoring a woman because of romantic interest is not sex discrimination** even when the male is more qualified for the job. Here, the decision to fire the male and hire the female was purely personal and not based on a belief that women were superior workers. *Preston v. Wisconsin Health Fund,* 397 F.3d 539 (7th Cir. 2005).

♦   A Colorado employee worked as a meat wrapper for a company's retail stores. Subsequently, she was given the opportunity to work as a temporary project employee. The assignment was not considered a promotion, and she was not given higher pay or better benefits. She stayed in temporary assignments for nearly two years. Her supervisor then told her he did not need her anymore, and she was returned to her meat-wrapping position, again with no change in salary or benefits. She sued for sex discrimination under Title VII, alleging that two male employees with less experience were kept in the temporary assignment to complete the work she had been told was done. A federal court dismissed her lawsuit on the grounds that the company had not taken "adverse action" against her, but the Tenth Circuit reversed. **The reassignment could be an adverse action because it resulted in a reduction in responsibility.** A trial was required. *Stinnett v. Safeway, Inc.*, 337 F.3d 1213 (10th Cir. 2003).

♦   A Nevada casino instituted a "Personal Best" program under which female bartenders and beverage servers had to wear makeup and nail polish, while male bartenders and beverage servers had to keep their hair short and have clean, trimmed fingernails. A female bartender with excellent performance reviews refused to comply with the makeup policy and never applied for a position that did not require makeup. She was fired, and then sued the casino under Title VII, alleging sex discrimination. A federal court and the Ninth Circuit ruled against her. The policy did not burden female servers more than males. **Different grooming standards are discriminatory only when they impose a greater burden on one sex than the other.** Accordingly, the casino could legally enforce its personal appearance policy. *Jespersen v. Harrah's Operating Co.*, 392 F.3d 1076 (9th Cir. 2004).

♦   In a lawsuit brought by the EEOC against a restaurant for gender discrimination, a Florida federal court found that the restaurant intentionally discriminated against four women even though they did not apply for jobs during the period covered by the lawsuit. The restaurant appealed to the Eleventh Circuit, which affirmed in part. The Eleventh Circuit held when a **plaintiff has not actually applied and been rejected for a job**, a case of discrimination can be established by showing 1) a real and present interest in the job, and 2) that she was effectively deterred from applying by the employer's discriminatory practices. Here, two of the women were unable to show that they had a real and present interest in applying for the jobs during the applicable time period. The other two women showed that they had a real and present interest that was effectively deterred by the restaurant's male-servers-only policy. Those two plaintiffs were entitled to back pay and prejudgment interest. *EEOC v. Joe's Stone Crabs, Inc.*, 296 F.3d 1265 (11th Cir. 2002).

♦   A Washington federal court held that a company could not offer a health plan with a comprehensive prescription medicine benefits package that excluded prescription contraceptives. The court stated that **employers cannot exclude benefits that are available only to women.** Denying prescription contraceptives here was tantamount to denying employee benefits on the basis of sex, in violation of Title VII. *Erickson v. Bartell Drug Co.*, 141 F.Supp.2d 1266 (W.D. Wash. 2001).

2. Pregnancy

♦   AT & T based pension calculations on a seniority system that gave less retirement credit for pregnancy absences than it did for medical leave generally. After the Pregnancy Discrimination Act took effect, the company changed its policy prospectively, but did not make any retroactive adjustments. A group of female employees and their union sued the company under Title VII, alleging sex and pregnancy discrimination. A California federal court ruled for the employees, but the U.S. Supreme Court ultimately reversed. **The Pregnancy Discrimination Act did not apply retroactively, and the company could calculate retirement benefits in part by using the prior system.** *AT & T Corp. v. Hulteen*, 129 S.Ct. 1962, 173 L.Ed.2d 898 (U.S. 2009).

♦   A company manufactured batteries made primarily from lead. In 1982, the company began a policy of excluding pregnant women and women capable of bearing children from jobs involving lead exposure. In 1984, a group of affected employees initiated a class action suit against the company, challenging its fetal protection policy as sex discrimination that violated Title VII. A Wisconsin federal court granted pretrial judgment to the company, finding that it had established a business necessity defense. The U.S. Court of Appeals, Seventh Circuit, affirmed, and the case reached the U.S. Supreme Court.

The Court noted that **there was a clear bias in the company's policy allowing fertile men but not women the choice of risking their reproductive health**. Thus, there was clear sex discrimination involved. Even though there was no malevolent motive involved, the policy could not be termed "neutral." Accordingly, the only way for the company to justify the discrimination was by establishing that gender was a bona fide occupational qualification, which it could not do. Decisions about the welfare of future children must be left to parents rather than employers. Since the company complied with the lead standard developed by the Occupational Safety and Health Administration and issued warnings to its female employees about the dangers of lead exposure, it was not negligent, and a future court would have difficulty finding it liable. The Court reversed the lower court decisions and struck down the company's fetal protection policy. *Int'l Union, UAW v. Johnson Controls, Inc.*, 499 U.S. 187, 111 S.Ct. 1196, 113 L.Ed.2d 158 (1991).

♦   An Iowa bank hired a pregnant teller, who rushed to the bathroom with nausea four to 11 times each morning after arriving at work. She rejected the bank's offer of a later start time. The bank then fired her and she sued for pregnancy discrimination, but she lost when the Eighth Circuit held that **the bank did not need to treat her more favorably than its non-pregnant employees**. Since the bank did not tolerate any teller leaving her station that many times – including once while in the middle of a transaction with a customer – it could fire her without violating Title VII. *Elam v. Regions Financial Corp.*, 601 F.3d 873 (8th Cir. 2010).

♦   A South Dakota medical clinic fired an employee after the managing partner found out she was pregnant. It also refused to hire a pregnant applicant.

It claimed that the reason it took both actions was because both women's absences would coincide with its busy season (a legitimate reason). Both women contacted the EEOC, which sued on their behalf. A jury awarded the employee $15,341 in back pay and gave the applicant $5,757. The Eighth Circuit upheld the awards and also ruled that the jury should have been allowed to consider awarding punitive damages because there was evidence that the clinic's managers knew they were violating the law and acted in reckless disregard of it. *EEOC v. Siouxland Oral Maxillofacial Surgery Associates, LLP,* 578 F.3d 921 (8th Cir. 2009).

♦ A pregnant insurance company employee in Pennsylvania asked about time off for doctor's appointments and was told by a vice president (and part owner) that they would "play it by ear." The company required her to call in every day she was going to be absent. She later learned that her baby had deformities and decided to terminate the pregnancy. Her husband called the vice president and allegedly was told that she could take time off for the abortion and the funeral. However, when she called in after the funeral, she was told she was fired. She sued under the Pregnancy Discrimination Act (PDA). A federal court granted pretrial judgment to the company, but the Third Circuit reversed. It held that **the PDA protects a woman who decides to terminate a pregnancy**, and that there was evidence the employee was treated more harshly than male employees who needed time off for medical reasons. *Doe v. C.A.R.S. Protection Plus, Inc.,* 527 F.3d 358 (3d Cir. 2008).

♦ A Michigan fire safety officer claimed that she was promised the supervisor position at Chrysler's Auburn Hills facility. However, when she filled out forms explaining that she was pregnant and needed a new uniform that would fit, she was offered a promotion that was significantly inferior to the one at Auburn Hills. She began a three-month maternity leave several weeks later and did not return to work. Instead, she sued for sex discrimination under state law. A jury found that she was discriminated against because she was pregnant, but it rejected her claim of constructive discharge. The Sixth Circuit affirmed the ruling in her favor, but modified the award, noting that **she was only entitled to pay for the time between when she was offered the inferior position and when she quit**. *Lulaj v. The Wackenhut Corp.,* 512 F.3d 760 (6th Cir. 2008).

♦ A company in Washington advertised for a clerk/order checker, and a woman applied for the job. Although the job had no documented description of its requirements, the applicant was told it had a 25-pound lifting requirement. She was offered the job contingent on passing a preemployment physical. At the exam, she informed the company doctor that she was pregnant, and was told to get a release from her doctor. After she obtained the release allowing her to lift between 20 and 30 pounds, she was told that the lifting requirement was 40 pounds. When she got her doctor to raise her lifting restriction to 40 pounds, an internal expert at the company determined that the lifting requirement was actually 60 pounds. The company then refused to hire the applicant, and she sued for pregnancy discrimination. The Washington Supreme Court ruled in her favor, finding that the company violated state law. **It failed to show that the lifting requirement was a business necessity.** *Hegwine v. Longview Fibre Co.,* 172 P.3d 688 (Wash. 2007).

♦ A railroad offered a health care plan that excluded coverage for all male and female contraceptive methods, both prescription and non-prescription, when those methods were used solely for contraception. The plan allowed coverage for contraception when it was medically necessary for a non-contraceptive purpose. A number of female employees sued for sex discrimination under the Pregnancy Discrimination Act, and a Nebraska federal court ruled in their favor. The Eighth Circuit reversed. Here, **the plan was gender-neutral, excluding all contraception methods.** Further, since contraception prevents pregnancy, it is not "related to pregnancy" as meant by the act. *In re Union Pacific Railroad Co.,* 479 F.3d 936 (8th Cir. 2007).

♦ A New York employee sued her employer seeking benefits for her infertility treatments. She alleged violations of Title VII, the Pregnancy Discrimination Act and state law based on the employer's refusal to cover certain infertility procedures under its health benefits plan. Although the plan covered some treatments, it expressly excluded surgical impregnation procedures. A federal court ruled in favor of the employer, and the Second Circuit affirmed. Here, **the employer limited coverage equally between men and women**, so there was no violation of Title VII or the Pregnancy Discrimination Act. Despite the fact that surgical implantation procedures would be performed only on women, both male and female employees were denied coverage for such a procedure. *Saks v. Franklin Covey Co.,* 316 F.3d 337 (2d Cir. 2003).

♦ A loan collector with generally outstanding performance goals was forced to miss work due to pregnancy-related problems. As a result, she fell short of her performance goals and was placed on a 90-day probation. Although she was able to improve the status of her accounts, she failed to meet specific performance goals and was fired. She sued the company under Title VII for pregnancy discrimination, and a jury awarded her $1,500 in compensatory damages, $30,000 in back pay and $230,000 in punitive damages. The Fourth Circuit Court of Appeals upheld the award against the company. There was evidence that **the employee was treated differently than non-pregnant employees** with respect to performance goals following a medical leave, and she was fired before the expiration of her 90-day probationary period. Even though the company had an EEO policy, there was evidence that the company was not committed to enforcing it. *Golson v. Green Tree Financial Servicing Corp.,* 26 Fed.Appx. 209 (4th Cir. 2002).

♦ An Arizona employee, who had a difficult relationship with her supervisor, became pregnant and informed her supervisor. She was fired a month before the baby was due. After the child's birth, she unsuccessfully sought substitute employment for several months before deciding to stay home with the baby. When she sued the company for pregnancy discrimination under Title VII and state law, a jury ruled in her favor. The court awarded her $15,000 in back pay and $50,000 in punitive damages. In the appeal that followed, the Ninth Circuit held that **the award of back pay had been properly limited** to the time between her firing and when she decided to stay home with the baby. Also, she was not entitled to more than $50,000 under Title VII because of the cap in 42 U.S.C. § 1981a is applicable to employers with fewer than 101 employees. *Caudle v. Bristow Optical Co.,* 224 F.3d 1014 (9th Cir. 2000).

♦   A New Hampshire business was sold and subsequently restructured by its new owner. A production manager, who was retained after the takeover, assumed the duties of two other management employees. The manager later became pregnant and requested maternity leave. Although her supervisor advised her that her position was secure, the company determined during her leave that her job duties could be performed by other employees. Before her six weeks of leave was over, the company advised the manager that her position would be eliminated. The employee sued, and the First Circuit held that the decision to eliminate the manager's position had been based on business judgment and did not reflect a discriminatory motive. **The Pregnancy Discrimination Act did not prohibit the employer from firing her while she was on maternity leave.** A pregnant employee can be fired for legitimate reasons. *Smith v. F.W. Morse & Co., Inc.,* 76 F.3d 413 (1st Cir. 1996).

F. Q&As

The following questions and answers will help you understand your obligations under the Pregnancy Discrimination Act. They were prepared by the Equal Employment Opportunity Commission.

1. What is the effective date of the Pregnancy Discrimination Act?

The Act became effective on October 31, 1978, except that with respect to fringe benefit programs in effect on that date, the Act will take effect 180 days thereafter, that is, April 29, 1979.

To the extent that title VII already required employers to treat persons affected by pregnancy-related conditions the same as persons affected by other medical conditions, the Act does not change employee rights arising prior to October 31, 1978, or April 29, 1979. Most employment practices relating to pregnancy, childbirth and related conditions—whether concerning fringe benefits or other practices—were already controlled by title VII prior to this Act. For example, title VII has always prohibited an employer from firing, or refusing to hire or promote, a woman because of pregnancy or related conditions, and from failing to accord a woman on pregnancy-related leave the same seniority retention and accrual accorded those on other disability leaves.

2. If an employer had a sick leave policy in effect on October 31, 1978, by what date must the employer bring its policy into compliance with the Act?

With respect to payment of benefits, an employer has until April 29, 1979, to bring into compliance any fringe benefit or insurance program, including a sick leave policy, which was in effect on October 31, 1978. However, any such policy or program created after October 31, 1978, must be in compliance when created.

With respect to all aspects of sick leave policy other than payment of benefits, such as the terms governing retention and accrual of seniority, credit for vacation, and resumption of former job on return from sick leave, equality of treatment was required by title VII without the Amendment.

3. *Must an employer provide benefits for pregnancy-related conditions to an employee whose pregnancy begins prior to April 29, 1979, and continues beyond that date?*

As of April 29, 1979, the effective date of the Act's requirements, an employer must provide the same benefits for pregnancy-related conditions as it provides for other conditions, regardless of when the pregnancy began. Thus, disability benefits must be paid for all absences on or after April 29, 1979, resulting from pregnancy-related temporary disabilities to the same extent as they are paid for absences resulting from other temporary disabilities. For example, if an employee gives birth before April 29, 1979, but is still unable to work on or after that date, she is entitled to the same disability benefits available to other employees. Similarly, medical insurance benefits must be paid for pregnancy-related expenses incurred on or after April 29, 1979.

If an employer requires an employee to be employed for a predetermined period prior to being eligible for insurance coverage, the period prior to April 29, 1979, during which a pregnant employee has been employed must be credited toward the eligibility waiting period on the same basis as for any other employee.

As to any programs instituted for the first time after October 31, 1978, coverage for pregnancy-related conditions must be provided in the same manner as for other medical conditions.

4. *Would the answer to the preceding question be the same if the employee became pregnant prior to October 31, 1978?*

Yes.

5. *If, for pregnancy-related reasons, an employee is unable to perform the functions of her job, does the employer have to provide her an alternative job?*

An employer is required to treat an employee temporarily unable to perform the functions of her job because of her pregnancy-related condition in the same manner as it treats other temporarily disabled employees, whether by providing modified tasks, alternative assignments, disability leaves, leaves without pay, etc. For example, a woman's primary job function may be the operation of a machine, and, incidental to that function, she may carry materials to and from the machine. If other employees temporarily unable to lift are relieved of these functions, pregnant employees also unable to lift must be temporarily relieved of the function.

6. *What procedures may an employer use to determine whether to place on leave as unable to work a pregnant employee who claims she is able to work or deny leave to a pregnant employee who claims that she is disabled from work?*

An employer may not single out pregnancy-related conditions for special procedures for determining an employee's ability to work.

However, an employer may use any procedure used to determine the ability of all employees to work. For example, if an employer requires its employees to submit a doctor's statement concerning their inability to work before granting leave or paying sick benefits, the employer may require employees affected by pregnancy-related conditions to submit such statement. Similarly, if an employer allows its employees to obtain doctor's statements from their personal physicians for absences due to other disabilities or return dates from other disabilities, it must accept doctor's statements from personal physicians for absences and return dates connected with pregnancy-related disabilities.

7. *Can an employer have a rule which prohibits an employee from returning to work for a predetermined length of time after childbirth?*

No.

8. *If an employee has been absent from work as a result of a pregnancy-related condition and recovers, may her employer require her to remain on leave until after her baby is born?*

No. An employee must be permitted to work at all times during pregnancy when she is able to perform her job.

9. *Must an employer hold open the job of an employee who is absent on leave because she is temporarily disabled by pregnancy-related conditions?*

Unless the employee on leave has informed the employer that she does not intend to return to work, her job must be held open for her return on the same basis as jobs are held open for employees on sick or disability leave for other reasons.

10. *May an employer's policy concerning the accrual and crediting of seniority during absences for medical conditions be different for employees affected by pregnancy-related conditions than for other employees?*

No. An employer's seniority policy must be the same for employees absent for pregnancy-related reasons as for those absent for other medical reasons.

11. *For purposes of calculating such matters as vacations and pay increases, may an employer credit time spent on leave for pregnancy-related reasons differently than time spent on leave for other reasons?*

No. An employer's policy with respect to crediting time for the purpose of calculating such matters as vacations and pay increases cannot treat employees on leave for pregnancy-related reasons less favorably than employees on leave for other reasons. For example, if employees on leave for medical reasons are credited with the time spent on leave when computing entitlement to vacation or pay raises, an employee on leave for pregnancy-related disability is entitled to the same kind of time credit.

12. Must an employer hire a woman who is medically unable, because of a pregnancy-related condition, to perform a necessary function of a job?

An employer cannot refuse to hire a women because of her pregnancy-related condition so long as she is able to perform the major functions necessary to the job. Nor can an employer refuse to hire her because of its preferences against pregnant workers or the preferences of co-workers, clients, or customers.

13. May an employer limit disability benefits for pregnancy-related conditions to married employees?

No.

14. If an employer has an all female work force or job classification, must benefits be provided for pregnancy-related conditions?

Yes. If benefits are provided for other conditions, they must also be provided for pregnancy-related conditions.

15. For what length of time must an employer who provides income maintenance benefits for temporary disabilities provide such benefits for pregnancy-related disabilities?

Benefits should be provided for as long as the employee is unable to work for medical reasons unless some other limitation is set for all other temporary disabilities, in which case pregnancy-related disabilities should be treated the same as other temporary disabilities.

16. Must an employer who provides benefits for long-term or permanent disabilities provide such benefits for pregnancy-related conditions?

Yes. Benefits for long-term or permanent disabilities resulting from pregnancy-related conditions must be provided to the same extent that such benefits are provided for other conditions which result in long-term or permanent disability.

17. If an employer provides benefits to employees on leave, such as installment purchase disability insurance, payment of premiums for health, life or other insurance, continued payments into pension, saving or profit sharing plans, must the same benefits be provided for those on leave for pregnancy-related conditions?

Yes, the employer must provide the same benefits for those on leave for pregnancy-related conditions as for those on leave for other reasons.

18. Can an employee who is absent due to a pregnancy-related disability be required to exhaust vacation benefits before receiving sick leave pay or disability benefits?

No. If employees who are absent because of other disabling causes receive sick leave pay or disability benefits without any requirement that they first exhaust vacation benefits, the employer cannot impose this requirement on an employee absent for a pregnancy-related cause.

19. Must an employer grant leave to a female employee for childcare purposes after she is medically able to return to work following leave necessitated by pregnancy, childbirth or related medical conditions?

While leave for childcare purposes is not covered by the Pregnancy Discrimination Act, ordinary title VII principles would require that leave for childcare purposes be granted on the same basis as leave which is granted to employees for other non-medical reasons.

For example, if an employer allows its employees to take leave without pay or accrued annual leave for travel or education which is not job related, the same type of leave must be granted to those who wish to remain on leave for infant care, even though they are medically able to return to work.

20. If State law requires an employer to provide disability insurance for a specified period before and after childbirth, does compliance with the State law fulfill the employer's obligation under the Pregnancy Discrimination Act?

Not necessarily. It is an employer's obligation to treat employees temporarily disabled by pregnancy in the same manner as employees affected by other temporary disabilities. Therefore, any restrictions imposed by State law on benefits for pregnancy-related disabilities, but not for other disabilities, do not excuse the employer from treating the individuals in both groups of employees the same. If, for example, a State law requires an employer to pay a maximum of 26 weeks benefits for disabilities other than pregnancy-related ones but only six weeks for pregnancy-related disabilities, the employer must provide benefits for the additional weeks to an employee disabled by pregnancy-related conditions, up to the maximum provided other disabled employees.

21. If a State or local government provides its own employees income maintenance benefits for disabilities, may it provide different benefits for disabilities arising from pregnancy-related conditions than for disabilities arising from other conditions?

No. State and local governments, as employers, are subject to the Pregnancy Discrimination Act in the same way as private employers and must bring their employment practices and programs into compliance with the Act, including disability and health insurance programs.

22. Must an employer provide health insurance coverage for the medical expenses of pregnancy-related conditions of the spouses of male employees? Of the dependents of all employees?

Where an employer provides no coverage for dependents, the employer is not required to institute such coverage. However, if an employer's insurance program covers the medical expenses of spouses of female employees, then it must equally cover the medical expenses of spouses of male employees, including those arising from pregnancy-related conditions.

But the insurance does not have to cover the pregnancy-related conditions of other dependents as long as it excludes the pregnancy-related conditions of the dependents of male and female employees equally.

23. Must an employer provide the same level of health insurance coverage for the pregnancy-related medical conditions of the spouses of male employees as it provides for its female employees?

No. It is not necessary to provide the same level of coverage for the pregnancy-related medical conditions of spouses of male employees as for female employees. However, where the employer provides coverage for the medical conditions of the spouses of its employees, then the level of coverage for pregnancy-related medical conditions of the spouses of male employees must be the same as the level of coverage for all other medical conditions of the spouses of female employees.

For example, if the employer covers employees for 100 percent of reasonable and customary expenses sustained for a medical condition, but only covers dependent spouses for 50 percent of reasonable and customary expenses for their medical conditions, the pregnancy-related expenses of the male employee's spouse must be covered at the 50 percent level.

24. May an employer offer optional dependent coverage which excludes pregnancy-related medical conditions or offers less coverage for pregnancy-related medical conditions where the total premium for the optional coverage is paid by the employee?

No. Pregnancy-related medical conditions must be treated the same as other medical conditions under any health or disability insurance or sick leave plan available in connection with employment, regardless of who pays the premiums.

25. Where an employer provides its employees a choice among several health insurance plans, must coverage for pregnancy-related conditions be offered in all of the plans?

Yes. Each of the plans must cover pregnancy-related conditions.

For example, an employee with a single coverage policy cannot be forced to purchase a more expensive family coverage policy in order to receive coverage for her own pregnancy-related condition.

26. On what basis should an employee be reimbursed for medical expenses arising from pregnancy, childbirth or related conditions?

Pregnancy-related expenses should be reimbursed in the same manner as are expenses incurred for other medical conditions. Therefore, whether a plan reimburses the employees on a fixed basis, or a percentage of reasonable and customary charge basis, the same basis should be used for reimbursement of expenses incurred for pregnancy-related conditions. Furthermore, if medical costs for pregnancy-related conditions increase, reevaluation of the reimbursement level should be conducted in the same manner as are cost reevaluations of increases for other medical conditions.

Coverage provided by a health insurance program for other conditions must be provided for pregnancy-related conditions. For example, if a plan provides major medical coverage, pregnancy-related conditions must be so covered. Similarly, if a plan covers the cost of a private room for other conditions, the plan must cover the cost of a private room for pregnancy-related conditions. Finally, where a health insurance plan covers office visits to physicians, pre-natal and post-natal visits must be included in such coverage.

27. May an employer limit payment of costs for pregnancy-related medical conditions to a specified dollar amount set forth in an insurance policy, collective bargaining agreement or other statement of benefits to which an employee is entitled?

The amounts payable for the costs incurred for pregnancy-related conditions can be limited only to the same extent as are costs for other conditions. Maximum recoverable dollar amounts may be specified for pregnancy-related conditions if such amounts are similarly specified for other conditions, and so long as the specified amounts in all instances cover the same proportion of actual costs. If, in addition to the scheduled amount for other procedures, additional costs are paid for, either directly or indirectly, by the employer, such additional payments must also be paid for pregnancy-related procedures.

28. May an employer impose a different deductible for payment of costs for pregnancy-related medical conditions than for costs of other medical conditions?

No. Neither an additional deductible, an increase in the usual deductible, nor a larger deductible can be imposed for coverage for pregnancy-related medical costs, whether as a condition for inclusion of pregnancy-related costs in the policy or for payment of the costs when incurred. Thus, if pregnancy-related costs are the first incurred under the policy, the employee is required to pay only the same deductible as would otherwise be required had other medical costs been the first incurred. Once this deductible has been paid, no additional deductible can be required for other medical procedures. If the usual deductible has already been paid for other medical procedures, no additional deductible can be required when pregnancy-related costs are later incurred.

29. *If a health insurance plan excludes the payment of benefits for any conditions existing at the time the insured's coverage becomes effective (pre-existing condition clause), can benefits be denied for medical costs arising from a pregnancy existing at the time the coverage became effective?*

Yes. However, such benefits cannot be denied unless the pre-existing condition clause also excludes benefits for other pre-existing conditions in the same way.

30. *If an employer's insurance plan provides benefits after the insured's employment has ended (i.e. extended benefits) for costs connected with pregnancy and delivery where conception occurred while the insured was working for the employer, but not for the costs of any other medical condition which began prior to termination of employment, may an employer (a) continue to pay these extended benefits for pregnancy-related medical conditions but not for other medical conditions, or (b) terminate these benefits for pregnancy-related conditions?*

Where a health insurance plan currently provides extended benefits for other medical conditions on a less favorable basis than for pregnancy-related medical conditions, extended benefits must be provided for other medical conditions on the same basis as for pregnancy-related medical conditions. Therefore, an employer can neither continue to provide less benefits for other medical conditions nor reduce benefits currently paid for pregnancy-related medical conditions.

31. *Where an employer's health insurance plan currently requires total disability as a prerequisite for payment of extended benefits for other medical conditions but not for pregnancy-related costs, may the employer now require total disability for payment of benefits for pregnancy-related medical conditions as well?*

Since extended benefits cannot be reduced in order to come into compliance with the Act, a more stringent prerequisite for payment of extended benefits for pregnancy-related medical conditions, such as a requirement for total disability, cannot be imposed. Thus, in this instance, in order to comply with the Act, the employer must treat other medical conditions as pregnancy-related conditions are treated.

32. *Can the added cost of bringing benefit plans into compliance with the Act be apportioned between the employer and employee?*

The added cost, if any, can be apportioned between the employer and employee in the same proportion that the cost of the fringe benefit plan was apportioned on October 31, 1978, if that apportionment was nondiscriminatory. If the costs were not apportioned on October 31, 1978, they may not be apportioned in order to come into compliance with the Act. However, in no circumstance may male or female employees be required to pay unequal apportionments on the basis of sex or pregnancy.

33. In order to come into compliance with the Act, may an employer reduce benefits or compensation?

In order to come into compliance with the Act, benefits or compensation which an employer was paying on October 31, 1978 cannot be reduced before October 31, 1979 or before the expiration of a collective bargaining agreement in effect on October 31, 1978, whichever is later.

Where an employer has not been in compliance with the Act by the times specified in the Act, and attempts to reduce benefits, or compensation, the employer may be required to remedy its practices in accord with ordinary title VII remedial principles.

34. Can an employer self-insure benefits for pregnancy-related conditions if it does not self-insure benefits for other medical conditions?

Yes, so long as the benefits are the same. In measuring whether benefits are the same, factors other than the dollar coverage paid should be considered. Such factors include the range of choice of physicians and hospitals, and the processing and promptness of payment of claims.

35. Can an employer discharge, refuse to hire or otherwise discriminate against a woman because she has had an abortion?

No. An employer cannot discriminate in its employment practices against a woman who has had an abortion.

36. Is an employer required to provide fringe benefits for abortions if fringe benefits are provided for other medical conditions?

All fringe benefits other than health insurance, such as sick leave, which are provided for other medical conditions, must be provided for abortions. Health insurance, however, need be provided for abortions only where the life of the woman would be endangered if the fetus were carried to term or where medical complications arise from an abortion.

37. If complications arise during the course of an abortion, as for instance excessive hemorrhaging, must an employer's health insurance plan cover the additional cost due to the complications of the abortion?

Yes. The plan is required to pay those additional costs attributable to the complications of the abortion. However, the employer is not required to pay for the abortion itself, except where the life of the mother would be endangered if the fetus were carried to term.

38. May an employer elect to provide insurance coverage for abortions?

Yes. The Act specifically provides that an employer is not precluded from providing benefits for abortions whether directly or through a collective bargaining agreement, but if an employer decides to cover the costs of abortion, the employer must do so in the same manner and to the same degree as it covers other medical conditions.

G. Statutes and Regulations

Title VII of the Civil Rights Act of 1964 prohibits sex discrimination.

It is enforced primarily by the Equal Employment Opportunity Commission, which has promulgated the implementing regulations. These regulations are located in the Code of Federal Regulations at 29 C.F.R. Part 1604.

V. RACE/COLOR DISCRIMINATION

A. Overview

Title VII of the Civil Rights Act of 1964 prohibits employers that retain at least 15 employees from discriminating against applicants and employees on the basis of race or color. Race and color overlap under Title VII, but they are not the same thing. Under Title VII employers cannot discriminate against applicants or employees based on their racial background or their skin shade or tone. Nor can they discriminate based on characteristics that are linked to race, such as hair texture. The prohibition extends to all employment decisions, including those relating to hiring, firing, promotion, compensation and all other privileges and benefits of employment. Title VII prohibits two types of race/color discrimination: namely, discrimination that is intentional and discrimination that results from when neutral job policies have a disproportionately negative impact on people of a certain color or race.

B. Defining "Race" Discrimination

Title VII prohibits employers from discriminating on the basis of "race," but it does not specifically say what "race" means. The federal Office of Management and Budget uses the following five categories to collect data relating to race: American Indian or Alaska Native; Asian; Black or African-American; Native Hawaiian or other Pacific Islander; and White. Under Equal Employment Opportunity Commission guidelines, race discrimination under Title VII includes discrimination based on any of the following:

- Racial or ethnic ancestry.
- Physical characteristics associated with race, such as color, hair and facial features.
- Race-linked illness, such as sickle cell anemia.

- Cultural characteristics linked to race or ethnicity, such as name, dress, grooming practices, accent or manner of speech.
- Perception that an individual is a member of a particular racial group.
- Association with a person of a particular race. For example, an employer cannot discriminate against a white person because he is married to an African-American.
- Membership in a subgroup of a particular racial group. For example, an employer cannot take a negative job action against an African-American woman with a preschool-age child while not taking a similar action against a White woman with a preschool-age child.
- "Reverse" discrimination. The law prohibits discrimination against all people, including Caucasians.

C. Defining "Color" Discrimination

Title VII separately lists "color" as a basis of prohibited discrimination. Title VII does not specifically define "color," but courts have interpreted it to mean complexion, pigmentation, or skin shade or tone. Discrimination on the basis of color can occur between people of different races or ethnicities. It can also occur between people of the same race or ethnicity.

D. Judicial Decisions

The following case summaries provide examples of issues that can arise in cases alleging race or color discrimination under Title VII and how they were resolved by the courts.

♦ An Indiana car salesman was fired by the dealer's new Pakistani Muslim manager for failing to meet production goals. He was later rehired to work at a different dealership. He then filed EEOC charges relating to his earlier termination. When the manager at the new dealership discovered the charges, he threatened to fire the employee unless he withdrew the charges. The employee agreed to drop the charges but never did so. He stayed away from work even though his manager called several times to inform him that he still had a job. When he sued for race discrimination and retaliation, a jury awarded him $1.1 million, but the Seventh Circuit reversed, noting that **even though the manager got angry with the employee and threatened him, the company repeatedly informed him that he wasn't fired.** *Chapin v. Fort-Rohr Motors, Inc.,* 621 F.3d 673 (7th Cir. 2010).

♦ An African-American store manager in Pennsylvania received a final warning for performance problems. She received a second final warning for missing a mandatory meeting and bringing her grandson to work with her. Later, she asked her district manager if she could close her store early because her son was having a medical emergency. The district manager apparently gave a vague answer that she took for permission to close. When she was fired, she sued for race discrimination, but a federal court and the Third Circuit ruled against her. Here, **the company followed the progressive discipline in the handbook,**

which also clearly stated that employment was at will. And a white manager who was not fired for closing his store early had no prior disciplinary incidents. *Coleman v. Blockbuster, Inc.,* 352 Fed.Appx. 676 (3d Cir. 2009).

♦ A company in Pennsylvania invited an African-American to attend a training session for an independent contractor traveling sales job. The invitee attended the training and signed an agreement at the end of the session. However, she refused to shake the recruiter's hand, and he then said, "You ain't nothing but the N word." When she asked if he was calling her a "nigga," he allegedly smirked. The company then made the decision not to retain the independent contractor as a sales rep. She sued under 42 U.S.C. § 1981. A federal court granted pretrial judgment to the company, but the Third Circuit reversed. **It joined the First, Seventh and Eleventh Circuits in holding that independent contractors are protected by Section 1981**, and it also held that fact issues required a trial over whether race was involved in the decision. *Brown v. J. Kaz, Inc.,* 581 F.3d 175 (3d Cir. 2009).

♦ An African-American applicant for a position in Ohio interviewed for the job but was not hired. She claimed race discrimination, asserting that she had been asked different questions than two white applicants, one of whom already worked for the company in a different position. When she sued under Title VII she lost. A federal court and the Sixth Circuit held that **the company could ask different follow-up questions** based on how interviewees responded to questions about experience and familiarity with the company's hands-off management style. *Alexander v. CareSource,* 576 F.3d 551 (6th Cir. 2009).

♦ A black employee of a Maryland power company received consistently good reviews until she was transferred to a new department and got a new supervisor – a co-worker with whom she had clashed in the past. For two years the relationship deteriorated. Then the employee was fired after accusing her supervisor of being a bigot. She sued under Title VII, but a federal court found no evidence of race bias. **The company documented her insubordinate, confrontational and indifferent behavior and her unwillingness to improve her job performance.** *Alston v. Baltimore Gas & Electric Co.,* 2008 WL 5428126 (D. Md. 12/31/08).

♦ An African-American truck driver complained of race discrimination when he learned that a white driver received a raise. Because he made more money than the other drivers, the black driver did not receive a raise himself. He filed a charge with the EEOC. Seven months later, a customer complained that he was harassing its employees. The driver received a warning letter and then sued, claiming race discrimination and retaliation. An Arkansas federal court ruled against him, and the Eighth Circuit affirmed. Here, even though he claimed a discriminatory motive, **his employer was allowed to believe the customer and issue the disciplinary warning**. *Littleton v. Pilot Travel Centers, LLC,* 568 F.3d 641 (8th Cir. 2009).

♦ A black department manager at a Best Buy store in Ohio made at least two complaints about favorable treatment for white employees. The store later discovered a new computer and a purchase order for a display computer together and tied them to the department manager. It believed he tried to take a larger employee discount than policy allowed and fired him. He sued under Title VII, alleging race discrimination and retaliation. He claimed that he had written up another purchase order reflecting the proper price. A federal court and the Sixth Circuit ruled against him, finding no evidence of a Title VII violation. Here, **the store conducted a reasonable investigation and properly believed he had violated its policy on employee discounts.** *Graham v. Best Buy Stores,* 298 Fed.Appx. 487 (6th Cir. 2008).

♦ A Massachusetts production supervisor from Jamaica decided to have urgent dental work done in Jamaica. He got another supervisor to cover for him and sent his boss an email confirming the time he'd be off. However, he did not submit a written request for the time off as required by company policy. Once in Jamaica, he realized he needed another week off and left a voice mail message with his boss, but again failed to fill out a computer spreadsheet, as required by company policy. His manager, who had told him he hated Jamaicans and Jamaican music a year earlier, notified HR of his failure to follow company procedures. When the supervisor returned to work, he met with managers to explain his absence. A separate review committee fired him, and he sued under Title VII. A federal court and the First Circuit ruled against him, noting that there was **no evidence of race discrimination in the termination process.** His boss had minimal input into the termination decision. *Thompson v. The Coca-Cola Co.,* 522 F.3d 168 (1st Cir. 2008).

♦ A black manager at a UPS facility in Indiana dated and then married a white employee who worked in another department. This was in violation of the company's anti-fraternization policy. After UPS fired the manager, he sued under Title VII, **claiming that he was fired because the company didn't want him associating with a white woman.** A federal court granted pretrial judgment for UPS, and the Seventh Circuit affirmed. Here, the manager was warned to "rectify" the situation and failed to do so. Also, he failed to show that similarly situated white couples were treated differently. Another white manager who refused to end a relationship with an employee was fired too. *Ellis v. United Parcel Service,* 523 F.3d 823 (7th Cir. 2008).

♦ A white assistant coach for a New York university married a black woman and was fired four years later, when the team's performance slipped. The university also fired a black assistant coach, but retained the most junior assistant coach, who was white. When the coach sued under Title VII, **claiming he had been discriminated against because of his association with a black woman**, the Second Circuit held that there were fact issues for a jury as to whether the reason offered by the university was a pretext for discrimination. The coach offered evidence that a vice president was biased against blacks and that there was pressure to fire him to appeal to the university's mostly white alumni. *Holcomb v. Iona College,* 521 F.3d 130 (2d Cir. 2008).

♦ A black assistant store manager at a Walgreen store in Illinois was twice offered the manager position at a predominantly black, low-income store. He turned down both offers. **When a manager position opened up in a predominantly white, affluent neighborhood, he sought that promotion.** His supervisor told him that the store "was possibly not ready to have a black manager." A white candidate was selected, and the assistant manager was given differing reasons for why he didn't get the job. He sued. After a federal court granted pretrial judgment to the company, the Seventh Circuit reversed, finding that a jury could conclude that the real reason for the non-promotion was racial bias. *Simple v. Walgreen Co.,* 511 F.3d 668 (7th Cir. 2007).

♦ A black employee of a rapidly growing company was promoted from sales clerk to assistant manager, but then had an argument with her manager. Although the manager was fired, the assistant manager was passed up for several promotions in favor of less-qualified white candidates. She sued for discrimination and an Arkansas federal court ruled in her favor, awarding her damages of $16,000. The Eighth Circuit largely affirmed, noting that **the company did not have written criteria for the manager position so as to justify its refusal to consider the black assistant manager.** Further, the argument with the manager could not be used as a reason for the non-promotion because a white employee who argued with her manager received a promotion. *Allen v. Tobacco Superstore, Inc.,* 475 F.3d 931 (8th Cir. 2007).

♦ An African-American security employee with a Colorado company was fired after a video camera showed him leaving two hours early, and after there was a discrepancy in his weekly log. Not until after he sued for discrimination under Title VII did he offer an explanation for why he had walked out of the store early (to check gas tanks behind the building). A federal court and the Tenth Circuit ruled against him. Here, **the company conducted a reasonable investigation and honestly believed he engaged in misconduct.** His explanation casting doubt on the decision came too late. *Young v. Dillon Companies,* 468 F.3d 1243 (10th Cir. 2006).

♦ An African-American team leader at a Tennessee plant was fired after cursing at subordinates. He also allegedly falsified time cards and intimidated his subordinates to the point that they sought transfers. A white team leader who also cursed at subordinates wasn't fired, and a Title VII lawsuit erupted. The case reached the Sixth Circuit, which ruled for the company. Here, the two employees' misconduct was not substantially identical. **The white employee only cursed, while the African-American employee allegedly committed other misconduct as well.** And the investigation, while not optimal, led the company to believe the employee had committed the misconduct alleged. *Haughton v. Orchid Automation,* 206 Fed.Appx. 524 (6th Cir. 2006).

♦ A black woman from Zimbabwe who had permanent resident status worked for a Colorado company. She complained of race discrimination after a comment by her supervisor. Three months later, her supervisor gave her a positive annual review. Five months after that, the employee went to Zimbabwe for a vacation and had a problem with her immigration papers that delayed her return. She reached the company by phone to explain the problem but failed to call in for the next several days, apparently because of problems with international telephone lines. The company considered her to have abandoned her job and discharged her. She sued for race and national origin discrimination, and retaliation under Title VII. A federal court and the Tenth Circuit ruled against her. **The company followed its employee handbook on job abandonment**, and the discharge was not causally connected to the earlier complaint. It came nine months later and after a positive review from her supervisor. *Antonio v. The Sygma Network,* 458 F.3d 1177 (10th Cir. 2006).

◆ An African-American poker dealer applied for a job at a casino in Mississippi. Even though he was certified and his skills were considered above average, he was not hired. He sued under Title VII for race discrimination. Another dealer at the casino testified that one of her supervisors commented that he didn't like to hire black dealers because the customers wouldn't like it. A federal judge found her testimony not credible and refused to let a jury have the case. The Fifth Circuit reversed, noting that the credibility of the witness was for a jury to determine. The lawsuit was allowed to proceed.

The comment was direct evidence of discrimination even though the employee could not remember which manager made the statement. *Jones v. Robinson Property Group, d/b/a/ Horseshoe Casino & Hotel,* 427 F.3d 987 (5th Cir. 2005).

◆ Over two weekends in July 2001, bomb threats were made against a telemarketing center in Missouri. When a sales manager played a tape of one of the phone calls to his team leaders, nine of them identified the voice as belonging to an African-American employee. The company fired the employee and he then sued under Title VII, alleging race discrimination. A federal court and the Eighth Circuit ruled against him. The company may have mistakenly believed he made the calls, but **it had legitimate reasons to believe he had made the threats**, including the voice recognition and the fact that the calls were made to a number that only employees were likely to know. *Johnson v. AT&T Corp.,* 422 F.3d 756 (8th Cir. 2005).

◆ A black female employed by a company in South Carolina applied for a managerial position, which was eventually given to a white woman. The black woman sued for race discrimination, claiming that she was more qualified because she had prior management experience and a master's degree in public administration. The selected candidate did not have a college degree and had been with the company for less than 18 months. The case reached the Fourth Circuit, which ruled in favor of the company. Here, although **the selection process was subjective**, it relied on nine factors for evaluating candidates, and the white employee scored higher in every category. *Diamond v. Colonial Life & Accident Insurance Co.,* 416 F.3d 310 (4th Cir. 2005).

◆ An African-American FedEx driver in Tennessee began a pallet-recycling program to earn money for company parties and other events. He also collected

252 DISCRIMINATION

pallets while off duty and sold them to earn spare cash. When the driver later complained about how African-American employees were being treated, he was accused of stealing money from the company. He admitted during a lengthy interrogation that he may have made a few small mistakes in calculating the number of pallets sold. His supervisors then reported that he had confessed to the theft, and the regional manager fired him without verifying the truth of the information she received. When he sued for race discrimination and retaliation under Title VII, a jury awarded him $15,000 in back pay and $100,000 in punitive damages. The Sixth Circuit upheld the award, noting that **the company managers failed to act in good faith**. *Tisdale v. Federal Express Corp.*, 415 F.3d 516 (6th Cir. 2005).

♦ A telephone marketing and calling company in Alabama hired a black employee to work on a gubernatorial campaign to "get out the vote." At the request of the candidates, the company engaged in "race-matched calling," which meant that black callers called only black voters and white callers called only white voters in order to lure the voter groups to the polls on election day. During the race-matched calling, callers were segregated by whom they called. They were also physically separated by race in separate rooms. After the election, the employee was laid off, and she sued the company under 42 U.S.C. § 1981. The court found that the race-matched calling and segregation of the work force violated Section 1981. **Employers are forbidden by Section 1981 from assigning work based on stereotyped assumptions.** On appeal, the Eleventh Circuit held that even though the company had no malicious intent in separating its workers, its actions amounted to intentional segregation of black and white workers. However, punitive damages were not justified. *Ferrill v. Parker Group, Inc.*, 168 F.3d 468 (11th Cir. 1999).

E. Checklists

☑ CHECKLIST

Proactive Prevention

This checklist will help you take proactive measures to reduce the chances of a Title VII violation in your organization. It is derived from Section 15 of the Equal Employment Opportunity Commission's compliance manual.

❑ The employer has a strong EEO policy that is embraced by the CEO and top executives.

❑ The employer trains managers and employees on the content of the EEO policy, enforces the policy, and holds company managers accountable.

❑ The employer makes sure that decisions relating to enforcement of the policy are documented and transparent to the greatest feasible extent.

❑ The employer utilizes recruitment, hiring and promotion practices that are designed to diversify the pool of candidates considered for employment openings.

❏ The employer periodically conducts self-analyses to determine whether its practices create disadvantages for people of a particular race or color.

❏ The employer creates objective and job-related qualification standards that it consistently applies.

❏ The employer provides training and mentoring to give employees with different backgrounds an equal chance to perform well and advance.

❏ The employer makes sure that job openings and promotion criteria are made known and communicated to all eligible employees.

❏ The employer monitors compensation practices and performance appraisal systems for patterns of potential discrimination.

❏ The employer fosters open communication and early dispute resolution.

❏ The employer provides assurances that employees who complain of job bias or participate in an investigation will be protected from retaliation.

F. Statutes and Regulations

Title VII of the Civil Rights Act prohibits discrimination on the basis of race and color.

VI. NATIONAL ORIGIN DISCRIMINATION

A. Overview

Discrimination on the basis of national origin is prohibited by Title VII of the Civil Rights Act. National origin discrimination includes discrimination based on an individual's place of origin or the place of origin of his or her ancestors. It also includes discrimination based on the fact that an individual has the physical, cultural or linguistic characteristics of a particular ethnic group. In addition, it encompasses discrimination against an individual because he or she is associated with an individual of a particular national origin. As with all other characteristics protected from discrimination under Title VII, discrimination is prohibited on the basis of national origin with respect to all aspects of the employment relationship. In addition, the prohibition is meant to include discrimination that is purposeful as well as discrimination that results when the application of facially neutral policies adversely impacts the members of a particular national origin group.

B. Definition of "National Origin Group"

Title VII bars discrimination against any individual based on membership in a "national origin group." Under Title VII, a "national origin group" is a group of individuals who share a common language, ancestry, culture or other similar characteristics of a social nature. A national origin group is also referred to as an "ethnic group."

C. Specific Examples of National Origin Discrimination

Prohibited discrimination based on national origin includes discrimination based on membership in a particular ethnic group, such as Hispanic. National origin discrimination also includes discrimination based on linguistic, physical or cultural characteristics that are closely associated with a particular national origin group. An individual can claim national origin discrimination if he or she is only perceived by the employer to be a member of a particular national origin group, even if the employer's perception is mistaken. In its regulations implementing Title VII's prohibition of discrimination on the basis of national origin, the Equal Employment Opportunity Commission states that national origin discrimination includes discrimination based on all of the following:

- Marriage to or association with people of a particular national origin group
- Membership in or association with an organization identified with or seeking to promote the interests of national origin groups
- Attendance at or participation in schools, churches, temples or mosques that are generally used by people of a particular national origin group, and
- The fact that a person's name or spouse's name is associated with a particular national origin group.

D. Overlap with Other Protected Classes

The prohibition of discrimination based on national origin sometimes overlaps with the prohibition of discrimination based on race or religion. For example, discrimination based on an individual's physical traits may constitute both national origin discrimination and race discrimination.

E. "English-only" Rules

The position of the Equal Employment Opportunity Commission is that an employer cannot adopt an "English-only" rule unless the rule is needed for it to operate safely or efficiently. The agency regulation implementing Title VII distinguishes two types of English-only rules: one that requires only English to be spoken at all times, and one that requires only English to be spoken at certain times. When an employer requires only English to be spoken at all times, the agency presumes that the rule violates Title VII and it will be difficult for the employer to justify. When an employer requires that only English be spoken at certain times, such as when hazardous materials are being handled, the rule will be upheld as long as the employer can show it is justified by business necessity.

F. Harassment

Title VII prohibits harassment based on national origin. National origin harassment can consist of slurs, graffiti or other offensive conduct. In determining whether an employer can be held liable for harassment based on national origin, the following factors are relevant:

- Whether the conduct was threatening
- The frequency of the conduct and whether it was hostile
- The context of the conduct, and
- How management responded to the conduct.

G. Judicial Decisions

Here are some case summaries dealing with the issue of national origin discrimination.

♦   Right after a West Virginia company told a Lebanese-American supervisor that he was being demoted for using profanity, the supervisor claimed that he had been harassed because of his Lebanese background. However, he refused to provide details of the harassment unless his demotion was removed. When the company refused to reconsider, he quit then sued for national origin discrimination. The case reached the West Virginia Supreme Court of Appeals, which ruled that the company was justified in demoting the supervisor because its investigation into employee complaints of mismanagement verified that he was the only supervisor at his branch using profane language. And **it couldn't be liable for the harassment he claimed because officials didn't know about it**. *Ford Motor Credit Co. v. West Virginia Human Rights Comm'n*, 696 S.E.2d 282 (W. Va. 2010).

♦   Three white Illinois employees went to breakfast at a restaurant with a Filipino and a Hispanic on a Saturday while working an overtime shift. The following Monday, the white employees and the Filipino told their group leader that they had not taken a lunch break. They were paid for a full shift. The Hispanic employee did not work that Monday. About a month later, a supervisor asked the Hispanic employee about that day and he told the supervisor that they had gone to breakfast. After an investigation, the three white employees and the Filipino were fired. The three white employees sued for discrimination and lost. A federal court and the Seventh Circuit held that **they were not similarly situated to the Hispanic employee because they had lied about their hours**, asserting they had not taken a break that day. *Antonetti v. Abbott Laboratories*, 563 F.3d 587 (7th Cir. 2009).

♦   An engineer of Indian ethnicity was fired after numerous complaints about his performance and reports from colleagues about insubordination. He sued under Title VII, claiming that his supervisor made a handful of slurs about people of Asian origin. He claimed national origin harassment and wrongful discharge. An Illinois federal court and the Seventh Circuit ruled for the company, noting that **the engineer never complained about the slurs** and that they weren't pervasive enough to amount to harassment anyway. Further, the numerous complaints about his performance justified his termination. *Andonissamy v. Hewlett-Packard Co.*, 547 F.3d 841 (7th Cir. 2008).

♦   A Muslim car salesman in Texas endured a number of harassing comments from his supervisor and co-workers. **His supervisor called him Taliban and**

Arab even though he was from India, and also mocked his religious dietary restrictions and his need to pray during the workday. After September 11, his co-workers suggested that he was involved in the terrorist attacks, and one told him he should go back to where he came from because of his beliefs. The supervisor also issued him a written warning for acting like a "Muslim extremist," and banged on his office partition to startle the salesman every time he walked by. When the salesman complained, he was fired. He filed a complaint with the EEOC, which sued for national origin discrimination on his behalf. A federal court granted pretrial judgment to the dealership, but the Fifth Circuit reversed, noting that all these incidents, when added together, could amount to a hostile work environment under Title VII. A trial was required. *EEOC v. WC & M Enterprises*, 496 F.3d 393 (5th Cir. 2007).

♦ An accountant from Peru who spoke rudimentary English emigrated to America and got a job as a credit union clerk after interviewing for the job in Spanish. Many of the credit union's customers spoke Spanish. Less than a year later, a new CEO took over and the clerk was fired because the CEO couldn't understand the clerk's limited English. The clerk sued for national origin discrimination and the credit union sought pretrial judgment. The District of Columbia Court of Appeals refused to award pretrial judgment to the credit union, finding issues of fact that required a trial. Here, there was evidence that **the CEO may have selectively enforced the credit union's bilingual language requirement against the clerk**, and that the requirement may have been added after the clerk was hired. *Estenos v. PAHO/WHO Federal Credit Union*, 952 A.2d 878 (D.C. Ct. App. 2008).

♦ An Iraqi supervisor at an Ohio manufacturing plant was fired because of numerous complaints about the demeaning way he communicated with his subordinates and because his superiors saw him ignore potential safety problems. He sued under Title VII, asserting that the real reason was national origin discrimination. He pointed out that employees discussed the Iraq war over lunch, and that, at his termination meeting, the operations manager said, "Maybe it's the people of Northwest Ohio who have a problem with you." A federal court and the Sixth Circuit held that the company provided ample evidence to support its decision to fire the supervisor. **The single comment, in the context of a discussion about his personality and management conflicts, could be construed as a statement about Midwestern congeniality.** The termination was upheld. *Abdulnour v. Campbell Soup Supply Co.*, LLC, 502 F.3d 496 (6th Cir. 2007).

♦ An Egyptian-born Muslim worked as a manager trainee at a Minnesota convenience store. After the busy holiday season, he was demoted to assistant trainee based on reports of insubordination. His hours were also cut back. He walked off the job after being accused of harassment, then sued under Title VII, claiming discrimination on the basis of his Arabic race. A federal court and the Eighth Circuit ruled against him. The company had a **legitimate reason for demoting him** and for cutting back his hours. Also, derogatory comments by an assistant manager could not be attributed to the company because the assistant manager was not involved in the decision to demote him. *Elnashar v. Speedway SuperAmerica, LLC,* 484 F.3d 1046 (8th Cir. 2007).

♦   A Kansas company learned that the Immigration and Naturalization Service was going to inspect its facility and became concerned because it had hired 300 people in a short time and knew it might not have completed I-9 forms for them. A Hispanic employee who had been hired under a more careful screening process was **suspended until he provided documentation of his eligibility to work**. After providing the documentation, he demanded a written apology and a complete explanation of why he had been suspended. The HR manager believed the demand amounted to a voluntary resignation and told the employee to leave the office. The employee, believing he had been fired, sued under Title VII. The case reached the Tenth Circuit Court of Appeals, which ruled in favor of the company. Here, the suspension was legitimate. Further, the HR manager's belief that the employee would not return to work without a written apology justified the termination decision. And the employee failed to show that this reason was actually a pretext for national origin discrimination. *Zamora v. Elite Logistics,* 478 F.3d 1160 (10th Cir. 2007).

♦   An international manufacturer hired an employee to work at its Brazilian facility, later transferring him to its Indiana facility. He worked as a buyer and eventually learned that he was making less than two senior buyers who had just been hired. His supervisor told him that he might be getting a lower salary because he was Brazilian. He sued for national origin discrimination, claiming that the supervisor's comment proved bias by the company. A federal court and the Seventh Circuit ruled against him. The company proffered a legitimate reason for the difference in pay – the greater education and experience of the senior buyers. **The supervisor's statement was not direct evidence of discrimination because he did not determine the employee's salary.** *Cardoso v. Robert Bosch Corp.,* 427 F.3d 429 (7th Cir. 2005).

♦   An employee of a security company in Pennsylvania was fired when he refused to remove or cover Confederate flag stickers on his lunch box and pickup truck. He sued the company under Title VII, asserting discrimination on the basis of religion and national origin, based on his claim as a "Confederate Southern-American." A federal court dismissed his case and the Third Circuit affirmed. Although national origin usually refers to a country of origin, it could be expanded to include a region. However, **even if "Confederate Southern-American" was a valid national origin, the employee's claim still failed**. The Confederate flag sends out a message that stigmatizes African-Americans by representing the belief that white men have the right to own black slaves. And the employee was not fired because of his status or beliefs, but because he refused to remove or cover the stickers. *Storey v. Burns Int'l Security Services,* 390 F.3d 760 (3d Cir. 2004).

♦   A Hispanic parts salesman for a truck dealership in Alabama was subjected to numerous derogatory nicknames. When the president of the company heard about the situation, he ordered a review of the dealership's anti-discrimination policies. Subsequently, all but one of the salesman's co-workers stopped using the ethnic slurs. After the salesman was fired, he sued the company under Title VII, alleging national origin discrimination in the form of a hostile work environment. A jury awarded him $25,000 in compensatory damages and $50,000 in punitive damages. The Eleventh Circuit affirmed in part but vacated the award of punitive damages. Here, there was sufficient evidence that **the harassment occurred multiple times each day, thus altering the conditions of employment**. Also, the manager had constructive notice of the harassment because he was present on some of the occasions. Finally, the manager was high enough up the corporate ladder to justify imposing liability on the company. However, there was insufficient evidence of malice or reckless indifference on the company's part, so the punitive damages award could not stand. *Miller v. Kenworth of Dothan, Inc.*, 277 F.3d 1269 (11th Cir. 2002).

♦   A citizen of Mexico, who resided lawfully in the United States, sought employment as a seamstress with a manufacturing company. Her application was rejected due to a longstanding policy against the employment of aliens. After exhausting her administrative remedies with the EEOC, the applicant sued the company in a Texas federal court, asserting that the company had discriminated against her on the basis of national origin in violation of Title VII. The court granted pretrial judgment to the applicant, but the U.S. Court of Appeals, Fifth Circuit, reversed. It determined that the phrase "national origin" did not include citizenship.

The case then came before the U.S. Supreme Court. The Supreme Court held that the company's refusal to hire the woman because of her citizenship was not national origin discrimination in violation of Title VII. Even though it protects aliens against discrimination because of race, color, religion, sex, or national origin, **Title VII does not prohibit discrimination against aliens on the basis of alienage.** Here, the company had not refused to hire the applicant because of her Mexican ancestry, but because she was not a United States citizen. This was not forbidden by Title VII. The Court affirmed the court of appeals' decision against the applicant. *Espinoza v. Farah Manufacturing Co.*, 414 U.S. 86, 94 S.Ct. 334, 38 L.Ed.2d 287 (1973).

H. Statutes and Regulations

The federal statute prohibiting employment discrimination based on national origin is Title VII of the Civil Rights Act. It is the same statute that also bars employers from discriminating based on race, color, religion and sex. Title VII's rule against discrimination on the basis of national origin is enforced primarily by the Equal Employment Opportunity Commission, which has promulgated implementing regulations. These regulations are located in the Code of Federal Regulations at 29 C.F.R. Part 1606.

VII. DISCRIMINATION BASED ON RELIGION

A. Overview

Title VII of the Civil Rights Act prohibits employers from discriminating on the basis of religion. As with all other characteristics and classifications protected by Title VII, the prohibition applies to all aspects of the employment relationship, including hiring, firing and all other terms and conditions of employment. Under Title VII, employers must reasonably accommodate the sincerely held religious beliefs of employees unless doing so would create an undue hardship. Title VII's prohibition of discrimination based on religion encompasses a bar on religion-based harassment. In addition, employers cannot retaliate against an individual for opposing discriminatory practices, filing a discrimination charge or participating in an investigation.

B. Definition of "Religious Practice"

It is important for employers to note that the Equal Employment Opportunity Commission, which is the federal agency with primary enforcement responsibility for Title VII and its prohibition of harassment based on religion, takes a broad view of practices that can qualify for protection from religious discrimination under the statute. Specifically, the EEOC defines "religious practices" to include any moral or ethical belief that is related to what is right and wrong and that is "sincerely held with the strength of traditional religious views." This means an employee's practices may be protected as "religious practices" under Title VII even if they do not correspond with or find a basis in the practices of a traditional religious group. Under Title VII, "religious practices" include observances as well as practices.

C. Duty to Provide "Reasonable Accommodation"

Under Title VII, employers must accommodate the religious practices of applicants and employees unless doing so would create an undue hardship. This means an employee's request for accommodation of religious preferences must be granted unless the employer can show that allowing it would result in "more than *de minimis* cost." The Equal Employment Opportunity Commission, which is primarily responsible for enforcing Title VII, interprets this phrase to mean costs that exceed ordinary administrative costs. Whether granting an accommodation results in more than *de minimis* cost depends in part on the employer's size and operating costs. It also depends in part on the number of employees who are seeking the accommodation. An employee's religious beliefs can be accommodated in many ways, including flexible scheduling, voluntary substitutions or swaps, job reassignments and lateral transfers.

D. Rearrangement of Work Schedules

Many if not most requests for accommodation of religious practices relate to conflicts between an employee's religious practices and his work schedule.

There are several ways to accommodate these requests. One way for an employer to accommodate such a request is to assist in arranging for voluntary substitutes and swaps. Employers should take steps to make it easier for the employee seeking the scheduling accommodation to find a voluntary substitute with similar qualifications. For example, employers should publicize a policy regarding accommodation and voluntary substitution. Employers can also provide a means by which employees needing substitutes can be matched with potential voluntary substitutes, such as a bulletin board or central file. Another way to accommodate a requests relating to scheduling is to create a flexible work schedule for employees seeking this accommodation. Flexible arrival and departure times, floating or optional holidays, flexible work breaks, use of lunch time in exchange for early departure, staggered work hours and allowing an employee to make up time are all examples of flexibility in job scheduling.

E. Religious Dress or Personal Appearance

Title VII's prohibition of discrimination based on religion may require employers to accommodate an employee's religious dress or personal appearance. These requests for accommodation must be granted unless they would impose an undue hardship. Whether a particular request for accommodation imposes an "undue hardship" depends on the specific factual circumstances of each case. As a general rule, an employer does not need to accommodate a request relating to dress or appearance if granting the request would create a safety hazard. For example, an employer would not be required to grant a request to permit an employee to wear a long gown if the gown could easily be caught in workplace machinery.

F. Seniority Rights

An employer can deny a request for religious accommodation under Title VII if granting the request would deny another employee a job or shift preference he is entitled to under a bona fide seniority system.

G. Harassment Prohibited

Title VII's ban on discrimination based on religion encompasses a ban on harassment based on religion. An employer's anti-harassment policy should include religion as a prohibited basis for harassment.

H. Judicial Decisions

The following case summaries provide examples of issues relating to discrimination based on religion that can arise under Title VII and how they were resolved by the courts.

◆ An employee of an airline belonged to a religion known as the Worldwide Church of God. It proscribed work from sunset Friday to sunset Saturday. Because of the employee's seniority, the airline was able to accommodate his religious beliefs until he transferred to a new position with low seniority. The airline agreed to permit the union to seek a change of work assignments, but it was unwilling to violate the seniority system. The airline then rejected a proposal that the employee work only four days a week, stating that this would impair critical functions in its operations. Eventually, the employee was discharged for refusing to work on Saturdays. He sued both the union and the airline under Title VII, claiming religious discrimination. A Missouri federal court ruled in favor of the defendants, and the U.S. Court of Appeals affirmed in part. However, it did hold that the airline failed to satisfy its duty to accommodate the employee's religious needs. On appeal to the U.S. Supreme Court, it was held that the airline made reasonable efforts to accommodate the religious beliefs of others. The Court reversed the court of appeals' decision and held in favor of the airline. *Trans World Airlines, Inc. v. Hardison,* 432 U.S. 63, 97 S.Ct. 2264, 53 L.Ed.2d 113 (1977).

◆   An employee of a chain of New England retail stores managed a clothing department at a location in Connecticut. When the store began to keep Sunday hours, the employee worked occasional Sundays for two years. He then notified his employer that he would no longer work on that day because it was his Sabbath. A Connecticut law stated that employers could not require their employees to work on their Sabbath days, and refusal to work on the Sabbath was not grounds for dismissal. The employer demoted the employee to a clerical position. The employee then resigned and filed a grievance administratively. He was found to have been discharged in violation of the statute, and a state trial court upheld that decision. The Connecticut Supreme Court reversed, and the case came before the U.S. Supreme Court, which held that the Connecticut law violated the Establishment Clause of the First Amendment. Essentially, it **imposed on employers an absolute duty to conform their business practices to the particular religious practices of their employees.** Under this law, Sabbath religious concerns automatically controlled all secular interests at the workplace. The primary effect of this law, then, was the advancement of religion, which is forbidden by the Establishment Clause. The Court affirmed the state supreme court's decision. *Estate of Thornton v. Caldor, Inc.,* 472 U.S. 703, 105 S.Ct. 2914, 86 L.Ed.2d 557 (1985).

◆   A temporary placement agency refused to refer a Muslim woman to a client that ran a commercial printing operation because the woman wore a khimar (a scarf that covers the head and can extend to the waist) and the client's dress code policy prohibited workers from wearing headwear or loose clothing that could get caught in the machines. The woman filed a religious discrimination complaint with the EEOC, which sued the temp agency for violating Title VII. A Minnesota federal court and the Eighth Circuit ruled for the temp agency, noting that **the client's legitimate and facially neutral safety policy** justified the refusal to refer the woman for employment. *EEOC v. Kelly Services, Inc.,* 598 F.3d 1022 (8th Cir. 2010).

◆   Two editorial writers for an Indiana paper claimed that they were **fired or forced to resign because of their religious belief that homosexuality is a sin.**

When they sued under Title VII, a federal court and the Seventh Circuit ruled against them. The court noted that one of the writers repeatedly violated the newspaper's overtime policy, continuing to work overtime without obtaining permission first. And the other writer made numerous spelling and reporting errors that required retractions or apologies to involved parties. The newspaper put forth legitimate, nondiscriminatory reasons for its decisions and thus was not liable under Title VII. *Patterson v. Indiana Newspapers, Inc.,* 589 F.3d 357 (7th Cir. 2009).

♦ A Jiffy Lube technician in Massachusetts practiced Rastafarianism, which prohibited him from cutting his hair or shaving. When a new grooming policy took effect, requiring employees who had customer contact to be clean-shaven and to keep their hair neatly trimmed, he asked for an accommodation so he could continue to work with customers rather than simply working in the lower bay. The company's vice president refused to discuss the matter and assigned him to the lower bay. He quit and then sued for religious discrimination. A state court granted pretrial judgment to the company, but the Supreme Judicial Court of Massachusetts reversed. Here, because **the company failed to engage in the interactive process**, it could not show that exempting the technician from the policy was the only possible accommodation and that doing so would impose an undue hardship on its business. The case required a trial. *Brown v. F.L. Roberts & Co., Inc.,* 896 N.E.2d 1279 (Mass. 2008).

♦ A North Carolina employee observed the Sabbath from sundown Friday to sundown Saturday. He also observed 20 religious days during the year, 14 of which did not coincide with his Sabbath. He met with HR to discuss possible accommodations, including transferring to a different shift or job, leaving his shift uncovered during his Sabbath, and being excused from the part of his shift that conflicted with his Sabbath. Ultimately, the HR manager decided that those accommodations wouldn't work because he lacked the seniority to transfer. He was allowed to use vacation, holiday and 60 hours of unpaid leave under the company's no-fault attendance policy. However, after exhausting all his leave options, he missed 11 days of work and was fired. When he sued for religious discrimination, he lost. The Fourth Circuit held that **Title VII's obligation to reasonably accommodate doesn't require a company to "totally" accommodate a religious request**. *EEOC v. Firestone Fibers & Textiles Co.,* 515 F.3d 307 (4th Cir. 2008).

♦ A secretary for an Alabama medical center was required to work alternate weekends. However, as a Seventh-Day Adventist, she could not work her Friday or Saturday shifts from 3:00 p.m. to 11:00 p.m. With the center's approval, she managed to swap all her Saturday shifts with co-workers. However, she failed to show up for her scheduled Friday shifts for three months and was placed on an involuntary leave of absence. Rather than immediately firing her, the center offered her a flexible certified nursing assistant position, which would allow her to work on Sundays instead of Fridays and Saturdays. **It offered her the transfer even though she had not been employed for at least 12 months – a requirement the center was willing to waive** in her case. When she never responded to the offers, the center deemed her to have voluntarily resigned. She sued for religious discrimination under Title VII, but a federal court and the Eleventh Circuit ruled against her. The center met Title VII's reasonable accommodation requirement. *Morrissette-Brown v. Mobile Infirmary Medical Center,* 506 F.3d 1317 (11th Cir. 2007).

♦   A software developer for a company in California claimed that she was **passed over for promotion because she did not belong to the same religion** (the Fellowship of Friends) as the hiring manager, who allegedly exercised his decision-making authority in favor of members of the same religion. When she sued for discrimination under Title VII, a federal court granted pretrial judgment to the company, noting that it offered legitimate nondiscriminatory reasons for the non-promotion. However, the Ninth Circuit reversed, finding issues of fact that required a trial. Here, she presented evidence that she was more qualified, that she was paid less than a Fellowship member in the same job and that the hiring manager told other managers she wasn't interested in the job. *Noyes v. Kelly Services,* 488 F.3d 1163 (9th Cir. 2007).

♦   A Home Depot employee in New York could not work Sundays because of his religion. His managers accommodated him for a year until a new store manager took over. She told him he needed to be "fully flexible" and offered him afternoon or evening shifts so he could attend church in the morning. He refused, explaining that he couldn't work on Sundays at all. After he was fired for missing a Sunday shift, he sued for religious discrimination under Title VII. A federal court granted pretrial judgment for Home Depot, but the Second Circuit reversed, finding an issue of fact that required a trial. **The offer to let the employee have Sunday mornings off was no accommodation at all.** *Baker v. The Home Depot,* 445 F.3d 541 (2d Cir. 2006).

♦   An Iowa employee alleged that the woman in the next cubicle propositioned her and then, after becoming religious, sought to convert her. The day before a mediation session to work out these and other problems, the employee took FMLA leave. She was fired when she failed to return to work, and sued under Title VII and state law. A federal court and the Eighth Circuit ruled against her. The claimed sexual harassment was not severe or pervasive enough to alter her working conditions, and the religious harassment stopped when she asked the co-worker to stop proselytizing. **The only continued "offensive" conduct was the posting of religious material in the next cubicle, which management determined did not violate company policy.** *Powell v. Yellow Book USA, Inc.,* 445 F.3d 1074 (8th Cir. 2006).

♦   A Muslim from Afghanistan claimed that he was subjected to continuing harassment by co-workers at the Maine meat plant where he worked. He sued for race, national origin and religious harassment under Title VII, citing a number of incidents. A jury agreed that the company knew or should have known about the harassment, but refused to award damages, finding **no evidence that the employee sought medical treatment for counseling or lost work as a result of the harassment.** The First Circuit Court of Appeals upheld the jury's findings. Although the jury could have awarded damages, it was not compelled to do so. *Azimi v. Jordan's Meats, Inc.*, 456 F.3d 228 (1st Cir. 2006).

♦ A cashier in Massachusetts with multiple body piercings and tattoos claimed that she was **required by her religion – the Church of Body Modification – to display her body piercings** to the public. Her employer had a dress code policy that forbade the wearing of any facial jewelry except earrings. It rejected her suggested accommodation that she cover her eyebrow piercings with a flesh-colored Band-Aid and fired her for unexcused absences as well as failure to comply with the dress code. During Equal Employment Opportunity Commission mediation, the employer offered to let her return to work with her jewelry covered, but she then took the position that she should be exempted from the dress code for religious reasons. When she sued under Title VII, a federal court ruled against her and the First Circuit Court of Appeals affirmed the ruling. Granting such an exemption would be an undue hardship to the employer because it would adversely affect the employer's public image. *Cloutier v. Costco Wholesale Corp.*, 390 F.3d 126 (1st Cir. 2004).

♦ An evangelical Christian quality assurance manager in Arizona counseled an openly gay female employee to stop dating other women. She also brought up the employee's sexual orientation at the employee's performance review. Subsequently, she was fired for violating the company's harassment policy, which prohibited harassment on the basis of sexual orientation. The policy also subjected the harasser to immediate termination for coercing, intimidating or threatening a co-worker. When she sued the company for religious discrimination under Title VII, a federal court and the Ninth Circuit ruled against her. The termination was not religious discrimination in violation of Title VII. **Her harassment of her subordinate made her discharge legitimate and nondiscriminatory.** *Bodett v. CoxCom, Inc.*, 366 F.3d 736 (9th Cir. 2004).

♦ A custodial supervisor made lewd sexual comments to a janitor who was a former pastor. Later, the supervisor made religious insults against the janitor, who complained to the company's human resources department on six occasions. He was told there was nothing that could be done about it, and that if he didn't like it, he could quit. The day after the supervisor harassed the janitor about not working overtime on Sundays, the janitor resigned. He then sued the company under Title VII, and a jury ruled in his favor. The First Circuit affirmed, finding that **the religious harassment violated Title VII**. The damage award of $300,000 against the company was upheld. *Johnson v. Spencer Press of Maine, Inc.*, 364 F.3d 368 (1st Cir. 2004).

♦ An Idaho employee hung anti-homosexual biblical passages in his cubicle in response to the company's diversity campaign, part of which encouraged tolerance for gay rights. The passages were large enough to be visible by co-workers, customers and others who passed through an adjacent corridor. After a supervisor removed them, the employee met with company officials, where he admitted that he intended the passages to be hurtful to gays by condemning gay behavior. He put the passages back up and was fired, then sued under Title VII for religious discrimination. A federal court ruled for the company, and the Ninth Circuit Court of Appeals affirmed. Here, **the company did not fire the employee because of his religious beliefs**. Rather, it fired him because his messages were demeaning to co-workers and in conflict with the company's diversity policy. *Peterson v. Hewlett-Packard Co.*, 358 F.3d 599 (9th Cir. 2004)

I. Statutes and Regulations

The federal statute prohibiting employment discrimination based on religion is Title VII of the Civil Rights Act. It is the same statute that also bars employers from discriminating based on race, color, religion and sex.

Title VII's rule against discrimination on the basis of religion is enforced primarily by the Equal Employment Opportunity Commission, which has promulgated the implementing regulations. These regulations are located in the Code of Federal Regulations at 29 C.F.R. Part 1605.

VIII.   DISCRIMINATION AGAINST VETERANS

The Uniformed Services Employment and Reemployment Rights Act (USERRA) guarantees the right of military reservists to return to their jobs with their rights of seniority, status, pay and other benefits as if they had not been absent due to reserve obligations. It also prohibits denials of hiring, retention and promotion because of reserve obligations.

A. Judicial Decisions

The following cases illustrate issues faced by employers relating to veterans' rights.

♦   A hospital technician in Illinois also served in the Army Reserves. He got a new supervisor, who required him to work rotating weekends even though she knew that would conflict with his military obligations. She later wrote him up three times, after which an HR vice president conducted a brief investigation and then fired him. He sued under USERRA, claiming that he would not have been fired but for his supervisor's illegal bias. He presented evidence that his supervisor exaggerated one incident and lied about another. A jury awarded him $57,640, but the Seventh Circuit reversed, finding that **the supervisor's bias did not "singularly" influence the discharge decision**. The Seventh Circuit rejected the argument that the supervisor's bias only had to be a "motivating factor" in the discharge decision. *Staub v. Proctor Hospital*, 560 F.3d 647 (7th Cir. 2009), cert. granted 4/19/10.

♦   Supervisors at a company in Puerto Rico made jokes about a military reservist. One complained about having to schedule shifts around his military leave. After he returned from military service, the company deducted from his pay the amounts necessary to offset his military income for days he received both a military and civilian paycheck. Three weeks after it finished recouping its pay, it fired him without notice. When he sued under USERRA, a federal court granted pretrial judgment to the company. The First Circuit reversed, holding that **the burden of proof was on the employer to show that it would have fired the reservist even if he wasn't in the military.** *Velazquez-Garcia v. Horizon Lines of Puerto Rico, Inc.*, 473 F.3d 11 (1st Cir. 2007).

♦ A computer technician for a Virginia company was formally reprimanded several times prior to her call-up for active military duty. When she returned to work six months later, some of her job duties changed because of the company's contract with an outside federal agency. The change affected all similar employees. Four months later, after being warned again about her performance and attitude, she was fired when she left the office without authorization to attend to a customer at an off-site location. She sued under USERRA, but a federal court and the Fourth Circuit ruled against her. **The employee's refusal to correct her misconduct justified the firing.** *Francis v. Booz, Allen & Hamilton, Inc.*, 452 F.3d 299 (4th Cir. 2006).

♦ An Arkansas employee, who was also a member of the U.S. Army, took 15 military leaves in three years. **Although company policy allowed employees to use accrued leave for emergency military leave, the plant manager where the employee worked claimed to be unaware of the policy.** After the employee returned from an emergency military leave, he asked to have his accrued sick leave applied to the time off. The plant manager suspended him, then fired him for "stealing" sick days. When he sued under USERRA, a federal court granted pretrial judgment to the company. The Eighth Circuit Court of Appeals reversed, finding an issue of fact over the real reason for the termination. Even though the manager claimed to be unaware of the policy allowing sick leave use, a human resources manager testified that all managers had been instructed on it. *Maxfield v. Cintas Corp. No. 2*, 427 F.3d 544 (8th Cir. 2005).

♦ An employee of Circuit City in Texas claimed that he was fired solely because of his status as a Marine Reserve officer. He sued the company under USERRA, and the company sought to compel arbitration. A federal court ruled that USERRA superseded the arbitration agreement, but the Fifth Circuit reversed. It noted that nothing in USERRA prevented a court from enforcing an arbitration agreement (which dealt with procedural, not substantive rights). **The employee had to arbitrate his USERRA claim.** *Garrett v. Circuit City Stores, Inc.*, 449 F.3d 672 (5th Cir. 2006).

♦ A customer support technician for a company in North Dakota took a military leave of 14 months to go overseas. While he was gone, the company lost the account he had been working on, and it sent him a layoff notice. When he returned from overseas, he filled out a job application, indicating that he would not be available to work until May 4, 2004. A human resources manager told him there were no jobs available and that he was not the only one looking for work. The technician's attorney then faxed a letter to the head of the company's compliance office demanding the technician's immediate rehire. Within 48 hours the company notified the technician that he should report to work on May 4. He sued the company for violating USERRA, but a federal court ruled against him. **His reemployment occurred "promptly" under USERRA, which does not require immediate reinstatement following military leave in excess of one year.** *Vander Wal v. Sykes Enterprises, Inc.*, 377 F.Supp.2d 738 (D.N.D. 2005).

♦ When a reservist from Colorado returned home from active duty, the company he worked for as a design consultant gave him a modified assignment because the unit he had previously worked in was in the middle of developing a plan for 2004. Four months later, the company fired him as part of a cost-cutting move. He sued under USERRA, and a federal court ruled in his favor. The company first violated USERRA by assigning him to a position with less responsibilities even though he kept his title, salary and benefits. Secondly, the company **violated USERRA by firing him less than a year after his return.** It could legitimately do so under the act only if it had "cause," which it did not have here. *Duarte v. Agilent Technologies, Inc.*, 366 F.Supp.2d 1039 (D. Colo. 2005).

♦ A provision of USERRA requires a returning military member to notify his employer of the intent to return to work no later than the next first full calendar day of regularly scheduled work after the expiration of eight hours from the return to the person's residence. When a New Jersey reservist stopped at his convenience store employer to pick up his paycheck on the way home from weekend duties, the manager ordered him to work that night's late shift or be fired. The reservist worked the shift, then fell asleep behind the wheel, crashed his car and died. His mother sued under USERRA and lost. The Third Circuit held that **USERRA did not give the reservist the right to an eight-hour rest period between returning from reservist duty and returning to work.** *Gordon v. Wawa, Inc.*, 388 F.3d 78 (3d Cir. 2004).

B. Statutes and Regulations

The USERRA statute is located in the U.S. Code at Title 38, Section 4301 *et seq.* The implementing regulation is 20 C.F.R. Part 1002. The statute is administered by the U.S. Department of Labor.

CHAPTER SEVEN

Posting and Recordkeeping Requirements

I. POSTING REQUIREMENTS

A. Overview

Many federal statutes and regulations enforced by the federal Department of Labor require employers to provide certain notices to their employees and/or post such notices in the workplace. The required notices must be posted where they can easily be seen by employees, such as in an employee dining area. These posters can be acquired directly from the Department of Labor or purchased from private vendors.

The Department of Labor has noted that posting requirements vary by statute and that not all employers are covered by the various applicable federal statutes. As a result, different posting requirements are applicable to different employers.

Employers who fail to post notices as required by law are subject to fines and other penalties.

II. RECORDKEEPING REQUIREMENTS

A. Overview

Many federal and state laws require employers to hold on to specified employee records for designated time periods. Examples of the types of records that must be retained include records relating to wages and hours, I-9 forms and records relating to applicants for employment.

B. Judicial Decisions

♦   A cashier at an Indiana store was quickly promoted to assistant store manager and, after the store manager was fired, she took on some of the manager's responsibilities while still remaining an hourly employee. Six weeks later she was promoted to store manager and held that position for four months until she requested a transfer. The following month she was fired. She then sued for overtime under the FLSA. A federal court noted that she couldn't specifically identify the hours or even days she worked overtime without pay. The court granted pretrial judgment to the store. However, the Seventh Circuit reversed, noting that **when an employer fails to keep proper records required by the FLSA, an employee can still proceed with her claim**. Here, although employees submitted accurate time sheets, the company could and apparently did use a computer to alter the hours employees said they worked. The store even showed the manager clocking out before closing time on several occasions even though she was the only employee who could lock up. *Brown v. Family Dollar Stores of Indiana, LP,* 534 F.3d 593 (7th Cir. 2008).

♦   After a Texas husband and wife were fired, they sued their former employer under the FLSA, asserting that they were entitled to unpaid wages. They put together records documenting their hours worked. The employer submitted her own records, which were not fully complete. Nevertheless, the court used the employer's records because **the employees' records were a reconstruction after the fact and were insufficient to allow a "just and reasonable inference" of hours worked**. Also, witness testimony supported the employer's version. The Fifth Circuit U.S. Court of Appeals ruled that the employer's records had properly been used to determine hours worked. *Rosales v. Lore,* 149 Fed.Appx. 245 (5th Cir. 2005).

♦   A husband and wife took a job with a Virginia storage facility. They lived on the premises and agreed to be paid for 40 hours a week each as a reasonable estimate of the time they would have to work. If unusual circumstances caused them to exceed a 40-hour week, they were supposed to notify the owner within 24 hours. They submitted only one such notification and were paid accordingly. Four years later they were fired. They sued under the FLSA, seeking overtime for many other weeks, but a federal court and the Fourth Circuit ruled against them. The agreement they had signed was reasonable under 29 CFR § 785.23 – a regulation applying to situations where employees reside on the owner's premises – and they chose not to adhere to it. *Garofolo v. Donald B. Heslep Associates, Inc.*, 405 F.3d 194 (4th Cir. 2005).

♦   Waiters at a chain of Tennessee steakhouses filed a lawsuit under the FLSA, claiming that they were entitled to unpaid minimum wages for a three-year period when they were assigned during some shifts to make salads instead of waiting on tables. They claimed they were not "tipped" employees under the FLSA when they worked in this capacity because they performed exclusively behind-the-scenes food preparation. As such, they argued that they were entitled to recoup the 50% of the $4.25 per hour minimum wage that the employer claimed for itself under the FLSA as a tip credit.

The Sixth Circuit Court of Appeals agreed that the waiters were not "tipped" employees when they worked as salad makers. However, although each waiter was entitled to payment of the full $4.25 per hour for all work time logged during those shifts, ultimately they could not legally recoup the payment because they failed to disclose the precise hours of each salad-making shift worked. The burden was on them to prove their salad-making hours, because the restaurant's records were in proper order. **Thus, the waiters failed to prove the specific amount they were owed.** Nor did the restaurant forfeit its entitlement to a tip credit for any of the waiters' work hours because it habitually deducted a 3% service charge from each tip when a customer charged the tip to a credit card. The practice is not necessarily inconsistent with Section 203(m) of the FLSA, which commands that a tipped employee be permitted to retain all tips, except tips shared in a pooling arrangement. When tips are charged to credit cards, the employer can deduct the amount the credit card company charges without violating the FLSA. *Myers v. Copper Cellar Corp.*, 192 F.3d 546 (6th Cir. 1999).

♦   A janitorial service in Maryland and Washington, D.C., failed to pay its workers overtime. The employer kept records for total hours worked per shift rather than on a workweek basis as required by FLSA regulations. This recordkeeping method made it extremely difficult to determine whether overtime pay was due. A group of employees sued, claiming violations of the FLSA. The court rejected evidence prepared by the employees' attorney designed to show that each claimant was owed unpaid overtime wages. It determined that the methodology was improper and that the employer's policy of issuing make-up checks for overtime wages adequately compensated employees. The U.S. Court of Appeals, D.C. Circuit, found that the district court had erroneously placed the burden on the employees to prove their overtime hours and wages. **Where employer records are inadequate or inaccurate, courts may not penalize employees by denying them recovery based on inability to precisely prove their damages.** Because the employer failed to maintain accurate records, the evidence presented by the employees was sufficient to establish damages. The court vacated and remanded the case. *Arias v. United States Service Industries, Inc.*, 80 F.3d 509 (D.C. Cir. 1996).

C. Paperwork Retention Guide

File	Law	Where	Length of time	Notes
Job applications and resumes	ADA	Personnel file	1 year	Keep SSN safe if included
Employment actions (hires, promotion, termination, etc.)	Title VII, ADA, ADEA (age), PDA (pregnancy)	Personnel file	1 year from the date of the action	If a legal action occurs, keep records for the duration of the action
Time sheets	FLSA	Personnel file	2 years	Keep accessible
Payroll	FLSA	Personnel file	3 years	Keep accessible
I-9s	Immigration and Nationality Act	None prescribed	3 years after hire or 1 year after termination, whichever is later	Keep in a separate file
Health plan materials	ERISA, HIPAA	Separate from personnel file if medical info is included	6 years	For Form 5500, that's 6 years after filing for a total of 8 years
Medical info (accommodation requests, injury reports)	ADA, OSHA, HIPAA	Separate from personnel file	1 year (ADA), duration of employment +30 years (OSHA), 6 years (HIPAA)	Keep secure and confidential
Family and medical leave (such as medical certifications)	FMLA	Separate confidential file (amount of leave taken can be in personnel file)	3 years	Medical info must be kept separate and confidential

III. STATUTES AND REGULATIONS

A. Job Safety and Health Protection

**29 C.F.R. Sec. 1903.2 Posting of notice;
availability of the Act, regulations and applicable standards.**

(a)

(1) Each employer shall post and keep posted a notice or notices, to be furnished by the Occupational Safety and Health Administration, U.S. Department of Labor, informing employees of the protections and obligations provided for in the Act, and that for assistance and information, including copies of the Act and of specific safety and health standards, employees should contact the employer or the nearest office of the Department of Labor. Such notice or notices shall be posted by the employer in each establishment in a conspicuous place or places where notices to employees are customarily posted. Each employer shall take steps to insure that such notices are not altered, defaced, or covered by other material.

(2) Where a State has an approved poster informing employees of their protections and obligations as defined in Sec. 1952.10 of this chapter, such poster, when posted by employers covered by the State plan, shall constitute compliance with the posting requirements of section 8(c)(1) of the Act. Employers whose operations are not within the issues covered by the State plan must comply with paragraph (a)(1) of this section.

(3) Reproductions or facsimiles of such Federal or State posters shall constitute compliance with the posting requirements of section 8(c)(1) of the Act where such reproductions or facsimiles are at least 8 1/2 inches by 14 inches, and the printing size is at least 10 pt. Whenever the size of the poster increases, the size of the print shall also increase accordingly. The caption or heading on the poster shall be in large type, generally not less than 36 pt.

(b) Establishment means a single physical location where business is conducted or where services or industrial operations are performed. (For example: A factory, mill, store, hotel, restaurant, movie theatre, farm, ranch, bank, sales office, warehouse, or central administrative office.) Where distinctly separate activities are performed at a single physical location (such as contract construction activities from the same physical location as a lumber yard), each activity shall be treated as a separate physical establishment, and a separate notice or notices shall be posted in each such establishment, to the extent that such notices have been furnished by the Occupational Safety and Health Administration, U.S. Department of Labor. Where employers are engaged in activities which are physically dispersed, such as agriculture, construction, transportation, communications, and electric, gas and sanitary services, the notice or notices required by this section shall be posted at the location to which employees report each day. Where employees do not usually work at, or report to, a single establishment, such as longshoremen, traveling salesmen, technicians, engineers, etc., such notice or notices shall be posted at the location from which the employees operate to carry out their activities. In all cases, such notice or notices shall be posted in accordance with the requirements of paragraph (a) of this section.

(c) Copies of the Act, all regulations published in this chapter and all applicable standards will be available at all Area Offices of the Occupational Safety and Health Administration, U.S. Department of Labor. If an employer has obtained copies of these materials, he shall make them available upon request to any employee or his authorized representative for review in the establishment where the employee is employed on the same day the request is made or at the earliest time mutually convenient to the employee or his authorized representative and the employer.

(d) Any employer failing to comply with the provisions of this section shall be subject to citation and penalty in accordance with the provisions of section 17 of the Act.

B. Equal Employment Opportunity

41 C.F.R. Sec. 60-1.42 Notices to be posted.

(a) Unless alternative notices are prescribed by the Deputy Assistant Secretary, the notices which contractors are required to post by paragraphs (1) and (3) of the equal opportunity clause in Sec. 60-1.4 will contain the following language and be provided by the contracting or administering agencies:

Equal Employment Opportunity is the Law – Discrimination is Prohibited by the Civil Rights Act of 1964 and by Executive Order No. 11246.

Title VII of the Civil Rights Act of 1964 – administered by the Equal Employment Opportunity Commission – prohibits discrimination because of Race, Color, Religion, Sex, or National Origin by Employers with 15 or more employees, by Labor Organizations, by Employment Agencies, and by Apprenticeship or Training Programs.

Any person who believes he or she has been discriminated against should contact the Equal Employment Opportunity Commission, 1801 L Street NW, Washington, DC 20507.

Executive Order No. 11246 – administered by the Office of Federal Contract Compliance Program prohibits discrimination because of Race, Color, Religion, Sex, or National Origin, and requires affirmative action to ensure equality of opportunity in all aspects of employment.

By all Federal Government Contractors and Subcontractors, and by Contractors Performing Work Under a Federally Assisted Construction Contract, regardless of the number of employees in either case.

Any person who believes he or she has been discriminated against should contact the Office of Federal Contract Compliance Programs, U.S. Department of Labor, Washington, DC 20210.

(b) The requirements of paragraph (3) of the equal opportunity clause will be satisfied whenever the prime contractor or subcontractor posts copies of the notification prescribed by or pursuant to paragraph (a) of this section in conspicuous places available to employees, applicants for employment, and representatives of each labor union or other organization representing his employees with which he has a collective-bargaining agreement or other contract or understanding.

Sec. 60-741.5 Equal opportunity clause.

(a) Government contracts. Each contracting agency and each contractor shall include the following equal opportunity clause in each of its covered Government contracts or subcontracts (and modifications, renewals, or extensions thereof if not included in the original contract):

Equal Opportunity for Workers With Disabilities

1. The contractor will not discriminate against any employee or applicant for employment because of physical or mental disability in regard to any position for which the employee or applicant for employment is qualified. The contractor agrees to take affirmative action to employ, advance in employment and otherwise treat qualified individuals with disabilities without discrimination based on their physical or mental disability in all employment practices, including the following:

   i. Recruitment, advertising, and job application procedures;

   ii. Hiring, upgrading, promotion, award of tenure, demotion, transfer, layoff, termination, right of return from layoff and rehiring;

   iii. Rates of pay or any other form of compensation and changes in compensation;

   iv. Job assignments, job classifications, organizational structures, position descriptions, lines of progression, and seniority lists;

   v. Leaves of absence, sick leave, or any other leave;

   vi. Fringe benefits available by virtue of employment, whether or not administered by the contractor;

   vii. Selection and financial support for training, including apprenticeship, professional meetings, conferences, and other related activities, and selection for leaves of absence to pursue training;

   viii. Activities sponsored by the contractor including social or recreational programs; and

   ix. Any other term, condition, or privilege of employment.

2. The contractor agrees to comply with the rules, regulations, and relevant orders of the Secretary of Labor issued pursuant to the act.

3. In the event of the contractor's noncompliance with the requirements of this clause, actions for noncompliance may be taken in accordance with the rules, regulations, and relevant orders of the Secretary of Labor issued pursuant to the act.

4. The contractor agrees to post in conspicuous places, available to employees and applicants for employment, notices in a form to be prescribed

by the Deputy Assistant Secretary for Federal Contract Compliance Programs, provided by or through the contracting officer. Such notices shall state the rights of applicants and employees as well as the contractor's obligation under the law to take affirmative action to employ and advance in employment qualified employees and applicants with disabilities. The contractor must ensure that applicants and employees with disabilities are informed of the contents of the notice (e.g., the contractor may have the notice read to a visually disabled individual, or may lower the posted notice so that it might be read by a person in a wheelchair).

C. Fair Labor Standards Act

29 C.F.R. Sec. 516.4 Posting of notices.

Every employer employing any employees subject to the [Fair Labor Standards] Act's minimum wage provisions shall post and keep posted a notice explaining the Act, as prescribed by the Wage and Hour Division, in conspicuous places in every establishment where such employees are employed so as to permit them to observe readily a copy. Any employer of employees to whom section 7 of the Act does not apply because of an exemption of broad application to an establishment may alter or modify the poster with a legible notation to show that the overtime provisions do not apply. For example: Overtime Provisions Not Applicable to Taxicab Drivers (section 13(b)(17)).

D. Employee Rights for Workers with Disabilities/Special Minimum Wage Poster

29 C.F.R Sec. 525.14 Posting of notices.

Every employer having workers who are employed under special minimum wage certificates shall at all times display and make available to employees a poster as prescribed and supplied by the Administrator. The Administrator will make available, upon request, posters in other formats such as Braille or recorded tapes. Such a poster will explain, in general terms, the conditions under which special minimum wages may be paid and shall be posted in a conspicuous place on the employer's premises where it may be readily observed by the workers with disabilities, the parents and guardians of such workers, and other workers. Where an employer finds it inappropriate to post such a notice, this requirement may be satisfied by providing the poster directly to all employees subject to its terms.

E. Family and Medical Leave Act

29 C.F.R. Sec. 825.300 Employer notice requirements.

(a) General notice.

(1) Every employer covered by the FMLA is required to post and keep posted on its premises, in conspicuous places where employees are employed, a notice explaining the Act's provisions and providing

information concerning the procedures for filing complaints of violations of the Act with the Wage and Hour Division. The notice must be posted prominently where it can be readily seen by employees and applicants for employment. The poster and the text must be large enough to be easily read and contain fully legible text. Electronic posting is sufficient to meet this posting requirement as long as it otherwise meets the requirements of this section. An employer that willfully violates the posting requirement may be assessed a civil money penalty by the Wage and Hour Division not to exceed $110 for each separate offense.

(2) Covered employers must post this general notice even if no employees are eligible for FMLA leave.

(3) If an FMLA-covered employer has any eligible employees, it shall also provide this general notice to each employee by including the notice in employee handbooks or other written guidance to employees concerning employee benefits or leave rights, if such written materials exist, or by distributing a copy of the general notice to each new employee upon hiring. In either case, distribution may be accomplished electronically.

(4) To meet the requirements of paragraph (a)(3) of this section, employers may duplicate the text of the notice contained in Appendix C of this part or may use another format so long as the information provided includes, at a minimum, all of the information contained in that notice. Where an employer's workforce is comprised of a significant portion of workers who are not literate in English, the employer shall provide the general notice in a language in which the employees are literate. Prototypes are available from the nearest office of the Wage and Hour Division or on the Internet at http://www.wagehour.dol.gov. Employers furnishing FMLA notices to sensory-impaired individuals must also comply with all applicable requirements under Federal or State law.

(b) Eligibility notice.

(1) When an employee requests FMLA leave, or when the employer acquires knowledge that an employee's leave may be for an FMLA-qualifying reason, the employer must notify the employee of the employee's eligibility to take FMLA leave within five business days, absent extenuating circumstances. See Sec. 825.110 for definition of an eligible employee. Employee eligibility is determined (and notice must be provided) at the commencement of the first instance of leave for each FMLA-qualifying reason in the applicable 12-month period (see Sec. Sec. 825.127(c) and 825.200(b)). All FMLA absences for the same qualifying reason are considered a single leave and employee eligibility as to that reason for leave does not change during the applicable 12-month period.

(2) The eligibility notice must state whether the employee is eligible for FMLA leave as defined in Sec. 825.110(a). If the employee is not eligible for FMLA leave, the notice must state at least one reason why the employee is not eligible, including as applicable the number of months the employee has been employed by the employer, the number of hours of service worked for the employer during the 12-month period, and whether

the employee is employed at a worksite where 50 or more employees are employed by the employer within 75 miles of that worksite. Notification of eligibility may be oral or in writing; employers may use Appendix D of this part 825 to provide such notification to employees. The employer is obligated to translate this notice in any situation in which it is obligated to do so in Sec. 825.300(a)(4).

(3) If, at the time an employee provides notice of a subsequent need for FMLA leave during the applicable 12-month period due to a different FMLA-qualifying reason, and the employee's eligibility status has not changed, no additional eligibility notice is required. If, however, the employee's eligibility status has changed (e.g., if the employee has worked less than 1,250 hours of service for the employer in the 12 months preceding the commencement of leave for the subsequent qualifying reason or the size of the workforce at the worksite has dropped below 50 employees), the employer must notify the employee of the change in eligibility status within five business days, absent extenuating circumstances.

(c) Rights and responsibilities notice.

(1) Employers shall provide written notice detailing the specific expectations and obligations of the employee and explaining any consequences of a failure to meet these obligations. The employer is obligated to translate this notice in any situation in which it is obligated to do so in Sec. 825.300(a)(4). This notice shall be provided to the employee each time the eligibility notice is provided pursuant to paragraph (b) of this section. If leave has already begun, the notice should be mailed to the employee's address of record. Such specific notice must include, as appropriate:

(i) That the leave may be designated and counted against the employee's annual FMLA leave entitlement if qualifying (see Sec. Sec. 825.300(c) and 825.301) and the applicable 12-month period for FMLA entitlement (see Sec. Sec. 825.127(c), 825.200(b), (f), and (g));

(ii) Any requirements for the employee to furnish certification of a serious health condition, serious injury or illness, or qualifying exigency arising out of active duty or call to active duty status, and the consequences of failing to do so (see Sec. Sec. 825.305, 825.309, 825.310, 825.313);

(iii) The employee's right to substitute paid leave, whether the employer will require the substitution of paid leave, the conditions related to any substitution, and the employee's entitlement to take unpaid FMLA leave if the employee does not meet the conditions for paid leave (see Sec. 825.207);

(iv) Any requirement for the employee to make any premium payments to maintain health benefits and the arrangements for making such payments (see Sec. 825.210), and the possible consequences of failure to make such payments on a timely basis (i.e., the circumstances under which coverage may lapse);

(v) The employee's status as a "key employee" and the potential consequence that restoration may be denied following FMLA leave, explaining the conditions required for such denial (see Sec. 825.218);

(vi) The employee's rights to maintenance of benefits during the FMLA leave and restoration to the same or an equivalent job upon return from FMLA leave (see Sec. Sec. 825.214 and 825.604); and

(vii) The employee's potential liability for payment of health insurance premiums paid by the employer during the employee's unpaid FMLA leave if the employee fails to return to work after taking FMLA leave (see Sec. 825.213).

(2) The notice of rights and responsibilities may include other information–e.g., whether the employer will require periodic reports of the employee's status and intent to return to work–but is not required to do so.

(3) The notice of rights and responsibilities may be accompanied by any required certification form.

(4) If the specific information provided by the notice of rights and responsibilities changes, the employer shall, within five business days of receipt of the employee's first notice of need for leave subsequent to any change, provide written notice referencing the prior notice and setting forth any of the information in the notice of rights and responsibilities that has changed. For example, if the initial leave period was paid leave and the subsequent leave period would be unpaid leave, the employer may need to give notice of the arrangements for making premium payments.

(5) Employers are also expected to responsively answer questions from employees concerning their rights and responsibilities under the FMLA.

(6) A prototype notice of rights and responsibilities is contained in appendix D of this part; the prototype may be obtained from local offices of the Wage and Hour Division or from the Internet at *www.wagehour. dol.gov.* Employers may adapt the prototype notice as appropriate to meet these notice requirements. The notice of rights and responsibilities may be distributed electronically so long as it otherwise meets the requirements of this section.

(d) Designation notice.

(1) The employer is responsible in all circumstances for designating leave as FMLA-qualifying, and for giving notice of the designation to the employee as provided in this section. When the employer has enough information to determine whether the leave is being taken for a FMLA-qualifying reason (e.g., after receiving a certification), the employer must notify the employee whether the leave will be designated and will be counted as FMLA leave within five business days absent extenuating circumstances. Only one notice of designation is required for each FMLA-qualifying reason per applicable 12-month period, regardless of whether the leave taken due to the qualifying reason will be a continuous block of leave or intermittent or reduced schedule leave. If the employer determines that the leave will not be designated as FMLA-qualifying

(e.g., if the leave is not for a reason covered by FMLA or the FMLA leave entitlement has been exhausted), the employer must notify the employee of that determination. If the employer requires paid leave to be substituted for unpaid FMLA leave, or that paid leave taken under an existing leave plan be counted as FMLA leave, the employer must inform the employee of this designation at the time of designating the FMLA leave.

(2) If the employer has sufficient information to designate the leave as FMLA leave immediately after receiving notice of the employee's need for leave, the employer may provide the employee with the designation notice at that time.

(3) If the employer will require the employee to present a fitness-for-duty certification to be restored to employment, the employer must provide notice of such requirement with the designation notice. If the employer will require that the fitness-for-duty certification address the employee's ability to perform the essential functions of the employee's position, the employer must so indicate in the designation notice, and must include a list of the essential functions of the employee's position. See Sec. 825.312. If the employer handbook or other written documents (if any) describing the employer's leave policies clearly provide that a fitness-for-duty certification will be required in specific circumstances (e.g., by stating that fitness-for-duty certification will be required in all cases of back injuries for employees in a certain occupation), the employer is not required to provide written notice of the requirement with the designation notice, but must provide oral notice no later than with the designation notice.

(4) The designation notice must be in writing. A prototype designation notice is contained in appendix E of this part; the prototype designation notice may be obtained from local offices of the Wage and Hour Division or from the Internet at *http://www.wagehour.dol.gov.* If the leave is not designated as FMLA leave because it does not meet the requirements of the Act, the notice to the employee that the leave is not designated as FMLA leave may be in the form of a simple written statement.

(5) If the information provided by the employer to the employee in the designation notice changes (e.g., the employee exhausts the FMLA leave entitlement), the employer shall provide, within five business days of receipt of the employee's first notice of need for leave subsequent to any change, written notice of the change.

(6) The employer must notify the employee of the amount of leave counted against the employee's FMLA leave entitlement. If the amount of leave needed is known at the time the employer designates the leave as FMLA-qualifying, the employer must notify the employee of the number of hours, days, or weeks that will be counted against the employee's FMLA leave entitlement in the designation notice. If it is not possible to provide the hours, days, or weeks that will be counted against the employee's FMLA leave entitlement (such as in the case of unforeseeable intermittent leave), then the employer must provide notice of the amount of leave counted against the employee's FMLA leave entitlement upon the

request by the employee, but no more often than once in a 30-day period and only if leave was taken in that period. The notice of the amount of leave counted against the employee's FMLA entitlement may be oral or in writing. If such notice is oral, it shall be confirmed in writing, no later than the following payday (unless the payday is less than one week after the oral notice, in which case the notice must be no later than the subsequent payday). Such written notice may be in any form, including a notation on the employee's pay stub.

(e) Consequences of failing to provide notice. Failure to follow the notice requirements set forth in this section may constitute an interference with, restraint, or denial of the exercise of an employee's FMLA rights. An employer may be liable for compensation and benefits lost by reason of the violation, for other actual monetary losses sustained as a direct result of the violation, and for appropriate equitable or other relief, including employment, reinstatement, promotion, or any other relief tailored to the harm suffered (see Sec. 825.400(c)).

29 C.F.R. Sec. 825.402 Violations of the posting requirement.

Section 825.300 describes the requirements for covered employers to post a notice for employees that explains the Act's provisions. If a representative of the Department of Labor determines that an employer has committed a willful violation of this posting requirement, and that the imposition of a civil money penalty for such violation is appropriate, the representative may issue and serve a notice of penalty on such employer in person or by certified mail. Where service by certified mail is not accepted, notice shall be deemed received on the date of attempted delivery. Where service is not accepted, the notice may be served by regular mail.

F. Uniformed Services Employment and Reemployment Rights Act

38 U.S.C. 4334. Notice of rights and duties

(a) Requirement To Provide Notice.— Each employer shall provide to persons entitled to rights and benefits under this chapter a notice of the rights, benefits, and obligations of such persons and such employers under this chapter. The requirement for the provision of notice under this section may be met by the posting of the notice where employers customarily place notices for employees.

(b) Content of Notice.— The Secretary shall provide to employers the text of the notice to be provided under this section.

G. Federal or Federally Financed Construction Projects

Sec. 5.5 Contract provisions and related matters.

(a) The Agency head shall cause or require the contracting officer to insert in full in any contract in excess of $2,000 which is entered into for the actual construction, alteration and/or repair, including painting and decorating, of a public building or public work, or building or work financed in whole or in part from Federal funds or in accordance with guarantees of a Federal agency or financed from funds obtained by pledge of any contract of a Federal agency to make a loan, grant or annual contribution (except where a different meaning is expressly indicated), and which is subject to the labor standards provisions of any of the acts listed in Sec. 5.1, the following clauses (or any modifications thereof to meet the particular needs of the agency, Provided, That such modifications are first approved by the Department of Labor):

(1) Minimum wages.

(i) All laborers and mechanics employed or working upon the site of the work (or under the United States Housing Act of 1937 or under the Housing Act of 1949 in the construction or development of the project), will be paid unconditionally and not less often than once a week, and without subsequent deduction or rebate on any account (except such payroll deductions as are permitted by regulations issued by the Secretary of Labor under the Copeland Act (29 CFR part 3)), the full amount of wages and bona fide fringe benefits (or cash equivalents thereof) due at time of payment computed at rates not less than those contained in the wage determination of the Secretary of Labor which is attached hereto and made a part hereof, regardless of any contractual relationship which may be alleged to exist between the contractor and such laborers and mechanics.

Contributions made or costs reasonably anticipated for bona fide fringe benefits under section 1(b)(2) of the Davis-Bacon Act on behalf of laborers or mechanics are considered wages paid to such laborers or mechanics, subject to the provisions of paragraph (a)(1)(iv) of this section; also, regular contributions made or costs incurred for more than a weekly period (but not less often than quarterly) under plans, funds, or programs which cover the particular weekly period, are deemed to be constructively made or incurred during such weekly period. Such laborers and mechanics shall be paid the appropriate wage rate and fringe benefits on the wage determination for the classification of work actually performed, without regard to skill, except as provided in Sec. 5.5(a)(4). Laborers or mechanics performing work in more than one classification may be compensated at the rate specified for each classification for the time actually worked therein: Provided, That the employer's payroll records accurately set forth the time spent in each classification in which work is performed. The wage determination (including any additional classification and wage rates conformed under paragraph (a)(1)(ii) of this section) and the Davis-Bacon poster (WH-1321) shall be posted at all times by the contractor and its subcontractors at the site of the work in a prominent and accessible place where it can be easily seen by the workers.

H. Employees Working on Government Contracts

Sec. 4.6 Labor standards clauses for Federal service contracts exceeding $2,500.

The clauses set forth in the following paragraphs shall be included in full by the contracting agency in every contract entered into by the United States or the District of Columbia, in excess of $2,500, or in an indefinite amount, the principal purpose of which is to furnish services through the use of service employees:

....

(e) The contractor and any subcontractor under this contract shall notify each service employee commencing work on this contract of the minimum monetary wage and any fringe benefits required to be paid pursuant to this contract, or shall post the wage determination attached to this contract. The poster provided by the Department of Labor (Publication WH 1313) shall be posted in a prominent and accessible place at the worksite. Failure to comply with this requirement is a violation of section 2(a)(4) of the Act and of this contract.

Sec. 4.184 Posting of notice.

Posting of the notice provided by the Wage and Hour Division shall be in a prominent and accessible place at the worksite, as required by Sec. 4.6(e). The display of the notice in a place where it may be seen by employees performing on the contract will satisfy the requirement that it be in a "prominent and accessible place". Should display be necessary at more than one site, in order to assure that it is seen by such employees, additional copies of the poster may be obtained without cost from the Division. The contractor or subcontractor is required to notify each employee of the compensation due or attach to the poster any applicable wage determination specified in the contract listing all minimum monetary wages and fringe benefits to be paid or furnished to the classes of service employees performing on the contract.

I. Employee Polygraph Protection Act

29 C.F.R. Sec. 801.6 Notice of protection.

Every employer subject to EPPA shall post and keep posted on its premises a notice explaining the Act, as prescribed by the Secretary. Such notice must be posted in a prominent and conspicuous place in every establishment of the employer where it can readily be observed by employees and applicants for employment. Copies of such notice may be obtained from local offices of the Wage and Hour Division.

J. Migrant and Seasonal Agricultural Worker Protection Act

29 C.F.R. Sec. 500.75 Disclosure of information.

(a) Where disclosure is required, Department of Labor optional forms may be used to satisfy the requirements of disclosure under the Act.

(b) Each farm labor contractor, agricultural employer, and agricultural association which recruits any migrant agricultural worker shall ascertain to the best of his ability and disclose, in writing to the extent that he has obtained such information, to such worker at the time of recruitment, the following information:

(1) The place of employment (with as much specificity as practical, such as the name and address of the employer or the association);

(2) The wage rates (including piece rates) to be paid;

(3) The crops and kinds of activities on which the worker may be employed;

(4) The period of employment;

(5) The transportation, housing, and any other employee benefits to be provided, if any, and any costs to be charged for each of them;

(6) Whether state workers' compensation or state unemployment insurance is provided:

(i) If workers' compensation is provided, the required disclosure must include the name of the workers' compensation insurance carrier, the name(s) of the policyholder(s), the name and telephone number of each person who must be notified of an injury or death, and the time period within which such notice must be given.

(ii) The information requirement in paragraph (b)(6)(i) of this section may be satisfied by giving the worker a photocopy of any workers' compensation notice required by State law.

(7) The existence of any strike or other concerted work stoppage, slowdown, or interruption of operations by employees at the place of employment; and

(8) The existence of any arrangements with any owner or agent of any establishment in the area of employment under which the farm labor contractor, the agricultural employer, or the agricultural association is to receive a commission or any other benefit resulting from any sales by such establishment to the workers.

(c) Each farm labor contractor, agricultural employer and agricultural association which employs any migrant agricultural worker shall post (and maintain) in a conspicuous place at the place of employment a poster provided by the Secretary of Labor, which sets out the rights and protections for workers required under the Act.

(d) The employer (other than a farm labor contractor) of any migrant agricultural worker, shall provide at the place of employment on request of the worker, a written statement of the conditions of employment. A farm labor contractor shall provide such information in accordance with Sec. 500.60(b) of these regulations.

(e) In a joint employment situation, each employer is equally responsible for displaying and maintaining the poster and for responding to worker requests for written statements of the conditions of employment which are made during the course of employment. This joint responsibility, however, does not require needless duplication, such as would occur if each employer posted the same poster or provided the same written statement with respect to the same employment conditions. Failure to provide the information required by a joint employment relationship, however, will result in all joint employers being responsible for that failure.

(f) Each farm labor contractor, agricultural employer and agricultural association which provides housing for any migrant agricultural worker shall post in a conspicuous place (at the site of the housing) or present in the form of a written statement to the worker the following information on the terms and conditions of occupancy of such housing, if any:

(1) The name and address of the farm labor contractor, agricultural employer or agricultural association providing the housing;

(2) The name and address of the individual in charge of the housing;

(3) The mailing address and phone number where persons living in the housing facility may be reached;

(4) Who may live at the housing facility;

(5) The charges to be made for housing;

(6) The meals to be provided and the charges to be made for them;

(7) The charges for utilities; and

(8) Any other charges or conditions of occupancy.

(g) If the terms and conditions of occupancy are posted, the poster shall be displayed and maintained during the entire period of occupancy. If the terms and conditions of occupancy are disclosed to the worker through a statement (rather than through a posting), such statement shall be provided to the worker prior to occupancy. Department of Labor optional forms may be used to satisfy this requirement.

Sec. 500.76 Disclosure of information.

(a) Where disclosure is required, Department of Labor optional forms may be used to satisfy the requirements of disclosure under the Act.

(b) Each farm labor contractor, agricultural employer and agricultural association, which recruits any seasonal agricultural worker for employment on a farm or ranch to perform field work related to planting, cultivating or harvesting operations, shall ascertain and, upon request, disclose in writing the following information to such worker when an offer of employment is made:

(1) The place of employment (with as much specificity as practical, such as the name and address of the employer or the association);

(2) The wage rates (including piece rates) to be paid;

(3) The crops and kinds of activities on which the worker may be employed;

(4) The period of employment;

(5) The transportation and any other employee benefits to be provided, if any, and any costs to be charged for each of them;

(6) Whether state workers' compensation or state unemployment insurance is provided:

> (i) If workers' compensation is provided, the required disclosure must include the name of the workers' compensation insurance carrier, the name(s) of the policyholder(s), the name and telephone number of each person who must be notified of an injury or death, and the time period within which such notice must be given.

> (ii) The information requirement in paragraph (b)(6)(i) of this section may satisfied giving the worker a photocopy of any workers' compensation notice required by State law.

(7) The existence of any strike or other concerted work stoppage, slowdown, or interruption of operations by employees at the place of employment; and

(8) The existence of any arrangements with any owner or agent of any establishment in the area of employment under which the farm labor contractor, the agricultural employer, or the agricultural association is to receive a commission or any other benefit resulting from any sales by such establishment to the workers.

(c) Each farm labor contractor, agricultural employer and agricultural association which recruits any seasonal agricultural worker for employment through the use of day-haul operation in canning, packing, ginning, seed conditioning or related research, or processing operations, shall ascertain and disclose in writing to the worker at the time of recruitment the information on employment conditions set out in paragraph (b) of this section.

(d)

> (1) Each farm labor contractor, agricultural employer and agricultural association which employs any seasonal agricultural worker shall post (and maintain) at the place of employment in a conspicuous place readily accessible to the worker a poster provided by the Secretary of Labor which sets out the rights and protections for such worker required under the Act.

> (2) Such employer shall provide, on request of the worker, a written statement of the information described in paragraph (b) of this section.

(e) In a joint employment situation, each employer is equally responsible for displaying and maintaining the poster and for responding to worker requests for written statements of the conditions of employment which are made during the course of employment. This joint responsibility, however, does not require needless duplication, such as would occur if each employer posted the same poster or provided the same written statement with respect to the same employment conditions.

K. Notification of Employee Rights Under Federal Labor Laws

29 C.F.R. Sec. 471.2 What employee notice clause must be included in Government contracts?

(a) Government contracts. With respect to all contracts covered by this part, Government contracting departments and agencies must, to the extent consistent with law, include the language set forth in appendix A to subpart A of part 471 in every Government contract, other than those contracts to which exceptions are applicable as stated in Sec. 471.3.

(b) Inclusion by reference. The employee notice clause need not be quoted verbatim in a contract, subcontract, or purchase order. The clause may be made part of the contract, subcontract, or purchase order by citation to 29 CFR part 471, appendix A to subpart A.

(c) Adaptation of language. The Director of OLMS may find that an Act of Congress, clarification of existing law by the courts or the National Labor Relations Board, or other circumstances make modification of the contractual provisions necessary to achieve the purposes of the Executive Order and this part. In such circumstances, the Director of OLMS will promptly issue rules, regulations, or orders as are needed to ensure that all future government contracts contain appropriate provisions to achieve the purposes of the Executive Order and this part.

(d) Physical posting of employee notice. A contractor or subcontractor that posts notices to employees physically must also post the required notice physically. Where a significant portion of a contractor's workforce is not proficient in English, the contractor must provide the notice in the language employees speak. The employee notice must be placed:

(1) In conspicuous places in and about the contractor's plants and offices so that the notice is prominent and readily Seen by employees. Such conspicuous placement includes, but is not limited to, areas in which the contractor posts notices to employees about the employees' terms and conditions of employment; and

(2) Where employees covered by the National Labor Relations Act engage in activities relating to the performance of the contract. An employee shall be considered to be so engaged if:

(i) The duties of the employee's position include work that fulfills a contractual obligation, or work that is necessary to, or that facilitates, performance of the contract or a provision of the contract; or

(ii) The cost or a portion of the cost of the employee's position is allowable as a cost of the contract under the principles set forth in the Federal Acquisition Regulation at 48 CFR Ch. 1, part 31: Provided, That a position shall not be considered covered by this part by virtue of this provision if the cost of the position was not allocable in whole or in part as a direct cost to any Government contract, and only a de minimis (less than 2%) portion of the cost of the position was allocable as an indirect cost to Government contracts, considered as a group.

(e) Obtaining a poster with the employee notice. A poster with the required employee notice, including a poster with the employee notice translated into languages other than English, will be printed by the Department, and will be provided by the Federal contracting agency or may be obtained from the Division of Interpretations and Standards, Office of Labor-Management Standards, U.S. Department of Labor, 200 Constitution Avenue, NW., Room N-5609, Washington, DC 20210, or from any field office of the Department's Office of Labor-Management Standards or Office of Federal Contract Compliance Programs. A copy of the poster in English and in languages other than English may also be downloaded from the Office of Labor-Management Standards website at *http://www.olms.dol.gov*. Additionally, contractors may reproduce and use exact duplicate copies of the Department's official poster.

(f) Electronic postings of employee notice. A contractor or subcontractor that customarily posts notices to employees electronically must also post the required notice electronically. Such contractors or subcontractors satisfy the electronic posting requirement by displaying prominently on any website that is maintained by the contractor or subcontractor, whether external or internal, and customarily used for notices to employees about terms and conditions of employment, a link to the Department of Labor's website that contains the full text of the poster. The link to the Department's website must read, "Important Notice about Employee Rights to Organize and Bargain Collectively with Their Employers." Where a significant portion of a contractor's workforce is not proficient in English, the contractor must provide the notice required in this subsection in the language the employees speak. This requirement will be satisfied by displaying prominently on any website that is maintained by the contractor or subcontractor, whether external or internal, and customarily used for notices to employees about terms and conditions of employment, a link to the Department of Labor's website that contains the full text of the poster in the language the employees speak. In such cases, the Office of Labor-Management Standards will provide translations of the link to the Department's website that must be displayed on the contractor's or subcontractor's website.

CHAPTER EIGHT

Forms

Form I-1: Sample Hiring Policy

Employers should have a brief, written policy concerning how it handles hiring. A sample:

(Company name) is an Equal Opportunity Employer. We make employment decisions based on individuals' qualifications and ability to perform specific job requirements.

Employment with the Company is considered to be "at will," which means either party may terminate the relationship at any time and for any lawful reason.

All applicants must complete an employment application. The Company may also require a resume and letters of reference depending on the position being applied for.

Following the Company's review of all completed applications, the employer will begin interviewing the most qualified candidates. Those who do not meet our employment requirements for whatever reason will remain classified as applicants.

The Company will make conditional offers of employment to those candidates selected during the interview process. The conditional aspect of the job offer depends on the employee's agreeing to acknowledge company policies in writing, consenting and passing all necessary drug, background and reference checks, and finally any other condition that should be met before the candidate may consider him/herself an employee.

Form III-1: Handbooks

Employers should always ask staff members to sign a form stating that they've read and understood the company handbook. Here's an example of an employee handbook acknowledgment form, courtesy of the Florida Department of Juvenile Justice:

ACKNOWLEDGEMENT OF RECEIPT

This is to acknowledge that I have received the [business name] Employee Handbook. I acknowledge that I have a responsibility to read and understand this handbook, including the policy on discipline and standards of conduct. I understand that the topics discussed in this handbook represent the general policies of the State and that my employing agency may impose additional requirements, depending upon the nature of my position and the authority granted to the agency.

Employee Name:_____

Employee Signature:_____

Date: _____

Source: http://www.djj.state.fl.us/forms/personnel/sof_employee_handbook_03-10-03.pdf

Form III-2: Sample Internet Policy

Here's a sample Internet policy, courtesy of Business Link:

Use of the Internet by employees of [business name] is permitted and encouraged where such use supports the goals and objectives of the business.

However, [business name] has a policy for the use of the Internet whereby employees must ensure that they:
- comply with current legislation
- use the internet in an acceptable way, and
- do not create unnecessary business risk to the company by their misuse of the Internet.

In particular the following is deemed unacceptable use or behavior by employees:
- visiting Internet sites that contain obscene, hateful, pornographic or otherwise illegal material
- using the computer to perpetrate any form of fraud, or software, film or music piracy
- using the Internet to send offensive or harassing material to other users
- downloading commercial software or any copyrighted materials belonging to third parties, unless this download is covered or permitted under a commercial agreement or other such licence
- hacking into unauthorized areas
- publishing defamatory and/or knowingly false material about [business name], your colleagues and/or our customers on social networking sites, 'blogs' (online journals), 'wikis' and any online publishing format
- revealing confidential information about [business name] in a personal online posting, upload or transmission - including financial information and information relating to our customers, business plans, policies, staff and/or internal discussions
- undertaking deliberate activities that waste staff effort or networked resources
- introducing any form of malicious software into the corporate network

If you produce, collect and/or process business-related information in the course of your work, the information remains the property of [business name]. This includes such information stored on third-party websites such as webmail service providers and social networking sites, such as Facebook and LinkedIn.

[business name] accepts that the use of the Internet is a valuable business tool. However, misuse of this facility can have a negative impact upon employee productivity and the reputation of the business.

In addition, all of the company's Internet-related resources are provided for business purposes. Therefore, the company maintains the right to monitor the volume of internet and network traffic, together with the internet sites visited. The specific content of any transactions will not be monitored unless there is a suspicion of improper use.

Where it is believed that an employee has failed to comply with this policy, they will face the company's disciplinary procedure. If the employee is found to have breached the policy, they will face a disciplinary penalty ranging from a verbal warning to dismissal. The actual penalty applied will depend on factors such as the seriousness of the breach and the employee's disciplinary record. [These procedures will be specific to your business. They should reflect your normal operational and disciplinary processes. You should establish them from the outset and include them in your acceptable use policy.]

All company employees, contractors or temporary staff who have been granted the right to use the company's Internet access are required to sign this agreement confirming their understanding and acceptance of this policy.

Source: http://www.businesslink.gov.uk/bdotg/action/detail?itemId= 1076142205&type=RESOURCES

Form III-3: Sample Email Use Policy

Here's a sample email use policy, courtesy of Business Link

Use of email by employees of [business name] is permitted and encouraged where such use supports the goals and objectives of the business.

However, [business name] has a policy for the use of email whereby the employee must ensure that they:

- comply with current legislation
- use email in an acceptable way, and
- do not create unnecessary business risk to the company by their misuse of the Internet.

Unacceptable behavior includes the following

- use of company communications systems to set up personal businesses or send chain letters
- forwarding of company confidential messages to external locations
- distributing, disseminating or storing images, text or materials that might be considered indecent, pornographic, obscene or illegal
- distributing, disseminating or storing images, text or materials that might be considered discriminatory, offensive or abusive, in that the context is a personal attack, sexist or racist, or might be considered as harassment
- accessing copyrighted information in a way that violates the copyright
- breaking into the company's or another organization's system or unauthorized use of a password/mailbox
- broadcasting unsolicited personal views on social, political, religious or other non-business related matters
- transmitting unsolicited commercial or advertising material
- undertaking deliberate activities that waste staff effort or networked resources
- introducing any form of computer virus or malware into the corporate network

[business name] accepts that the use of email is a valuable business tool. However, misuse of this facility can have a negative impact upon employee productivity and the reputation of the business.

In addition, all of the company's email resources are provided for business purposes. Therefore, the company maintains the right to examine any systems and inspect any data recorded in those systems.

In order to ensure compliance with this policy, the company also reserves the right to use monitoring software in order to check upon the use and content of emails. Such monitoring is for legitimate purposes only and will be undertaken in accordance with a procedure agreed with employees.

Where it is believed that an employee has failed to comply with this policy, he or she will face the company's disciplinary procedure. If the employee is found to have breached the policy, he or she will face a disciplinary penalty ranging from a verbal warning to dismissal. The actual penalty applied will depend on factors such as the seriousness of the breach and the employee's disciplinary record. [These procedures will be specific to your business. They should reflect your normal operational and disciplinary processes. You should establish them from the outset and include them in your acceptable use policy.]

All company employees, contractors or temporary staff who have been granted the right to use the company's email services are required to sign this agreement confirming their understanding and acceptance of this policy.

Source: http://www.businesslink.gov.uk/bdotg/action/detail?itemId= 1076142227&type=RESOURCES

Form III-4: Drug and Alcohol Policy

Here's an example of an alcohol and drug test consent form, courtesy of the State of Nevada:

EMPLOYER: If applicable, state objective facts giving rise to the belief that the employee is under the influence of alcohol or a controlled substance.

_____

_____

I, _____ pursuant to a request by my appointing authority or as a condition of employment with the [business name] hereby give my consent to and authorize the testing laboratory to perform analytical tests deemed necessary to determine the absence or the presence of alcohol and/or drugs in my urine, blood, or breath as specified by statute and regulation.

I give my consent to release the results of the test(s) and other related medical information from the laboratory to individuals who have a need to know of the alcohol and drug testing results and to the use of all such reports or other medical information in its assessment of my employment application and/or employment status. I understand the results of the test may not be used in any criminal proceeding.

I understand that:

The appointing authority may request proof that I am taking a controlled substance as directed pursuant to a lawful prescription issued in my name. If requested, I must provide such proof within 72 hours.

I have the right to request a re-test of the initial specimen at a licensed laboratory of my choice when I have a positive test for drugs. All requests for a re-test of the sample must be made within ten (10) working days of the receipt of the original positive test result. The results of the sample must be forwarded to me by the appointing authority of the agency.

A positive test for alcohol and/or drugs, or my refusal to authorize the test(s) by signing this form, taking the specified test(s) or producing a specimen, may result in the following action:

Applicants – rejection of my employment application

Employees – referral to an employee assistance program and/or disciplinary action up to and including termination in accordance with any applicable policy.

Applicant/Employee Signature: _____

Date:_____

Supervisor's Signature
(if employee refuses to sign): _____

Date:_____

Witness' Signature
(if employee refuses to sign): _____

Date:_____

Source: dop.nv.gov/forms/ts-76.doc

Form VI-1: Employment Policy Regarding Individuals with Disabilities

A federal law called the Americans with Disabilities Act (ADA) prohibits employers from discriminating against qualified applicants and employees on the basis of disability. This law also requires employers to provide reasonable accommodations to qualified applicants and employees with disabilities, unless doing so would create an undue hardship. It is our policy to comply with this law's requirements and the requirements of all other federal, state and local laws.

We will not discriminate against qualified individuals with disabilities with respect to any condition, benefit or privilege of employment. These conditions, benefits and privileges of employment include but are not limited to those related to hiring, pay, promotion and training. In addition, it is our policy to engage in an interactive process to determine an appropriate and effective reasonable accommodation in the event that such an accommodation may be needed to enable an individual with a disability to perform essential job accommodation.

An individual with a disability who poses a direct threat to the health or safety of himself or others in the workplace is not a qualified individual with a disability under the ADA. It is our policy not to hire or retain individuals who pose a direct health or safety threat.

This policy will be implemented by the department of human resources.

Form VI-2: Request for Job Accommodation

Name of employee: _____

Job title or position: _____

Name of supervisor: _____

Date: _____

Instructions to employee: Complete this form and submit it to your supervisor or to human resources.

1. What is the physical or mental condition that requires a job accommodation?

2. How does this condition affect your ability to perform your job duties?

3. If you are requesting a specific accommodation, please identify it:

4. How will this accommodation help you perform your job?

5. Are there other alternative accommodations that you are aware of?

6. If you are requesting specific equipment and/or services, please provide any information you may have regarding vendors, cost, etc., including addresses and telephone numbers.

I understand that I may be required to submit documentation from a qualified health care or rehabilitation professional, if my disability and/or my need for accommodation are not obvious.

SIGNED: _____

DATE: _____

Form VI-3: Sample Policy Regarding Request
for Religious Accommodation

The company recognizes its legal responsibility to extend reasonable accommodation to the religious practices of its employees under Title VII of the Civil Rights Act. Pursuant to that responsibility, the company has developed this policy relating to the accommodation of potential conflicts between our employees' work schedules and religious practices. It is the company's policy to permit and encourage employees whose religious practices conflict with their work schedules to seek out a voluntary substitute in such instances. The voluntary substitute must possess substantially similar qualifications as the employee who is seeking the substitution. The company also will aid in the arrangement of a voluntary substitute where such substitution is feasible, by, for example, maintaining a central file of employees who are willing to serve as voluntary substitutes. The company will also consider flexible scheduling and transfer as potential means of accommodation where appropriate. Employees seeking accommodation under this policy should consult with their immediate supervisor.

APPENDIX A

Supreme Court Decisions
Relating to Employment Law

I. HIRING PRACTICES

♦ **The Tucker Act allows a federal contract employee to sue the United States for damages resulting from a breach of the contract in federal court. However, federal courts lack jurisdiction to hear claims for money damages by an employee not hired pursuant to an express or implied contract.**

While employed in a data processing position with the Army and Air Force Exchange Service (AAFES), an employee was selected for participation in the Executive Management Program (EMP). A regulation provided that EMP status could be withdrawn for "conduct off the job reflecting discredit on the AAFES." Subsequently, the employee was arrested off the base for possession of controlled substances. He pled guilty to four misdemeanor counts of violating state drug laws. The AAFES then discharged him. After his administrative appeal was denied, he sued in federal court, alleging that his due process rights and his right to a free and impartial appeal pursuant to AAFES regulations were infringed. The district court dismissed the case, but the U.S. Court of Appeals reversed, finding that the Tucker Act (which gives federal courts jurisdiction over certain suits against the United States founded upon express or implied contracts) provided a basis for jurisdiction. The U.S. Supreme Court granted review.

The Supreme Court held that the Tucker Act did not confer jurisdiction over the ex-employee's claim for money damages. The ex-employee had not worked for the AAFES under an express contract. Rather, he had been appointed to his positions. Thus, the court of appeals had erred by implying a contract based on the AAFES regulations. Tucker Act jurisdiction could not be imposed as a result of those regulations. The Court reversed the appellate court's decision, holding that the ex-employee was not allowed to sue in federal court over his termination. *Army and Air Force Exchange Service v. Sheehan*, 456 U.S. 728, 102 S.Ct. 2118, 72 L.Ed.2d 520 (1982).

♦ **The Privileges and Immunities Clause allows discrimination against citizens of another state if the governmental body doing the discriminating has a substantial reason for the difference in treatment and if the degree of discrimination bears a close relationship to the reason.**

Acting pursuant to a statewide affirmative action program, the Camden,

New Jersey, City Council adopted an ordinance setting minority hiring goals on all public works contracts. In addition, the ordinance required at least 40% of the employees of contractors and subcontractors working on city construction projects to be Camden residents. After the state treasury department approved the ordinance, an association of labor organizations filed an appeal. The New Jersey Supreme Court rejected the unions' challenges to the ordinance's validity. The court held that the Privileges and Immunities Clause of the Constitution did not apply because the ordinance only discriminated on the basis of municipal residency, not state residency.

On appeal to the U.S. Supreme Court, the Court noted that the municipal ordinance was properly subject to the restrictions and commands of the Privileges and Immunities Clause. A municipality is merely a political subdivision of a state; what the state cannot do directly, the municipality cannot do by derived authority. Even though the ordinance mostly affected New Jersey residents who lived outside Camden (who could not bring a Privileges and Immunities Clause challenge because that was only for citizens of other states), there were some out-of-state residents affected to bring the challenge. The Court reversed and remanded for a determination of whether the city's justification for the ordinance was sufficient to allow the difference in treatment for out-of-state residents. *United Building & Construction Trades Council v. Mayor and Council of City of Camden,* 465 U.S. 208, 104 S.Ct. 1020, 79 L.Ed.2d 249 (1984).

II. COMPENSATION AND BENEFITS

A. Compensation

1. Fair Labor Standards Act (FLSA)

a. Scope

♦   The FLSA was amended in 1974 to exempt from minimum wage and maximum hours rules persons "employed in domestic service employment to provide companionship services for individuals ... unable to care for themselves." A Department of Labor regulation includes in the exemption companionship workers employed by an agency other than the family or household using the services. A domestic worker in New York who provided companionship services sued her former employer (a third-party agency) for minimum and overtime wages. The case reached the U.S. Supreme Court, which held that the third-party regulation was valid and binding, meaning **the worker was not entitled to minimum or overtime wages**. *Long Island Care at Home, Ltd. v. Coke,* 551 U.S. 158, 127 S.Ct. 2339, 168 L.Ed.2d 54 (2007).

♦   Employees of meat and poultry processing plants in Washington and Maine brought class action lawsuits against the company who owned the plants, alleging FLSA violations. They asserted that the company owed them for the time they spent waiting to change into and out of required specialized clothing and safety gear, and that it owed them for the time it took to walk between the locker room and the production floor. The case reached the U.S. Supreme Court, which determined that **the time spent walking between the locker room and the production floor was compensable**. The Portal-to-Portal Act does not exclude such time from the FLSA's coverage. Further, the time spent waiting to doff the protective gear was covered by the FLSA. However, the time spent waiting to don the protective gear before the start of each shift was not compensable. Donning and doffing gear that is integral and indispensable to employees' work is a "principal activity" under the Portal-to-Portal Act, but waiting to don the first piece of gear is two steps removed from the productive activity on the assembly line. *IBP, Inc. v. Alvarez,* 546 U.S. 21, 126 S.Ct. 514, 163 L.Ed.2d 288 (2005).

♦ **In *National League of Cities v. Usery,* a case that has since been overruled, the Supreme Court held that the Fair Labor Standards Act's (FLSA's) 1974 amendments (which made the FLSA applicable to almost all public employees) were invalid with respect to employees working in traditional governmental function jobs. The Court stated that the law impaired the states' abilities to structure their employer-employee relations.**

In 1974, Congress amended the FLSA and broadened its coverage to include almost all public employees. Various cities and states and the National League of Cities brought an action in a federal district court to challenge the validity of the amendments, asserting that intergovernmental immunity prevented Congress from so amending the act. A three-judge district court convened and dismissed the complaint. Further appeal was taken to the U.S. Supreme Court. On appeal, the Supreme Court held that the 1974 amendments operated to obstruct the states' abilities to structure their employer-employee relationships with respect to areas of traditional government functions. The amendments were invalid because they impaired the states' abilities to function effectively in a federal system. Essentially, the Court determined that Congress could not directly force the states to utilize only Congress' means of conducting integral governmental functions. The Court thus reversed the three-judge court's decision and held the amendments invalid. *National League of Cities v. Usery,* 426 U.S. 833, 96 S.Ct. 2465, 49 L.Ed.2d 245 (1976).

♦ **The following case overturned *National League of Cities v. Usery,* above, by holding that it was permissible to require state and local government employers to comply with the Fair Labor Standards Act (FLSA) despite the fact that many of the jobs were in areas that were traditionally governmental. Forcing compliance did not destroy states' sovereignty.**

The San Antonio Metropolitan Transit Authority (SAMTA), a public mass-transit authority, provided transportation to the San Antonio area with the help of substantial financial assistance under the Urban Mass Transportation Act. In 1979, the Wage and Hour Administration of the Department of Labor issued an opinion that SAMTA's operations were not immune from the minimum wage and overtime requirements of the FLSA. SAMTA filed a suit in federal district court, asserting under *National League of Cities v. Usery* that it was exempt from the requirements of the FLSA. The district court agreed, and appeal was taken directly to the U.S. Supreme Court.

The Supreme Court noted that drawing boundaries between areas of traditional governmental functions and those areas that were not traditionally run by the government was not only unworkable, but inconsistent with established principles of federalism. Forcing local governments to comply with the FLSA in areas not traditionally governmental, and allowing state immunity for functions that were deemed traditionally governmental, would lead to inconsistent results. Further, the Court noted that the FLSA requirements were not destructive of state sovereignty or violative of the Constitution. Accordingly, the Court overruled *National League of Cities* and reversed the decision of the district court. *Garcia v. San Antonio Metropolitan Transit Authority*, 469 U.S. 528, 105 S.Ct. 1005, 83 L.Ed.2d 1016 (1985).

◆   **In 1985, the Supreme Court held that the Fair Labor Standards Act (FLSA) applied to a nonprofit religious organization. The "associates" involved with the organization were really employees and thus had to be paid at least minimum wage (either in the form of cash or benefits). If they chose to, they could return any payments made to them, but the decision had to be theirs.**

A nonprofit religious organization derived most of its income from the operation of commercial businesses staffed by its "associates." These people, former drug addicts and criminals, received no cash salaries, but were provided with food, clothing, shelter and other benefits. The Secretary of Labor filed an action in federal court against the organization and its officers, alleging violations of the FLSA. The district court held that the organization was an "enterprise" within the meaning of the FLSA. Further, under the economic reality test of employment, the associates were employees of the organization protected by the FLSA. The U.S. Court of Appeals affirmed the finding of liability by the district court, and the case reached the U.S. Supreme Court.

The Court noted that the FLSA contained no express or implied exception for commercial activities conducted by religious or other nonprofit organizations. Further, even though the associates here involved claimed that they were not employees, they did expect compensation of a sort for their work; thus, the economic reality was that they were employees under the FLSA. Finally, the Court held that application of the FLSA did not violate the Free Exercise Clause or the Establishment Clause. The FLSA did not require the payment of cash wages, so the employees could still be paid in the form of benefits. Also, they could return any payments made to them if they so wished, and provided it was voluntary, this would not violate the FLSA. Nor did the FLSA's recordkeeping requirements inhibit religious activities undertaken with a business purpose. The Court therefore determined that the FLSA applied to the organization, and affirmed the lower court's decision. *Tony & Susan Alamo Foundation v. Secretary of Labor,* 471 U.S. 290, 105 S.Ct. 1953, 85 L.Ed.2d 278 (1985).

b. Procedures

♦ **The Supreme Court upheld the civil penalty provisions of the Fair Labor Standards Act (FLSA) against constitutional attack because, even though the agency that assessed the fines received the fines, no government official stood to gain from their imposition.**

A corporation that managed about 40 restaurants was found to have committed over 150 violations of the FLSA's child labor provisions. The administrator who assessed the fine against the corporation added an amount for willful violation of the FLSA. However, an administrative law judge reviewed the evidence and determined that the violations were not willful. He reduced the total assessment. The corporation then brought suit in federal court, challenging the civil penalty provisions of the FLSA as violative of due process because the fines went to the agency that assessed them (as reimbursement for enforcement expenses) and this created an impermissible risk of bias. The district court granted summary judgment to the employer, and the U.S. Supreme Court consented to review the case.

The Court held that the section of the FLSA that provided for civil penalties did not violate the Due Process Clause. No government official stood to profit economically from the vigorous enforcement of the FLSA's child labor provisions. Thus, there was little chance that the administrator's judgment would be distorted by the prospect of gain. Further, the agency's administration of the FLSA minimized any potential for bias. Accordingly, the Court reversed the district court's decision and remanded the case. *Marshall v. Jerrico, Inc.,* 446 U.S. 238, 100 S.Ct. 1610, 64 L.Ed.2d 182 (1980).

♦ **Rights arising out of the Fair Labor Standards Act (FLSA) are individual rights. They cannot be waived by the existence of a collective bargaining system. If an employee believes that his or her employer is violating the FLSA, the question can be litigated in court despite a collective bargaining agreement to the contrary.**

Truck drivers, employed by a freight company, were required to conduct safety inspections of their trucks, and transport them to a repair facility if they failed the inspections. They were not paid for their time doing this. Their union filed a grievance on their behalf, but a joint committee rejected the grievance. The truck drivers then filed suit in federal district court, asserting that their time was compensable under the FLSA. They also claimed that the union had breached its duty of fair representation. The court addressed only the fair representation claim, holding against the truck drivers. The U.S. Court of Appeals affirmed, and the case came before the U.S. Supreme Court.

The Court held that the drivers' claims under the FLSA were not barred by the submission of their grievance to the joint committee. Here, the rights at issue arose out of a federal statute, not out of the collective bargaining agreement. The district court should have addressed their claims under the FLSA. The collective bargaining process applies to members of a collective organization, but the rights asserted here were individual rights protected by Congress. They could not be waived. FLSA rights are best protected in a judicial forum, not by an arbitrator. The Court reversed the court of appeals' decision. *Barrentine v. Arkansas-Best Freight System*, 450 U.S. 728, 101 S.Ct. 1437, 67 L.Ed.2d 641 (1981).

♦ **In *McLaughlin*, below, the Court held that in order to apply the three-year statute of limitations for willful violations of the Fair Labor Standards Act (FLSA), the employer had to know or show reckless disregard for the matter of whether its conduct was prohibited by the FLSA. This was the same standard as enunciated earlier in *Trans World Airlines, Inc. v. Thurston*, 469 U.S. 111, 105 S.Ct. 613, 83 L.Ed.2d 523 (1985).**

A shoe manufacturer employed seven mechanics to maintain and repair its equipment. In 1984, the Secretary of Labor filed a complaint against the company, alleging that it had failed to pay those employees overtime compensation as required by the FLSA. The company asserted that the two-year statute of limitations precluded the action, but the secretary maintained that the three-year statute (for willful violations of the FLSA) applied. A federal district court agreed with the secretary, but the U.S. Court of Appeals, Third Circuit, vacated its decision, holding that only where the employer knew or showed reckless disregard for the matter of whether its conduct was prohibited by the FLSA would the three-year statute of limitations apply. On further appeal to the U.S. Supreme Court, this standard was upheld. *McLaughlin v. Richland Shoe Co.*, 486 U.S. 128, 108 S.Ct. 1677, 100 L.Ed.2d 115 (1988).

♦ **The Court held that a company could remove a Fair Labor Standards Act (FLSA) action to federal court over the objections of the employee who filed the action in state court.**

A concrete company employee brought a lawsuit in a Florida state court under the FLSA, seeking unpaid wages, liquidated damages, prejudgment interest and attorneys' fees against his employer. The company removed the case to federal court, and the employee sought to have the case remanded to state court, citing 29 U.S.C. § 216(b), which provides that an action for relief under the FLSA "may be maintained ... in any Federal or State court of competent jurisdiction." The court denied his motion, and the Eleventh Circuit affirmed. The U.S. Supreme Court also affirmed. It held that Section 216(b) did not bar removal of a case from state to federal court. Here, despite the employee's argument that an action for a small amount could be hindered by removal to a distant federal court (thereby increasing litigation costs) where it would be more difficult for employees to vindicate their rights effectively, the Court refused to rule that the employee could block removal of the case to federal court. *Breuer v. Jim's Concrete of Brevard, Inc.*, 538 U.S. 691, 123 S.Ct. 1882, 155 L.Ed.2d 923 (2003).

c. Overtime

♦ **In the following case, the Supreme Court ruled that marine engineers and members of an engineering department aboard a seafood processing vessel were "seamen" and thus exempted from the overtime provisions of the Fair Labor Standards Act (FLSA).**

A group of employees who worked in the engineering department of a seafood company on a barge that processed fish sued their employer to recover overtime benefits under the FLSA. The employees did not perform any hands-on processing or packing of fish. As members of the engineering department, they were responsible for maintaining all systems for support and continuous operation of the vessel while at moorage or under way. They were on call 24 hours a day to perform work at a moment's notice if necessary to keep the vessel operating. Also, they each performed tasks that conformed to those expected of Coast Guard licensed personnel. However, they maintained that they were not seamen because their duties did not "primarily aid navigation of the vessel." A federal district court held that they were not entitled to protection under the FLSA because they were "seamen" and thus exempted from the provisions of the act. The U.S. Court of Appeals, Ninth Circuit, reversed, holding that the employees were not seamen, but instead were industrial maintenance employees. Accordingly, the court found that the FLSA applied to them. Appeal was taken to the U.S. Supreme Court. The Court held that the court of appeals had improperly arrived at its judgment. The appellate court should only have overturned the district court's findings of fact if they were clearly erroneous. Here, each of the employees was a crew member who performed maritime work in navigable waters. Thus, they had been properly deemed seamen by the district court. *Icicle Seafoods, Inc. v. Worthington,* 475 U.S. 709, 106 S.Ct. 1527, 89 L.Ed.2d 739 (1986).

♦ **Section 15(a)(1) of the Fair Labor Standards Act (FLSA) prohibits "any person" from introducing into interstate commerce goods produced in violation of the minimum wage or overtime pay provisions of the act. In the case below, the Supreme Court held that "any person" included secured creditors of violators who acquired "hot goods" under a security agreement.**

A corporation acquired a security interest in a manufacturer's inventory. When the manufacturer began to fail financially, the corporation took possession. However, because some of the inventory had been manufactured during a period in which employees were not paid, the Department of Labor sought to prohibit the sale or transportation of the "hot goods" in interstate commerce. The case came before the U.S. Supreme Court, which held that Section 15(a)(1) of the FLSA, which prohibits "any person" from introducing into interstate commerce goods produced in violation of the minimum wage or overtime provisions of the act, applied to the corporation here. Even though the corporation was just a secured creditor, it was still subject to the restrictions set forth by the act. *Citicorp Industrial Credit, Inc. v. Brock,* 483 U.S. 27, 107 S.Ct. 2694, 97 L.Ed.2d 23 (1987).

♦ **The Fair Labor Standards Act (FLSA) allows public employers to compensate their employees with extra time off in lieu of overtime pay – either under collective bargaining agreements or under individual agreements between employers and employees. The Court held that a Texas public employer could provide compensatory time off pursuant to individual agreements even though the employees had designated a union** representative (because the state prohibited public sector collective bargaining). The FLSA requires employers to pay employees at least time-and-one-half for all overtime hours. However, a congressionally enacted exception allows public employers to compensate their employees with extra time off (comp time) instead of overtime pay. The relevant subsection of the congressional amendment allows comp time "in lieu of" overtime pay when the public agency and representatives of the employees reach such an agreement. In the case of employees not covered by the above provision, an employer and an employee may individually agree to such an arrangement. A Texas sheriff's union represented more than 400 deputy sheriffs. However, the union was prohibited by Texas law from entering into collective bargaining agreements with the county. Each employee was bound by form agreements individually entered into with the county. These form agreements provided, in part, that employees working overtime would be compensated with extra time off. The union filed suit in a U.S. district court alleging that the workers' representation by the union precluded the individual agreements providing for comp time rather than overtime pay. The district court entered summary judgment for the county and the U.S. Court of Appeals, Fifth Circuit, affirmed, albeit on different reasoning. The union appealed to the U.S. Supreme Court.

The issue on appeal was "whether a public employer in a state that prohibits public sector collective bargaining may take advantage of that exception when its employees have designated a union representative." First, the Court rejected the narrow reading of the statute espoused by the county. The county had argued that individual agreements were precluded only when the employees were bound by applicable provisions of a collective bargaining agreement. The Court deemed such an interpretation contrary to the statute's overall structure. Congress had attempted to restrict use of individual agreements "to a limited class of employee." The Court also rejected the union's argument that the mere selection of a representative, regardless of his or her ability to enter into an agreement, precluded individual agreements between the employee and the county. Instead, it determined that individual agreements were precluded only when an elected representative had the authority to negotiate the use of comp time via a collective bargaining agreement. Since the union did not have authority under local law to enter into a collective bargaining agreement, individual agreements authorizing comp time were permitted. The holding of the court of appeals was affirmed. *Moreau v. Klevenhagen*, 508 U.S. 22, 113 S.Ct. 1905, 123 L.Ed.2d 584 (1993).

♦ **Under the Fair Labor Standards Act (FLSA), the employer must engage in an actual practice of making pay deductions or maintain an employment policy that creates a significant likelihood of such deductions in order to remove the employee from the exemption for salaried employees. An inadvertent deduction or deduction for reasons other than lack of work will not remove the exemption if the employer reimburses the employee for the deductions and promises to comply in the future.**

Several Missouri police officers employed by the St. Louis Police Department filed suit against the Board of Police Commissioners in federal district court, seeking payment of overtime wages under the FLSA. The officers contended that they did not meet the exemption for salaried employees because under the terms of the department manual their compensation could be reduced for disciplinary infractions related to the "quality or quantity" of work performed. They also claimed that they did not meet the other requirement for exempt status: that their duties be of an executive, administrative or professional nature. The district court found that the officers were paid on a salary basis, although not all of the officers satisfied the duties criteria. The U.S. Court of Appeals, Eighth Circuit, affirmed in part and reversed in part, holding that both the salary basis and duties tests were satisfied as to all the officers. The U.S. Supreme Court granted certiorari.

The Court found that the "no disciplinary deductions" element of the salary basis test applied to public sector employees. Moreover, the Secretary of Labor had reasonably interpreted the salary basis test to deny exempt status when either an actual practice of making pay deductions exists or an employment policy creates a "significant likelihood" of such deductions. An inadvertent deduction or deduction for reasons other than lack of work will not remove the exemption if the employer reimburses the employee for such deductions and promises to comply in the future. Furthermore, the regulations do not require immediate payment of the reimbursement. The Court affirmed the decision of the court of appeals. *Auer v. Robbins*, 519 U.S. 452, 117 S.Ct. 905, 137 L.Ed.2d 79 (1997).

♦ **In a decision affecting all state and local government employers, the U.S. Supreme Court rejected the appeal of a group of Texas county deputy sheriffs who asserted that their employer could not force them to use accumulated compensatory time under the Fair Labor Standards Act Amendments of 1985. The court held that the Fair Labor Standards Act (FLSA) does not prevent public employers from specifying when employees may use their comp time.**

Congress amended the FLSA in 1985 to permit states and their political subdivisions to compensate their employees for working overtime at one and one-half their rate of pay for every hour in excess of 40 per week. Employers may agree with their employees either orally or in writing to provide compensatory time off work instead of cash compensation. The act requires employers to honor requests to use compensatory time within a reasonable time period, so long as it does not disrupt the employer's operations. FLSA regulations limit the compensatory time that an employee may accrue. After the maximum is reached, the employer must pay the employee for additional hours worked. A group of Texas county deputy sheriffs agreed individually to accept compensatory time off in lieu of cash compensation for working overtime. The county implemented a budgetary protection policy under which supervisors set a maximum number of hours that could be accumulated by an employee. Employees were advised of the maximum and asked to take voluntary steps to reduce comp time accumulations. Supervisors could specify that employees take their compensatory time at scheduled times. The deputies sued the county in a federal district court, alleging that the compelled use of comp time violated the FLSA. The court awarded summary judgment in their favor, but the county obtained reversal of the order on appeal to the U.S. Court of Appeals for the Fifth Circuit.

The deputies, with the support of the U.S. Department of Labor, appealed to the U.S. Supreme Court, contending that the FLSA implicitly prohibits public employers from compelling their employees to take accrued comp time. The court found that the FLSA establishes "a minimum guarantee that an employee will be able to make some use of compensatory time when he requests to use it." However, the law does not expressly or impliedly limit a public employer from scheduling employees to take time off work with full pay. Because the FLSA was silent on the matter of employer-compelled comp time usage, the Court refused to find that the county policy violated the statute, holding that "under the FLSA an employer is free to require an employee to take time off work and an employer is also free to use the money it would have paid in wages to cash out accrued compensatory time." The court affirmed the Fifth Circuit's judgment. *Christensen v. Harris County*, 529 U.S. 576, 120 S.Ct. 1655, 146 L.Ed.2d 621 (2000).

B. Benefits

1. Health Benefits

◆   **In the following case, the Supreme Court held that a state law requiring the provision of certain minimal healthcare benefits was not preempted by the National Labor Relations Act (NLRA) or the Employee Retirement Income Security Act (ERISA).**

A Massachusetts law required that certain minimum mental healthcare benefits be provided to residents of the state who were insured under a general healthcare plan that covered hospital and surgical expenses. Two insurers who provided health insurance to unions or employers contended that they did not have to comply with the law because ERISA or the NLRA preempted it. A trial court required the insurers to provide the coverage mandated by the law, and the Supreme Judicial Court of Massachusetts affirmed.

The U.S. Supreme Court heard the case and determined that the Massachusetts law was a law that regulated insurance. Accordingly, it was not preempted by ERISA. Further, the law was not subject to the NLRA because even though it set a minimum employment standard, it was unrelated to the collective bargaining process and had only an indirect effect on the right of self organization established by the NLRA – it did not limit that right. Accordingly, the lower court's decision was affirmed, and the state law was upheld. The insurers had to provide the minimum coverage mandated by the statute. *Metropolitan Life Insurance Co. v. Massachusetts*, 471 U.S. 724, 105 S.Ct. 2380, 85 L.Ed.2d 728 (1985).

◆   **The Supreme Court held that self-funded employee benefit plans are not "insurance" for the purpose of interpreting state insurance laws. Such laws are "saved" from preemption by the Employee Retirement Income Security Act (ERISA). In the following case, the Court held that since the plan was not insurance, ERISA preempted state regulation of it.**

A corporation operated a self-funded healthcare plan under which plan members agreed to reimburse it for benefits paid if the member recovered on a claim in a liability action against a third party. The daughter of a plan member was seriously injured in an automobile accident, and the plan paid part of her medical expenses. A negligence action against the driver of the vehicle in which the daughter was injured settled. The plan member refused to reimburse the plan, asserting that Pennsylvania law precluded subrogation by the plan. The member sought and obtained a declaratory judgment that the state statute prohibited the plan from enforcing the subrogation provision. The U.S. Court of Appeals affirmed, and the case came before the U.S. Supreme Court.

The Court stated that ERISA preempted the application of the Pennsylvania law, and that the plan could seek subrogation. Since Congress clearly intended to exempt from state regulation ERISA employee benefit plans, the state statute could not stand here. State laws that directly regulate insurance are "saved" from preemption, but this does not apply to self-funded employee benefit plans because they are not insurance for purposes of such laws. *FMC Corp. v. Holliday*, 498 U.S. 52, 111 S.Ct. 403, 112 L.Ed.2d 356 (1990).

♦ **Section 402(b)(3) of the Employee Retirement Income Security Act (ERISA) requires every employee benefit plan to provide a procedure for amending the plan, and for identifying the persons who have authority to amend the plan. The Supreme Court held that a plan could state: "the company reserves the right to amend the plan." This satisfied the requirements of Section 402(b)(3).**

A corporation maintained and administered a single-employer health plan for its employees. In response to rising healthcare costs, it discontinued coverage for retirees upon the termination of operations at the facility from which they had retired. After closing a New Jersey facility, the corporation's executive vice president notified retirees of the facility by letter that their post-retirement health benefits were being terminated. The retirees filed a lawsuit against the corporation in the U.S. District Court for the District of New Jersey, alleging that the termination of benefits violated Section 402(b)(3) of ERISA, 29 U.S.C. § 1102(b)(3). Section 402(b)(3) required employee benefit plans to have "a procedure for amending such plan, and for identifying the persons who have authority to amend the plan." The retirees claimed that the company's summary plan description lacked a valid amendment procedure and that its action constituted a plan amendment. The district court agreed with the retirees, and ordered the corporation to pay them over $2.6 million in benefits. The U.S. Court of Appeals, Third Circuit, affirmed the district court's decision and the corporation appealed to the U.S. Supreme Court.

The Supreme Court agreed with the corporation that the minimal language in its summary plan description satisfied the amendment procedure requirement of ERISA Section 402(b)(3). Under the plan description, the corporation "reserve[d] the right at any time to amend the plan..." ERISA created no substantive entitlement to employer-provided welfare benefits and employers were allowed to freely modify, amend or terminate welfare plans under most circumstances. The Court reasoned that a plan that simply identified the person or persons having authority to amend a plan necessarily indicated the amendment procedure. The reservation clause contained in the corporation's summary plan description identified "the company" as the person having amendment authority. It was then only necessary to apply corporate law principles to identify the particular individual or corporate committee with decision-making authority. It was unnecessary to further specify the names of individuals or committees within a corporation to satisfy ERISA, and for single-employer health plans it was sufficient to identify the employer as the entity having amendment authority. The Court reversed and remanded the court of appeals' decision, directing the court to consider on remand whether the corporation had complied with its valid amendment procedure. Under this fact inquiry, the court was to apply corporate law principles to determine whether the appropriate corporate officials had actually approved the amendments contained in the revised summary plan description. *Curtiss-Wright Corp. v. Schoonejongen,* 514 U.S. 73, 115 S.Ct. 1223, 131 L.Ed.2d 94 (1995).

♦ **The Supreme Court found that the Consolidated Omnibus Budget Reconciliation Act of 1985 (COBRA) amendments require group health plan sponsors, including employers, to provide continuation coverage to an employee covered under his or her spouse's plan.**

COBRA amended the Employee Retirement Income Security Act (ERISA) by authorizing qualified beneficiaries of employer group health plans to obtain continuation coverage in specified circumstances including employment termination. A Missouri medical corporation discharged an employee with cancer who was covered under its group health plan. It informed the employee that he had COBRA continuation coverage rights under the plan and could remain covered if he elected to do so and made the necessary payments. The former employee participated in the plan for six months, at which time the employer notified him that he was not entitled to COBRA benefits because he was already covered by a group health plan supplied by his wife's employer as of his election date. The former employee commenced a federal district court action against his former employer, health plan and plan administrators for wrongful denial of coverage. The award of summary judgment to the employer was affirmed by the U.S. Court of Appeals, Eighth Circuit. The employee appealed to the U.S. Supreme Court.

The Court stated that the COBRA amendments to ERISA require group health plan sponsors, including employers, to provide continuation coverage when plan beneficiaries might otherwise lose coverage upon the occurrence of a qualifying event, such as employment termination or divorce. COBRA coverage may cease on the date on which the qualified beneficiary first becomes covered, after the date of election, under any other group health plan which does not limit or exclude a beneficiary's preexisting health conditions. The former employer and plan argued that the employee was "first" covered by his wife's plan after the time of the election. The Court disagreed, finding that the employee had been continuously covered by his wife's group health plan and did not "first become" covered under the wife's plan after the date of election. Because the former employer could not cut off the former employee's COBRA coverage, the Court vacated and remanded the lower court judgments. *Geissal v. Moore Medical Corp.,* 524 U.S. 74, 118 S.Ct. 1869, 141 L.Ed.2d 64 (1998).

♦ **The U.S. Supreme Court determined that an employee benefit plan cannot sue in federal court to recoup medical expenses paid to a beneficiary who later won a settlement from a third party.**
A woman was left a quadriplegic after a 1994 car accident. At the time, the woman was covered by her then-husband's health insurance plan from Great-West Life & Annuity Insurance Co., which paid out more than $411,000 in medical expenses. However, the plan included a reimbursement provision that permitted Great-West to recover any third-party payments made to the woman up to the amount of benefits paid out by the plan. In 1993 the woman sued Hyundai Motors and other parties allegedly responsible for the accident. An agreement was reached for $650,000, and the California Superior Court approved the settlement. The court ordered the woman to pay Great-West $13,828 as her share of the medical costs. Great-West did not accept this payment, instead electing to sue the woman in Los Angeles federal court, seeking total reimbursement for the benefits it had paid out under the Employee Retirement Income Security Act (ERISA). A federal district court granted the woman summary judgment after finding that the fiduciary of a plan may only be reimbursed for a *pro rata* share of a beneficiary's medical expenses. The Ninth Circuit affirmed in a unanimous opinion.

The Supreme Court, in a 5–4 decision, concluded the Ninth Circuit was correct in finding that under ERISA the benefit plan was blocked from dipping into the personal injury settlement. Under Section 502(a)(3) of ERISA, Great West was only entitled to equitable relief. Because the relief Great-West was seeking, reimbursement for benefits paid, was not equitable relief, Great-West's suit was not permitted under ERISA. The Court rejected Great-West's assertions that the relief sought was equitable, finding no support for this argument. The amicus U.S.'s assertion that Great-West's suit should be deemed one for equitable relief under the common law of trusts was also rejected. *Great-West Life & Annuity Insurance Co. v. Knudson,* 534 U.S. 204, 122 S.Ct. 708, 151 L.Ed.2d 635 (2002).

III. DISCRIMINATION

A. Race and National Origin Discrimination

1. Scope and Standard of Proof

♦ Two African-American employees in Alabama sued under Title VII when they were passed over for promotions in favor of two white employees. The plant manager called them "boy" when talking to them. A jury ruled in their favor, but the Eleventh Circuit held that the use of the word "boy" by itself was not evidence of discrimination. The U.S. Supreme Court held that **the use of the word "boy" by itself could evidence racial animus**, given the context of the remark, inflection or tone of voice, local custom and historical usage. Also, the employees did not have to prove that their qualifications were so superior to the white employees' that the difference virtually jumped off the page and slapped the court in the face. A better test was needed for determining pretext in the qualifications context – e.g., were the plaintiff's qualifications "clearly superior"? Or could no reasonable person have chosen the selected candidate over the plaintiff? The Court remanded the case. *Ash v. Tyson Foods, Inc.*, 546 U.S. 454, 126 S.Ct. 1195, 163 L.Ed.2d 1053 (2006).

♦   **One of the most important Supreme Court cases in the area of civil rights is *Griggs v. Duke Power Co.*, where the Court held that Title VII forbids not only practices adopted with a discriminatory *motive*, but also those that have a discriminatory effect. Upon showing discriminatory effect, the burden shifts to the employer to prove that business necessity required the employment practice.**

In *Griggs*, a group of black employees at a North Carolina power plant sued under Title VII of the Civil Rights Act of 1964, challenging their employer's requirement that employees possess a high school diploma or pass an intelligence test as a condition of employment in or transfer to jobs at the plant. Section 703 of the act authorized the use of an ability test, so long as it was not intended or used to discriminate. The district court held that the employer's prior policy of racial discrimination had ended, and the U.S. Court of Appeals, Fourth Circuit, upheld that determination. The employees appealed to the U.S. Supreme Court.

The Supreme Court held that Title VII requires the elimination of artificial, arbitrary, and unnecessary barriers to employment that discriminate on the basis of race. If a practice excludes minorities and cannot be shown to be related to job performance, it is prohibited, even if the employer lacked discriminatory intent. Title VII does not preclude the use of testing or measuring procedures so long as they are demonstrably a reasonable measure of job performance. In this case, the procedures were not related to job performance. Therefore, they violated Title VII. The Court reversed the lower court decisions. *Griggs v. Duke Power Co.*, 401 U.S. 424, 91 S.Ct. 849, 28 L.Ed.2d 158 (1971).

♦   **The Supreme Court case that established the standard of proof for discrimination lawsuits is *McDonnell Douglas Corp. v. Green*, where the Court stated that an employee alleging discrimination must show that he or she belongs to a protected minority, has applied and is qualified for an available position, was rejected, and that the employer continued to seek applicants with the complainant's qualifications.**

In this case, a black civil rights activist engaged in disruptive and illegal activity against his former employer as part of his protest that his discharge, and the employer's general hiring practices, were racially motivated. Soon after, the employer advertised for qualified personnel, but rejected the activist's reemployment application on the grounds of his illegal conduct. The activist filed a complaint with the Equal Employment Opportunity Commission (EEOC), claiming a Title VII violation. The EEOC found that there was reasonable cause to believe that the discharge violated Section 704(a) of Title VII, which forbids discrimination against applicants or employees for protesting against discriminatory employment conditions. The activist eventually sued, and a federal district court ruled that his activity was not protected by Section 703(a). The court dismissed the Section 703 claim because the EEOC had made no finding with respect to that section. The court of appeals affirmed, and also stated that Section 703(a)(1), which prohibits discrimination in any employment decision, could also be used to make a viable claim. The employer sought review from the U.S. Supreme Court.

The Supreme Court held that a reasonable cause finding by the EEOC is not necessary in order for a party to raise Section 703(a)(1) at trial. It further held that in a private, nonclass-action complaint under Title VII the complaining party has the burden of establishing a *prima facie* case, which can be satisfied by showing that he belongs to a racial minority, has applied and was qualified for a job the employer was trying to fill, was rejected, and the employer continued to seek applicants with the complainant's qualifications. Even though the employee had done this, the employer carried its burden in showing that it had a reason for rejecting the applicant. The Court remanded the case, but allowed the activist an opportunity to show that the employer's reason for refusal was simply a pretext for a racially discriminatory decision. *McDonnell Douglas Corp. v. Green,* 411 U.S. 792, 93 S.Ct. 1817, 36 L.Ed.2d 668 (1973).

◆ **In 1974, the Supreme Court held that an employee could seek a trial under Title VII after having submitted a claim of discrimination to arbitration. However, even though the arbitration was not binding, the arbitrator's decision could be introduced as evidence in the Title VII suit.**

A company fired a black drill operator for producing too many defective or unusable parts. The employee filed a grievance under the collective bargaining agreement (CBA) in force, claiming racial discrimination. He also filed a complaint with the Colorado Civil Rights Commission. Following an arbitration hearing, conducted pursuant to the CBA, the arbitrator found that the discharge had been for cause. When the EEOC found no reasonable cause to believe Title VII had been violated, the employee brought suit in federal court. The court granted summary judgment to the company, holding that the employee was bound by the decision at the arbitration hearing. The U.S. Court of Appeals affirmed, and the case came before the U.S. Supreme Court.

The Supreme Court held that the employee's right to a new trial was not foreclosed by the prior submission of his claim to arbitration. Title VII was designed to supplement existing laws and instructions relating to employment discrimination. The right to sue in court was an independent right not precluded by arbitration. The Court also held, however, that the arbitrator's decision could be admitted as evidence against the employee in the Title VII suit. The Court reversed the lower courts' decisions. *Alexander v. Gardner-Denver Co.,* 415 U.S. 36, 94 S.Ct. 1011, 39 L.Ed.2d 147 (1974).

◆ **In *Albermarle Paper Co. v. Moody,* the Supreme Court held that employment testing which, although it appeared to be neutral on its face, was discriminatory against minorities, had to be justified by business necessity. The complaining party could then demonstrate that there were other less discriminatory means of achieving the same result available to the employer.**

A group of black employees sued their North Carolina employer and the employees' union for Title VII violations. The major issues were the plant's seniority system, its program of employment testing, and back pay. The federal district court found that the employees had been locked in the lower-paying job classifications and ordered a new system of plant-wide seniority. The court refused to order back pay. It also refused to limit the plant's testing program, stating that the tests were job related. The employees appealed the back pay and employment issues, and the court of appeals ruled in their favor. The plant appealed to the U.S. Supreme Court.

The Supreme Court held that if there is unlawful discrimination, back pay should only be denied for reasons that would not frustrate the purposes of Title VII. The absence of bad faith on the employer's part is not a sufficient reason for denying back pay. In this case, however, there was some question about the timing of the demand for back pay, so the issue would remain open on remand. With regard to employment testing, the Court stated that testing must be correlated with important elements of work or be relevant to the job. The testing in this case was defective because it failed to meet these standards. *Albemarle Paper Co. v. Moody,* 422 U.S. 405, 95 S.Ct. 2362, 45 L.Ed.2d 280 (1975).

♦   **In 1976, the Supreme Court stated that Title VII and 42 U.S.C. § 1981 apply to whites as well as to nonwhites in the private employment context. When policies are applied unevenly to different races, Title VII is violated, regardless of whether the class more heavily impacted is whites.**

Two white employees of a transportation company were discharged for misappropriating cargo from one of the company's shipments. However, a black employee, charged with the same offense, was not terminated. After grievance proceedings were unsuccessful, the two employees sued the company and their union for discriminating against them by retaining the black employee while letting them go. A federal district court dismissed the complaint, finding that 42 U.S.C. § 1981 (which prohibits discrimination in the making and enforcement of contracts) did not apply to discrimination against whites, and that no valid claim had been stated under Title VII. The U.S. Court of Appeals affirmed, and the case reached the U.S. Supreme Court.

The Supreme Court held that both Title VII and Section 1981 apply to whites as much as to nonwhites in the private employment context. While theft of cargo may warrant discharging an employee, such a policy must be applied evenly to both whites and nonwhites or Title VII is violated. Here, if all other things were equal, then the union and the company would have unlawfully discriminated against the employees – the union by shirking its duty to properly represent the employees, and the company by discharging only the white employees. Since the case should not have been dismissed, the Court reversed and remanded it. *McDonald v. Santa Fe Trail Transportation Co.,* 427 U.S. 273, 96 S.Ct. 2574, 49 L.Ed.2d 493 (1976).

♦   **In a 1977 employment discrimination case, the Court stated that under Title VII employers accused of employment discrimination were entitled to meet the complaining parties' evidence with their own evidence to rebut an inference of discrimination.**

A suburban St. Louis, Missouri, school district had a racial composition of only 1.8 percent black teachers, compared to an area-wide rate of 15.4%. School principals in the suburban district had almost unlimited discretion in their hiring policies. The district's attendance rate was only 2% black compared to 50% black students in the nearby St. Louis city school district. The U.S. government sued the suburban school district on the theory that the district had a pattern or practice of racially discriminatory hiring practices. The government based its case on statistical disparities, subjective hiring practices and evidence from 55 unsuccessful black teaching applicants. The court ruled that there was no pattern or practice of discrimination in the district's hiring practices. It noted that the district had never operated a racially segregated dual school system, and that the small percentage of black employees corresponded with the small number of black students in the district. On appeal, the U.S. Court of Appeals, Eighth Circuit, reversed the district court's decision ruling that teacher-student ratios were irrelevant and that the correct comparison was between the district's black employment rate and that of the local labor market. The district petitioned to the U.S. Supreme Court, which granted certiorari.

The Court held that employment statistics were relevant in establishing a pattern or practice of race discrimination under Title VII. However, the court of appeals erroneously substituted its judgment for the district court's when it held that the government had successfully proven its case. The court of appeals should have permitted the district to meet the government's evidence with its own evidence in rebuttal to contradict the evidence of employment discrimination. Title VII was inapplicable to public employers until March 24, 1972, and employers who used nondiscriminatory policies after that date were not in violation of the act despite prior transgressions. The district had hired progressively more black teachers in years after 1972, making necessary a remand to the district court for further findings consistent with the Court's opinion. *Hazelwood School Dist. v. U.S.*, 433 U.S. 299, 97 S.Ct. 2736, 53 L.Ed.2d 768 (1977).

♦ **In *Gulf Oil Co. v. Bernard*, where a company sought to limit communication between class action plaintiffs and potential class members, the Supreme Court held that there would have to be sufficient grounds for the imposition of such an order because such interference would hinder the class plaintiffs.**

An oil company and the Equal Employment Opportunity Commission (EEOC) entered into a conciliation agreement with respect to alleged discrimination against black and female employees at a refinery. The company began to notify potential discriminatees, offering settlements in return for a full release. A group of black present and former employees, and rejected applicants, then sued under Title VII. The company sought an order to limit communications between the named plaintiffs and potential class members who were not actual parties to the litigation. A federal district court issued the order, requiring court approval before such communications could be made. The U.S. Court of Appeals reversed, holding that the order was an unconstitutional prior restraint on free speech in violation of the First Amendment.

The U.S. Supreme Court agreed that the district court had exceeded its authority in entering the order. Since the order interfered with class representatives' efforts to inform potential class members of the existence of the lawsuit against the company, and since it made it more difficult for class representatives to obtain information about the merits of the case, there would have to be sufficient grounds to impose the order. Here, the record did not reveal any such grounds. The Court affirmed the court of appeals' decision striking down the order. *Gulf Oil Co. v. Bernard,* 452 U.S. 89, 101 S.Ct. 2193, 68 L.Ed.2d 693 (1981).

◆ **An employer who granted special treatment to certain black candidates who passed a written examination for promotion could not use that as a defense in a lawsuit which alleged that the exam was discriminatory to blacks. An employer cannot discriminate against one part of a class of minorities while granting preferential treatment to another part of the class.**

Black employees of a Connecticut state agency received provisional promotions to supervisor status. To attain permanent status, they had to participate in a selection process that required a passing score on a written examination. Fifty-four percent of black candidates passed, compared to 68% of the white candidates. The failing black employees sued, claiming a violation of Title VII. While the case was pending, the employer promoted 22.9% of the black candidates who passed the test, but only 13.5% of the white candidates. The employer argued that this was a complete defense to the suit. The district court agreed, but the U.S. Court of Appeals, Second Circuit, reversed. Appeal was then taken to the U.S. Supreme Court.

The Court held that the eventual hiring of a greater percentage of blacks did not preclude a Title VII lawsuit, and was not a defense. The pass-fail barrier created a *prima facie* case of employment discrimination. The employer needed to show that the barrier was not an artificial, arbitrary or unnecessary barrier, but rather measured skills related to effective performance as a supervisor. No special treatment of part of a class could be used to justify discrimination against another part. The case was remanded for further proceedings. *Connecticut v. Teal,* 457 U.S. 440, 102 S.Ct. 2525, 73 L.Ed.2d 130 (1982).

◆ **The Supreme Court clarified in the following case that once the employer produces a legitimate nondiscriminatory reason for its action toward an employee, the burden falls on the employee to show that the stated reason for the action is a mere pretext.**

A black Washington, D.C., post office employee was turned down for a promotion. Although he possessed the minimum qualifications necessary, the postal service selected a non-minority candidate. It asserted that he was not promoted because he had turned down several lateral transfers that would have broadened his postal service experience. He filed suit against the post office under Title VII, 42 U.S.C. § 2000e *et seq.,* claiming that he had been discriminated against by race. The federal district court ruled in favor of the postal service, but the court of appeals reversed. It held that the district court had erred in requiring the employee to offer direct proof of discriminatory intent.

On appeal, the U.S. Supreme Court noted that once the employee established a *prima facie* case that the postal service had discriminated against him, and the postal service had produced a legitimate, nondiscriminatory reason for not promoting him, the burden fell on the employee to show that the reason given for rejecting him was pretextual. However, it was not necessary for him to submit direct evidence of discriminatory intent. Rather, he merely had to persuade the judge that the postal service's reason was not the real reason for his rejection. Because the district court had used the wrong standard to determine whether the postal service was liable, the Court vacated the court of appeals' decision and remanded the case to the district court. *U.S. Postal Service Board of Governors v. Aikens,* 460 U.S. 711, 103 S.Ct. 1478, 75 L.Ed.2d 403 (1983).

♦ **A plaintiff in a Title VII suit need not prove discrimination with scientific certainty. The burden is just to prove discrimination by a preponderance of the evidence.**

Certain black employees of the North Carolina Agricultural Extension Service and the United States sued the service in a federal district court, alleging a pattern and practice of racial discrimination in employment and provision of services. The district court found no pattern to certify the action as a class action, and further held that no individual discrimination had taken place. The U.S. Court of Appeals, Fourth Circuit, affirmed, and a further appeal was taken to the U.S. Supreme Court. The Supreme Court held that, under Title VII, the service had a duty to eradicate salary disparities between white and black workers that had their origin prior to the enactment of Title VII. Here, the employees had shown by a preponderance of the evidence that discrimination had occurred, even though they had not proven it with scientific certainty. Since it was more likely than not that discrimination had played a part in the salary discrepancies, the Court determined that the employees were entitled to the relief they sought. The Court thus affirmed in part and reversed in part, and remanded the case for a proper determination of damages. *Bazemore v. Friday,* 478 U.S. 385, 106 S.Ct. 3000, 92 L.Ed.2d 315 (1986).

♦ **In *Watson v. Fort Worth Bank and Trust*, the Supreme Court determined that a disparate impact (discriminatory effect) analysis could be applied to subjective employment criteria. Now an employee would no longer have to prove discriminatory intent on the part of the employer to successfully maintain a lawsuit under Title VII.**

A Texas woman of African-American heritage was rejected in favor of white applicants for four promotions to supervisory positions in the bank where she worked. Rather than use specified standards in the selection process, the bank was relying on the subjective judgment of various white supervisors. The employee exhausted her administrative remedies, then brought suit against the bank in a federal district court, alleging violations of Title VII. The district court dismissed her claim, holding that she had not met her burden of proof that the bank had acted with the intent to discriminate against her personally. The U.S. Court of Appeals, Fifth Circuit, affirmed. The employee sought review from the U.S. Supreme Court. On appeal, she argued that the district court should have applied a disparate impact analysis to her claims. In other words, she would only have to show that the bank had adopted a facially neutral policy without a discriminatory motive which had the effect of discriminating against her. The Supreme Court held that, when analyzing subjective or discretionary employment practices, a court may, in appropriate cases, analyze the practice under the disparate impact approach. This would solve the problem of prohibited conduct caused by subconscious stereotypes and prejudices. The Court remanded the case for evaluation under the disparate impact approach. *Watson v. Fort Worth Bank and Trust,* 487 U.S. 977, 108 S.Ct. 2777, 101 L.Ed.2d 827 (1988).

♦   **In 1993, the Court held that even though the trier of fact had rejected an employer's asserted reasons for discharging an employee, this did not mean that the employee was entitled to judgment as a matter of law. The employee still had the ultimate burden of persuasion as to whether the employer intentionally discriminated against him.**

A Missouri halfway house employed an African-American correctional officer. After being demoted and ultimately discharged, the officer filed suit alleging that these actions had been taken because of his race in violation of Title VII. At trial, the federal district court found that the officer had established, by a preponderance of the evidence: 1) a *prima facie* case of racial discrimination; 2) that the employer had rebutted the presumption by introducing evidence of two legitimate nondiscriminatory reasons for its actions; and 3) that the employer's reasons were pretextual. However, the district court held that the employee had failed to carry his ultimate burden of proving that the adverse actions were racially motivated, and found for the halfway house. The employee then appealed to the U.S. Court of Appeals, Eighth Circuit. The Eighth Circuit reversed the decision of the trial court and held that the employee was entitled to judgment as a matter of law once he proved that all of the employer's proffered reasons were pretextual. The halfway house appealed to the U.S. Supreme Court.

The Supreme Court reinstated the district court's decision, stating that the judge's rejection of an employer's asserted reasons for its actions does not entitle a plaintiff to judgment as a matter of law. Under *McDonnell Douglas Corp. v. Green,* 411 U.S. 792, 93 S.Ct. 1817, 36 L.Ed.2d 668 (1973), once the employee established a *prima facie* case of discrimination, a presumption arose that the employer unlawfully discriminated against him, requiring judgment in his favor unless the employer came forward with an explanation. This presumption placed upon the employer the burden of proving that the adverse actions were taken for legitimate, nondiscriminatory reasons. However, the ultimate burden of persuasion remained at all times with the employee. The trier of fact was required to decide whether the employee had proven that the employer intentionally discriminated against him because of race. Accordingly, the Supreme Court upheld the district court's decision for the halfway house. *St. Mary's Honor Center v. Hicks,* 509 U.S. 502, 113 S.Ct. 2742, 125 L.Ed.2d 407 (1993).

On remand, the district court ruled against the officer, who appealed again to the U.S. Court of Appeals, Eighth Circuit. The court of appeals affirmed the district court and reiterated the Supreme Court's mandate that an appropriate factfinder must determine that the employer has unlawfully discriminated.

The district court had determined that the officer's unfair treatment was because of personal animosity and was not race-related. The court affirmed the decision in favor of the employer. *Hicks v. St. Mary's Honor Center,* 90 F.3d 285 (8th Cir. 1996).

2. Affirmative Action

♦ **In an effort to eradicate the discriminatory effect that test-taking had on blacks and Hispanics, the County of Los Angeles sought to use a random selection process to hire applicants. The county was ordered to undertake affirmative action efforts and eventually found a non-random, nondiscriminatory method.**

In 1969, persons seeking employment with the Los Angeles County Fire Department were required to take a written examination as well as a physical test. Applicants were ranked according to their performance on the tests and selected for interviews on the basis of their scores. Those who passed the oral interviews were placed on a hiring-eligible list. Because blacks and Hispanics did poorly on the written exams, this method resulted in disparate impact (a facially neutral policy that has a discriminatory effect) on minority hiring. In 1972, the county administered a new test it had designed, which was graded on a pass-fail basis solely to screen out illiterates. It then intended to select 500 passing applicants at random to interview. However, prior to doing so, the county was sued because its random selection process violated Civil Service regulations.

A hiring freeze was instituted, and as a result of the ensuing manpower shortage, the county next sought to use a prior graded test to meet the needs of the fire department. At this point, a class action suit was filed on behalf of present and future black and Mexican-American applicants in a federal district court. It was alleged that the hiring procedure violated 42 U.S.C. § 1981. The court found that violations had occurred and ordered affirmative action efforts. The court of appeals affirmed this decision, and the U.S. Supreme Court agreed to hear the case. However, by the time the case reached the Court, the district court had found an efficient and non-random way to screen applicants and increase minority representation in the fire department. Because the Supreme Court determined that a successful system was being used and the chances of reverting to the old invalidated system were now very slim, it held that the case should be dismissed on grounds of mootness. Accordingly, it dismissed the case. *County of Los Angeles v. Davis,* 440 U.S. 625, 99 S.Ct. 1379, 59 L.Ed.2d 642 (1979).

♦ **In 1979, the Court stated that even though Title VII prohibits race discrimination, not all private, voluntary affirmative action plans are invalid. The Court upheld a private affirmative action plan in the following case.**

A union and a company entered into a collective bargaining agreement, which included an affirmative action plan designed to raise the percentage of black craftworkers in the company's plants to the percentage of blacks in the local labor force. After some junior black employees were selected for in-plant craft training programs over some senior white employees, a lawsuit was brought in federal district court, alleging that the affirmative action program violated Title VII. The court held that the plan violated Title VII, and the U.S. Court of Appeals affirmed. The U.S. Supreme Court then granted certiorari.

The Court first stated that Title VII's prohibition against racial discrimination did not condemn all private, voluntary, race-conscious affirmative action plans. To do so would defeat the very purpose of Title VII. The Court then noted that the affirmative action plan in this case was permissible. It opened employment opportunities for blacks in areas that were traditionally closed to them, and it did not unnecessarily trammel the interests of white employees. Finally, the Court stated that the plan was a temporary measure, designed only to eliminate a manifest racial imbalance. The Court reversed the court of appeals' decision and upheld the plan. *United Steelworkers v. Weber,* 443 U.S. 193, 99 S.Ct. 2721, 61 L.Ed.2d 480 (1979).

♦ **The Supreme Court invalidated an affirmative action plan approved by a Michigan school board and teachers' association that enhanced minority teacher rights in the event of a layoff. The plan would have permitted layoffs of more senior whites in an attempt to preserve the racial balance of the teaching force.**

White Michigan teachers sued their board of education for attempting to implement a collective bargaining agreement provision under which their seniority rights were impaired in favor of less-senior minority teachers in the event of a layoff. They sued in a federal district court under the Equal Protection Clause and Title VII of the 1964 Civil Rights Act, as well as state law. The district court ruled that the importance of providing minority teachers as role models for minority students as a remedy for past societal discrimination justified the layoff provision. The U.S. Court of Appeals, Sixth Circuit, affirmed the district court's decision, and the white teachers appealed to the U.S. Supreme Court. By a five to four vote the justices reversed the lower court decisions and held that the white teachers had been unfairly discriminated against in violation of the Equal Protection Clause. A total of six different opinions were filed in the case as the justices failed to agree on an appropriate standard of review for government affirmative action programs.

The majority opinion rejected the school board's argument that race-based layoffs were necessary to remedy the effects of societal discrimination. Clear and convincing evidence must be presented to prove that the government entity in question had engaged in past racial discrimination. Similarly, the Supreme Court rejected the role model justification for retaining minority teachers, because it would allow racially based layoffs long after they were needed to cure the ills of past discrimination. "Carried to its logical extreme, the idea that black students are better off with black teachers could lead to the very system the Court rejected in *Brown v. Board of Education....*"

The majority opinion held that even if the school board had sufficient justification for engaging in remedial or benign racial discrimination, laying off white teachers was too drastic and intrusive a remedy. While hiring goals and promotion policies favorable to minorities were acceptable under the Equal Protection Clause, the actual laying off of a certain race of employees was unconstitutional. "Denial of future employment is not as intrusive as loss of an existing job." The layoffs made by the school board were impermissible, and the lower court rulings were reversed. *Wygant v. Jackson Board of Educ.*, 476 U.S. 267, 106 S.Ct. 1842, 90 L.Ed.2d 260 (1986).

♦ **In 1989, the Court held that an affirmative action plan in Virginia had to be narrowly tailored to achieve a compelling governmental interest. Since the plan could not pass this strict scrutiny, it had to be struck down.**

The city of Richmond, Virginia adopted a plan requiring prime contractors awarded city construction contracts to subcontract at least 30 percent of the dollar amount of each contract to one or more minority business enterprises (MBEs). These were defined as businesses from anywhere in the country that were owned and controlled (at least 51%) by black, Spanish-speaking, Asian, Indian, Eskimo, or Aleut citizens. The plan purported to be remedial in nature, but no direct evidence was presented at the hearing prior to its adoption that the city had discriminated on the basis of race in letting contracts. After the sole bidder on a city contract was denied a waiver of the MBE requirement and lost its contract, it sued the city under 42 U.S.C. § 1983, alleging that the plan was unconstitutional under the Fourteenth Amendment's Equal Protection Clause. The federal court upheld the plan, and the U.S. Court of Appeals, Fourth Circuit, affirmed. The U.S. Supreme Court vacated and remanded for further consideration in light of *Wygant v. Jackson Board of Educ.*, 476 U.S. 267, 106 S.Ct. 1842, 90 L.Ed.2d 260 (1986). On remand, the court of appeals held that the plan violated the Constitution. The case again came before the U.S. Supreme Court.

The Court held that the city had failed to demonstrate a compelling governmental interest through evidence of past discrimination in the city's construction industry. It is not enough to generally assert that past discrimination has occurred. Next, the Court held that the plan was not narrowly tailored to remedy the effects of prior discrimination since it allowed minority entrepreneurs from anywhere in the country to obtain a preference over other citizens based solely on race. The lower court decision was affirmed. *City of Richmond v. J.A. Croson Co.*, 488 U.S. 469, 109 S.Ct. 706, 102 L.Ed.2d 854 (1989).

♦ **After *City of Richmond v. J.A. Croson Co.* was decided, a similar affirmative action plan came before the Supreme Court. In this case, a Florida city asserted that the case was moot because the plan had been repealed and replaced by another plan. The Court held that the case was not moot and that an association had standing to challenge the city's plan.**

A Florida city passed an ordinance requiring that it set aside 10% of all city contracts for minority business enterprises (MBEs). Under the ordinance, an MBE was a business at least 51% owned by persons who were "black, Spanish-speaking, Oriental, Indian, Eskimo, Aleut or handicapped." Women-owned firms were also considered MBEs under the ordinance. The ordinance did not require "mathematical certainty" when designating contracts awarded to MBEs, but required that the city come as close as possible to 10%. The ordinance provided that this be reduced in certain limited situations. An association of

Florida construction firms sued the city in a U.S. district court alleging that the set asides provided by the ordinance violated the Equal Protection Clause of the Fourteenth Amendment. The district court entered summary judgment for the association. On appeal, the U.S. Court of Appeals, Eleventh Circuit, reversed, holding that the association lacked standing to bring suit. The association appealed to the U.S. Supreme Court. After the Supreme Court agreed to hear the case, the city repealed the ordinance and enacted a second ordinance which: 1) provided that only women and African-Americans were eligible for the set asides, 2) changed the set asides' percentage goals, and 3) provided "five alternative methods for achieving participation goals."

The city contended that the "challenged statutory language" had been repealed and therefore the case was moot. The Supreme Court disagreed, ruling that the ordinance had not been "sufficiently altered" to moot the present lawsuit. It declined to adopt a per se rule that all statutory changes, however insignificant, would moot a lawsuit. Next, the association argued that it had standing to challenge the ordinance. The Supreme Court agreed, noting that to have standing to challenge the ordinance the association had to demonstrate: "an injury in fact," a causal connection between the injury and the challenged conduct, and "a likelihood that the injury would be redressed by a favorable decision." Under the principles established in *Regents of Univ. of California v. Bakke,* 438 U.S. 265, 98 S.Ct. 2733, 57 L.Ed.2d 750 (1978), an individual denied an equal opportunity need not allege that he would have obtained the desired benefit absent the denial in order to have standing. Rather, the challenging party need only establish that he or she was denied an "opportunity to compete." Here, the denial of equal treatment with respect to the city contracts was sufficient to establish an injury. Further, the ordinance prevented the association from competing on an equal footing in its quest for a benefit. Since, absent the ordinance, the association members would have bid on the set aside contracts, and since a judicial decree would "redress the injury," the association had standing to challenge the ordinance. The holding of the appellate court was reversed. *Northeastern Florida Chapter of the Associated General Contractors of America v. City of Jacksonville,* 508 U.S. 656, 113 S.Ct. 2297, 124 L.Ed.2d 586 (1993).

◆   **In the following case, the Supreme Court reaffirmed the application of strict scrutiny to all racial classifications for federal, state and local governments. Moreover, the Court narrowed affirmative action program requirements to ensure a sufficiently detailed examination.**

The Federal Lands Highway Division, part of the U.S. Department of Transportation, awarded a highway construction contract to a Colorado contractor. The contractor received additional compensation for hiring a subcontractor controlled by "socially and economically disadvantaged individuals." The highway division construed the relevant federal statute as containing a presumption that African-American, Hispanic, Asian-Pacific, Subcontinent Asian, Native American, and female individuals were socially and economically disadvantaged. The contractor rejected the low bidder on the subcontract, because it was not controlled by disadvantaged persons. The subcontractor filed suit in a federal district court, claiming that the race-based presumption violated its right to equal protection. The district court granted the U.S. government's motion for summary judgment, and the U.S. Court of Appeals, Tenth Circuit, affirmed. The subcontractor appealed to the U.S. Supreme Court.

The Supreme Court reversed the Tenth Circuit decision, ruling that the standard of review for federal, state and local governments should be strict scrutiny. Affirming the principles laid out in *City of Richmond v. J.A. Croson Co.*, 488 U.S. 469, 109 S.Ct. 706, 102 L.Ed.2d 854 (1989), the Court held that the Fifth and Fourteenth Amendments require that all racial classifications be narrowly tailored to further a compelling government interest. The Court rejected the government's plea for a less rigorous standard, ruling that only strict scrutiny would submit racial classifications to a sufficiently detailed examination. It noted that heightened scrutiny would "smoke out illegitimate uses of race by assuring that the legislative body is pursuing a goal important enough to warrant use of a highly suspect tool." The Court reversed and remanded the case to determine whether the use of the subcontractor compensation clauses could be properly described as compelling. *Adarand Constructors, Inc. v. Pena*, 515 U.S. 200, 115 S.Ct. 2097, 132 L.Ed.2d 158 (1995).

3. Relief

♦ **Title VII requires the courts to "make whole" victims of discrimination. In the following case, the applicants who had not been hired were not only entitled to jobs, but also to retroactive seniority to the date when they should have been hired.**
        A black over-the-road (OTR) truck driver applied for a job with a transportation company, but was not hired. He then brought a class action suit against the company and his union, alleging various racially discriminatory employment practices in violation of Title VII. After a trial, the federal district court found that the company had engaged in a pattern of discrimination. It ordered the company to stop its illegal practices and to notify class members of their right to priority consideration of OTR jobs. However, it declined to award back pay and seniority status retroactive to the date of application for unnamed members of the class. The U.S. Court of Appeals affirmed the order in part, but held that back pay should have been awarded. On further review, the U.S. Supreme Court held that unnamed members of the class should have been granted seniority in addition to being hired. To require an employer only to hire a class victim of discrimination falls short of the "make whole" purpose of Title VII. The only way to allow the victim of discrimination to obtain his rightful place in the hierarchy of seniority was to grant him seniority status retroactive to the date of application. The Court reversed and remanded the case. *Franks v. Bowman Transportation Co., Inc.*, 424 U.S. 747, 96 S.Ct. 1251, 47 L.Ed.2d 444 (1976).

♦ **A year after *Franks v. Bowman Transportation Co.*, the Court held that retroactive seniority could not be given to a date earlier than the effective date of Title VII. The Court also stated that a bona fide seniority system**

will not be held unlawful merely because it perpetuates pre-Title VII discrimination.

The United States sued a nationwide common carrier of motor freight and a union representing a large group of the company's employees, claiming that the company engaged in a pattern of discriminating against blacks and Hispanics. The government claimed that the minority members were hired as local city drivers, a lower-paying and less desirable position than line drivers (long distance drivers). The government also claimed that the collective bargaining agreements between the union and company "locked-in" the effects of racial discrimination, because a transferred city driver forfeited all seniority he had earned. The district court held that the union and company had violated Title VII and enjoined both from committing further violations thereof. The district court stated that the affected class of discriminatees included all minority members hired as city drivers at every terminal with a line-driver operation, whether or not they were hired before the effective date of Title VII. Stating that they had been injured to varying degrees, the court divided the affected class into three groups. The court of appeals rejected this approach, and review was sought from the U.S. Supreme Court.

The Supreme Court held that the government had successfully shown that discrimination had occurred. The Court also held that retroactive seniority may be awarded as relief for post-Title VII discriminatees, even if the seniority system agreement makes no provision for such relief. However, it stated that the union's conduct in agreeing to the seniority system did not violate Title VII. Employees who suffered only pre-Title VII discrimination were not entitled to relief, and no person could be given retroactive seniority to a date earlier than the act's effective date. Therefore, the union's injunction was vacated. A bona fide seniority system does not become unlawful simply because it perpetuates pre-Title VII discrimination. The seniority system was made in good faith and applied to all members. Every post-Title VII minority member was entitled to relief unless the company could show that it did not discriminate. Non-applicants had to be allowed to prove that they should be treated as applicants and entitled to relief. They would have to show that they would have applied for a line-driver position, but for the discriminatory policy. *Int'l Brotherhood of Teamsters v. U.S.*, 431 U.S. 324, 97 S.Ct. 1843, 52 L.Ed.2d 396 (1977).

♦ **Federal courts should not impose hiring methods on companies for the purpose of increasing minority employment until it has been shown that the employers have violated Title VII.**

Three black bricklayers sought employment with a construction company. The company hired superintendents for specific jobs and let them hire their own work force. The superintendent involved in this case hired only one of the three applicants, and at a date much later than the application. The applicants sued, claiming a violation of Title VII. A federal district court dismissed the suit, holding that no discrimination had been proven. The U.S. Court of Appeals reversed, finding that a *prima facie* case had been made out, and that the company had not effectively rebutted it. The appellate court devised an "appropriate" hiring procedure for the company, and an appeal was taken to the U.S. Supreme Court.

The Court first agreed that the applicants had made out a *prima facie* case of discrimination. It then held, however, that the appellate court should not have imposed a hiring method to enable the company to consider more minority employees until a violation of Title VII was proven. Further, the company should have been allowed to offer statistics showing that its work force was racially balanced. While not conclusive, such evidence was one factor to be considered in determining whether discrimination was a motive in the hiring practices of the company. The Court reversed and remanded the case. *Furnco Construction Corp. v. Waters*, 438 U.S. 567, 98 S.Ct. 2943, 57 L.Ed.2d 957 (1978).

♦ **In 1983, the Court examined lawsuits brought by private plaintiffs under Title VI (which outlaws discrimination in programs that receive federal financial assistance). The Court held that only equitable relief was available in such lawsuits. To obtain money damages, plaintiffs would have to bring suit under 42 U.S.C. § 1983.**

A group of black and Hispanic police officers challenged several written examinations administered by the city of New York, which were found to have a discriminatory impact and not to be job-related. Each officer was hired anyway, but later than similarly situated white officers. Then, when the police department laid off people on a "last-hired, first-fired" basis, the black and Hispanic officers were disproportionately affected by the layoffs. A federal court granted relief to the officers under Title VI and Title VII. The Second Circuit Court of Appeals affirmed the relief granted under Title VII, but reversed as to Title VI.

On appeal to the U.S. Supreme Court, the Court first held that discriminatory intent was not an essential element of a Title VI violation. The Court then stated that only injunctive, non-compensatory relief could be recovered for a defendant's unintentional violation of Title VI where private plaintiffs were involved. This meant that private plaintiffs in such cases could not obtain money damages unless they could bring their suit under 42 U.S.C. § 1983 (where the defendant acts under color of state law). By suing under Title VI, which outlaws discrimination in programs that receive federal financial assistance, the plaintiffs would be limited to non-monetary relief. *Guardians Ass'n v. Civil Service Comm'n of City of New York*, 463 U.S. 582, 103 S.Ct. 3221, 77 L.Ed.2d 866 (1983).

♦ **The Supreme Court held that a federal district court could not modify a layoff plan where the modification went beyond the terms of a consent decree, because the effects of the modification were felt by employees who had not been parties to the lawsuit when the consent decree was entered.**

A black firefighter challenged the hiring and promotion practices of the Memphis, Tennessee, Fire Department. Subsequently, a consent decree was entered into for the purpose of remedying the department's hiring and promotion practices with respect to blacks. After this occurred, budget deficits required a reduction of city employees. A federal district court entered an order for an injunction to prevent the fire department from following its seniority system in the impending layoffs. A modified layoff plan was approved, and some white employees with more seniority than black employees were laid off. In the challenge to this modification of the consent decree, the U.S. Court of Appeals affirmed the district court's modification.

On appeal to the U.S. Supreme Court, the Court held that the injunction was an invalid exercise of the district court's powers. Here, the modification went beyond the terms of the consent decree. Further, its effects were felt by the union and certain white employees who had not been parties to the suit when the consent decree was entered. Since this was not a valid Title VII remedial order, the Court reversed the court of appeals' decision and struck down the injunction. *Firefighters Local Union No. 1784 v. Stotts*, 467 U.S. 561, 104 S.Ct. 2576, 81 L.Ed.2d 483 (1984).

♦ **In 1986, six members of the Supreme Court agreed that a district court could, in appropriate circumstances, order preferential relief to individuals who were not the actual victims of race discrimination as a remedy for violations of Title VII.**

A sheet metal workers' union and its apprenticeship committee engaged in a continuing practice of discrimination toward black and Hispanic individuals for a number of years. After numerous court orders were unsuccessful in reversing the practice of the union, the Equal Employment Opportunity Commission (EEOC) initiated an action against the union under Title VII. The district court ordered the union to end its discriminatory practices, and established a 29% nonwhite membership goal (based on the percentage of nonwhites in the relevant labor pool in New York City). After several more court actions, the union was found guilty of civil contempt for disobeying earlier court orders. The court then imposed a fine on the union to be placed in a special fund for the purpose of increasing nonwhite membership in the union. The U.S. Court of Appeals affirmed, and the union appealed to the U.S. Supreme Court.

On appeal, the Supreme Court noted that Title VII allowed the kind of affirmative, race-conscious relief that the district court had ordered in this case. A court need not order relief only for actual victims of past discrimination, but can also order relief of a broader scope to satisfy the purposes of Title VII. The Supreme Court also found that the imposition of fines (and the special fund) was designed to coerce compliance and was thus a proper remedy for civil contempt. It affirmed the lower court decisions. *Local 28 of Sheet Metal Workers v. EEOC*, 478 U.S. 421, 106 S.Ct. 3019, 92 L.Ed.2d 344 (1986).

♦ **Race-conscious relief may by provided by consent decrees, which involve court-approved voluntary agreements among parties.**

An organization of black and Hispanic firefighters employed by the city of Cleveland filed a complaint against the city, charging it with discrimination on the basis of race and national origin in the hiring, assignment and promotion of firefighters in violation of Title VII. The firefighters' labor union was able to intervene in the suit, but it objected to the consent decree entered into between the organization and the city. The U.S. Court of Appeals upheld the decree as valid, and the union appealed to the U.S. Supreme Court.

The Court first noted that Title VII did not preclude entry of a consent decree that benefited individuals who were not the actual victims of the employer's discriminatory practices. Title VII prohibited a court from ordering the hiring or promotion of an individual who was refused employment or promotion for any reason other than discrimination. However, past discriminatory practices by an employer might justify relief for non-victims of the same class in certain contexts. Next, the Court stated that since the consent decree was voluntary, there was no Title VII violation in the adoption of it by the parties and the court. Finally, the Court stated that the consent decree was valid even though the intervenor-union did not consent to it because the decree did not bind the union to do or not do anything. The Court affirmed the appellate court's decision. *Local No. 93, Int'l Ass'n of Firefighters v. City of Cleveland,* 478 U.S. 501, 106 S.Ct. 3063, 92 L.Ed.2d 405 (1986).

♦ **The Supreme Court upheld a 50% promotion requirement for blacks to eradicate the discriminatory exclusion of blacks from certain positions. This relief was justified by a compelling governmental interest and was narrowly tailored to achieve its purposes.**

In 1972, a federal district court determined that the Alabama Department of Public Safety had systematically excluded blacks from employment as state troopers in violation of the Fourteenth Amendment and issued a hiring quota order. By the early 1980s, there were still no blacks who had been promoted to the rank of corporal. The district court determined that the test used for promotions had an adverse impact on blacks and ordered the department to promote at least 50% blacks to the rank of corporal if qualified black candidates were available. It also ordered the department to submit a realistic schedule for the development of promotional procedures for all ranks above the entry level. The United States appealed the order, asserting that it violated the Equal Protection Clause of the Fourteenth Amendment. The U.S. Court of Appeals affirmed the order, and the question came before the U.S. Supreme Court.

The Supreme Court held that the one-black-for-one-white promotion requirement was permissible under the Fourteenth Amendment. There was a compelling governmental interest in eradicating the department's pervasive and continuing discriminatory exclusion of blacks. Further, the order provided for promotions only when openings were available and did not require gratuitous promotions. Also, the requirement could be waived if no qualified black troopers were available. Finally, the requirement was only a temporary measure and was contingent on the department's successful implementation of valid promotional procedures. Accordingly, the Court found that the requirement did not impose an unacceptable burden on whites and was thus constitutional. The Court affirmed the lower courts' rulings. *United States v. Paradise,* 480 U.S. 149, 107 S.Ct. 1053, 94 L.Ed.2d 203 (1987).

4. Other Considerations

♦ **Liability under 42 U.S.C. § 1981 may not be imposed absent intentional discrimination, whereas under Title VII, liability may be imposed where facially neutral policies have a discriminatory effect.**

In contracts between a union and certain construction industry employers, an exclusive hiring hall was established. Also, the parties created an apprenticeship program between the union and several trade associations. After the union engaged in a pattern of intentional race discrimination with respect to the administration of the system, the state of Pennsylvania brought suit in a federal court under 42 U.S.C. § 1981 against the union, the employers, and the trade associations. The district court found that even though the employers and the trade associations had not intentionally discriminated against minority workers, they were nevertheless liable under Section 1981 for the purpose of imposing an injunctive remedy. Because the hiring procedure had been delegated to the union (which had intentionally discriminated), the employers and the trade associations were liable under the doctrine of *respondeat superior* (vicarious liability). The U.S. Court of Appeals affirmed, and further appeal was taken to the U.S. Supreme Court.

The Supreme Court determined that liability could not be imposed under Section 1981 without proof of intentional discrimination. Because the district court had not found any discriminatory intent on the part of the employers and the trade associations, they could not be vicariously liable for the union's acts. They did not control the union's activities, and no agency relationship existed. Further, the district court had improperly allocated to the employers and the trade associations a portion of the costs of the remedial decree. Without a supportable finding of liability, it did not have the power to do so. The Court reversed and remanded the case. *General Building Contractors Ass'n v. Pennsylvania*, 458 U.S. 375, 102 S.Ct. 3141, 73 L.Ed.2d 835 (1982).

◆　**After a court found that an employer had not systematically engaged in a discriminatory pattern of conduct toward certain employees, the Supreme Court determined that the employees were not precluded from bringing individual claims against the employer under 42 U.S.C. § 1981. It was possible that isolated cases of discrimination existed, and this could be litigated despite the earlier ruling.**

The Equal Employment Opportunity Commission brought an action in a federal district court against the Federal Reserve Bank of Richmond, Virginia, alleging that one of the bank's branches had violated Title VII by engaging in discriminatory employment practices. Four black employees were allowed to intervene and received certification as a class. They then notified other class members who joined in the suit. The court found discrimination with respect to employees in certain specified pay grades, but not with respect to employees above those grades. The court denied other employees' motions to intervene because they were in the higher grades, and they then filed separate actions under 42 U.S.C. § 1981. The U.S. Court of Appeals, Fourth Circuit, reversed the district court's finding of discrimination in the class action and further determined that the judgment in the class action precluded the individual suits from being litigated.

The U.S. Supreme Court granted certiorari. The Court noted that, while the class members were bound by the judgment against them in the class action, they were not precluded from bringing individual claims against the bank. Even though it had not been shown that the bank had systematically engaged in a discriminatory pattern of conduct, the individuals might be able to show isolated cases of discrimination. The Court thus reversed the court of appeals' decision and allowed the individual claims. *Cooper v. Federal Reserve Bank of Richmond*, 467 U.S. 867, 104 S.Ct. 2794, 81 L.Ed.2d 718 (1984).

♦   **Part of the Civil Rights Act, as codified at 42 U.S.C. § 1981, states that "[a]ll persons … shall have the same right to make and enforce contracts … as is enjoyed by white citizens…" In 1987, the Court ruled that although originally intended to vindicate the rights of former slaves, Section 1981 extended to persons of Arab ancestry and other ethnic groups as well.**

A private college in Pennsylvania denied tenure to a professor it had employed under a one-year non-renewable contract. The professor was a Muslim who was born in Iraq but was a U.S. citizen. He claimed that the college had refused to grant tenure on the basis of his national origin and religion in violation of state and federal civil rights laws, including Section 1981. The professor sued the college in a federal district court, which dismissed many of the claims because they were too late to meet local statutes of limitations. The court also dismissed the Section 1981 claim, ruling that the act did not extend to the professor. It ruled that Section 1981, which forbids racial discrimination in the making and enforcement of any contract, does not reach claims of discrimination based on Arab ancestry. The court stated that Arabs were Caucasians, and that since Section 1981 was not enacted to protect whites, an Arab professor could not rely upon the statute. The professor appealed to the U.S. Court of Appeals, Third Circuit. The appeals court affirmed the district court's decision that the professor's Title VII claim was untimely, but reversed its decision regarding the Section 1981 claim. The college appealed to the U.S. Supreme Court, which agreed to review only the Section 1981 claim.

In affirming the court of appeals' decision, the Supreme Court noted that although Section 1981 does not use the word "race," the Court has construed the statute to forbid all racial discrimination in the making of private as well as public contracts. It observed that persons who might be thought of as Caucasian today were not thought to be of the same race at the time Section 1981 became law. The Court cited several dictionary and encyclopedic sources to support its decision that for the purposes of Section 1981, Arabs, Englishmen, Germans and certain other ethnic groups are not to be considered a single race. Based on the history of Section 1981 the Court reasoned that Congress "intended to protect from discrimination identifiable classes of persons who are subjected to intentional discrimination solely because of their ancestry or ethnic characteristics." If the professor could prove that he was subjected to intentional discrimination because he was an Arab, rather than solely because of his place of origin or his religion, the lawsuit could proceed under Section 1981. The court of appeals' decision in favor of the professor was affirmed and the case was remanded for trial. *St. Francis College v. Al-Khazraji*, 481 U.S. 604, 107 S.Ct. 2022, 97 L.Ed.2d 749 (1987).

♦   **A requirement for permanent employment that is based on length of employment will probably pass constitutional muster. In the case below, a 45-week requirement for attaining permanent employee status was held to be a component of a valid seniority system.**

A multi-employer brewery industry collective bargaining agreement accorded greater benefits, with respect to hiring and layoffs, to permanent employees than it did to temporary employees. To become a permanent employee, an employee had to work at least 45 weeks in a single calendar year. A black temporary employee of a brewing company filed a class action suit against the brewers association and several unions, alleging that the collective bargaining agreement's 45-week requirement operated to preclude him and members of his class from achieving permanent status. A federal district court dismissed the claim, and the U.S. Court of Appeals reversed. It held that the 45-week requirement was not a seniority system under Title VII (which allows differences in terms, conditions and privileges of employment that are not the result of an intent to discriminate).

On appeal to the U.S. Supreme Court, the Court found that the 45-week requirement was a component of a valid seniority system. Since it was based on length of employment rather than education standards, aptitude or physical tests, or other standards that give effect to subjectivity, it was valid and enforceable. The Court remanded the case so that the employee could try to show that the system was not bona fide or that the differences were the result of an intent to discriminate. *California Brewers Ass'n v. Bryant,* 444 U.S. 598, 100 S.Ct. 814, 63 L.Ed.2d 55 (1980).

♦ **In 1982, the Court held that bona fide seniority systems that were adopted after the effective date of Title VII and that merely had a discriminatory effect (as opposed to being intentionally discriminatory) were entitled to the immunity provided by Section 703(h) of Title VII.**

Prior to 1963, a tobacco company and a union engaged in overt race discrimination. However, discrimination continued even after that by means of a seniority system that segregated whites and blacks. In a lawsuit brought by the Equal Employment Opportunity Commission (EEOC) and a class of black employees, a federal district court held that the seniority system was not a bona fide seniority system. The U.S. Court of Appeals held that Congress intended the immunity accorded to bona fide seniority systems to run only to those that were in place at the time of Title VII's effective date. On appeal to the U.S. Supreme Court, the Court determined that the bona fide seniority system immunity was not limited to those systems in place before the adoption of Title VII. Section 703(h), which granted this immunity, did not make a distinction between pre- and post-act discrimination impact. Dissenting, Justice Brennan stated that the Court's holding meant that seniority plans adopted after Title VII became effective would not be subject to challenge under the disparate impact standard of *Griggs v. Duke Power Co.*, 401 U.S. 424, 91 S.Ct. 849, 28 L.Ed.2d 158 (1971). Thus, the employees challenging the seniority system would have to show more than discriminatory effect; they would have to show discriminatory intent. *American Tobacco Co. v. Patterson*, 456 U.S. 63, 102 S.Ct. 1534, 71 L.Ed.2d 748 (1982).

♦ **Likewise, in *Pullman-Standard v. Swint*, an otherwise valid seniority system in place prior to Title VII's enactment that was merely discriminatory in its *effect* on minorities was upheld.**

In 1971, black employees at a manufacturing company in Alabama brought suit against the company and their union, alleging violations of the Civil Rights Act of 1964 under Title VII. Prior to 1965, the company had openly pursued a racially discriminatory policy of job assignments. A seniority system was adopted in 1954 that measured length of continuous service in a particular department. The lawsuit alleged that the seniority system violated Title VII. A federal district court judge found that the system was the result of "colorblind objectives" and that it did not foster discrimination. The U.S. Court of Appeals reversed, and the case reached the U.S. Supreme Court, which held that a showing of disparate impact alone was not sufficient to invalidate the seniority system if it did not have a discriminatory purpose. Here, the court of appeals had improperly reversed the district court. The question of whether the system was intended to discriminate was a question of fact that should have been left to the district court to resolve. The Court thus reversed the court of appeals' decision and remanded the case. *Pullman-Standard v. Swint*, 456 U.S. 273, 102 S.Ct. 1781, 72 L.Ed.2d 66 (1982).

B. Sex Discrimination

1. Discrimination

♦ **Title VII of the Civil Rights Act also protects against sex discrimination. In a 1971 case, the Supreme Court held that if men with pre-school-age children were hired by a company, then the company could not refuse to hire women with pre-school-age children. However, a bona fide occupational qualification can justify an otherwise discriminatory requirement.**

A Florida woman sued a company under Title VII claiming that she had been denied employment because of her sex. The company refused to accept job applications from women with pre-school-age children. The district court granted summary judgment to the company, noting that 70-75% of the applicants were women and 75-80% of those hired for the position were women. It reasoned that no question of bias was presented. The court of appeals affirmed. The U.S. Supreme Court granted review. The Court stated that Section 703(a) of the Civil Rights Act of 1964 requires that persons of like qualifications be given equal employment opportunities irrespective of their sex. There cannot be one hiring policy for women and one for men. Only if the requirement was a bona fide occupational qualification, reasonably necessary to the normal operation of the business, could it be justified. The Court remanded for full development of the issue. *Phillips v. Martin Marietta Corp.*, 400 U.S. 542, 91 S.Ct. 496, 27 L.Ed.2d 613 (1971).

♦ **An airline that refused to credit a returning employee with seniority from her earlier days with the company was held not to have violated Title VII despite the fact that it had forced the employee to resign in violation of Title VII. The Court determined that the seniority system in place was bona fide.**

A flight attendant for an airline company was forced to resign in 1968 when she married. When the airline's policy of "single only" flight attendants was found to be violative of Title VII, it abated the policy. The flight attendant was rehired by the airline in 1972 as a new employee, without seniority from her days with the airline prior to 1968. She sued the company in a federal district court, alleging that, by refusing to credit her with pre-1972 seniority, the airline was guilty of a present, continuing violation of Title VII. The court dismissed the case, but the U.S. Court of Appeals reversed. The U.S. Supreme Court granted certiorari. The Supreme Court noted that the violation alleged by the flight attendant was not a continuing violation because she had not asserted that the seniority system in place discriminated against female employees or that it treated former employees who were discharged for discriminatory reasons differently from other former employees. Since the flight attendant had not shown intentional discrimination on the part of the airline, her claim for relief was barred. The Court held that it is permissible to treat employees differently according to a bona fide seniority system if the differences are not the result of intentional discrimination. The Court reversed the court of appeals' decision. *United Air Lines, Inc. v. Evans,* 431 U.S. 553, 97 S.Ct. 1885, 52 L.Ed.2d 571 (1977).

◆ **In *Dothard v. Rawlinson,* the Supreme Court held that height and weight restrictions were discriminatory against women. However, it allowed the employer to use sex as a bona fide occupational qualification because of the nature of the job.**

An applicant for employment at an Alabama prison was rejected because she failed to meet its 120-pound weight requirement. The statute that established the weight requirement also established a minimum height of 5 feet 2 inches. She sued, challenging the requirements as establishing gender criteria for assigning correctional counselors to "contact" positions. A federal district court found for the applicant, noting that 40% of the female population, but only 1% of the male population, would be excluded by the requirements. The court rejected the employer's bona fide occupational qualification (BFOQ) defense, ruling that being a male was not a legitimate qualification.

The U.S. Supreme Court held that the district court was correct with regard to the finding of discrimination. The applicant had established a *prima facie* case of discrimination, which the employer failed to rebut. The Court noted that Title VII was an effort by Congress to remove artificial, arbitrary and unnecessary barriers to employment such as race and sex. The district court had committed no error in finding that the height and weight restrictions were discriminatory as applied to female applicants. The state had failed to justify the correlation between height (and weight) and strength or to show that height and weight were essential to job performance. However, the Court noted that a state regulation enacted after the commencement of the lawsuit was not a violation of Title VII. The regulation, which described prisoner contact jobs in male penitentiaries as too dangerous for women, was permissible as a measure of controlling inmates and safety at male prisons. The Court held that the state regulation outlined a BFOQ and reversed that part of the district court's judgment. *Dothard v. Rawlinson,* 433 U.S. 321, 97 S.Ct. 2720, 53 L.Ed.2d 786 (1977).

♦   In the following case, the Supreme Court held that an employer could not require female employees to pay more into their pension funds than male employees, despite the fact that women live longer than men. This generalization could not be used to justify discrimination against individual women.

The Los Angeles Department of Water and Power required its female employees to make larger contributions to their retirement pension funds than male employees. Upon retirement, each employee eligible for monthly retirement benefits received an amount computed as a fraction of salary multiplied by years of service, funded entirely by their own contributions. The department justified the disparity in contribution by the use of mortality tables and experience that showed that females lived longer than males, necessarily increasing the average pension of retired females. The monthly pension contribution required of female employees was $14.84 higher than that of male employees. A group of aggrieved female employees filed a Title VII discrimination complaint against the department in a federal district court, seeking an injunction against the disparate contributions and a refund of their excess contributions. Meanwhile, the California state legislature enacted a law prohibiting municipal agencies from requiring higher contributions based upon sex. The department then amended its plan so that both sexes paid the same retirement contribution. The court granted the employees' motion for summary judgment on federal law grounds and ordered restitution of the excess funds. The department appealed to the U.S. Court of Appeals, Ninth Circuit, which affirmed the district court decision. The department appealed to the U.S. Supreme Court, which granted a writ of certiorari.

Before the Supreme Court, the department argued that the difference in required contributions was based upon mortality tables, which constituted a factor other than sex under the 1963 Equal Pay Act, and therefore was not unlawful discrimination. The Court held that while there was a legitimate basis in fact for the distinction drawn by the department, the distinction involved a generalization that was not true in each individual case. Not every individual female lived longer than every individual male. Because Title VII prohibited unlawful discrimination against any *individual* with respect to compensation, terms, conditions or privileges of employment, courts were required to focus on alleged discrimination against individuals and to disregard generalizations about classes of persons. The lower courts had correctly ruled that the distinction drawn by the department was unlawful discrimination based upon sex. However, the lower courts had inappropriately awarded restitution of excess contributions to the aggrieved female employees. The pension fund had taken the disparate contributions in the good faith belief that the mortality tables would justify them. Employers should be given time to adjust to the requirements of Title VII, and there was no reason to penalize the funds and possibly jeopardize them for a good faith error. The Court remanded the case for proceedings consistent with its opinion. *City of Los Angeles Dep't of Water v. Manhart*, 435 U.S. 702, 98 S.Ct. 1370, 55 L.Ed.2d 657 (1978).

♦   In an employment discrimination lawsuit filed under Title VII, the aggrieved party bears the burden of proving that the employer's refusal to

hire is a pretext for unlawful discrimination.

In an employment discrimination case against a state college, a federal district court ruled that the college had discriminated against a professor on the basis of sex. The U.S. Court of Appeals, Fifth Circuit, affirmed the decision, ruling that Title VII of the 1964 Civil Rights Act, 42 U.S.C. § 2000e *et seq.*, required the college to prove absence of discriminatory motive. In a *per curiam* opinion, the U.S. Supreme Court held that this burden was too great. It ruled that in an employment discrimination case, the employer need only "articulate some legitimate, nondiscriminatory reason for the employee's rejection." In other words, the employee has the burden of proving that the reason for the employee's rejection was a mere pretext. The Court vacated the court of appeals' decision and remanded the case for reconsideration under the lesser standard. *Trustees of Keene State College v. Sweeney,* 439 U.S. 24, 99 S.Ct. 295, 58 L.Ed.2d 216 (1978).

♦ **In *Texas Dep't of Community Affairs v. Burdine,* the Court clarified the standard required for proving discrimination. After the employee states a *prima facie* case, and after the employer articulates a legitimate, nondiscriminatory reason for its action, the employee must prove that the reason proffered by the employer is a mere pretext for discrimination.**

A Texas woman with several years of experience in employment training was hired by the state's department of community affairs. She received one promotion, and subsequently applied for a supervisor's position, which she did not receive. The department then fired her in a staff reduction. However, it later rehired, transferred and promoted her, keeping her salary commensurate with what she would have received had she gotten the first promotion. She nevertheless sued the department in a federal district court, asserting that the failure to promote and the decision to terminate her were based on gender discrimination. The district court ruled for the department, and she appealed to the U.S. Court of Appeals, Fifth Circuit, which held that she had not been discriminated against in the nonpromotion, but that she had been discriminated against in the termination. The department petitioned the U.S. Supreme Court for review.

The Supreme Court first stated that the employee had the burden of showing a *prima facie* case of discrimination, namely: that she belonged to a protected minority, she was qualified for the job, she was rejected despite her qualifications, and after her rejection the department continued to look at candidates with the same qualifications. The burden would then shift to the department to "articulate some legitimate, nondiscriminatory reason for the employee's rejection." If it was successful, the employee would then have to prove that the reasons given by the department were a pretext for discrimination. Because the court of appeals had not used this standard, the Supreme Court vacated its decision and remanded the case for a determination based on this. *Texas Dep't of Community Affairs v. Burdine,* 450 U.S. 248, 101 S.Ct. 1089, 67 L.Ed.2d 207 (1981).

♦ **The Supreme Court held that the prohibition in Title VII against sex-based wage discrimination was not limited to claims for equal pay for equal** work. Even where a lawsuit could not be filed under the Equal Pay Act because of job differences, a Title VII lawsuit was not necessarily precluded. However, an employer may use the affirmative defenses set out in the Equal Pay Act when defending a Title VII suit.

Female guards at an Oregon county jail were paid substantially less than male guards at the same facility. The county eliminated the female section of the jail, transferred its prisoners to a neighboring county and terminated the employment of the female guards. The terminated guards sued the county in a federal district court under Title VII of the 1964 Civil Rights Act, 42 U.S.C. § 2000e *et seq.,* seeking back pay and alleging that they had been unlawfully paid unequal wages for substantially similar work as that performed by the male guards. The court held that the male guards supervised over 10 times as many prisoners and did less clerical work than their female counterparts. It ruled that the females were not entitled to equal pay because they did not perform substantially similar work, and that the pay inequity was not attributable to sex discrimination. The court held that because the females had not met the standard of the 1963 Equal Pay Act, 29 U.S.C. § 206(d), no Title VII action was possible. The female employees appealed to the U.S. Court of Appeals, Ninth Circuit, which reversed, holding that alleged sex discrimination victims were entitled to Title VII protection. The county appealed to the U.S. Supreme Court.

The Court first noted that the case did not involve a comparable worth analysis, but was simply a sex discrimination case. It stated that the court of appeals had correctly ruled that Title VII wage discrimination claims could be brought in this situation, and that the female guards were not limited to remedies under the Equal Pay Act. Title VII by its terms barred sex-based wage discrimination but permitted differentials if such differentials could be justified under the Equal Pay Act. This included seniority, merit, quantity or quality of work or other bona fide factors. Title VII claims for sex-based wage discrimination were thus permissible. In this case, the county had evaluated the female guards' job worth at 95% of the male guards, yet had paid them only 70% as much. The court of appeals had correctly ruled that this presented a viable Title VII complaint for sex discrimination. *County of Washington v. Gunther,* 452 U.S. 161, 101 S.Ct. 2242, 68 L.Ed.2d 751 (1981).

◆ **Title IX of the 1972 Education Amendments, 20 U.S.C. § 1681 *et seq.,* prohibits gender discrimination in education programs and activities that receive federal financial assistance. Sanctions for noncompliance include termination of funding for specific future grants. In 1982, the Supreme Court ruled that Title IX's nondiscrimination requirements applied not only to students and academic policies, but to employment as well.**

In 1975, the U.S. Department of Education issued regulations prohibiting gender-based employment discrimination in all federally funded education programs. The regulations pertained to many employment practices including job classification and pregnancy leave. A tenured Connecticut public school teacher took a one-year maternity leave. The school, which received Title IX funds, refused to rehire her and she filed an administrative appeal, resulting in an education department request to investigate school district employment practices. The district refused the request for an investigation and sued the U.S.

government in a federal district court, which granted an injunction against enforcing the nondiscrimination regulations. The court ruled that Title IX's nondiscrimination mandate applied only to discrimination practices against students and not to teachers and employment practices. The district court also rejected another Title IX complaint by a Connecticut public school guidance counselor who claimed that her school district gave her discriminatory work assignments and failed to renew her contract on the basis of her sex. The U.S. Court of Appeals, Second Circuit, consolidated the two cases and reversed the district court decisions. The U.S. Supreme Court granted certiorari.

The Court found no reason to limit Title IX to discrimination complaints by students alone. Section 901(a) of the statute broadly stated that "No person in the United States shall, on the basis of sex, be excluded from participation in, be denied the benefits of, or be subjected to discrimination under any education program or activity receiving Federal financial assistance...." An extensive review of the statute's legislative history revealed evidence that employment practices were within the scope of Title IX. The Court affirmed the appeals court's decision, although it rejected the court's attempt to expand potential funding termination beyond the particular program that was found to be in noncompliance. The Court remanded the case with instructions to apply the act to the cases, permitting funding termination on a program-specific basis only, if the records justified a finding of gender-based discrimination in a federally funded program. *North Haven Board of Educ. v. Bell*, 456 U.S. 512, 102 S.Ct. 1912, 72 L.Ed.2d 299 (1982).

♦ **In *Ford Motor Co. v. EEOC*, the Court held that applicants who had been offered unconditional employment after being discriminated against were only eligible for back pay up until the date of the offers.**

Three women applied for "picker-packer" positions at an automobile company's warehouse, positions that no women had held before. The company hired three men instead, and a discrimination charge was filed with the Equal Employment Opportunity Commission (EEOC). The company later offered two of the women the job for which they had been turned down, but without seniority to the date of the applications. The women declined the offers. The EEOC then sued the company in a federal district court, which held that the company had violated Title VII. The court ordered the company to pay back pay from the date of the applications to the date of its order. The U.S. Court of Appeals affirmed the decision, and further appeal went to the U.S. Supreme Court. The Court held that an unconditional offer of employment will toll the continuing accrual of back pay liability under Title VII even if the employer does not offer seniority retroactive to the date of the alleged discrimination. Accordingly, for the two women who had been offered employment after they were initially rejected by the company, back pay was only due up until the time of the offer by the company. The Court reversed the lower courts' rulings, effectively requiring claimants to minimize their damages by accepting unconditional offers. *Ford Motor Co. v. EEOC*, 458 U.S. 219, 102 S.Ct. 3057, 73 L.Ed.2d 721 (1982).

♦   **If an employer provides benefits for its employees, it may not do so in a discriminatory manner. In the following case, the Supreme Court applied Title VII even though elevation to partnership status was not an "offer of employment."**

A woman lawyer was hired by a law firm as an associate. She took the job because the firm apparently represented that she would make partner if her work was satisfactory. The firm decided not to make her a partner, maintaining its all-male partnership status. After filing a charge with the Equal Employment Opportunity Commission, the lawyer sued the firm (her employment had terminated when she did not make partner), alleging discrimination under Title VII. A federal district court dismissed the complaint on the ground that Title VII was inapplicable to the selection of partners by a partnership. The U.S. Court of Appeals affirmed, and the case came before the U.S. Supreme Court. The Supreme Court reversed the court of appeals, finding that the lawyer had stated a cognizable claim under Title VII. Where an employer provides its employees with benefits, it may not do so in a discriminatory manner. If it is a term, condition or privilege of employment, discrimination by the employer is unlawful. Further, even if elevation to partnership status is not an offer of employment, Title VII still applies to bar discrimination in such a context. The Court remanded the case for further proceedings. *Hishon v. King & Spalding*, 467 U.S. 69, 104 S.Ct. 2229, 81 L.Ed.2d 59 (1984).

♦   **In *Anderson v. Bessemer City*, the Supreme Court upheld a district court's discrimination ruling, and stated that the U.S. Court of Appeals had improperly re-examined the evidence. Since there was sufficient evidence to support the charge, the district court's ruling should not have been overturned.**

A North Carolina city developed a new job for managing the city's recreational facilities. Four men and one woman composed the mayoral committee responsible for selecting an applicant. After considering eight applicants, the four men voted to hire a 24-year-old man who had recently graduated from college with a physical education degree. The sole female committee member voted to hire the only female applicant, a 39-year-old teacher with degrees in social studies and education. The female applicant filed a sex discrimination complaint under Title VII against the city, claiming that she had not been hired solely on the basis of her sex.

The federal district court in which the matter was filed held in the applicant's favor, finding that she had a broader range of experience than the male applicant. The court also held that the male committee members were biased against the female applicant and that one male committee person had stated that he would not have wanted his wife to perform the recreation director's job duties. There was also evidence that the committee had actively solicited male applicants but had made no attempt to recruit females. Finally, the reasons given for hiring the male applicant were pretextual. The city appealed to the U.S. Court of Appeals, Fourth Circuit, which reversed the lower court's decision. The applicant appealed to the U.S. Supreme Court, which held that the court of appeals had improperly weighed the district court findings by attempting to conduct a new evaluation of the evidence. There was sufficient evidence of sex bias and discrimination in the district court record, and the court of appeals should not have denied relief to the applicant. The Court reversed the court of appeals' judgment. *Anderson v. Bessemer City,* 470 U.S. 564, 105 S.Ct. 1504, 84 L.Ed.2d 518 (1985).

◆   **In 1987, the Supreme Court held that an affirmative action plan that took sex into account as one factor in the hiring decision was valid. The plan was not a quota system, and it presented a case-by-case approach. Further, the Court reaffirmed its decision in** *United Steelworkers v. Weber,* **443 U.S. 193, 99 S.Ct. 2721, 61 L.Ed.2d 480 (1979), that an employer seeking to implement an affirmative action plan need not point to its own prior discriminatory practices, but need only point to a conspicuous imbalance in traditionally segregated job categories.**

A California county transportation agency voluntarily adopted an affirmative action plan. The plan allowed the agency to consider, as one factor, the sex of an applicant in making promotions. The long-term goal of the plan was to achieve a work force whose composition reflected the proportion of women and minorities in the area labor force. When a road dispatcher position opened up, the agency promoted one of the qualified female applicants. A male employee who was passed over sued the agency in a federal district court. The court found that the woman had been selected because of her sex and invalidated the agency's plan. The court of appeals reversed this decision, and the man further appealed the case to the U.S. Supreme Court.

The Supreme Court held that the agency had appropriately taken the woman's sex into account as one factor in determining that she be promoted. It found that the agency plan was flexible and presented a case-by-case approach to effecting a gradual improvement in the representation of women and minorities in the agency. Thus, the plan was fully consistent with Title VII. Even though the male candidate had shown a *prima facie* case of discrimination on the part of the agency, the agency had shown a nondiscriminatory rationale for its decision, namely the affirmative action plan. Further, the Court noted that an employer need not point to its own prior discriminatory practices to justify its adoption of such a plan. It need only point to a conspicuous imbalance in traditionally segregated areas of employment. Since the plan had taken into account distinctions in qualifications to provide guidance, the agency had not merely engaged in blind hiring by the numbers. The Court affirmed the court of appeals' decision and upheld the affirmative action plan. *Johnson v. Transportation Agency, Santa Clara County,* 480 U.S. 616, 107 S.Ct. 1442, 94 L.Ed.2d 615 (1987).

◆   **The Supreme Court stated that employers might be liable for punitive damages under Title VII even where an employee does not prove that the employer engaged in some extraordinarily egregious behavior. However, it also held that employers cannot be vicariously liable where managers act contrary to the employer's good-faith efforts to comply with Title VII.**

A male and a female employee who had both received "distinguished" performance ratings competed for a promotion. After she was rejected, the female employee sued for gender discrimination, claiming that the other candidate had been "pre-selected." A federal jury found discrimination and awarded the employee $52,718 in back pay. But the district court judge refused to allow the jury to consider punitive damages, and the employee appealed. The U.S. Court of Appeals, D.C. Circuit, affirmed, and the case reached the Supreme Court.

The Court noted that punitive damages could be awarded without a showing of egregious behavior independent of the employer's state of mind. Where the employer acts with malice or with reckless indifference to the employee's federally protected rights, punitive damages are a proper form of relief.

Punitive damages would not be warranted, the Court said, where the employer is unaware of the relevant federal prohibition, or where the employer discriminates with the distinct belief that the discrimination is lawful, such as where it reasonably believes a bona fide occupational qualification is satisfied. The Court also noted that an employer cannot be held vicariously liable under Title VII (for punitive damages) for the discriminatory decisions of its management employees where those decisions are contrary to the employer's good-faith efforts to comply with the statute. *Kolstad v. American Dental Ass'n*, 527 U.S. 526, 119 S.Ct. 2118, 144 L.Ed.2d 494 (1999).

♦ **In a case decided late in the 2000-2001 term, the Supreme Court held that the Civil Rights Act of 1991 does not contemplate the inclusion of front pay as part of a compensatory damage award in federal anti-discrimination cases. Thus, an employee who prevailed against her employer in an employment discrimination case filed under Title VII was allowed to increase a $300,000 compensatory damage award for lost compensation represented by front pay.**

A federal district court held that the employee was subjected to sexual harassment by co-workers and that supervisors were aware of the harassment. She took a medical leave of absence to obtain psychological assistance and was discharged for failing to return to work. The court awarded the employee more than $100,000 in back pay and benefits, more than $250,000 in attorneys' fees and $300,000 in compensatory damages, which represented the maximum amount under the 1991 act's limit for employers with more than 500 employees. The U.S. Court of Appeals for the Sixth Circuit affirmed the district court judgment, finding flagrant sex discrimination that the employer's managers and supervisors did not take adequate steps to prevent.

The employee appealed to the U.S. Supreme Court, arguing that her compensatory damage award had been improperly capped at $300,000 and that she was entitled to a further award representing "front pay." The Supreme Court explained that front pay is generally money awarded to an employee for lost compensation during the period between a judgment and reinstatement. Courts also order front pay as a substitute for reinstatement in cases where reinstatement is not possible.

The court stated that victims of sex discrimination have traditionally been entitled to remedies under Title VII such as injunctions, reinstatement, back pay, lost benefits and attorneys' fees. The Civil Rights Act of 1991 expanded traditional Title VII remedies to include compensatory and punitive damage awards. When read as a whole, the 1991 act was best interpreted as excluding front pay from the meaning of compensatory damages. Under that construction, front pay was not included in the statutory damage limit and the employee was entitled to a front pay award to supplement the $300,000 awarded by the district court. According to the Court, Congress sought to expand available remedies when amending the Civil Rights Act by permitting employees to recover compensatory and punitive damages, including front pay. The Court reversed the lower court decisions and remanded the case for further proceedings. *Pollard v. E.I. du Pont de Nemours & Co.*, 532 U.S. 843, 121 S.Ct. 1946, 150 L.Ed.2d 62 (2001).

2. Sexual Harassment

◆   An employee at a Louisiana café quit after 10 months, claiming she had been forced to quit due to sexual harassment. She sued under Title VII, and a jury awarded her $40,000. Two weeks later, the café sought to have the action dismissed because it did not have 15 employees. It claimed the federal court thus had no jurisdiction to hear the case. A federal court and the Fifth Circuit agreed, but the U.S. Supreme Court reversed. It ruled that **the 15-employee requirement was not jurisdictional**. In other words, the café had a duty to raise that defense at or before trial. Having failed to do so, it could not later try to assert the defense. *Arbaugh v. Y&H Corp.*, 546 U.S. 500, 126 S.Ct. 1235, 163 L.Ed.2d 1097 (2006).

◆   **The Supreme Court has held that sexual harassment constitutes a form of sex discrimination protected by Title VII. Sexual harassment creates a hostile work environment and need not be sex related; any form of harassment against an employee because of the employee's sex will be considered harassment.**

A woman worked for a bank in various capacities over a four-year period. Her supervisor allegedly harassed her during this period, demanding sexual favors and forcibly raping her on several occasions. When the employee took an indefinite sick leave, the bank discharged her. She then brought suit against the bank, claiming that she had been subjected to sexual harassment in violation of Title VII. On conflicting trial testimony, a federal district court ruled for the bank, finding that the bank did not have notice of any harassment, and that its policies forbade such behavior. The U.S. Court of Appeals reversed, and appeal was taken to the U.S. Supreme Court.

The Supreme Court first noted that sexual harassment is clearly a form of sex discrimination prohibited by Title VII. It then stated that while absence of notice of harassment will not necessarily shield an employer from liability, employers are not always automatically liable for sexual harassment by their supervisor employees. The Court determined that Congress intended agency principles to apply to some extent. The Court also held that it was not improper to admit into evidence the complainant's "sexually provocative speech and dress." Even though voluntariness in the sense of consent is not a defense to a sexual harassment claim, such information bears on the issue of whether the complainant has found particular sexual advances unwelcome. The Court affirmed the court of appeals' holding, and remanded the case. *Meritor Savings Bank, FSB v. Vinson*, 477 U.S. 57, 106 S.Ct. 2399, 91 L.Ed.2d 49 (1986).

♦ **Conduct can be actionable as "abusive work environment" harassment even where it does not seriously affect an employee's psychological well-being or lead the employee to suffer injury.**

A Tennessee woman worked as a manager of a rental equipment company. The president of the company often insulted her because of her gender and frequently made her the target of unwanted sexual innuendoes. The employee subsequently quit and sued the company, claiming that the president's conduct had created an abusive work environment because of her gender. The federal district court found that, although this was a "close case," the president's conduct did not create an abusive environment because while some of the conduct would offend a reasonable woman, it was not so severe as to be "expected to seriously affect the manager's psychological well-being." The U.S. Court of Appeals, Sixth Circuit, affirmed, and the manager appealed to the U.S. Supreme Court.

The Supreme Court reaffirmed the standard set forth in *Meritor Savings Bank, FSB v. Vinson*, 477 U.S. 57, 106 S.Ct. 2399, 91 L.Ed.2d 49 (1986), that "Title VII is violated when the workplace is permeated with discriminatory behavior that is sufficiently severe or pervasive to create a hostile environment." The Court noted that the standard required only an objectively hostile environment – one that a reasonable person would find hostile – as well as the victim's subjective perception that the environment was abusive. Further, the court held that the determination of whether the environment was hostile could only be reached by looking at all the circumstances, which include frequency, severity, whether the conduct was humiliating, whether it unreasonably interfered with the employee's performance, and the psychological harm to the victim. The court reversed and remanded the case with instructions for the trial court to consider the psychological harm to the victim as but one factor to be considered in looking at all the circumstances. *Harris v. Forklift Systems, Inc.*, 510 U.S. 17, 114 S.Ct. 367, 126 L.Ed.2d 295 (1993).

♦ **In 1998, the Supreme Court extended Title VII protections to same-sex harassment.**

A Louisiana offshore service employed a roustabout to work on oil platforms in the Gulf of Mexico. He claimed that he was forcibly subjected to sex-related humiliating actions, assault and threats of rape by co-workers, including two employees with supervisory authority. When he complained to the employer's safety compliance clerk, the clerk did nothing and stated that he had also been subjected to abuse by the co-workers. Eventually, the roustabout quit and sued the employer in the U.S. District Court for the Eastern District of Louisiana, alleging sex discrimination in violation of Title VII of the Civil Rights Act of 1964. The court granted summary judgment to the employer, holding that the roustabout had no viable cause of action under Title VII since the harassment was caused by same-sex co-workers. The U.S. Court of Appeals, Fifth Circuit, affirmed the judgment and the roustabout appealed to the U.S. Supreme Court.

The Court stated that sex discrimination in the form of same-sex harassment that is so objectively offensive that it alters the conditions of employment is actionable under Title VII. The Court found no language in Title

VII that bars a sex discrimination claim when the complaining party and alleged perpetrators are of the same sex, and it rejected the employer's assertion that allowing the claim would transform Title VII into a general code of workplace civility. The Court noted that not all verbal or physical harassment in the workplace is prohibited by Title VII, since it does not cover conduct that is not severe or pervasive enough to create an objectively hostile or abusive work environment. The Court reversed the lower court decisions and remanded the case. *Oncale v. Sundowner Offshore Services, Inc.*, 523 U.S. 75, 118 S.Ct. 998, 140 L.Ed.2d 201 (1998).

♦   **In the case below, the Supreme Court held that Title VII imposes vicarious liability on an employer for sexual harassment by supervisors.**

An Illinois employee of a corporation alleged that she was subjected to constant *quid pro quo* sexual harassment from one of her supervisors, a mid-level manager who had the authority to hire and promote, subject to higher approval, but who was not considered a policymaker. The employee refused all of the supervisor's advances, but suffered no tangible retaliation and was even promoted once. Despite her knowledge of the employer's sexual harassment policy, she never complained to upper-level management about the supervisor's behavior. The employee resigned and sued the employer in a federal district court alleging sexual harassment and constructive discharge in violation of Title VII of the Civil Rights Act of 1964. The district court granted the employer's motion for summary judgment and the U.S. Court of Appeals, Seventh Circuit, reversed. The U.S. Supreme Court granted review.

The Supreme Court held that Title VII imposes vicarious liability on an employer for actionable discrimination caused by a supervisor with authority over an employee. When a supervisor discriminates in the terms and conditions of a subordinate's employment, his actions draw upon his superior position over the subordinate. However, in cases where there is no tangible employment action taken against the employee, the employer may assert a two-pronged affirmative defense. First, the employer must prove that it exercised reasonable care to prevent and promptly correct any sexual harassment. Second, the employer must prove that the employee unreasonably failed to avail herself of any employer remedies or failed to avoid harm otherwise. However, the affirmative defense is not available to the employer when the supervisor's harassment culminates in a tangible employment action such as discharge or demotion. The Court remanded the case for further consideration in light of its holding. *Burlington Industries, Inc. v. Ellerth*, 524 U.S. 742, 118 S.Ct. 2257, 141 L.Ed.2d 633 (1998).

♦   **In a different case decided on the same day as *Ellerth*, the Supreme Court found a city vicariously liable for the creation of a hostile work environment.**

A Florida woman worked as a lifeguard for a city. She had two male supervisors who controlled all aspects of her job, including work assignments and discipline. The lifeguard was subjected to severe and pervasive unwelcome touching, sexual comments, and other offensive behavior from the two supervisors. Although the city had a policy against sexual harassment, it completely failed to disseminate the policy to the lifeguard's department. Also, the policy did not assure that any harassing supervisors could be bypassed in registering complaints. The employee did not report this harassment to higher management, from whom she was completely isolated. She eventually resigned and sued the city alleging sexual harassment in violation of Title VII of the Civil Rights Act of 1964 and 42 U.S.C. § 1983. The district court found the city liable for the harassment. The U.S. Court of Appeals, Eleventh Circuit, reversed. Using the same holding as it did in *Ellerth,* the Supreme Court found the city vicariously liable for the hostile environment created by the lifeguard's supervisors. The Court reversed the court of appeals' decision and remanded the case for reinstatement of the district court decision. *Faragher v. City of Boca Raton,* 524 U.S. 775, 118 S.Ct. 2275, 141 L.Ed.2d 662 (1998).

♦   **The Supreme Court reversed a decision in favor of a school employee who claimed sexual harassment by male co-workers and retaliation by the district, finding she failed to show any causality between the alleged harassing incident and the allegedly retaliatory job transfer.**

A school district employee met with two male co-workers to review psychological evaluation reports from job applicants seeking employment with the district. She alleged that during one meeting, her supervisor read from a report that one applicant had commented to a co-worker, "I hear making love to you is like making love to the Grand Canyon," and that the supervisor then said, "I don't know what that means." According to the complaining employee, the other employee responded, "Well, I'll tell you later," and then both male employees chuckled. The employee asserted that when she complained about this incident, she was transferred to another position in retaliation. The transfer took place 20 months after the alleged harassment.

A federal court awarded summary judgment to the school district, and the employee appealed. The U.S. Court of Appeals, Ninth Circuit, reversed, observing that the employee had a reasonable belief that the harassing incident violated Title VII and that the Equal Employment Opportunity Commission (EEOC) had issued a right-to-sue letter within three months of the job transfer, making summary judgment improper.

The U.S. Supreme Court accepted the school district's petition for review concerning the question of the employee's reasonable belief that a Title VII violation had occurred. It held that no reasonable person could have believed that the single incident giving rise to the lawsuit violated Title VII. Sexual harassment is actionable only if it is so severe or pervasive as to alter the conditions of the victim's employment and create an abusive working environment. According to the Court, simple teasing, offhand comments and isolated incidents that are not extremely serious will not amount to discriminatory changes in the terms and conditions of employment. In this case, the employee's job required that she review the offensive statement. She conceded that it did not upset her to read the written remark in the applicant's file. Significantly, the supervisor's comment and the male employee's response was at worst "an isolated incident" that could not remotely be considered serious under recent Supreme Court precedents.

The Court found "no causality at all" between the job transfer proposed by the school district and the employee's complaint. It noted that there must be a very close proximity in time between an employer's knowledge of an employee's protected conduct and an adverse employment action if this is the employee's only evidence of retaliation. The Court reversed the Ninth Circuit's judgment. *Clark County School Dist. v. Breeden,* 532 U.S. 268, 121 S.Ct. 1508, 149 L.Ed.2d 509 (2001).

3. Pregnancy Discrimination

♦ AT&T based pension calculations on a seniority system that gave less retirement credit for pregnancy absences than it did for medical leave generally. After the Pregnancy Discrimination Act took effect, the company changed its policy prospectively, but did not make any retroactive adjustments. A group of female employees and their union sued the company under Title VII, alleging sex and pregnancy discrimination. A California federal court ruled for the employees, but the U.S. Supreme Court ultimately reversed. **The Pregnancy Discrimination Act did not apply retroactively, and the company could calculate retirement benefits in part by using the prior system.** *AT&T Corp. v. Hulteen,* 129 S.Ct. 1962, 173 L.Ed.2d 898 (U.S. 2009).

♦ **In 1974, three teachers challenged school district rules that required them to take mandatory unpaid leaves of absence at specified times during and after childbirth. The Supreme Court held that the mandatory cutoff dates were arbitrary and bore no rational relationship to the state interest in continuity of instruction. Because the rules created an irrebuttable presumption of physical incompetency by pregnant teachers even where contrary medical evidence was present, the rules violated the Due Process Clause of the U.S. Constitution.**
Two public school teachers in Ohio and one in Virginia brought lawsuits challenging their school districts' maternity leave of absence rules. The Cleveland, Ohio, school board rule required a pregnant school teacher to take unpaid maternity leave five months before the expected childbirth. The teacher could return to work at the next regular school semester following the date when her child attained the age of three months. The Chesterfield County, Virginia, school board rule required a teacher to take leave of absence four months before the anticipated childbirth with reemployment guaranteed no later than the first day of the school year following the date she was declared re-eligible. Both rules required a physician's written statement prior to reemployment. The teachers challenged the constitutionality of the mandatory leave of absence rules.
The U.S. Supreme Court held that the rules of both school boards regarding leave of absence at mandatory and fixed time periods violated the Due Process Clause of the Fourteenth Amendment. The Court said that the arguments advanced by the school districts in defense of their rules, such as continuity of classroom instruction, physical inability of teachers to teach, and health of the teacher and unborn child contained arbitrary irrebuttable presumptions. The arbitrary fourth or fifth month maternity leave rules bore no rational relationship to the state interest in continuity in the classroom, and could work against continuity by requiring that leaves be taken in mid-semester even when the

teacher could have finished the semester. The Court further held that the return to work provisions of the rules were valid with respect to physical examination before returning to work and the dates of reemployment. However, the Court struck down the Cleveland, Ohio, board's rule requiring teachers to wait for reemployment until the child was three months old. The Court found the rule in violation of due process because of the irrebuttable presumptions the rule contained bearing no rational relationship to any legitimate school interest. *Cleveland Board of Educ. v. LaFleur*, 414 U.S. 632, 94 S.Ct. 791, 39 L.Ed.2d 52 (1974).

♦ **The Court stated that an employer's disability benefits plan did not violate Title VII despite the fact that the plan failed to cover pregnancy-related disabilities. The Court determined that the benefits plan was merely less than all-inclusive and that this was acceptable. However, this case was overruled seven years later.**

A company provided its employees with a disability plan that paid weekly nonoccupational sickness and accident benefits; however, the plan excluded disabilities arising from pregnancy. A group of women employees brought a lawsuit against the company, asserting that its policy constituted sex discrimination in violation of Title VII. A federal district court held for the employees, and the U.S. Court of Appeals affirmed. The company petitioned for a writ of certiorari, which the U.S. Supreme Court granted.

The Supreme Court held that the company's disability benefits plan did not violate Title VII even though it failed to cover pregnancy-related disabilities. The Court noted that the plan did not exclude anyone because of gender; it merely removed one physical condition – pregnancy – from the list of disabilities that were covered. Even though pregnancy is confined to women, it is significantly different from the typical covered disease or disability. Gender-based discrimination does not result simply because a company's disability benefits plan is less than all-inclusive. Here, the company's plan was just an insurance package that covered some risks while excluding others. Since no pretext for discrimination was shown, the Court reversed the lower courts and upheld the plan. *General Electric Co. v. Gilbert*, 429 U.S. 125, 97 S.Ct. 401, 50 L.Ed.2d 343 (1976). *Newport News Shipbuilding and Dry Dock Co. v. EEOC*, below, overrules this case.

♦ **A pregnancy limitation in an employer's health plan that provided fewer pregnancy benefits for spouses of male employees than it did for female employees was held to violate the Pregnancy Discrimination Act. The case overruled *General Electric Co. v. Gilbert*, above, which allowed differential treatment of pregnancy as nongender-based discrimination.**

After Title VII was amended in 1978 by the Pregnancy Discrimination Act to prohibit discrimination on the basis of pregnancy, a company amended its health insurance plan to provide its female employees with hospitalization benefits for pregnancy-related conditions to the same extent as for other medical conditions. However, the plan provided less extensive pregnancy benefits for spouses of male employees. The company then filed an action in a Virginia federal district court challenging Equal Employment Opportunity Commission

(EEOC) guidelines that indicated that its health insurance plan was unlawful. The EEOC also sued, asserting that the plan was discriminatory. The district court ruled for the company, but the U.S. Court of Appeals reversed. The case then came before the U.S. Supreme Court.

The Supreme Court stated that pregnancy limitations for spouses of male employees discriminated against the men who worked for the company. The plan provided less protection to married male employees than it did to married female employees. The Pregnancy Discrimination Act provides that it is discriminatory to exclude pregnancy coverage from an otherwise inclusive benefits plan. The act not only overturned the holding of *General Electric Co. v. Gilbert*, which held that it was lawful to exclude disabilities caused by pregnancy from a disability plan that provided general coverage; it also rejected that Court's reasoning that differential treatment of pregnancy is not gender-based discrimination even though only women can become pregnant. The Court affirmed the court of appeals' decision in favor of the EEOC. *Newport News Shipbuilding and Dry Dock Co. v. EEOC,* 462 U.S. 669, 103 S.Ct. 2622, 77 L.Ed.2d 89 (1983).

♦ **In the case below, the Court determined that California's Fair Employment and Housing Act (which prohibits, among other things, discrimination on the basis of pregnancy) was not inconsistent with – and thus not preempted by – Title VII. Accordingly, employers could be required to abide by the state law without violating Title VII.**

The California Federal Savings and Loan Association, a federally chartered S&L, was an employer covered by both Title VII and Section 12945(b)(2) of the California Government Code. Section 12945(b)(2) prohibits employers from disallowing reasonable pregnancy leaves. The S&L employed a woman as a receptionist for several years. She took a pregnancy disability leave for four months, then notified the S&L that she was able to return to work. However, it informed her that her job had been filled and that no other similar positions were available. It maintained that just because it allowed employees to take unpaid leaves of absence, it was not required to reinstate the employees if similar positions did not exist when they chose to return. The employee filed a complaint with the Department of Fair Employment and Housing, which charged the S&L with violating Section 12945(b)(2). Before a hearing was conducted, the S&L brought suit in a federal district court, seeking a declaration that Section 12945(b)(2) was preempted by Title VII. It argued that compliance with Section 12945(b)(2) would open the door for a reverse discrimination suit by disabled males who took unpaid leaves. The district court agreed with the S&L, but the U.S. Court of Appeals, Ninth Circuit, reversed. Appeal was taken to the U.S. Supreme Court.

On appeal, the Court noted that the purpose of both Title VII and Section 12945(b)(2) was to achieve equality of employment opportunities. By requiring reinstatement after pregnancy leaves, Section 12945(b)(2) ensured that women would not lose their jobs on account of pregnancy. Further, the Court noted that the Pregnancy Discrimination Act, which amended Title VII, did not prohibit employment practices that favored pregnant women. The federal and state laws merely established a minimum standard which employers were required to abide by. Accordingly, the Supreme Court affirmed the court of appeals' decision and held that Section 12945(b)(2) was not preempted by Title VII. *California Federal Savings and Loan Ass'n v. Guerra*, 479 U.S. 272, 107 S.Ct. 683, 93 L.Ed.2d 613 (1987).

♦ **Discrimination on the basis of sex that is done without malevolent motive or for the protection of employees' health and well-being still violates Title VII. If a class of employees wishes to be exposed to risks that another class is encountering, the employer cannot prevent those employees from exposing themselves to those risks.**

A company manufactured batteries, the primary ingredient of which was lead. As a result, in 1982, the company began a policy of excluding pregnant women and women capable of bearing children from jobs involving lead exposure. In 1984, a group of affected employees initiated a class action against the company, challenging its fetal protection policy as sex discrimination that violated Title VII. A federal district court granted summary judgment to the company, finding that it had established a business necessity defense. The U.S. Court of Appeals, Seventh Circuit, affirmed, and the employees petitioned the U.S. Supreme Court for review.

The Court noted that there was a clear bias in the company's policy, allowing fertile men but not women the choice of risking their reproductive health. Thus, there was clear sex discrimination involved. Even though there was no malevolent motive involved, the policy could not be termed "neutral." Accordingly, the only way for the company to justify the discrimination was by establishing that gender was a bona fide occupational qualification (BFOQ). The Court then stated that the company could not show a valid BFOQ. Decisions about the welfare of future children must be left to parents rather than their employers. The Court next looked to the issue of tort liability and found that it was unlikely that a person could bring a negligence action against the company at a later date for prenatal injuries. Since the company complied with the lead standard developed by the Occupational Safety and Health Administration and issued warnings to its female employees about the dangers of lead exposure, it was not negligent and it would be difficult for a court to find liability against the company. The Court therefore reversed the lower courts' decisions and struck down the company's fetal protection policy. *Int'l Union, UAW v. Johnson Controls*, 499 U.S. 187, 111 S.Ct. 1196, 113 L.Ed.2d 158 (1991).

C. Age Discrimination

1. Generally

♦ A group of night watchmen in New York sued under the ADEA after they were removed from their positions and assigned to less desirable jobs as night porters and light-duty cleaners. The employer asserted that they should have arbitrated their claims as required by the collective bargaining agreement in place. The case reached the U.S. Supreme Court, which agreed with the employer that **the watchmen had to arbitrate their claims under the ADEA.** The union and the employer bargained in good faith and agreed that employment-related discrimination claims would be subject to arbitration. And the ADEA does not preclude the arbitration of such claims. As a result, the employees had to arbitrate their claims. They still retained the option of suing their union for breach of the duty of fair representation; they could also sue the union directly under the ADEA; and they could still bring individual claims to the EEOC or the NLRB. *14 Penn Plaza LLC v. Pyett,* 556 U.S. 247, 129 S.Ct. 1456, 173 L.Ed.2d 398 (2009).

◆   A 54-year-old claims administration director for a financial services company in Iowa was reassigned to a job as a claims project coordinator. The employer transferred many of his duties to a newly created position and gave the job to a woman in her early 40s whom the coordinator had previously supervised. He sued the company under the ADEA, presenting evidence that he was reassigned in part because of his age. The company claimed the reassignment was part of corporate restructuring. The case reached the U.S. Supreme Court, which held that **an employee can win an ADEA claim by only proving that age was the sole motivating factor for the adverse action.** *Gross v. FBL Financial Services, Inc.,* 129 S.Ct. 2343, 174 L.Ed.2d 119 (U.S. 2009).

◆   An atomic power laboratory in New York was ordered to reduce its work force. It did so in part by ranking employees on job performance, flexibility and criticality. The flexibility factor assessed whether the employees' skills were transferable to other assignments. The criticality factor assessed the importance of the employees' skills to the lab. When 30 of the 31 people laid off were age 40 or older, an ADEA lawsuit ensued. A jury ruled that the layoff process had a disparate impact on older employees, but the Second Circuit reversed, finding the employees should have been required to prove that the selection process was unreasonable. The Supreme Court vacated and remanded the case. Here, **the burden should have been on the employer to prove that its layoff process used reasonable factors other than age.** *Meacham v. Knolls Atomic Power Laboratory,* 554 U.S. 84, 128 S.Ct. 2395, 171 L.Ed.2d 283 (2008).

◆   After an older employee in Kansas was fired as part of a reduction in force, she sued for age discrimination. When she sought to introduce testimony from five other employees who claimed that their supervisors discriminated against them because of age, the court refused to allow the "me too" testimony. The Tenth Circuit reversed, but the Supreme Court reversed the court of appeals. It held that such **"me too" testimony can be admitted if it is relevant and not unduly prejudicial.** This is a fact-based inquiry that is best left to the trial court to ascertain. *Sprint/United Management Co. v. Mendelsohn,* 552 U.S. 379, 128 S.Ct. 1140, 170 L.Ed.2d 1 (2008).

◆   A group of senior, longtime police officers with a Mississippi city challenged the city's revised pay policy because it gave proportionately higher raises to officers with less than five years' tenure. They claimed that the revised policy had a disparate (discriminatory) impact on them. The U.S. Supreme Court held that **the officers could sue for disparate impact discrimination under the ADEA.** To win, the officers would have to identify a "specific test, requirement, or practice with the pay plan that ha[d] an adverse impact on older workers." The city claimed that the differential was justified by the need to make junior officers' salaries competitive with comparable positions in the market. Here, the Court determined that the policy was based on reasonable factors other than age and therefore did not violate the ADEA. *Smith v. City of Jackson*, 544 U.S. 228, 125 S.Ct. 1536, 161 L.Ed.2d 410 (2005).

♦ **In the *Trans World Airlines, Inc. v. Thurston* case, the Supreme Court held that an airline's retirement and transfer policy violated the Age Discrimination in Employment Act (ADEA). However, it could not be liable for double damages due to willful misconduct because it did not knowingly violate the ADEA.**

An airline was concerned that its retirement policy with respect to flight engineers violated the ADEA. It thus adopted a plan permitting any employee with "flight engineer status" to continue to work in that capacity. However, captains (pilots) had to obtain that status through bidding procedures outlined in the collective bargaining agreement prior to their 60th birthday and hope that a vacancy opened up prior to that time. Otherwise, the captain would be retired. Even though this was the policy for captains displaced by age, it was not the policy for those who were displaced for any other reason (like medical disability or reduction in manpower). Three pilots sued, claiming that this policy violated the ADEA. The district court held for the airline, but the U.S. Court of Appeals reversed, finding that the discrimination had been willful and awarding double damages against the airline.

On further appeal, the U.S. Supreme Court held that the airline's transfer policy denied 60-year-old captains a "privilege of employment" on the basis of age, and that this violated the ADEA. The only reason some captains were not allowed to "bump" less senior employees was because of their age. Further, there was no bona fide occupational qualification defense that the airline could establish to justify its actions. However, the Court held that the airline should not have been assessed double damages because it did not "know" that its conduct violated the ADEA. Nor did it adopt its transfer policy in "reckless disregard" of the ADEA's requirements. Accordingly, the Court upheld the finding that the airline had discriminated on the basis of age, but reversed the award of double damages because the airline had acted in good faith in attempting to determine whether its policy would violate the ADEA. *Trans World Airlines, Inc. v. Thurston*, 469 U.S. 111, 105 S.Ct. 613, 83 L.Ed.2d 523 (1985).

♦ **In 1993, the Supreme Court held that in a disparate treatment case under the Age Discrimination in Employment Act (ADEA), liability depends on whether age actually motivated the employer's decision. An adverse decision was insufficient to support an age discrimination claim where the decision was based on years of service, which could be distinguished from age.**

A Massachusetts manufacturing employee was fired when he was 62 years old and a few weeks shy of vesting for his pension benefits. He filed suit in a federal district court alleging violations of the ADEA and ERISA. The jury found for the employee on both violations and further determined that the

ADEA violation had been willful. Thus, the employee was entitled to liquidated damages. The district court granted the employer's motion for judgment notwithstanding the verdict with respect to the finding of willfulness. Both parties appealed to the U.S. Court of Appeals, First Circuit, which affirmed the jury's finding of a wilful violation of the ADEA. The employer appealed to the U.S. Supreme Court.

There were two issues on appeal to the Supreme Court: whether an employer's interference with the vesting of pension benefits was a violation of the ADEA and what standard of willfulness should be used under the ADEA. The ADEA was enacted to prevent discrimination based on age and also to "prohibit the problem of inaccurate and stigmatizing stereotypes about productivity and competence declining with age." However, when an employer's decision is wholly motivated by factors other than age, the stigmatizing stereotypes disappear. The court noted that this was true even when the motivating factor was correlated with age (such as pension status). Because age and years of service may be analytically distinct, an employer could take account of one while ignoring the other. Thus, the court reasoned that it was incorrect to say that a decision based on years of service was necessarily "age-based." Next, the Court analyzed the standard for willfulness under the ADEA. The Court ruled that once a willful violation had been shown, the employee need not additionally demonstrate that the employer's conduct was outrageous, prove direct evidence of the employer's motivation, or prove that age was the predominant factor in the employment decision. The Supreme Court remanded the case to the court of appeals to determine if the jury had sufficient evidence to find a violation of the ADEA. *Hazen Paper Co. v. Biggins,* 507 U.S. 604, 113 S.Ct. 1701, 123 L.Ed.2d 338 (1993).

♦ **After-acquired evidence of an employee's wrongdoing that would have led to the employee's discharge is not a complete bar to recovery under the Age Discrimination in Employment Act (ADEA). Where the employee was discharged in violation of the ADEA, such evidence merely limits the damages award available.**

A 62-year-old secretary worked for a Tennessee publishing company for over 30 years. She had access to company financial records and made copies of documents when she became concerned that the company would terminate her employment because of her age. The publishing company dismissed the secretary under a work force reduction plan. She filed a lawsuit against the publisher in the U.S. District Court for the Middle District of Tennessee under the ADEA, seeking back pay and other relief. During the course of pretrial discovery, the publisher learned that the secretary had copied company financial documents. Based on this information, it filed a motion for summary judgment, which the court granted on the basis of the secretary's misconduct. The U.S. Court of Appeals, Sixth Circuit, affirmed the decision and the secretary appealed to the U.S. Supreme Court.

The Court rejected the reasoning of the lower courts that the secretary's misconduct constituted proper grounds for termination based on the after-acquired evidence revealed in discovery. The important anti-discrimination objectives of the ADEA precluded the blanket denial of relief to the former secretary. Employee wrongdoing remained relevant and would preclude reinstatement or front pay as an appropriate remedy in this case. However, on remand, the district court could not impose an absolute rule barring the secretary's recovery of back pay. The remedy should calculate back pay from the date of the unlawful discharge to the date the publisher discovered the wrongdoing. The case was remanded for further proceedings. *McKennon v. Nashville Banner Publishing Co.,* 513 U.S. 352, 115 S.Ct. 879, 130 L.Ed.2d 852 (1995).

♦ **The Supreme Court, in *Commissioner of Internal Revenue v. Schleier,* viewed an Age Discrimination in Employment Act (ADEA) settlement as taxable. The Court distinguished the liquidated damages from tort damages for personal injury or sickness and analogized the damages to back wages.**

An airline employee was fired when he reached the age of 60 pursuant to company policy. He filed an age discrimination lawsuit against the airline in a federal district court under the ADEA. The parties reached a settlement prior to trial under which the airline paid the employee $145,000. The parties designated half of the payment as back pay and the other half as liquidated damages. The airline did not withhold any payroll or income tax from the liquidated damages portion of the settlement award. The former employee failed to pay any income tax on the liquidated damages portion of the settlement award, and the Commissioner of the IRS served him with a deficiency notice, stating that liquidated damages were includable in his gross income. The former employee filed a U.S. Tax Court action asserting that he had properly excluded the liquidated damage award and seeking a refund of tax paid on his back pay. The tax court held that the entire settlement award was excludable from income as damages received on account of personal injury or sickness within the meaning of the IRS Code. The U.S. Court of Appeals, Fifth Circuit, affirmed the tax court decision, and the commissioner appealed to the U.S. Supreme Court.

On appeal, the former employee argued that his settlement was attributable to a personal injury or sickness because it was based upon a tort or tort-type right under the ADEA. The court disagreed, finding that liquidated damages under the ADEA were distinguishable from tort damages for personal injury or sickness and were analogous to back wages that were of an economic character and therefore fully taxable. In order to exclude damage awards from taxation, taxpayers were required to demonstrate that the underlying cause of action was based upon a tort or tort-type right and that the damages were received on account of personal injury or sickness. Because the settlement award in this case failed both parts of the test, the lower court decisions were reversed. *Commissioner of Internal Revenue v. Schleier,* 515 U.S. 323, 115 S.Ct. 2159, 132 L.Ed.2d 294 (1995).

♦ **In *O'Connor v. Consolidated Coin Caterers Corp.,* the Supreme Court refined the McDonnell Douglas test. Specifically, the Court determined that the Age Discrimination in Employment Act (ADEA) prohibits discrimination on the basis of age, not class membership.**

A 56-year-old North Carolina employee was fired by his employer after 12 years of work and replaced by a 40-year-old man. The discharged employee filed a lawsuit against his former employer in the U.S. District Court for the Western District of North Carolina, alleging age discrimination in violation of the ADEA. The court held for the employer, and the U.S. Court of Appeals, Fourth Circuit, affirmed. The employee appealed to the U.S. Supreme Court, which agreed to review the questions of whether the employee was barred from proving age discrimination under the ADEA solely because he had been replaced by a worker who was 40 years old and also whether the employee was within the class of persons protected by the ADEA.

The Court observed that federal courts analyze ADEA cases under the framework first established in the case of *McDonnell Douglas Corp. v. Green*, 411 U.S. 792, 93 S.Ct. 1817, 36 L.Ed.2d 668 (1973). Complaining parties in such cases must demonstrate that they are in a protected group, are discharged or demoted despite competently performing their jobs and are replaced by someone outside the protected class. The Court stated that the evidence must be adequate to create an inference that an employment decision was based on an illegal discriminatory motive. It was nonsensical to prohibit an inference of discrimination based on the class status of the individual who replaces the complaining party. Under that logic, a 40-year-old worker replaced by a 39-year-old worker would be entitled to ADEA protection while the 56-year-old employee in this case would gain no relief despite being replaced by an individual who was 16 years younger. Because the ADEA prohibits discrimination on the basis of age, and not on the basis of class membership, the replacement of an employee by a substantially younger employee was a far more reliable indicator of age discrimination. The lower court decisions were reversed and remanded. *O'Connor v. Consolidated Coin Caterers Corp.*, 517 U.S. 308, 116 S.Ct. 1307, 134 L.Ed.2d 433 (1996).

♦ **Before an employer may obtain a waiver or release of potential Age Discrimination in Employment Act (ADEA) claims, the employer must comply with the specific statutory requirements outlined in the Older Workers Benefit Protection Act (OWBPA) amendments. If the employer does not comply with the statutory requirements, then the waiver or release becomes unenforceable despite the employee's failure to tender back the severance pay.**

The OWBPA imposes specific requirements upon employers who discharge employees and seek the waiver or release of potential claims against them under the ADEA. The requirements apply where an employee is offered a severance package in return for the waiver of claims against the employer. Among the requirements of a valid OWBPA waiver are a minimum 20-day notice to the employee to consider the waiver, written advice to consult an attorney prior to executing the waiver, a seven-day period after signature of the waiver in which to revoke consent and specific reference to rights or claims arising under the ADEA. A Louisiana employer presented an employee with a severance agreement and waiver after she received a poor performance rating. The employer did not comply with OWBPA requirements, giving her only 14 days to consider the waiver, failing to allow seven days after signing the release during which to change her mind, and making no reference to ADEA claims.

The employee signed the release, waiving all claims against the employer in return for $6,258. She then filed an age discrimination complaint against the employer in a federal district court, alleging constructive discharge in violation of the ADEA and state law. The court granted the employer's summary judgment motion, ruling that she had ratified the defective release by retaining the severance pay. The U.S. Court of Appeals, Fifth Circuit, affirmed. The U.S. Supreme Court agreed to review the case.

The Court found that the lower courts had improperly relied on general contract principles in concluding that the employee's retention of the severance pay effectively waived the ADEA claim. The Court observed that the OWBPA amended the ADEA with specific statutory commands forbidding the waiver of an ADEA claim unless the statutory requirements are met. The Court reversed and remanded the case since the release did not comply with OWBPA standards and was unenforceable. The failure to tender back the severance pay award did not excuse the employer's failure to comply with the OWBPA. *Oubre v. Entergy Operations, Inc.*, 522 U.S. 422, 118 S.Ct. 838, 139 L.Ed.2d 849 (1998).

♦ **Congress exceeded its constitutional authority under the Fourteenth Amendment when it included state employees within the coverage of the Age Discrimination in Employment Act (ADEA). The Supreme Court found that Congress had no reason to believe that the states unconstitutionally discriminated against employees on the basis of age, making the contested amendment to the ADEA improper.**

The U.S. Court of Appeals, Eleventh Circuit, consolidated three age discrimination cases in Florida filed against public employers and found that Congress did not effectively abrogate Eleventh Amendment immunity when it amended the ADEA to extend the act's protections to state employees. Two of the cases involved actions by current and former university employees against public universities. The other case involved the Florida Department of Corrections. The U.S Supreme Court agreed to hear the consolidated cases.

The Court initially explained that the Eleventh Amendment prohibits federal suits against nonconsenting states. Congress may abrogate state immunity only by making its intention unmistakably clear in statutory language, and only then as a valid exercise of constitutional authority. In this case, Congress had clearly stated its intent to abrogate Eleventh Amendment immunity by subjecting the states to potential liability for monetary damages in suits filed by individual employees. However, the court held that Congress lacked the power to do so when it amended the ADEA in 1974. Under the standard defined by *Seminole Tribe of Florida v. Florida*, 517 U.S. 44 (1996), Congress has no Article I commerce power to abrogate state immunity. Although Section 5 of the Fourteenth Amendment permits Congress to abrogate state immunity, this affirmative grant of power does not include the power to determine what constitutes a constitutional violation. The court has required a showing of a "congruence and proportionality" between the injury Congress seeks to prevent or remedy and the means adopted to achieve that end. Under the congruence and proportionality test, Congressional action will be struck down if it is out of proportion to a supposed remedial objective that cannot be understood as responsive to, or designed to prevent, unconstitutional behavior. Applying this test, the Supreme Court determined the ADEA as amended was not appropriate legislation under Section 5 of the Fourteenth Amendment, because its substantive requirements were found disproportionate to any perceived unconstitutional conduct by the states.

The Court previously held that age classifications do not violate the Equal Protection Clause. Unlike classifications based on race and gender, age classifications do not reflect prejudice or antipathy, and older persons have not been subjected to a history of purposeful or unequal treatment. Moreover, age classifications are presumptively rational, and states may discriminate on the basis of age without offending the Fourteenth Amendment, if the classification is rationally related to a legitimate state interest. The amended ADEA was out of proportion to its supposed remedial objective because it purported to prevent discrimination that was not protected by the Equal Protection Clause. The court characterized the legislative record of the ADEA as "an unwarranted response to a perhaps inconsequential problem." Congress identified no pattern of age discrimination by the states and had no reason to believe that state and local governments were unconstitutionally discriminating against their employees on the basis of age. Therefore, the employees could not pursue their lawsuits under the ADEA. *Kimel v. Florida Board of Regents*, 528 U.S. 62, 120 S.Ct. 631, 145 L.Ed.2d 522 (2000).

♦ **The Supreme Court held that the Age Discrimination in Employment Act (ADEA) did not protect against reverse age discrimination. Therefore, an employer can favor an older employee over a younger one.**

A company and a union entered into a collective bargaining agreement, which eliminated the company's obligation to provide health benefits to subsequently retired employees, except as to then-current workers at least 50 years old. Employees who were at least 40 and thus protected by the ADEA, but not yet 50 (so without the promise of health benefits) filed charges with the Equal Employment Opportunity Commission (EEOC), claiming that the bargaining agreement violated the ADEA by discriminating against them because of their age. When the company and union refused to settle, the employees sued in an Ohio federal court, which dismissed the action on the grounds that the ADEA did not cover "reverse age discrimination." The Sixth Circuit reversed, finding that the ADEA did not specifically limit its coverage to older workers. The U.S. Supreme Court granted review and held that the ADEA was never intended to prevent an employer from favoring an older worker over a younger one. Rather, Congress was concerned with discrimination that was directed at older workers. Hence, the over 40 provision in the statute. The Court overruled the EEOC's interpretive guidance, which told employers that they could not favor an older worker over a younger one. Reverse age discrimination is not barred by the ADEA. *General Dynamics Land Systems, Inc. v. Cline*, 540 U.S. 581, 124 S.Ct. 1236, 157 L.Ed.2d 1094 (2004).

2. Procedural Issues

♦ **In a 1989 case, the Court decided that district courts have discretion in Age Discrimination in Employment Act (ADEA) actions to facilitate notice to potential plaintiffs so long as they do not communicate any encouragement to join the suit or any approval of the suit's merits.**

A company ordered a reduction in work force and discharged or demoted approximately 1,200 workers. One of the discharged employees filed an age discrimination charge with the Equal Employment Opportunity Commission for himself and all similarly situated employees. A group of affected employees brought suit under the ADEA, and sought discovery of the names and addresses of all similarly situated employees. They also requested that a court-approved consent document be sent out. A federal district court ordered the company to comply with the discovery request, and authorized the sending of consent documents. The U.S. Court of Appeals affirmed, and the U.S. Supreme Court granted review. The Supreme Court held that district courts have discretion in ADEA actions to facilitate notice to potential plaintiffs. As had the court of appeals, the Court declined to examine the terms of the notice used in this case. It noted that the district court was correct to permit discovery of the discharged employees' names and addresses. The Court stated, however, that trial courts have to be careful to maintain neutrality by avoiding even the appearance of endorsement of the merits of an action. The Court affirmed the lower court decisions and remanded the case. *Hoffman-La Roche, Inc. v. Sperling*, 493 U.S. 165, 110 S.Ct. 482, 107 L.Ed.2d 480 (1989).

♦ **Federal employees wishing to pursue an age discrimination claim under the Age Discrimination in Employment Act (ADEA) may invoke the Equal Employment Opportunity Commission's (EEOC's) administrative process or they may file a lawsuit. For a direct suit, employees must give the EEOC notice of their intent to sue at least 30 days before bringing suit, and the notice must be filed within 180 days of the alleged unlawful practice.**

A 63-year-old man was accepted into a training program with the Internal Revenue Service (IRS). On April 26, 1987, he was informed that his performance was not satisfactory. He requested a demotion and transfer so that he could avoid termination. He felt that he had been a victim of age discrimination, and in September of 1987, attempted to gain relief through the Department of the Treasury. He also notified the IRS of an intent to sue if the matter was not resolved to his satisfaction. The appeal to the Department of the Treasury was dismissed because he had not acted within 30 days of the employer's action. He then appealed to the EEOC, which upheld the dismissal. In May 1988, a lawsuit was filed in a federal court. Again the claim was dismissed. The court held that the employee could either proceed directly to federal court within 180 days of the employer's action and notify the EEOC within 30 days of bringing suit, or attempt to gain relief through the appropriate agency and bring suit only after an exhaustion of administrative remedies. The suit was brought more than 180 days after the employer's action, so the court determined that it was untimely. The employee then appealed to the U.S. Court of Appeals, Fifth Circuit, which held that he was not required to bring suit within 180 days of the employer's action, but only needed to serve notice within that time. However, the dismissal was upheld because his notice to the EEOC was not within 30 days of his filing suit. The case then reached the U.S. Supreme Court.

The Supreme Court ruled that the requirement of notice to the EEOC was incorrectly applied. Section 15(d) of 29 U.S.C. § 633a(d) allows a federal employee to proceed directly to federal court by serving notice of the alleged unlawful practice on the employer within 180 days, and requires only that the employee notify the EEOC of the employee's intent to sue not less than 30 days from when the suit is brought. The man had met this requirement. He had served notice to his employer within 180 days, and had filed suit more than 30 days after notifying the EEOC. The case was reversed and remanded for trial. *Stevens v. Dep't of the Treasury*, 500 U.S. 1, 111 S.Ct. 1562, 114 L.Ed.2d 1 (1991).

◆ **The Supreme Court has held that employers may compel arbitration with respect to an age discrimination claim if the procedures are adequate and the arbitration agreement is not the result of unequal bargaining power.**

A corporation hired a middle-age man as its manager of financial services. As required by his employer, he then registered as a securities representative with several stock exchanges, including the New York Stock Exchange (NYSE). In 1987, at the age of 62, the manager was discharged. He filed a claim with the Equal Employment Opportunity Commission, then brought suit in a North Carolina federal district court under the Age Discrimination in Employment Act (ADEA). His employer filed a motion to compel arbitration because NYSE Rule 347 provided for arbitration of any controversy arising out of employment or termination of employment. The district court denied the motion, holding that "Congress intended to protect ADEA claimants from the waiver of a judicial forum." The U.S. Court of Appeals, Fourth Circuit, reversed. The manager appealed to the U.S. Supreme Court. The Court stated that there was no inconsistency between the public policy behind the ADEA and enforcing agreements to arbitrate age discrimination claims. The ADEA was enacted with the idea of providing a flexible approach to claim resolution. Further, the manager failed to show that the arbitration procedures were inadequate. Since he failed to meet the burden of proving that Congress intended to preclude arbitration of claims under the ADEA, the Court held that the arbitration clause could be enforced. *Gilmer v. Interstate/Johnson Lane Corp.*, 500 U.S. 20, 111 S.Ct. 1647, 114 L.Ed.2d 26 (1991).

◆ **State administrative agency findings with respect to the Age Discrimination in Employment Act (ADEA) which have not been judicially reviewed have no preclusive effect on federal proceedings.**

A 63-year-old New York man was dismissed from his position as a vice president in the mortgage department of a bank. He filed an age discrimination claim with the Equal Employment Opportunity Commission, which referred the matter to the New York State Division of Human Rights. This agency found no probable cause to believe the employee was discharged due to his age, and the Human Rights Appeal Board affirmed that decision. The employee then brought suit in a federal district court under the ADEA rather than appealing the administrative decision in state court. The district court granted the employer's motion for summary judgment, holding that the agency determination precluded the claim in federal court. The U.S. Court of Appeals, Second Circuit, reversed, and further appeal was taken to the U.S. Supreme Court. The Court held that the state administrative proceedings did not preclude the ADEA suit in this case because they had not been judicially reviewed. Both Section 626(d)(2) and Section 633(b) of the ADEA assume the possibility of federal consideration after state agencies have finished examining the case. However, if state agency actions were given preclusive effect, federal proceedings would be a mere formality. The Court affirmed the reversal of summary judgment and remanded the case. *Astoria Federal Savings and Loan Ass'n v. Solimino*, 501 U.S. 104, 111 S.Ct. 2166, 115 L.Ed.2d 96 (1991).

♦ **Preserving a jury's role in deciding ultimate questions of fact, a unanimous U.S. Supreme Court held that the jury in an Age Discrimination in Employment Act (ADEA) case did not need direct evidence of age discrimination to infer that the former employer intentionally violated the ADEA when it terminated an employee.**

An employee worked for a plumbing company for 40 years before being fired. He sued under the ADEA, claiming the reason he was terminated was his age: 57. At trial, the company argued that it fired the employee because he had failed to maintain accurate attendance records, but the employee countered with evidence establishing that his record-keeping was proper and, contrary to the company's assertions, he had never falsified any information. A jury agreed with the employee, awarding him $98,000 in damages. On appeal, the Fifth Circuit concluded that the evidence was sufficient to show that the plumbing company's explanation for the termination was pretextual, but was not enough under *St. Mary's Honor Center v. Hicks*, 509 U.S. 502 (1993), to prove intentional discrimination. Although the employee introduced additional evidence that the official who fired him said he "was so old [he] must have come over on the Mayflower," and that he "was too damn old to do [his] job," those comments were not made in the context of termination and could not prove intent, the Fifth Circuit reasoned.

On further appeal, the U.S. Supreme Court concluded that once the employee offered substantial evidence from which a jury could conclude that the company's explanation for the termination was not the real reason he was fired, the jury was then free to infer intentional discrimination and hold the company liable. The appeals court wrongly confined its review of the verdict to derogatory age-related comments that the official made to the employee, and to evidence that the official had singled the employee out for harsher treatment than younger workers. The Fifth Circuit "believed that only this additional evidence of discrimination was relevant to whether the jury's verdict should stand." However, the court of appeals improperly discounted the record as a whole, ignoring critical evidence that the official treated a worker who was substantially younger than the employee more leniently and that even though two other company officials joined him in the termination recommendation, the official wielded "absolute power" over all company decisions. *Reeves v. Sanderson Plumbing Products*, 530 U.S. 133, 120 S.Ct. 2097, 147 L.Ed.2d 105 (2000).

3. Mandatory Retirement

♦ **In 1976, the Supreme Court upheld a mandatory retirement law for state police officers against constitutional attack. The Court noted that age is not a "suspect class." As long as the law was rationally related to a legitimate governmental interest, it would be upheld.**

A Massachusetts law required automatic retirement at the age of 50 for its uniformed state police officers. An officer who was automatically retired sued the state board of retirement in a federal district court, asserting that the law denied him equal protection. Four months before his retirement, he had passed a rigorous examination and he stated that he was still capable of performing the duties of a uniformed officer. The district court agreed with the officer that compulsory retirement at age 50 was irrational and violated equal protection. The board then was granted leave to appeal the case to the U.S. Supreme Court.

The Court first determined that the proper standard to use in deciding whether the law violated equal protection was the "rational basis" standard. So long as the law was rationally related to a legitimate state interest, the Court would uphold it as valid because officers over 50 are not a "suspect class" of persons requiring heightened judicial scrutiny. It then noted that the Massachusetts law was rationally related to a legitimate state interest because physical ability generally declines with age. Further, the state's needs in protecting the public outweighed the interests of the few officers who were still capable of performing their duties after age 50. Although the state could have chosen a more individualized means to determine fitness than an arbitrary cutoff at age 50, its law did not violate equal protection merely because it was not perfect. The Court reversed the district court's decision and upheld the mandatory retirement law. *Massachusetts Board of Retirement v. Murgia,* 427 U.S. 307, 96 S.Ct. 2562, 49 L.Ed.2d 520 (1976).

♦ **Three years later, the Court again upheld a mandatory retirement statute – this time for participants in the foreign service.**

The U.S. Congress enacted a mandatory retirement age of 60 for participants in the foreign service retirement system. Employees covered by the civil service retirement system were not required to retire until age 70. A group of past and present foreign service employees sued in a federal district court, challenging the constitutionality of the classification requiring earlier retirement, and a special three-judge court was convened to hear the case. It held that the law was violative of equal protection and that no distinction should be made between civil service and foreign service employees. The government then sought review from the U.S. Supreme Court. The Supreme Court noted that so long as there was a rational basis for the law, it would be upheld, because foreign service personnel over age 60 were not members of a suspect class of people who required strict judicial scrutiny. The Court then determined that an earlier mandatory retirement furthered a legitimate governmental interest in two ways. First, it created incentives to morale and performance by assuring more predictable promotions. Second, it removed from service those who were too old for overseas duty. Even if the decision by Congress may not have been wise, Congress had chosen a rational means to achieve a legitimate end. The Court refused to find the law unconstitutional and reversed the district court's decision. *Vance v. Bradley*, 440 U.S. 93, 99 S.Ct. 939, 59 L.Ed.2d 171 (1979).

◆ **In the following case, the Court determined that the U.S. Court of Appeals had improperly interpreted the federal civil service statute when it ruled that age 55 was a bona fide occupational qualification for municipal firefighters.**

Six Maryland firefighters brought suit in a federal district court to challenge the city of Baltimore's municipal code provisions that established a mandatory retirement age lower than 70 for firefighters and police personnel. They asserted that the provisions violated the Age Discrimination in Employment Act (ADEA), which prohibited employers from discriminating on the basis of age against employees between the ages of 40 and 70 – the upper limit of 70 was removed by a 1986 amendment. The city maintained that age was a bona fide occupational qualification (BFOQ) for firefighters, and that it could thus require a lower retirement age. The district court found for the firefighters, but the U.S. Court of Appeals reversed.

On further appeal, the U.S. Supreme Court reversed. It held that even though the federal civil service statute established age 55 as the retirement age for federal firefighters, this did not mean that age 55 was a BFOQ for nonfederal firefighters. Congress had not determined that age was an employment qualification, but rather that it wished to maintain the image of a youthful work force by making early retirement attractive and financially rewarding. Thus, the court of appeals should not have given any weight to the civil service statute's provisions regarding retirement age. The case was remanded for further proceedings. *Johnson v. Mayor and City Council of Baltimore*, 472 U.S. 353, 105 S.Ct. 2717, 86 L.Ed.2d 286 (1985).

◆ **In 1985, the Supreme Court stated that the bona fide occupational qualification (BFOQ) exception to the Age Discrimination in Employment Act's (ADEA's) prohibition on age discrimination was intended to be extremely narrow. The age limit must be "reasonably necessary" to the safe performance of the job, not merely reasonable for the employer.**

An airline company required all cockpit crew members (pilots, copilots and flight engineers) to retire at the age of 60. A Federal Aviation Administration regulation prohibited persons from serving as pilots or copilots after turning 60, but made no similar provision for flight engineers. A group of flight engineers, and pilots who wished to become flight engineers, sued the airline in federal court, contending that the mandatory retirement provision violated the ADEA. The airline defended by arguing that the age 60 limit was a BFOQ that was reasonably necessary to the safe operation of the airline. A jury held for the employees, and the U.S. Court of Appeals affirmed. The U.S. Supreme Court granted certiorari.

The Court stated that the BFOQ exception to the ADEA's prohibition on age discrimination was intended to be extremely narrow. The BFOQ standard, held the Court, is one of "reasonable necessity," not reasonableness. Thus, even if it was "rational" for the airline to set age 60 as the limit for flight engineers, the airline still had to show that it had reasonable cause to believe that all or substantially all flight engineers over 60 would be unable to safely perform their job duties, or that it would be highly impractical to deal with older employees on an individual basis to determine whether they had the necessary qualifications for the job. Because the airline had not shown this, the Court affirmed the lower courts' decisions in favor of the employees. *Western Air Lines, Inc. v. Criswell*, 472 U.S. 400, 105 S.Ct. 2743, 86 L.Ed.2d 321 (1985).

♦ **Appointed state judges can be compelled to retire at a specified age because they are not protected by the Age Discrimination in Employment Act (ADEA). The ADEA does not cover appointees at the policymaking level, which includes judges.**

Four Missouri state judges filed suit in federal court, challenging the mandatory retirement provision of the Missouri Constitution under both the ADEA and the Equal Protection Clause. The court held that the judges were not protected by the ADEA because they were appointees on a policymaking level and thus were excluded from the ADEA's definition of "employee." The court also held that the Equal Protection Clause was not violated by the provision. The U.S. Court of Appeals affirmed the district court's decision, and the case came before the U.S. Supreme Court. The Court noted that when Congress extended the ADEA's provisions to include the states as employers, it redefined "employee" to exclude all elected and most high-ranking state officials, including appointees at the policymaking level. Since the Court determined that judges were presumptively appointees at the policymaking level, they were not covered by the ADEA. Further, mandatory retirement did not violate the Equal Protection Clause because there was a rational basis for distinguishing 70-year-old judges from other state employees for whom no mandatory retirement applied. The Court affirmed the lower court decisions and upheld the mandatory retirement provisions. *Gregory v. Ashcroft*, 501 U.S. 452, 111 S.Ct. 2395, 115 L.Ed.2d 410 (1991).

D. Disability Discrimination

♦ **Section 504 of the Rehabilitation Act, 29 U.S.C. § 794, prohibits discrimination against otherwise qualified individuals with disabilities solely because of their disabilities. In comparison, Title VI, 42 U.S.C. § 2000d *et seq.*, provides more limited protection because it only allows employment discrimination actions to be brought when the employer receives federal financial assistance primarily intended to provide employment.**

A railroad employee, working as a locomotive engineer, was involved in an accident that required amputation of his left hand and forearm in 1971. After being disabled, the railroad allegedly refused to employ him without justification for finding him unfit to work. In 1979, he sued the railroad's successor in interest (Conrail) for violating Section 504 of the Rehabilitation Act of 1973. That section provides that no otherwise qualified individual with a disability can be discriminated against solely because of his or her disability "under any program or activity receiving Federal financial assistance." A 1978 amendment to the act made available to such victims all the remedies set forth in Title VI of the Civil Rights Act. However, Title VI made employment discrimination actionable only when the employer received federal financial assistance "the primary objective of which [was] to provide employment."

A federal district court determined that the aid the government had given to Conrail did not have the primary objective of providing employment. The U.S. Court of Appeals reversed and remanded the case, finding that Section 504 was not limited in the same way as was Title VI. On further appeal, the U.S. Supreme Court agreed with the court of appeals that the financial assistance extended to Conrail did not have to have the primary objective of providing employment in order for the employee to continue the suit. Further, the fact that the employee had died after the start of the suit did not make it moot, for his estate was still entitled to back pay if the discrimination was proven. The amendment had not been intended to add the primary objective requirement of Title VI into the Rehabilitation Act. Accordingly, the Court affirmed the court of appeals' decision and held that the lawsuit against Conrail could be maintained. *Consolidated Rail Corp. v. Darrone*, 465 U.S. 624, 104 S.Ct. 1248, 79 L.Ed.2d 568 (1984).

◆ **In the *Arline* case, the Supreme Court held that a person with a contagious disease could be considered a "handicapped individual" within the meaning of Section 504 of the Rehabilitation Act.**

In a Florida case, the U.S. Supreme Court held that a teacher with tuberculosis qualified for protection under the Rehabilitation Act. The case involved an elementary school teacher who was discharged because of the continued recurrence of tuberculosis. She sued the school board under Section 504 but a federal district court dismissed her claims. However, the U.S. Court of Appeals, Eleventh Circuit, reversed the district court's decision and held that persons with contagious diseases fall within Section 504's coverage. The school board appealed this decision to the U.S. Supreme Court.

The Supreme Court noted that the regulations implementing Section 504 define an individual with a disability as "any person who (i) has a physical or mental impairment which substantially limits one or more major life activities, (ii) has a record of such impairment, or (iii) is regarded as having such an impairment." The regulations define "physical impairment" as a disorder affecting, among other things, the respiratory system and further define "major life activities" as "functions such as caring for one's self ... and working." Here, the teacher qualified as a person with a disability because her tuberculosis affected her respiratory system as well as her ability to work. Allowing discrimination based on the contagious effects of a physical impairment would be inconsistent with the underlying purpose of Section 504. The Court remanded the case to the district court to determine whether the teacher was otherwise qualified for her job and whether the school board could reasonably accommodate her. *School Board of Nassau County v. Arline*, 480 U.S. 273, 107 S.Ct. 1123, 94 L.Ed.2d 307 (1987).

On remand, the district court held that the teacher was otherwise qualified to teach. The teacher posed no threat of transmitting tuberculosis to her students. The court observed that at the time she was on medication, medical tests indicated a limited number of negative cultures. Her family members tested negative and she had limited contact with students. The court ordered her reinstatement or a front pay award of $768,724, representing her earnings until retirement. *Arline v. School Board of Nassau County*, 692 F.Supp. 1286 (M.D. Fla. 1988).

♦   **In a case involving a student at the Merchant Marine Academy, the Supreme Court determined that the U.S. government did not waive its immunity against monetary damages for Section 504(a) Rehabilitation Act violations.**

A first-year student at the U.S. Merchant Marine Academy was diagnosed with diabetes. He was separated from the Academy on the grounds that his diabetes was a disqualifying condition. He filed suit in federal district court against the Secretary of the Department of Transportation and others, alleging that they violated Section 504(a) of the Rehabilitation Act (Act). He requested reinstatement, compensatory damages, attorney's fees and costs. The district court granted the student summary judgment, finding that his separation from the Academy violated the Act, and ordered him reinstated. The government disputed the compensatory damages award, contending that it was protected by sovereign immunity. The district court found that the student was entitled to damages. Soon after, the U.S. Court of Appeals, District of Columbia Circuit, held in another case that the government had not waived its immunity against monetary damages for violations of Section 504(a). The district court then vacated part of its prior decision and denied compensatory damages. The student appealed and the D.C. Circuit Court of Appeals granted the government's motion for summary judgment.

The U.S. Supreme Court granted certiorari to determine whether Congress has waived the government's sovereign immunity against monetary damage awards for violations of Section 504(a). The Court found that a waiver of sovereign immunity must be clearly expressed in the statutory text. The Court found no such language in the text of Section 504(a). The student argued that Section 505(a)(2) of the Act states that the remedies set forth in Title VI of the Civil Rights Act of 1964 are "available to any person aggrieved by any act... by any recipient of Federal assistance or Federal provider of such assistance under [Section 504]." Because Title VI provides for monetary damages, the student claimed that read together, Section 505(a)2 and Section 504(a) establish a waiver of the government's immunity against monetary damages. The Court, however, found that this was not an unequivocal expression of a waiver of immunity. It also found that the Department of Transportation is not a provider of financial assistance to the Academy because it manages the Academy itself. Because there is no clear expression of the government's intent to waive its sovereign immunity, monetary damage awards are not allowed under Section 504(a) of the Act. The court of appeals' decision was affirmed. *Lane v. Pena*, 518 U.S. 187, 116 S.Ct. 2092, 135 L.Ed.2d 486 (1996).

♦   **While Section 504 of the Rehabilitation Act applies only to programs receiving federal funding, the Americans with Disabilities Act of 1990 (ADA) expands protection of individuals with disabilities to prohibit discrimination by both public and private employers. The ADA includes** many of the same concepts as Section 504, such as an employer's duty to provide reasonable accommodations to a disabled employee unless the accommodation would result in an undue hardship to the employer.

A Maine dentist examined an HIV-positive patient in his office and discovered that she had a cavity. He advised her that he maintained a policy against filling cavities of HIV-infected persons in his office, and offered to perform the work at a hospital. The patient filed suit in a federal district court against the dentist, alleging violations of the ADA, which prohibits discrimination against individuals with disabilities by a variety of service and public accommodations, including most employers. The court granted summary judgment to the patient, and the dentist appealed to the U.S. Court of Appeals, First Circuit, which affirmed. The court of appeals ruled that the patient's HIV was a disability even though it had not progressed to the symptomatic stage. Because of the patient's present lack of symptoms, the dentist's policy violated the ADA. The U.S. Supreme Court agreed to review the case and held that asymptomatic HIV is a physical impairment that substantially limits the major life activity of reproduction. Accordingly, the patient was disabled within the meaning of the ADA. The Court affirmed that portion of the judgment and remanded the case to the court of appeals for a determination of whether the patient's HIV infection posed a significant threat to the health and safety of others so as to justify the dentist's refusal to treat her in his office. *Bragdon v. Abbott,* 524 U.S. 624, 118 S.Ct. 2196, 141 L.Ed.2d 540 (1998).

♦ **The Supreme Court held that applying for and receiving Social Security disability benefits did not necessarily bar a person from suing for disability discrimination under the Americans with Disability Act (ADA). However, a benefits recipient cannot simply ignore her contention that she is too disabled to work.**

A Texas employee suffered a stroke and applied for Social Security benefits, alleging that she was disabled and unable to work. When her condition improved, she returned to work and notified the Social Security Administration (SSA), which then denied her claim for benefits. However, her employer fired her less than a week later, and she asked the SSA to reconsider the denial of benefits. She also sued her former employer in a Texas federal court for violating the ADA by refusing to provide a reasonable accommodation that would allow her to perform her job.

A week later, the SSA granted her request for benefits. The court then granted pretrial judgment to the employer, reasoning that because she had asserted that she was disabled in her application for and receipt of Social Security benefits, she had conceded that she was totally disabled. As a result, she could not now claim that she could perform the essential functions of her job. The U.S. Court of Appeals, Fifth Circuit, affirmed the lower court's decision, and the case reached the U.S. Supreme Court.

The Supreme Court held that the pursuit and receipt of Social Security Disability Insurance benefits does not automatically bar a person from litigating a claim under the ADA. However, the person must present a sufficient explanation of the seeming contradiction that she is disabled under the Social Security Act while not disabled under the ADA. Because the SSA does not take into account a reasonable accommodation when it determines whether a person is disabled for Social Security benefit purposes, qualifying for such benefits might not disqualify a person from suing under the ADA.

A person might qualify for Social Security benefits under SSA administrative rules and yet, due to special individual circumstances, remain capable of performing the essential functions of the job. Here, the employee had explained the discrepancy between her claim for Social Security benefits and her ADA claim that she could perform the essential functions of the position with the accommodation of training and additional time to do the job. As such, her claim should not have been dismissed at the pretrial stage. The Court also noted that American rules allow a person to plead alternatively where she is not sure under which theory she might succeed. It refused to apply a strong presumption against a recipient's ADA success. *Cleveland v. Policy Management Systems Corp.*, 526 U.S. 795, 119 S.Ct. 1597, 142 L. Ed. 2d 30 (1999).

♦ **Congress exceeded its authority by allowing state employees to sue for monetary damage awards under the Americans with Disabilities Act (ADA). Congress did not identify a history and pattern of irrational employment discrimination against individuals with disabilities by the states when it enacted the ADA. Therefore, states are entitled to Eleventh Amendment immunity from ADA suits by employees seeking money damages.**

Two Alabama state employees alleged that they were discriminated against by their employers in violation of the ADA. One was a state university nursing director who was demoted upon her return from a medical leave to undergo treatment for breast cancer. The other was a youth services department security officer with chronic asthma and sleep apnea who alleged that the department refused to provide him with reasonable accommodations to mitigate the effects of his disabilities. They sued the state for monetary damages under the ADA. A federal court granted summary judgment to the state.

The U.S. Court of Appeals, Eleventh Circuit, reversed the district court judgment, and the state appealed to the Supreme Court, arguing that the ADA did not validly abrogate Eleventh Amendment immunity in lawsuits seeking monetary relief. The Court explained that the Eleventh Amendment ensures that no state may be sued in a federal court without first consenting to be sued. However, Congress may abrogate this immunity where it does so unequivocally and under a valid grant of constitutional authority.

The Court analyzed the enforcement provisions of Section 5 of the Fourteenth Amendment to the U.S. Constitution. Legislation enacted under Section 5 must demonstrate "congruence and proportionality between the injury to be prevented or remedied and the means adopted to that end." In this case, there was no such congruence and proportionality. Congress identified negative attitudes and biases against individuals with disabilities as reasons for enacting the ADA, but did not identify a pattern of irrational discrimination by the states. Since there was no pattern of unconstitutional behavior by the states, the ADA failed the "congruence and proportionality" test for Eleventh Amendment analysis. The Court reversed the decision. *Board of Trustees of Univ. of Alabama v. Garrett*, 531 U.S. 356, 121 S.Ct. 955, 148 L.Ed.2d 866 (2001).

♦ **Employers can refuse to hire someone whose disability poses a direct threat to his health or safety on the job without violating the Americans with Disabilities Act (ADA).**
An individual worked for contractors of Chevron in the coker unit at a California refinery. Twice he applied to work directly for Chevron, which offered to hire him each time, provided he could pass a physical. Each time, the exam showed liver abnormalities or liver damage, which Chevron doctors said could be aggravated by continued exposure to toxins at the refinery. In each instance, Chevron withdrew the job offer. The second time, Chevron asked the contractor employing the individual to either reassign him to a job not involving exposure to toxins or to remove him from the refinery altogether. After the contractor laid him off, he filed a lawsuit in federal district court, claiming Chevron violated the ADA by refusing to hire him or let him continue to work at the refinery. The district court granted summary judgment to Chevron on the grounds that the company acted reasonably. The U.S. Court of Appeals, Ninth Circuit, reversed, finding Equal Employment Opportunity Commission (EEOC) regulation 29 C.F.R. § 1630.15(b), which allows employers to defend disability discrimination charges where a person's disability would create a direct threat to himself in the job, to be in conflict with the ADA.

The Supreme Court found no conflict between the regulation and the ADA. According to the justices, the ADA permitted Chevron to reject the individual for a position in its refinery under the "business necessity" defense after the post-offer medical exam revealed abnormalities in his liver, which his own physicians had diagnosed as hepatitis C. Chevron's doctors predicted that the individual could die from prolonged exposure to chemicals in the refinery. The failure of Congress to include the threat to self defense in the actual text of the ADA did not mean this defense was unavailable to employers. Although the ADA defines "direct threat" as applying only to a person whose disability creates a direct threat to others in the workplace, the law also allows employers to weed out applicants because of their disabilities based on qualification standards that are "job-related" and "consistent with business necessity." The disputed EEOC regulation strikes the right balance between the ADA and other health and safety obligations, and falls reasonably within the statute's parameters. Chevron wished to avoid time lost to sickness, excessive turnover from medical retirement or death, litigation under state tort law, and the risk of violating the Occupational Safety and Health Act (OSHA Act). Although it is unclear whether an employer would actually be liable for hiring a disabled individual who knowingly consented to work in a job likely to pose dangers to his health under the OSH Act, hiring the individual "would put Congress's policy in the ADA ... at loggerheads with the competing policy of OSHA." In providing for the threat-to-self defense, the EEOC did exactly what administrative agencies should do when Congress creates competing objectives. The Ninth Circuit decision was reversed and remanded for a determination of whether Chevron proved the threat-to-self defense under the circumstances of this case. *Chevron U.S.A. v. Echazabal,* 536 U.S. 73, 122 S.Ct. 2045, 153 L.Ed.2d 82 (2002).

♦ **The U.S. Supreme Court concluded that while a seniority system usually trumps a disabled worker's accommodation request for a particular job, the worker may still show that special circumstances make the accommodation reasonable in a particular situation.**

An airline cargo handler was placed in a mailroom position after he suffered a work-related back injury in 1990. He lost the mailroom job when his employer, US Airways, decided not to make an exception to its seniority policy for him and allowed non-disabled employees to bid on the position. The employee was unable to bid on any other jobs because of his injury. He filed suit under the Americans with Disabilities Act (ADA), claiming that he was an individual with a disability able to perform the essential functions of the mailroom job and that US Airways discriminated against him by not granting his request for the reasonable accommodation of staying in the mailroom position. The Ninth Circuit reviewed the case twice, ultimately finding that the presence of a seniority system is merely "a factor in the undue hardship analysis" under the ADA and that courts should determine whether the accommodation conflict presents an undue hardship on a case-by-case basis.

The Supreme Court held that under the ADA, an existing seniority system does not always make a disabled worker's conflicting accommodation request unreasonable. Nor does it mandate, as the employee argued, that "reasonable accommodation" means "effective accommodation," authorizing a court to consider *only* the individual's disability-related needs and not the impact on other employees. Rather, the ADA's objectives demand "reasonable responsive reaction" from both employers and employees. This means the act "will sometimes require affirmative conduct to promote entry of disabled people into the workforce." In most cases, the seniority system will prevail over an accommodation request, unless special circumstances exist. In order to show special circumstances, the plaintiff can demonstrate that despite the seniority system, the requested accommodation is reasonable. US Air's personnel handbook contains a disclaimer advising employees that its seniority policy does not create any legal rights and that the company "reserves the right to change any and all" portions of the seniority policy at will. US Air also conceded that point at oral argument. The employee claimed that from time to time, the airline makes exceptions to the policy for medical or other reasons. As a result, the Court, remanded the case for reconsideration. *US Airways, Inc. v. Barnett*, 535 U.S. 391, 122 S.Ct. 1516, 152 L.Ed.2d 589 (2002).

♦ **The Supreme Court adopted the Equal Employment Opportunity Commission's (EEOC's) six-factor standard for determining whether a director-shareholder should be counted as an employee under the Americans with Disabilities Act (ADA).**

A bookkeeper at a medical clinic in Oregon sued the clinic under the ADA after she was fired. The clinic sought to have the case dismissed, alleging that it did not have the necessary 15 employees to qualify it as a covered employer under the ADA because the four physician-shareholders who owned the clinic could not be counted as employees. A federal court agreed with the clinic and dismissed the case, but the Ninth Circuit reversed. The case reached the U.S. Supreme Court, which adopted the EEOC's standard for determining when a director-shareholder should be counted as an employee under the ADA. The standard provides six factors for ascertaining whether the organization has control over the individual:

- Whether the organization can hire or fire the individual or set the rules and regulations of the individual's work
- Whether and, if so, to what extent the organization supervises the individual's work
- Whether the individual reports to someone higher up in the organization
- Whether and, if so, to what extent the individual is able to influence the organization
- Whether the parties intended that the individual be an employee, as expressed in written agreements or contracts
- Whether the individual shared in the profits, losses and liabilities of the organization

The Court reversed and remanded the case for a determination of whether the doctor-shareholders should be counted as employees. *Clackamas Gastroenterology Associates, P.C. v. Wells,* 538 U.S. 440, 123 S.Ct. 1673, 155 L.Ed.2d 615 (2003).

♦ **The Supreme Court held that a company could refuse to rehire a recovering addict who violated company rules at the time of his firing.**

An employee tested positive for cocaine after managers saw him acting like he was under the influence and required him to take a drug test. He admitted to drinking beer and using cocaine the night before, and resigned in lieu of being fired. Three years later, he re-applied for his job, and attached two reference letters – one from his pastor, and one from an Alcoholics Anonymous counselor. When the company refused to rehire him based on his prior workplace misconduct, he sued under the Americans with Disabilities Act (ADA), claiming that the company was discriminating against him because of his condition as a recovering drug addict. An Arizona federal court granted pretrial judgment to the company, but the Ninth Circuit reversed, finding that the company's no-rehire rule was unlawful as applied to former drug addicts whose only work-related offense was testing positive because of an addiction. The case then reached the U.S. Supreme Court, which held that the company could refuse to rehire the employee even if he was a recovering addict. Refusing to rehire employees fired for violating company rules does not violate the ADA. The Court remanded the case for a determination of whether the company had actually refused to rehire the employee because of his record of drug addiction, which would violate the ADA. *Raytheon Co. v. Hernandez,* 540 U.S. 44, 124 S.Ct. 513, 157 L.Ed.2d 357 (2003).

E. Religious Discrimination

♦ **Employers must make reasonable efforts to accommodate the religious beliefs of their employees. However, they need not go beyond such good-faith efforts. If the accommodation will cause an undue hardship, employers**

will not have to alter their policies for the benefit of such employees.

An employee of an airline belonged to a religion known as the Worldwide Church of God. It proscribed work from sunset Friday to sunset Saturday. Because of the employee's seniority, the airline was able to accommodate his religious beliefs until he transferred to a new position with low seniority. The airline agreed to permit the union to seek a change of work assignments, but it was unwilling to violate the seniority system. The airline then rejected a proposal that the employee work only four days a week, stating that this would impair critical functions in its operations. Eventually, the employee was discharged for refusing to work on Saturdays. He sued both the union and the airline under Title VII, claiming religious discrimination. A federal court ruled in favor of the defendants, and the U.S. Court of Appeals affirmed in part, holding that the airline did not satisfy its duty to accommodate the employee's religious needs. On appeal to the U.S. Supreme Court, it was held that the airline did make reasonable efforts to accommodate the religious beliefs of others. The Court reversed the court of appeals' decision and held in favor of the airline. *Trans World Airlines, Inc. v. Hardison*, 432 U.S. 63, 97 S.Ct. 2264, 53 L.Ed.2d 113 (1977).

♦   **States may not impose an absolute duty on employers to conform their business practices to the religious practices of their employees. An absolute duty would advance religion, in violation of the Establishment Clause of the First Amendment.**

An employee of a chain of New England retail stores managed a clothing department at a location in Connecticut. Although the store was closed by law on Sundays, when state law allowed, it began to keep Sunday hours. After working occasional Sundays for two years, the employee notified his employer that he would no longer work on that day because it was his Sabbath. A Connecticut law stated that employers could not require their employees to work on their Sabbath days, and that refusal to work on the Sabbath was not grounds for dismissal. The employer demoted the employee to a clerical position. He then resigned and filed a grievance administratively. He was found to have been discharged in violation of the statute, and a state trial court upheld that decision. The Connecticut Supreme Court reversed, and the case came before the U.S. Supreme Court.

The Court held that the Connecticut law violated the Establishment Clause of the First Amendment. Essentially, it imposed on employers an absolute duty to conform their business practices to the particular religious practices of their employees. Under this law, Sabbath religious concerns automatically controlled over all secular interests at the workplace. The primary effect of this law, then, was the advancement of religion, which is forbidden by the Establishment Clause. The Court affirmed the state supreme court's decision in favor of the employer. *Estate of Thornton v. Caldor, Inc.*, 472 U.S. 703, 105 S.Ct. 2914, 86 L.Ed.2d 557 (1985).

♦   **When teachers select an exclusive bargaining representative, they impliedly surrender a measure of their personal choice, including religious accommodation. This follows from the premise that the state has a strong** interest in hearing only one voice in collective bargaining matters.

A Connecticut high school teacher belonged to a church that required its members to refrain from secular employment during designated holy days. This practice caused the teacher to miss approximately six school days each year for religious purposes. The teacher worked under terms of a bargaining agreement between the school board and his teachers' union that allowed only three days of leave for religious observation. The agreement also allowed leave for "necessary personal business," which could not be used for religious purposes. The teacher took either unauthorized leave for the extra three religious days he required, scheduled hospital visits on church holidays, or worked on those holidays. He repeatedly asked for permission to use three days of his "necessary personal business" leave for religious purposes. He also offered to pay for a substitute teacher if the school board would pay him for the extra days that he missed. These alternatives were rejected by the school board. When all administrative alternatives were exhausted, he filed a lawsuit alleging that the school board's policy regarding "necessary personal business" leave was discriminatory on the basis of religion. A U.S. district court dismissed the teacher's lawsuit and he appealed. The U.S. Court of Appeals, Second Circuit, said that the school board was bound to accept one of the teacher's proposed solutions unless "that accommodation causes undue hardship on the employer's conduct of his business."

The U.S. Supreme Court modified the appellate court's decision. It decided that the school district was not required to accept the teacher's proposals even if acceptance would not result in "undue hardship." The school board was only bound to offer a fair and reasonable accommodation of the teacher's religious needs. The bargaining agreement policy of allowing three days off for religious purposes was found to be reasonable. Because none of the lower courts had decided whether this policy had been administered fairly, the case was remanded for a determination of that question. *Ansonia Board of Educ. v. Philbrook*, 479 U.S. 60, 107 S.Ct. 367, 93 L.Ed.2d 305 (1986).

♦   **Title VII employment restrictions do not apply to religious educational institutions. In a 1987 decision, the Court ruled that religious schools were free from Title VII's scope even when the job involved was nonreligious.**

In a decision affecting private religious educational institutions, the U.S. Supreme Court ruled that such institutions may discriminate on the basis of religion in the hiring for nonreligious jobs involving nonprofit activities. The case involved a man who worked at a Mormon church-operated gymnasium for 16 years. After being discharged for failing to meet several church-related requirements for employment, he sued the church in a federal district court, alleging religious discrimination in violation of Title VII. The church moved for dismissal claiming that Section 702 of Title VII exempted it from liability. The man claimed that if Section 702 allowed religious employers to discriminate on religious grounds in hiring for nonreligious jobs, then Title VII would be in violation of the Establishment Clause of the First Amendment. The district court ruled for the man, and the church appealed directly to the U.S. Supreme Court.

The question before the Court was whether applying Section 702 to the secular nonprofit activities of religious organizations violated the Establishment

Clause. Section 702 provides that Title VII "shall not apply ... to a religious corporation, association [or] educational institution ... with respect to the employment of individuals of a particular religion to perform work connected with the carrying on by such [an organization] of its activities." In ruling for the church, the Supreme Court applied the three-part test set out in *Lemon v. Kurtzman*. *Lemon* requires first that a law serve a secular legislative purpose. Section 702 meets this test, said the Court, since it is a permissible legislative purpose to alleviate ... governmental interference with the ability of religious organizations to define and carry out their missions. The second test required that Section 702 have a primary effect that neither advances nor inhibits religion. Section 702 meets that requirement since a law is not unconstitutional simply because it *allows* churches to advance religion, stated the Court. Section 702 does not violate the third part of the *Lemon* test because it does not impermissibly entangle church and state. The Supreme Court reversed the district court's decision and upheld the right of nonprofit religious employers to impose religious conditions for employment in nonreligious positions involving nonprofit activities. *Corp. of the Presiding Bishop of the Church of Jesus Christ of Latter-Day Saints v. Amos*, 483 U.S. 327, 107 S.Ct. 2862, 97 L.Ed.2d 273 (1987).

F.   Retaliation

◆   A Tennessee school district employee answered questions about discrimination as part of an investigation into a sexual harassment complaint. Shortly thereafter, she was fired. She sued for retaliation under Title VII, but a federal court granted pretrial judgment to the county. After the Sixth Circuit affirmed, the U.S. Supreme Court reversed, holding that the employee could pursue her claim under **the "opposition" clause of Title VII**, which prohibits an employer from retaliating against an employee who opposes discrimination. *Crawford v. Metropolitan Government of Nashville and Davidson County*, 555 U.S. 271, 129 S.Ct. 846, 172 L.Ed.2d 650 (2009).

◆   A black assistant manager at an Illinois restaurant claimed he was fired because he complained that a white colleague fired a black subordinate for race-based reasons. He sued the restaurant for retaliation under 42 U.S.C. § 1981, which prohibits race discrimination in the making and enforcement of contracts. The case reached the U.S. Supreme Court, which held that **Section 1981 also prohibits employers from retaliating against employees who complain of race discrimination**. The right to "make and enforce contracts" also includes the right to complain of race discrimination without being retaliated against for doing so. *CBOCS West, Inc. v. Humphries*, 553 U.S. 442, 128 S.Ct. 1951, 170 L.Ed.2d 864 (2008).

◆   After a Tennessee female rail worker complained to company officials that her supervisor had repeatedly told her that women shouldn't be working in the yard and made insulting remarks to her in front of co-workers, she was reassigned to a less favorable position. She filed a retaliation charge with the EEOC and was shortly thereafter suspended for insubordination. After she filed a grievance with her union, the company found she had not been insubordinate and reinstated her with back pay. When she sued for retaliation, a jury awarded her $46,750. The U.S. Supreme Court upheld the award, noting that **reassignment of job duties can be retaliation if it is "materially adverse" to an employee.** It defined materially adverse as a harmful action that could dissuade a reasonable worker from making a charge of discrimination. The suspension was also materially adverse even though she was reinstated with back pay because a reasonable employee might choose not to file a discrimination charge knowing she could be out of work indefinitely. *Burlington Northern and Santa Fe Railway Co. v. White,* 548 U.S. 53, 126 S.Ct. 2405, 165 L.Ed.2d 345 (2006).

◆ An employee of an Illinois educational materials company filed a sex discrimination complaint against her employer with the U.S. Equal Employment Opportunity Commission (EEOC), asserting that she should have received a promotion. The employer then fired her. The EEOC filed a federal district court action on behalf of the employee against the employer for unlawful retaliation under Title VII. The employer moved to dismiss the case, stating that it did not have 15 employees during 20 weeks in the past two years and did not come within the coverage of the act. The court agreed with the employer, and the U.S. Court of Appeals, Seventh Circuit, affirmed. The U.S. Supreme Court agreed to review the case.

On appeal, the employer argued that an employer "has" an employee for Title VII purposes only when it is actually compensating an individual on a particular working day. The EEOC argued that the appropriate test for when an employer has an employee is whether the parties have an employment relationship on the day in question. This test was already used by the EEOC in age discrimination regulations and the U.S. Department of Labor in Family and Medical Leave Act regulations. The Court agreed with the EEOC that an employer has an employee if an employment relationship exists between the parties. Applying this test, the employer had employment relationships with 15 or more employees for 38 weeks of the calendar year in question and was an employer within the meaning of Title VII. The Court reversed and remanded the case. *Walters v. Metropolitan Educ. Enterprises, Inc.,* 519 U.S. 202, 117 S.Ct. 660, 136 L.Ed.2d 644 (1997).

◆ **In 1997, the Supreme Court held that Title VII protects former employees from retaliatory action by former employers.**

Title VII of the Civil Rights Act of 1964 makes it an unlawful employment practice for an employer to discriminate against employees or employment applicants on the basis of several specified grounds. An oil corporation fired an African-American employee, who then filed a complaint against it with the U.S. Equal Employment Opportunity Commission (EEOC), which enforces Title VII employment complaints. While the charge was pending, the former employee applied for work with another company. When the company contacted the oil corporation for an employment reference, the corporation gave him a negative reference, which he believed was in retaliation for having filed the EEOC charge. The former employee sued the corporation in a federal district court for retaliatory discrimination under Title VII. The court dismissed the case, ruling that Section 704(a) of Title VII does not protect the rights of former employees. The former employee appealed to the U.S. Court of Appeals, Fourth Circuit, which affirmed the district court decision. The U.S. Supreme Court agreed to review the case.

The Court found that Section 704(a) was ambiguous because it made no reference to past or present employment status. However, other sections in Title VII used the term "employee" to describe more than just a current employee. Sections 706(g)(1) and 717(b) of Title VII applied to the reinstatement or hiring of an employee, necessarily including former employees. In order to be consistent with Title VII's broad scope, the Court construed Section 704(a) as protecting former employees from retaliatory action by former employers. In doing so, it agreed with the EEOC that to exclude former employees from Section 704(a) protection would undermine Title VII by allowing retaliation against victims of discrimination. This might give an incentive to employers to fire employees who brought EEOC complaints. The Court reversed and remanded the court of appeals' decision. *Robinson v. Shell Oil Co.*, 519 U.S. 337, 117 S.Ct. 843, 136 L.Ed.2d 808 (1997).

IV. DISCIPLINE AND TERMINATION

A. Termination

The Due Process Clause of the Fourteenth Amendment to the U.S. Constitution prohibits states from depriving persons of life, liberty, or property without due process of law. In the context of public employment, due process generally means notice and an opportunity to be advised of the reason for employment termination, suspension or demotion.

The contract of employment, whether by collective bargaining agreement, state law or otherwise, determines the precise procedural guarantees that must be provided. Due process is not an inflexible legal standard. It simply requires fundamental fairness in view of the legal rights described in the employment contract.

1. Property or Liberty Interests

♦   **Two 1972 Supreme Court cases help to define the concept of due process in public employment. In *Perry v. Sindermann* and *Board of Regents v. Roth*, below, the Court held that liberty and property rights are *created* by contract or state law, and *protected* by the U.S. Constitution. Tenured teachers enjoy property interests in continued employment under state tenure laws. However, untenured teachers have no more than "a unilateral expectation" of reemployment.**

The Wisconsin state university system hired an assistant professor under a one-year contract. As the year drew to a close, the university notified the teacher that his contract would not be renewed. The notice conformed to university rules, which did not require any reason for nonretention or any hearing for the teacher. Wisconsin tenure law required teachers to have four years of service before becoming "permanent" employees. The teacher sued the state college board in a federal district court, alleging that he was being terminated for making critical statements about university administrators. The teacher also claimed that the failure of university officials to give any reason for nonretention violated his procedural due process rights. The court held for the teacher on his due process claim and the U.S. Court of Appeals, Seventh Circuit, affirmed this decision. The U.S. Supreme Court agreed to hear the university board's petition.

In dismissing the teacher's due process claims, the Supreme Court stated that no liberty interest was implicated because in declining to rehire the teacher, the university had not made any charge against him such as incompetence or immorality. Such a charge would have made it difficult for the teacher to gain employment elsewhere and thus would have deprived him of liberty. As no reason was given for the nonrenewal of his contract, the teacher's liberty interest in future employment was not impaired and he was not entitled to a hearing on these grounds. The Court declared that because the teacher had not acquired tenure he possessed no property interest in continued employment at the university. The teacher had a property interest in employment during the term of his one-year contract, but upon expiration the interest ceased to exist. The Court stated: "To have a property interest in a benefit, a person clearly must have more than an abstract need or desire for it. He must have more than a unilateral expectation of it. He must, instead, have a legitimate claim of entitlement to it." Because the teacher's contract secured no interest in reemployment for the following year, he had no property interest in reemployment. The Court reversed the lower court decisions and remanded the case. *Board of Regents v. Roth*, 408 U.S. 564, 92 S.Ct. 2701, 33 L.Ed.2d 548 (1972).

♦ **A fair and impartial hearing, conducted in accordance with procedural safeguards, must be given to a dismissed teacher if there is a property or a liberty interest involved or if the dismissal involves a stigma upon the character of the teacher.**

The *Sindermann* case involved a teacher employed at a Texas university for four years under a series of one-year contracts. When he was not rehired for a fifth year he brought suit contending that due process required a dismissal hearing. The Supreme Court held that "a person's interest in a benefit is a 'property' interest for due process purposes if there are such rules and mutually explicit understandings that support his claim of entitlement to the benefit that he may invoke at a hearing." Because the teacher had been employed at the university for four years, the Court felt that he may have acquired a protectable property interest in continued employment. The case was remanded to the trial court to determine whether there was an unwritten "common law" of tenure at the university. If so, the teacher would be entitled to a dismissal hearing. *Perry v. Sindermann*, 408 U.S. 593, 92 S.Ct. 2694, 33 L.Ed.2d 570 (1972).

♦ **Applying many of the principles of the *Roth* case, above, the Court found no protectable property interest in the following case involving a police officer who was an at-will employee. The employee also had no liberty**

interest to protect because the reasons for dismissal remained confidential.
A policeman in a North Carolina city was dismissed by the city manager
upon the recommendation of the chief of police. A city ordinance allowed for
the termination of a permanent employee, such as the officer, if he failed to
perform work up to the standard of his classification. Upon being discharged,
the officer sued, asserting that he had a constitutional right to a pretermination
hearing. He also argued that he had been deprived of property and liberty
interests by his dismissal. The district court ruled against the officer and the
court of appeals affirmed. The officer then appealed to the U.S. Supreme Court.
The Court held that the district court had correctly concluded that the officer
"held his position at the will and pleasure of the city." It also ruled that no
liberty interest had been violated because no stigma attached through a public
communication. The reasons for the officer's dismissal had been kept private.
Since he was an at-will employee, he also had no property interest to be
protected. The Court affirmed the lower court decisions, and held that no
pretermination hearing had been necessary. *Bishop v. Wood*, 426 U.S. 341, 96
S.Ct. 2074, 48 L.Ed.2d 684 (1976).

◆ **The Supreme Court held that an at-will employee could sue for
damages under 42 U.S.C. § 1985(2) on claims that two company officials
targeted him for termination for cooperating with federal agents in a
criminal investigation against the company.**
An at-will employee for a Georgia-based health care company cooperated
with federal agents investigating the company for Medicare fraud. The
employee attended the grand jury proceedings and was expected to appear as a
witness in a criminal trial after the company was indicted. After being fired, he
sued in federal court under 42 U.S.C. § 1985(2), alleging that three of the
company's officers conspired to intimidate him and to retaliate against him for
attending the grand jury proceedings and to keep him from testifying at the
criminal trial. Section 1985(2) prohibits people from entering into conspiracies
to "deter, by force, intimidation or threat," any witness from testifying in court.
It provides a cause of action when parties to a conspiracy cause the witness to
be "injured in his person or property."
The district court dismissed the lawsuit, holding that an at-will employee
has no constitutionally protected property interest in continued employment.
Therefore, an employee who loses his job pursuant to a conspiracy theory
proscribed by Section 1985(2) has not suffered an actual injury.
The U.S. Court of Appeals, Eleventh Circuit, affirmed, and the Supreme
Court accepted the case for review. The Court reversed the Eleventh Circuit's
decision, holding instead that the sort of harm alleged by the employee –
"essentially third-party interference with at-will employment relationships" –
states a claim for relief under Section 1985(2). The harm has long been
recognized under tort law as a compensable injury; Georgia, for example,
provides a cause of action against third parties for wrongful interference with
employment relations, and the Supreme Court refused to ignore that tradition.
Moreover, "[t]he gist of the wrong at which Section 1985(2) is directed is
not deprivation of property, but intimidation or retaliation against witnesses in
federal-court proceedings." Therefore, the fact that at-will employment is not

"property" for purposes of the Due Process Clause does not mean that an at-will employee who loses his job does not suffer injury to his "person or property" as contemplated by Section 1985(2). *Haddle v. Garrison*, 525 U.S. 121, 119 S.Ct. 489, 142 L.Ed.2d 502 (1998).

2. Procedural Safeguards

♦ **School boards derive their authority from state laws, and are generally authorized to make employment decisions including hiring, firing and negotiating employment contracts. The fact that school boards must negotiate with collective bargaining representatives as adversaries in contract negotiations does not deprive school boards of their status as impartial decision makers in employment matters. Without a showing of actual bias, boards are presumed to be impartial when they conduct hearings for employment termination.**

Wisconsin education law prohibited strikes by teachers. Under state law, school boards had sole authority to make hiring and firing decisions and were required to negotiate employment terms and conditions with authorized collective bargaining representatives. When contract negotiations between teachers and their local school board became protracted, the teachers called a strike. The board attempted to end the strike, noting that it was in direct violation of state law. When the teachers refused to return to work, the board held disciplinary hearings and fired the striking teachers. The teachers appealed to the Wisconsin courts, arguing that the school board was not an impartial decision maker and that their discharges had violated their due process rights. The Wisconsin Supreme Court ruled that due process under the Fourteenth Amendment required that the teachers' conduct and the board's response to that conduct be evaluated by an impartial decision maker and that the board itself was not sufficiently impartial to make the decision to discharge the teachers. The board appealed this decision to the U.S. Supreme Court.

The Supreme Court reversed the Wisconsin Supreme Court decision and held that there was no evidence that the board could not make an impartial decision in determining to discharge these teachers. The mere fact that the board was involved in negotiations with the teachers did not support a claim of bias. The board was the only body vested with statutory authority to employ and dismiss teachers. Moreover, participation in negotiations with the teachers was also required by law. This involvement prior to the decision to discharge the teachers was not a sufficient showing of bias to disqualify the board as a decision maker under the Due Process Clause of the Fourteenth Amendment. *Hortonville Joint School Dist. No. 1 v. Hortonville Educ. Ass'n*, 426 U.S. 482, 96 S.Ct. 2308, 49 L.Ed.2d 1 (1976).

♦ **Public employees are vested by state law with the right to notice and a hearing at some point in the termination process. The Court upheld an Ohio statute in which employees were limited to notice and an informal hearing in termination matters, but had no full administrative hearing rights until after the termination.**

Ohio law protected all civil service employees from dismissal except for "misfeasance, malfeasance, or nonfeasance in office." Employees who were terminated for cause were entitled to an order of removal stating the reasons for termination. Unfavorable orders could be appealed to a state administrative board whose determinations were subject to state court review. A security guard hired by a school board stated on his job application that he had never been convicted of a felony. Upon discovering that he had in fact been convicted of grand larceny, the school board dismissed him for dishonesty in filling out the job application. He was not afforded an opportunity to respond to the dishonesty charge or to challenge the dismissal until nine months later. In a second case, a school bus mechanic was fired because he had failed an eye examination. The mechanic appealed his dismissal after the fact because he had not been afforded a pretermination hearing. A federal district court rejected both of the employees' claims and they appealed to the U.S. Court of Appeals, Sixth Circuit, which reversed the district court's decisions. The U.S. Supreme Court consolidated the appeals by the school districts.

The Supreme Court held that the employees possessed a property right in their employment and were entitled to a pretermination opportunity to respond to the dismissal charges against them. The pretermination hearing, stated the Court, need not resolve the propriety of the discharge, but should be a check against mistaken decisions – essentially a determination of whether there are reasonable grounds to believe that the charges against the employee are true and support the proposed action. The Supreme Court upheld that portion of the lower court decisions that found the delay in the guard's administrative proceedings did not constitute a separate constitutional violation. The Due Process Clause requires a hearing "at a meaningful time," and here the delay stemmed in part from the thoroughness of the procedures afforded the guard. On the matter of the right to a pretermination hearing, however, both cases were remanded for further proceedings consistent with the Court's decision. *Cleveland Board of Educ. v. Loudermill*, 470 U.S. 532, 105 S.Ct. 1487, 84 L.Ed.2d 494 (1985).

♦ **The following case illustrates the importance of the employment contract (or a statute that addresses the employment relationship) in determining what process is due the employee. The Due Process Clause may be invoked by private employers, when a government agency issues an order determining employee-employer rights.**

A trucking company discharged one of its drivers, alleging that he had disabled several lights on his assigned truck in order to obtain extra pay while awaiting repairs. The driver filed a grievance, asserting that the discharge had been in retaliation for having complained of safety violations. He also filed a complaint with the Department of Labor, alleging that his firing violated Section 405 of the Surface Transportation Assistance Act, which forbids such action. A field investigator obtained statements substantiating the driver's claim, and offered the company the opportunity to submit a written statement detailing the basis for the employee's discharge, but it was not allowed to examine the substance of the investigator's evidence. A preliminary administrative order called for the employee's temporary reinstatement, and the company filed suit in a federal court, challenging the constitutionality of the department's order. The company charged that reinstatement prior to an evidentiary hearing violated its due process rights. The court ruled for the company. Appeal was taken directly to the U.S. Supreme Court, which affirmed in part and reversed in part. It stated that due process required pre-reinstatement notice of the employee's allegations, notice of the substance of the relevant supporting evidence, an opportunity to submit a written response, and an opportunity to meet with the investigator and present statements from rebuttal witnesses. Due process did not require employer confrontation and cross-examination before preliminary reinstatement if a prompt post-reinstatement evidentiary hearing was available. *Brock v. Roadway Express, Inc.*, 481 U.S. 252, 107 S.Ct. 1740, 95 L.Ed.2d 239 (1987).

♦ **Even in a case involving national security, public employees are entitled to have appropriate procedures for employment actions. Statutes and regulations describing appropriate procedures must be obeyed.**

The National Security Agency (NSA) terminated the employment of a cryptographic technician for engaging in homosexual relationships with foreign nationals. The NSA proposed terminating the employee according to its personnel regulations. The termination letter noted that the employee's "indiscriminate personal conduct" made his continued access to classified information impossible. After a hearing, the employee's security clearance was revoked and because this was a condition to NSA employment, his termination became final. The employee then requested a hearing before the Secretary of Defense, claiming that the 1959 NSA Act did not authorize termination without a hearing before the defense secretary. The secretary's response was that the removal was for cause under the NSA's regulations and did not require the secretary's authority. The employee sued the secretary in the U.S. District Court for the District of Columbia, claiming that the Act did not delegate authority to remove employees to the NSA's director. The district court granted the secretary's motion for summary judgment. The U.S. Court of Appeals, District of Columbia Circuit, reversed the district court's decision, ruling that the Act applied. The defense secretary appealed to the U.S. Supreme Court.

The Supreme Court noted that the NSA Act authorized the defense secretary or his designee to establish positions and make necessary appointments to carry out the function of the agency. The authority to appoint also implied a power to remove. The Act was not the exclusive means to remove NSA employees for national security reasons. The alternative selected by the NSA director was a correct procedure for removal because of permissive language in the Act. The secretary had broad discretion to terminate employees consistent with national security, just as discretion was present in the selection of NSA employees. The termination procedure selected by the NSA director provided a hearing equivalent to that provided under the NSA Act. The Court reversed the appeals court, permitting the secretary to terminate the technician's employment. *Carlucci v. Doe*, 488 U.S. 93, 109 S.Ct. 407, 102 L.Ed.2d 395 (1988).

3. Other Considerations

♦   A communications operator for the Pennsylvania State Police claimed that three of her supervisors subjected her to sexually harassing comments and gestures. She told the EEO officer about the harassment but never filed a complaint. Shortly thereafter, she was arrested for theft in the workplace and was interrogated. She was allowed to resign and then sued under Title VII. **The question of constructive discharge reached the U.S. Supreme Court**, which held that if the constructive discharge was not the result of an official act by the police, but instead the misconduct of a rogue supervisor, then the police could assert the Faragher/Ellerth defense. However, if the police sanctioned the actions leading to the constructive discharge, then a tangible employment action would have occurred so as to make the defense unavailable. The Court remanded the case for further proceedings. *Pennsylvania State Police v. Suders,* 542 U.S. 129, 124 S.Ct. 2342, 159 L.Ed.2d 204 (2004).

♦   **In the case below, the non-renewal of a tenured teacher's contract because of her failure to earn continuing education credits was held constitutionally allowable and not a deprivation of her substantive due process and equal protection rights.**
    A tenured Oklahoma teacher failed to earn required continuing education credits. This violated her school district's policy, and she forfeited salary increases to which she would have been otherwise entitled. The state legislature then mandated salary raises for teachers regardless of compliance with continuing education requirements. The district threatened to terminate the teacher's employment unless she fulfilled the continuing education requirements. When she refused, the district refused to renew her contract. She sued the district in a federal district court, which dismissed her case. However, the U.S. Court of Appeals, Tenth Circuit, reversed the district court's decision, and the district appealed to the U.S. Supreme Court.
    Regarding the Due Process Clause part of the teacher's claim, the Court said that the district's rule was endowed with a presumption of legislative validity and the teacher failed to rebut that presumption. The desire of the district to provide well-qualified teachers was not arbitrary – especially when it made every effort to give this specific teacher a chance to meet the requirements. The rule was reasonable, and the teacher's interest in continued employment did not outweigh the compelling state interest in public education. Nor was there a deprivation of equal protection, since all teachers were obligated to obtain the same credits. The sanction of contract non-renewal was rationally related to the district's objective of enforcing the continuing education obligation of its teachers. The Court reversed the court of appeals' decision, finding the district sanctions constitutional on both Due Process and Equal Protection Clause grounds. *Harrah Independent School Dist. v. Martin,* 440 U.S. 194, 99 S.Ct. 1062, 59 L.Ed.2d 248 (1979).

♦   **Where an employer takes improper action against an employee, and a union refuses to process the employee's grievance, both the union and the employer can be held liable for damages to the employee.**

A U.S. postal service employee was suspended without pay for fighting with a co-worker. He was a member of the American Postal Workers Union. After the employee was formally terminated, he filed a grievance with the union as provided by the collective bargaining agreement (CBA). The union chose not to take his grievance to arbitration, and he then sued the union and the postal service in a federal district court, asserting that the postal service had violated the CBA by dismissing him without just cause, and that the union had breached its duty of fair representation. A jury found for the employee and against both defendants and apportioned the damages between the two. On appeal to the U.S. Court of Appeals, Fourth Circuit, the court affirmed except for the award of damages against the union. The postal service then appealed to the U.S. Supreme Court.

The Supreme Court held that where damage had been caused by both the employer and the union, it was proper to apportion liability between the two according to the damage each had caused. Here, requiring the union to pay damages would not impose on it a burden inconsistent with national policy, but rather would provide an additional incentive to unions to process members' claims where warranted. The Court thus reversed the court of appeals' decision, and allowed apportionment of the damages between the postal service and the union. *Bowen v. United States Postal Service*, 459 U.S. 212, 103 S.Ct. 588, 74 L.Ed.2d 402 (1983).

♦ **The paramount interest of national security prevails over individual due process rights, as shown in the following case involving a work-related security clearance.**

The Navy hired a veteran's-preference civilian employee to work at its refit facility, which worked on the Trident submarine. All employee positions at the facility were classified as sensitive. While waiting for a security clearance, the employee performed only limited duties. His security clearance was denied after he had been at the facility for more than a year because the Navy discovered that he had several felony convictions. He was dismissed for cause after administrative proceedings were held, and he appealed. He argued that because he had been removed for cause and not for national security reasons, he had not been afforded sufficient procedural protections. The U.S. Court of Appeals agreed, and the Navy appealed to the U.S. Supreme Court. The Supreme Court held that the employee received sufficient procedural due process. It stated that the employee had been dismissed for cause because he did not have the necessary security clearance. The decision not to issue a security clearance was not reviewable in this case, where national security granted broad discretion to the Navy to determine who should have access to classified information. The Court held that since a security clearance was a requirement for employment at the facility, the clearance-denied employee had been dismissed for just cause. The Court reversed the court of appeals' decision. *Dep't of Navy v. Egan*, 484 U.S. 518, 108 S.Ct. 818, 98 L.Ed.2d 918 (1988).

♦ **In the case below, the Supreme Court found that a termination agreement could not prevent a former employee from testifying against his former employer. Despite a termination agreement, the state's court order**

could not extend beyond the parties' controversy to control proceedings brought in other states by other parties.

A longtime General Motors (GM) employee who worked on fuel line designs frequently testified for GM in product liability cases. In one Georgia case, he testified that a GM truck fuel system was an inferior product. He was then fired and he filed a Michigan trial court action against GM for wrongful discharge and other claims. GM counterclaimed for breach of a fiduciary duty not to disclose privileged and confidential information and for misappropriating documents. The parties reached a settlement agreement under which the former employee received payment in return for a permanent injunction prohibiting him from testifying as an expert witness in other GM product liability cases without prior written consent. However, the order did not affect the still pending Georgia litigation. A separate settlement agreement permitted the employee to testify in other cases if another tribunal ordered his appearance. Six years later, the former employee was subpoenaed to testify in a Missouri wrongful death action involving a GM vehicle fire. GM resisted his appearance, asserting that the Michigan court order barred his testimony. A federal district court allowed the employee to be deposed and to testify, and a jury awarded the victim's estate over $11 million in damages. The U.S. Court of Appeals, Eighth Circuit, reversed the district court judgment under the Full Faith and Credit Clause of the Constitution.

The Supreme Court accepted the estate's petition for review and found no public policy exception permitting a state court to resist the recognition of a foreign state court judgment. However, the Michigan court order could not extend beyond the parties' controversy to control proceedings brought in other states by other parties. Because the Michigan court had no power over the Missouri parties, it could not prevent the employee from testifying in the Missouri action. Moreover, the parties' agreement allowed the employee to testify where ordered by another court. The Court reversed the judgment and remanded the case. *Baker v. General Motors Corp.*, 522 U.S. 222, 118 S.Ct. 657, 139 L.Ed.2d 580 (1998).

♦   **A person may not bring suit under the federal Racketeer Influenced and Corrupt Organizations Act (RICO) for injuries caused by an overt act that is not an act of racketeering or otherwise unlawful under the statute.**

A company official discovered that several former senior officers and directors conspired to and engaged in racketeering. After he contacted regulators, he claimed the officers and directors orchestrated a scheme to remove him from the company. When he was fired, he sued, asserting, among other things, a Section 1964(c) cause of action for the officers and directors' alleged conspiracy to violate Sections 1962(a), (b), and (c) of RICO. He alleged that his injury was proximately caused by an overt act – the termination of his employment – done in furtherance of the conspiracy, and that Section 1964(c) therefore provided him with a cause of action under RICO. The court dismissed the RICO conspiracy claim, holding that employees who are terminated for refusing to participate in RICO activities, or who threaten to report RICO activities, do not have standing to sue under RICO for damages resulting from their loss of employment. In affirming, the U.S. Court of Appeals, Eleventh

Circuit, held that, because the overt act causing the injury was not an act of racketeering, it could not support a Section 1964(c) cause of action. The Supreme Court affirmed. "As at common law," the Court said, "a civil conspiracy plaintiff cannot bring suit under RICO based on injury caused by any act in furtherance of a conspiracy that might have caused the plaintiff injury. Rather, consistency with the common law requires that a RICO conspiracy plaintiff allege injury from an act that is analogous to an 'act of a tortious character,' … meaning an act that is independently wrongful under RICO. The specific type of act that is analogous to an act of a tortious character may depend on the underlying substantive violation the defendant is alleged to have committed." However, the alleged overt act in furtherance of the conspiracy here was not independently wrongful under any substantive provision of the statute. Because the termination was not independently wrongful under the disputed RICO provision, the official could not bring suit under Section 1964(c) in an attempt to recover damages resulting from the loss of his position. *Beck v. Prupis,* 529 U.S. 494, 120 S.Ct. 1608, 146 L.Ed.2d 561 (2000).

♦   **A unanimous Supreme Court held that the Merit Systems Protection Board (MSPB) could independently review a postal worker's three prior, but minor disciplinary actions to determine whether her termination based on a fourth incident was reasonable. The MSPB acted within its authority to do so even though the worker's challenges to the prior actions were subject to pending grievances in a collectively bargained-for procedure.**
Between April and August 1997, a letter carrier was disciplined three times: for disregarding a supervisor's instructions; delaying the mail; and various other violations including failure to deliver certified mail and attempting to receive unauthorized or unnecessary overtime. She filed grievances for each discipline under a procedure established by the postal service and her union, the National Association of Letter Carriers. While the grievances were pending, the letter carrier was disciplined one final time for requesting excessive overtime. In light of this violation and the past three incidents, she was fired. She appealed to the MSPB. An administrative law judge (ALJ) found that the prior disciplines were not clearly erroneous and that the termination was reasonable. The U.S. Court of Appeals, Federal Circuit, upheld the ALJ's factual findings but reversed the board's determination that the termination was reasonable.
The Supreme Court reversed, finding the MSPB has broad discretion in determining how it will review an eligible employee's appeal and that here, the board met the minimum standards set out by the Civil Service Reform Act, which governed the letter carrier's appeal. Those standards require that the postal service prove by a preponderance of evidence that misconduct occurred and that the penalty assessed – termination – was reasonable. There was nothing arbitrary about the MSPB's decision to independently review prior disciplinary actions to determine the reasonableness of the termination. The board had consistently done so for 19 years. The MSPB's approach was reasonable. Following the Federal Circuit's rule would require the board to either wait until pending grievance proceedings were completed before rendering a decision or to ignore the challenged disciplinary actions altogether. In reversing, the Supreme Court acknowledged that the MSPB's independent review of

disciplinary actions pending in grievance procedures may, at times, result in the board reaching a different conclusion than the arbitrator. This practice may also result in the terminated employee's grievance never being resolved, because some bargaining agreements require the union to withdraw the grievance when the MSPB finalizes the termination. The MSPB also has a policy of not relying on disciplinary actions that have been overturned in grievance proceedings at the time of review. Here, an arbitrator overturned the first discipline, and the postal service conceded that the case should be sent back to the Federal Circuit to determine the effect of this reversal on the letter carrier's termination. The Supreme Court agreed and remanded the case. *U.S. Postal Service v. Gregory,* 534 U.S. 1, 122 S.Ct. 431, 151 L.Ed.2d 323 (2001).

B. Suspension

♦ **The following case demonstrates that a determination of the appropriate procedure in a particular case can also determine the substantive outcome of the case.**

The U.S. Fish and Wildlife Service (FWS) hired a man as an administrative officer for a youth conservation camp. His position was to last for the duration of the program. Prior to that time, however, the FWS advised him that it intended to dismiss him for, among other things, his unauthorized use of a government vehicle. After he replied to the charges, the FWS dismissed him, but failed to advise him of his right to a formal hearing. Over a year later, the FWS concluded that it should only have suspended him for 30 days, and offered him back pay from the time the suspension would have ended to the time when the program had ended. He elected to sue in the claims court, asserting that the suspension was unwarranted. The claims court ruled that under the Civil Service Reform Act (CSRA) there should be no review of the personnel action. The employee successfully appealed to a federal district court, and the U.S. Court of Appeals denied the government's request for a rehearing. The case came before the U.S. Supreme Court, which held that the claims court had been correct in denying the employee a review of the personnel action taken against him. The Court stated that the CSRA had deliberately excluded employees in the nonpreference "excepted service" category from judicial review for a suspension action. It ruled that the employee's action could only be heard by either the Merit Systems Protection Board or the FWS. The Court reversed the appellate court's decision, and denied judicial review to the employee. *U.S. v. Fausto,* 484 U.S. 439, 108 S.Ct. 668, 98 L.Ed.2d 830 (1988).

♦ **The National Collegiate Athletic Association (NCAA) has been held not to be a state actor by the Supreme Court. In a 1988 Nevada case, the Court concluded that the NCAA did not have the power to discipline a university's coach, and thus could not be liable for sanctions imposed against him.**

Following a lengthy investigation of allegedly improper recruiting practices by the University of Nevada, Las Vegas (UNLV), the NCAA found 38 violations, including 10 by the school's head basketball coach. The NCAA proposed a number of sanctions and threatened to impose more if the coach was not suspended. UNLV decided to suspend the coach. Facing an enormous pay cut, the coach sued the NCAA under 42 U.S.C. § 1983 for violating his due process rights. The Nevada Supreme Court held that the NCAA's conduct constituted state action for constitutional purposes. It upheld a Nevada trial court's dismissal of the suspension and award of attorneys' fees. The NCAA appealed to the U.S. Supreme Court.

The Supreme Court held that the NCAA's participation in the events that led to the suspension did not constitute state action within the meaning of Section 1983. The NCAA was not a state actor on the theory that it misused the power it possessed under state law because UNLV (and not the NCAA) had suspended the coach. UNLV's decision to suspend the coach in compliance with the NCAA's rules and recommendations did not turn the NCAA's conduct into state action. This was because UNLV retained the power to withdraw from the NCAA and establish its own standards. The NCAA could not directly discipline the coach, but could threaten to impose additional sanctions against the school. It was the school's decision and not the NCAA's decision to suspend the coach. *NCAA v. Tarkanian*, 488 U.S. 179, 109 S.Ct. 454, 102 L.Ed.2d 469 (1988).

♦ **In the case below, the Supreme Court held that refusal to pay a suspended police officer (who had been charged with a felony) pending a hearing did not violate due process.**

A police officer employed by a Pennsylvania state university was arrested in a drug raid and charged with several felony counts related to marijuana possession and distribution. State police notified the university of the arrest and charges, and the university's human resources director immediately suspended the officer without pay pursuant to a state executive order requiring such action where a state employee is formally charged with a felony. Although the criminal charges were dismissed, university officials demoted the officer because of the felony charges. The university did not inform the officer that it had obtained his confession from police records and he was thus unable to fully respond to damaging statements in the police reports. He filed a federal district court action against university officials for failing to provide him with notice and an opportunity to be heard before his suspension without pay. The court granted summary judgment to the officials, but the U.S. Court of Appeals, Third Circuit, reversed and remanded the case.

The Supreme Court agreed to review the case, and stated that the court of appeals had improperly held that a suspended public employee must always receive a paid suspension under *Cleveland Board of Educ. v. Loudermill*, 470 U.S. 532 (1985). The Court held that the university did not violate due process by refusing to pay a suspended employee charged with a felony pending a hearing. It accepted the officials' argument that the Pennsylvania executive order made any pre-suspension hearing useless, since the filing of charges established an independent basis for believing that the officer had committed a felony. The Court noted that the officer here faced only a temporary suspension without pay, and not employment termination, as was the case in *Loudermill*. The Court reversed and remanded the court of appeals' judgment for consideration of the officer's arguments concerning a post-suspension hearing. *Gilbert v. Homar*, 520 U.S. 924, 117 S.Ct. 1807, 138 L.Ed.2d 120 (1997).

The Judicial System

In order to allow you to determine the relative importance of a judicial decision, the cases included in *The HR Handbook: Workplace Solutions from A to Z* identify the particular court from which a decision has been issued. For example, a case decided by a state supreme court generally will be of greater significance than a state circuit court case. Hence a basic knowledge of the structure of our judicial system is important to an understanding of school law.

Almost all the reports in this volume are taken from appellate court decisions. Although most employment law decisions occur at trial court and administrative levels, appellate court decisions have the effect of binding lower courts and administrators so that appellate court decisions have the effect of law within their court systems.

State and federal court systems generally function independently of each other. Each court system applies its own law according to statutes and the determinations of its highest court. However, judges at all levels often consider opinions from other court systems to settle issues which are new or arise under unique fact situations. Similarly, lawyers look at the opinions of many courts to locate authority that supports their clients' cases.

Once a lawsuit is filed in a particular court system, that system retains the matter until its conclusion. Unsuccessful parties at the administrative or trial court level generally have the right to appeal unfavorable determinations of law to appellate courts within the system. When federal law issues or constitutional grounds are present, lawsuits may be appropriately filed in the federal court system. In those cases, the lawsuit can be filed initially in the federal district court for that area.

On rare occasions, the U.S. Supreme Court considers appeals from the highest courts of the states if a distinct federal question exists and at least four justices agree on the question's importance. The federal courts occasionally send cases to state courts for application of state law. These situations are infrequent and, in general, the state and federal court systems should be considered separate from each other.

The most common system, used by nearly all states and also the federal judiciary, is as follows: a legal action is commenced in district court (sometimes called trial court, county court, common pleas court or superior court) where a decision is initially reached. The case may then be appealed to the court of appeals (or appellate court), and in turn this decision may be appealed to the supreme court.

Several states, however, do not have a court of appeals; lower court decisions are appealed directly to the state's supreme court. Additionally, some states have labeled their courts in a nonstandard fashion.

In Maryland, the highest state court is called the Court of Appeals. In the state of New York, the trial court is called the Supreme Court. Decisions of this court may be appealed to the Supreme Court, Appellate Division. The highest court in New York is the Court of Appeals. Pennsylvania has perhaps the most complex court system. The lowest state court is the Court of Common Pleas. Depending on the circumstances of the case, appeals may be taken to either the Commonwealth Court or the Superior Court. In certain instances the Commonwealth Court functions as a trial court as well as an appellate court. The Superior Court, however, is strictly an intermediate appellate court. The highest court in Pennsylvania is the Supreme Court.

While supreme court decisions are generally regarded as the last word in legal matters, it is important to remember that trial and appeals court decisions also create important legal precedents. For the hierarchy of typical state and federal court systems, please see the diagram below.

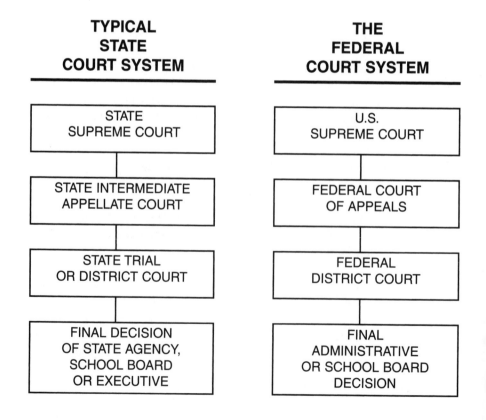

TYPICAL STATE COURT SYSTEM	THE FEDERAL COURT SYSTEM
STATE SUPREME COURT	U.S. SUPREME COURT
STATE INTERMEDIATE APPELLATE COURT	FEDERAL COURT OF APPEALS
STATE TRIAL OR DISTRICT COURT	FEDERAL DISTRICT COURT
FINAL DECISION OF STATE AGENCY, SCHOOL BOARD OR EXECUTIVE	FINAL ADMINISTRATIVE OR SCHOOL BOARD DECISION

Federal courts of appeals hear appeals from the district courts that are located in their circuits. Below is a list of states matched to the federal circuits in which they are located.

First Circuit	— Puerto Rico, Maine, New Hampshire, Massachusetts, Rhode Island
Second Circuit	— New York, Vermont, Connecticut
Third Circuit	— Pennsylvania, New Jersey, Delaware, Virgin Islands
Fourth Circuit	— West Virginia, Maryland, Virginia, North Carolina, South Carolina
Fifth Circuit	— Texas, Louisiana, Mississippi
Sixth Circuit	— Ohio, Kentucky, Tennessee, Michigan
Seventh Circuit	— Wisconsin, Indiana, Illinois
Eighth Circuit	— North Dakota, South Dakota, Nebraska, Arkansas, Missouri, Iowa, Minnesota
Ninth Circuit	— Alaska, Washington, Oregon, California, Hawaii, Arizona, Nevada, Idaho, Montana, Northern Mariana Islands, Guam
Tenth Circuit	— Wyoming, Utah, Colorado, Kansas, Oklahoma, New Mexico
Eleventh Circuit	— Alabama, Georgia, Florida
District of Columbia Circuit	— Hears cases from the U.S. District Court for the District of Columbia.
Federal Circuit	— Sitting in Washington, D.C., the U.S. Court of Appeals, Federal Circuit hears patent and trade appeals and certain appeals on claims brought against the federal government and its agencies.

How to Read a Case Citation

Generally, court decisions can be located in case reporters at law school or governmental law libraries. Some cases also can be located on the Internet through legal websites or official court websites.

Each case summary contains the citation, or legal reference, to the full text of the case. The diagram below illustrates how to read a case citation.

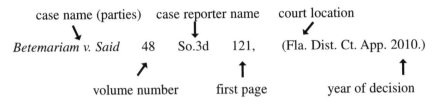

Some cases may have two or three reporter names, such as U.S. Supreme Court cases and cases reported in regional case reporters as well as state case reporters. For example, a U.S. Supreme Court case usually contains three case reporter citations.

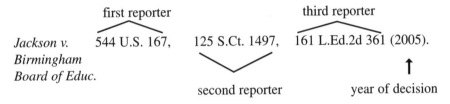

The citations still are read in the same manner as if only one citation has been listed.

Occasionally, a case may contain a citation that does not reference a case reporter. For example, a citation may contain a reference such as:

case name   year of decision   first page   year of decision

Ryan v.   No. 2009-CA-000858-MR, 2009   WL   1098330   (Ky. Ct. App. 2009).
Ryan

court file number   WESTLAW[1]   court location

The court file number indicates the specific number assigned to a case by the particular court system deciding the case. In our example, the Kentucky Court of Appeals has assigned the case of *Ryan v. Ryan* the case number of "No. 2009-CA-000858-MR," which will serve as the reference number for the case and any matter relating to the case. Locating a case on the Internet generally requires either the case name and date of the decision, and/or the court file number.

---

[1] WESTLAW® is a computerized database of court cases available for a fee.

Below, we have listed the full names of the regional reporters. As mentioned previously, many states have individual state reporters. The names of those reporters may be obtained from a reference law librarian.

P.	**Pacific Reporter**
	Alaska, Arizona, California, Colorado, Hawaii, Idaho, Kansas, Montana, Nevada, New Mexico, Oklahoma, Oregon, Utah, Washington, Wyoming
A.	**Atlantic Reporter**
	Connecticut, Delaware, District of Columbia, Maine, Maryland, New Hampshire, New Jersey, Pennsylvania, Rhode Island, Vermont
N.E.	**Northeastern Reporter**
	Illinois, Indiana, Massachusetts, New York, Ohio
N.W.	**Northwestern Reporter**
	Iowa, Michigan, Minnesota, Nebraska, North Dakota, South Dakota, Wisconsin
So.	**Southern Reporter**
	Alabama, Florida, Louisiana, Mississippi
S.E.	**Southeastern Reporter**
	Georgia, North Carolina, South Carolina, Virginia, West Virginia
S.W.	**Southwestern Reporter**
	Arkansas, Kentucky, Missouri, Tennessee, Texas

F.	**Federal Reporter**
	The thirteen federal judicial circuits courts of appeals decisions. *See, The Judicial System, p. 392* for specific state circuits.
F.Supp.	**Federal Supplement**
	The thirteen federal judicial circuits district court decisions. *See, The Judicial System, p. 392* for specific state circuits.
Fed. App.	**Federal Appendix**
	Contains unpublished decisions of the U.S. Circuit Courts of Appeal.

U.S.	**United States Reports**	
S.Ct.	**Supreme Court Reporter**	U.S. Supreme Court Decisions
L.Ed.	**Lawyers' Edition**	

INDEX